NO ZONING: ARTISTS ENGAGE HOUSTON

NO ZO

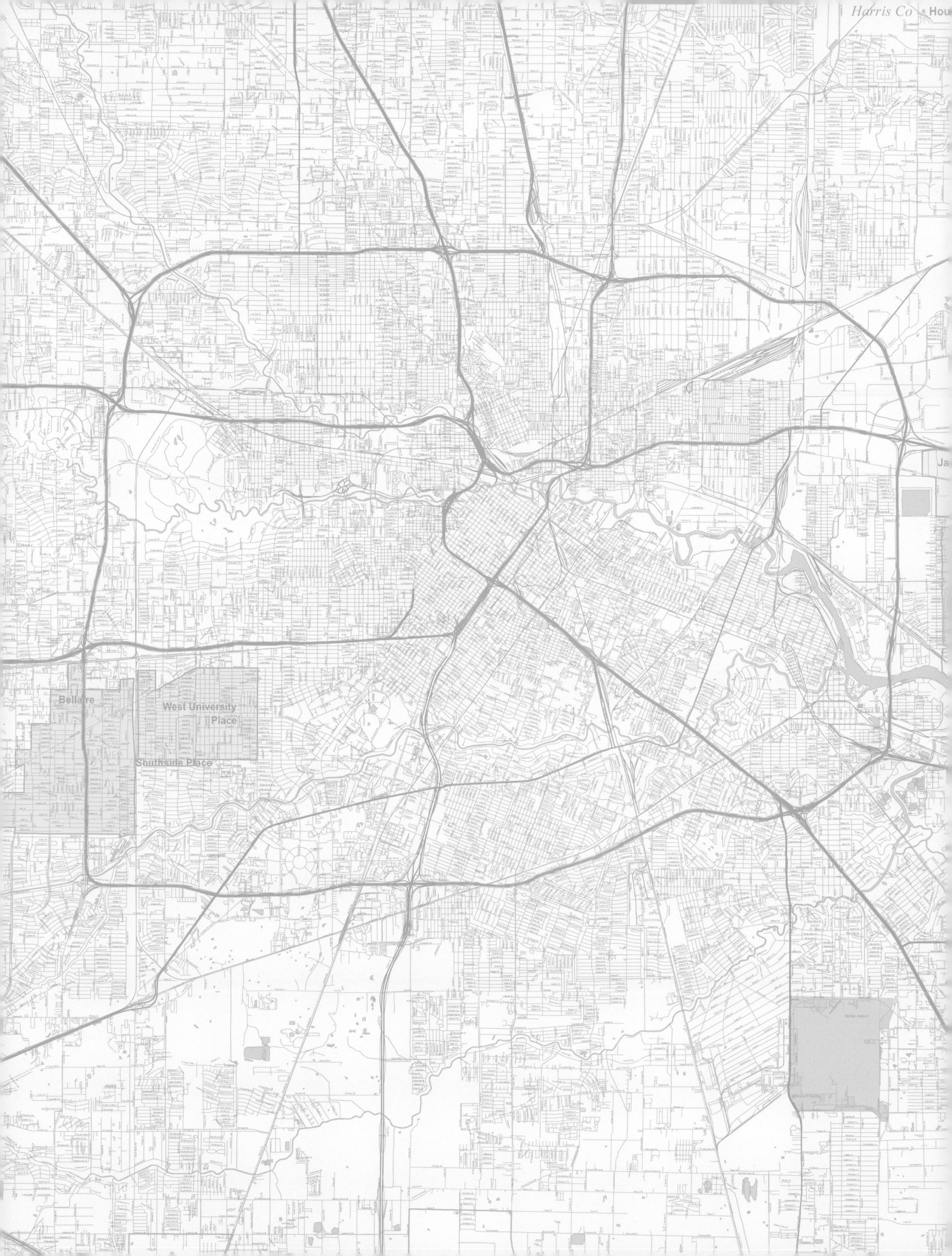
Harris Co
Bellaire
West University
Place
Southside Place

No Zoning: Artists Engage Houston has been made possible by generous support from the Union Pacific Foundation.

This exhibition has been supported by the patrons, benefactors, and donors to the Museum's Major Exhibition Fund:

Major Patron
Chinhui Juhn and Eddie Allen
Fayez Sarofim
Michael Zilkha

Patrons
Mr. and Mrs. A. L. Ballard
Mr. and Mrs. I. H. Kempner III
Ms. Louisa Stude Sarofim
Leigh and Reggie Smith

Benefactors
Marita and J. B. Fairbanks
George and Mary Josephine Hamman Foundation
Jackson Hicks / Jackson and Company
Elizabeth Howard
Marley Lott
Elisa and Cris Pye
Beverly and Howard Robinson
Swift + Company
The Susan Vaughan Foundation, Inc.

Donors
Baker Botts, LLP
Bergner and Johnson Design
Susie and Sanford Criner
Julia and Russell Frankel
Jo and Jim Furr
Mr. and Mrs. William Goldberg /
Bernstein Global Wealth Management
Louise D. Jamail
King & Spalding L.L.P.
KPMG, LLP
Judy and Scott Nyquist
Lauren Rottet
David I. Saperstein
Karen and Harry Susman
John and Becca Cason Thrash
Mark Wawro and Melanie Gray
Mr. and Mrs. Wallace Wilson

The catalogue accompanying the exhibition is made possible by a grant from The Brown Foundation, Inc.

The Museum's operations and programs are made possible through the generosity of the Museum's trustees, patrons, members, and donors. The Contemporary Arts Museum Houston receives partial operating support from the Houston Endowment, Inc., the City of Houston through the Houston Museum District Association, the National Endowment for the Arts, and the Texas Commission on the Arts.

Continental Airlines — Official airline of the Contemporary Arts Museum Houston.

This catalogue has been published to accompany the exhibition *No Zoning: Artists Engage Houston*, organized by Toby Kamps, Senior Curator, and Meredith Goldsmith, Curatorial Associate, for the Contemporary Arts Museum Houston, May 9 through October 4, 2009.

Library of Congress Control Number: 2009932517
ISBN 978-1-933619-19-4

Printed and bound in the United States of America.

Contemporary Arts Museum Houston
5216 Montrose Boulevard
Houston, Texas 77006-6547
Phone: (713) 284-8250
Fax: (713) 284-8275
www.camh.org

Available through D.A.P. / Distributed Art Publishers, Inc.
155 Sixth Avenue, 2nd Floor
New York, New York 10013
Tel: (212) 627-1999, Fax: (212) 627-9484
www.artbook.com

cover: George Hixson, *Shark Car* (detail), 1993. Gelatin silver print, 20 x 24 inches. Courtesy the artist

frontispiece: Don Quaintance, abandoned row houses on Elder Street, northwest of downtown Houston, 2009

Contents

Lenders to the Exhibition

The artists

Devin Borden Hiram Butler Gallery, Houston

Galerie Hubert Winter, Vienna

Inman Gallery, Houston

McClain Gallery, Houston

Poissant Gallery, Houston

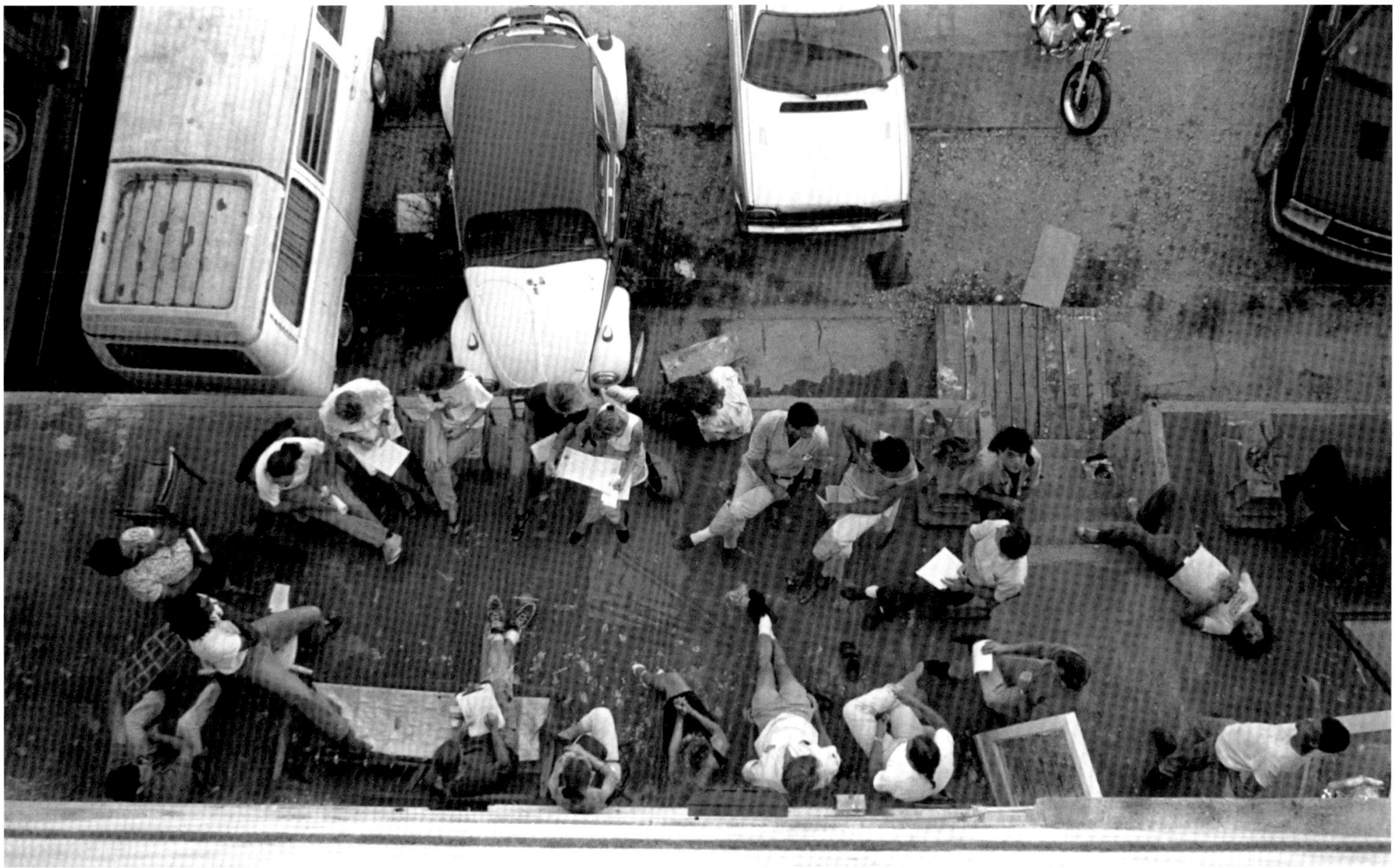

Group of Houston artists meeting on the front loading dock of Commerce Street Artists' Warehouse, 1990

Foreword

Upon arrival in Houston as newcomers, we learned right away about one of the city's most distinctive qualities: there are no official zoning regulations in Houston. Of course, that only contributes to its identity as the unruly and lawless "Wild West." And while there is a palpable respect for pragmatic thinking and entrepreneurship, we have found Houston to be a sophisticated, welcoming, and forward-thinking community that fully embraces the arts.

We are pleased to be co-authoring the foreword to the publication for *No Zoning: Artists Engage Houston*. Planning for the exhibition began during Linda Shearer's interim directorship, and its opening and subsequent run took place soon after Bill Arning took on the directorship in April 2009. It has been a pleasure for us to be involved in this project, which was the natural outgrowth of the 2007 exhibition *Nexus Texas*, a statewide presentation of talented artists, covering several generations and many styles. And, in difficult economic times, it is not uncommon to explore the creativity that exists in your own home territory. These projects have proved invaluable "crash courses" in a cultural scene with a unique flavor and history.

It was thanks to Senior Curator Toby Kamps and Curatorial Associate Meredith Goldsmith that these ideas coalesced into a serious and scholarly examination of a particular time and attitude unique to Houston. Just as the lack of zoning laws affected the design and nature of the city and its development, they also allowed artists to push the limits of their imaginations and go beyond the conventional presentation in galleries and museums. According to Kamps, this is an endeavor "examining projects by Houston artists using the city as inspiration, material, and site." While the traditional concept of a regionalist aesthetics based on isolation is no longer tenable in an age of unlimited connectivity, this curatorial approach examining what makes cultural production in Houston unique through the economic, social, and legal realities of this sprawling city promises to inform how future curators and critics understand these artists' activities.

The exhibition itself includes 21 artists working in this life-engaged mode today who are representative of the depth and range of the vast array of Houston artists. In addition to the exhibiting artists, the publication covers the historical background for this type of unzoned creative work in the city, and will prove to be an invaluable research document for Houston art lovers and historians as well. Kamps and his co-curator Goldsmith, who thought of the exhibition's provocative title, visited countless studios and collected numerous oral histories. Curatorial Manager Justine Waitkus and Director of Education and Public Programs Paula Newton must be singled out for their brave contributions towards a project that intrinsically requires a degree of both chaos and crowds well beyond a normal museum presentation.

Many different individuals assisted in this work; it became clear that the Houston art world is a supportive and collegial one. We would like to join *No Zoning*'s curators in thanking those countless Houstonians who contributed to making this exhibition possible and its publication a resource for future generations. In particular, we remain deeply grateful to The Brown Foundation, Inc.; since 1999, their steady support has enabled the CAMH to publish a catalogue for every exhibition it organizes. For a non-collecting museum, our publications document our exhibitions and become in essence the museum's "collection." Furthermore, they allow us to explore new areas of scholarship. Union Pacific has also proved to be a loyal sponsor of CAMH exhibitions and we salute its cultural leadership at this uncertain moment. To the many generous donors to the CAMH Major Exhibition Fund, we would like to express our enormous appreciation for their ongoing dedication to the CAMH and its exhibition program. A complete list of supporters is found on page 6. Our deepest gratitude goes to the artists who, without asking for permission from anyone, took it upon themselves to make Houston a more stimulating place!

Bill Arning
Director

Linda Shearer
Interim Director (2007–09)

Acknowledgments

"Houston is the only city in the United States without zoning laws!"

This is the first thing most people exclaim—more often with incredulity than admiration—in a discussion about the place. And this laissez-faire approach to land use was the first thing we—Toby Kamps and Meredith Goldsmith—had to wrap our heads around when we started working and living in this thoroughly disorganized yet mysteriously charming town two-and-a-half and three years ago, respectively. As we began our positions as Senior Curator at the Contemporary Arts Museum Houston (Toby) and Core Fellow in critical writing at the Glassell School of Art in 2007 and Curatorial Associate at the CAMH in 2006 (Meredith), we began acclimating ourselves to Houston's chaotic landscape, which veers abruptly from residential to industrial and from well-kempt to abject. We also had countless conversations with artists, museum visitors, critics, collectors, curators, and patrons about the many ways art, of the self-taught and academically trained varieties, exists outside of traditional museum, gallery, and sculpture park settings in Houston. Gradually, we learned to read the city—to appreciate the ways the *jolie* and the *laid* coexist and to see the ways creative individuals have shaped their immediate environments and, by extension, the city. When the opportunity arose to organize an exhibition looking at a salient feature of Houston's art world, we thought about these conversations and the "unzoned" aspects of Houston's art scene. Using a title suggested by Meredith during an early brainstorming session, we set about organizing a study of a group of freethinking and self-starting artists engaging the city itself as a backdrop for life-engaged projects. We tried to capture their spirit in an exhibition and catalogue that chronicles a selection of contemporary efforts and also places them in the context of the long tradition of extra-institutional art in Houston.

A project of this size and scope is possible only because of the efforts, generosity, and dedication of many. Our research, formal and informal, took many forms and drew on the memories and opinions of many Houston artists, writers, museum colleagues, and scene-sters. With sincere apologies to those whose large and small contributions we may have overlooked in the shuffle, we wish to thank the following individuals: Bob Abbinati and Que Imaging; Geraldine Aramanda; Chris Ballou; Diane Barber; Toni Beauchamp; Devin Borden; Stephen Bridges and The Orange Show Center for Visionary Art; Peter Brown; Hiram Butler; Kirk Farris; Mark Flood; Christa Forster; Stephen Fox; Sabrina Franzheim; Wayne Gilbert; GONZO247; Alison de Lima Greene; Nonya Grenader; Ann and James Harithas; Paul Hester; Fredericka Hunter; Kirsha Kaechele / KK Projects; Liz Kanistanaux and the Museum of Fine Arts, Houston; Karl Kilian; Paul Kittelson; Rainey Knudsen; Sharon and Gus Kopriva; Mark Larsen and The Artery; Cody Ledvina; Bert L. Long, Jr.; Meredith Long; Mik Maio; Peter Marzio; Robert McClain; Aaron Parazette; Michael Peranteau; Scott Peveto; Patrick Phipps; Scott Prescott; Charles Renfro; Mo Roberts; Michelangelo Sabatino; Jose Solis; Bill Stern; Terrie Sultan; Emily Todd; Cynthia Toles; ttweak (Dave Thompson and Randy Twaddle); Salle Werner Vaughn; Pat Waugh; Christine Jelson West; Michelle White; Amanda Wiles; and Clint Willour.

We extend great thanks to the Union Pacific Foundation, whose grant made this exhibition possible, and The Brown Foundation, Inc., for their generous support in the publication of this catalogue. An equal debt of gratitude is owed to the patrons, benefactors, and donors to the Museum's Major Exhibition Fund, including Major Patrons: Chinhui Juhn and Eddie Allen; Fayez Sarofim; and Michael Zilkha; Patrons: Mr. and Mrs. A. L. Ballard; Mr. and Mrs. I. H. Kempner III; Ms. Louisa Stude Sarofim; and Leigh and Reggie Smith; Benefactors: Marita and J. B. Fairbanks; The George and Mary Josephine Hamman Foundation; Jackson Hicks / Jackson and Company; Elizabeth Howard; Marley Lott; Elisa and Cris Pye; Beverly and Howard Robinson; Swift + Company; and The Susan Vaughan Foundation, Inc.; and Donors: Baker Botts, LLP; Bergner and Johnson Design; Susie and Sanford Criner; Julia and Russell Frankel; Jo and Jim Furr; Mr. and Mrs. William Goldberg / Bernstein Global Wealth Management; Louise D. Jamail; King & Spalding L.L.P.; KPMG, LLP; Judy and Scott Nyquist; Lauren Rottet; David I. Saperstein; Karen and Harry Susman; John and Becca Cason Thrash; Mark Wawro and Melanie Gray; and Mr. and Mrs. Wallace Wilson.

Many CAMH trustees have made important contributions to

the project as well. We would especially like to thank Marley Lott, Sissy Kempner, and Judy Nyquist for their research help and moral support as we explored the official and unofficial histories of art and culture in Houston.

Catalogue essayists Cameron Armstrong, The Art Guys (Michael Galbreth and Jack Massing), Caroline Huber, and Susanne Theis each contributed sensitive, revelatory texts that do ground-breaking work in documenting the history of city-based art and the effects of the city's unzoned landscape on its culture. Poet and University of Houston creative writing professor Tony Hoagland contributed the wonderful new poem "Because It Is Houston." For their outstanding efforts and the sensitive editorial eyes of Heather Brand and Polly Koch, we are grateful.

Designer Don Quaintance of Public Address Design did a fantastic job conceptualizing the exhibition's publication, as did Design/Production Assistant Elizabeth Frizzell, who was especially helpful with photo research for the chronology. Karen Powelson at CS Graphics, Singapore, assisted with the excellent printing.

Each member of the CAMH's talented staff has contributed in one way or another to realizing this ambitious project. First, we want to recognize the support of Interim Director Linda Shearer. Her early enthusiasm gave this project direction and momentum, which our new Director Bill Arning amplified in the project's final stretch. In the curatorial department, Curatorial Manager Justine Waitkus, Curator Valerie Cassel Oliver, and former Adjunct Curator Lynn M. Herbert were instrumental in both the logistical and conceptual aspects of the project. Intern Jennifer Teets contributed important early work on the catalogue's artist biographies and bibliographies. Education Director Paula Newton and Education Associate Carlos Lama applied their creative energies to developing an expansive and deeply enjoyable educational program of special events. And Registrar Tim Barkley and preparator Jeff Shore, along with Gallery Supervisor/Assistant Preparator Kenya Evans, Assistant Director Mike Reed, and temporary installation crew members Tierney Malone and Bret Shirley, managed complex logistics and construction with aplomb. As always, major contributions have been made by the development department and Karen Soh, development consultant, Kristina Spritzer, grants and gifts manager, and Amanda Bredbenner, development assistant. Communications and marketing manager Connie McAllister tirelessly publicized and assisted with the exhibition's myriad programs, and IT manager/webmaster Andy Balajadia deftly handled all computer and web-based logistics. The names of all staff are listed on page 134 of this book, and we extend our sincere gratitude to each of them.

Finally, though, we must reserve our deepest thanks to the artists in *No Zoning*: The Art Guys (Michael Galbreth and Jack Massing), Mary Ellen Carroll, Mel Chin (of The Fundred Dollar Bill Project), Bill Davenport, Ben Tecumseh DeSoto, Sharon Engelstein, Andrea Grover, collaborators Dan Havel and Dean Ruck, George Hixson, Lauren Kelley, KnittaPlease (Magda Sayeg and others), Eric Leshinsky, Lee Littlefield, Rick Lowe, Benjy Mason and Zach Moser, Jim Pirtle, Nestor Topchy, and Cleveland "The Flower Man" Turner. Their efforts, along with those of all artists weaving their work directly into the urban tapestry, are crucial in making Houston an exceptional home for the arts.

Toby Kamps
Senior Curator

Meredith Goldsmith
Curatorial Associate

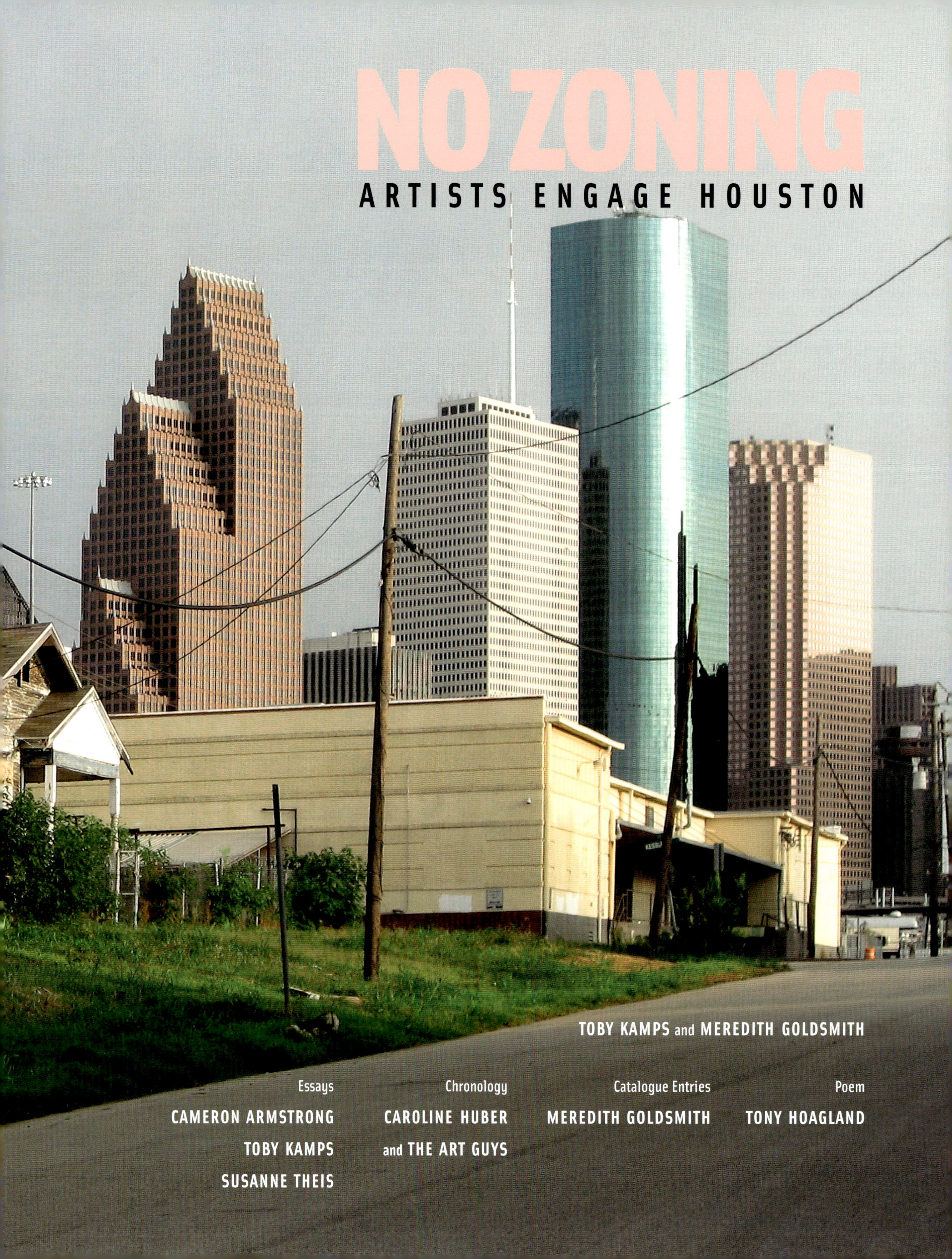

NO ZONING

ARTISTS ENGAGE HOUSTON

TOBY KAMPS and MEREDITH GOLDSMITH

Essays
CAMERON ARMSTRONG
TOBY KAMPS
SUSANNE THEIS

Chronology
CAROLINE HUBER
and THE ART GUYS

Catalogue Entries
MEREDITH GOLDSMITH

Poem
TONY HOAGLAND

Chronology and Essays

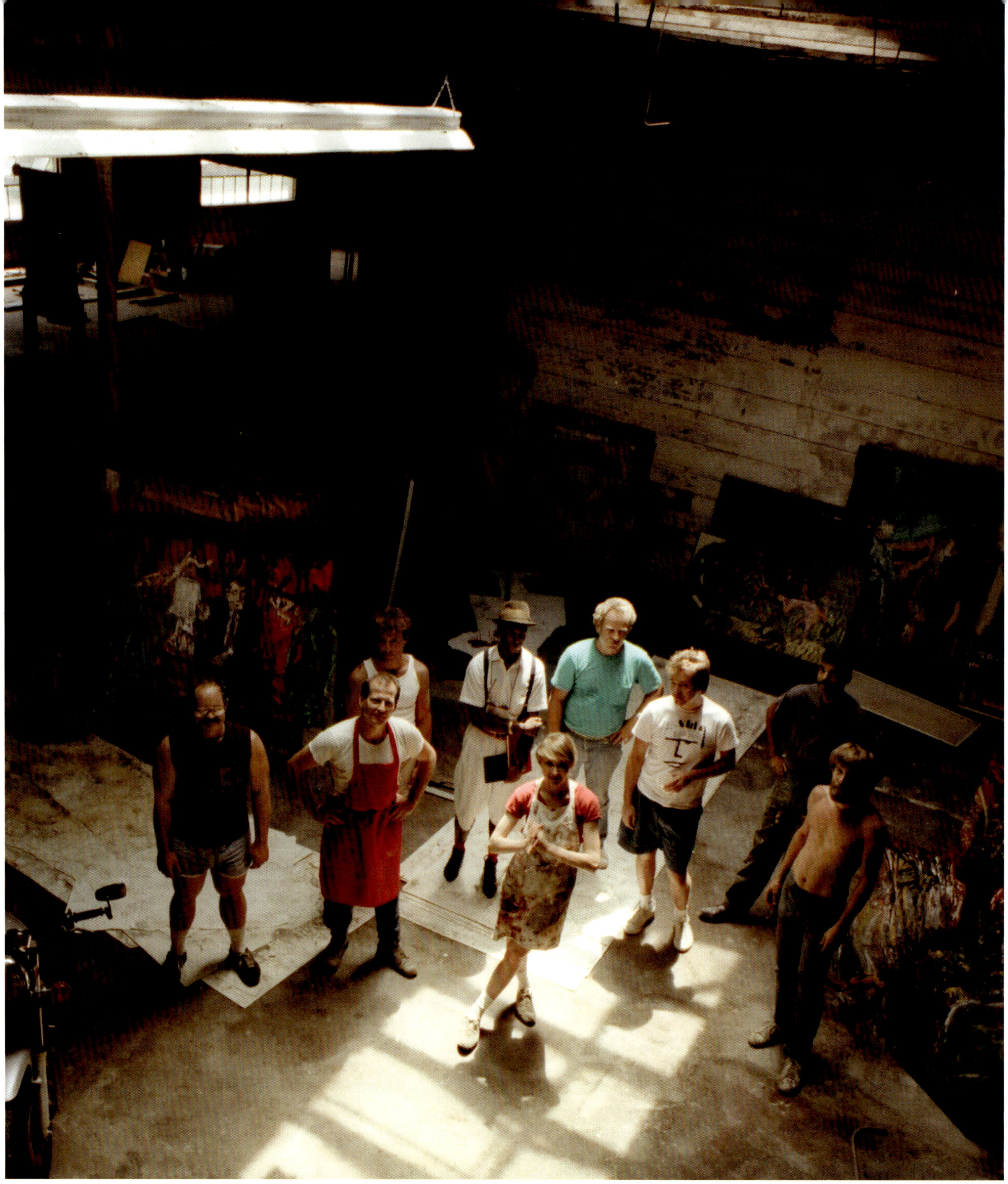

1930

1949

before 1970

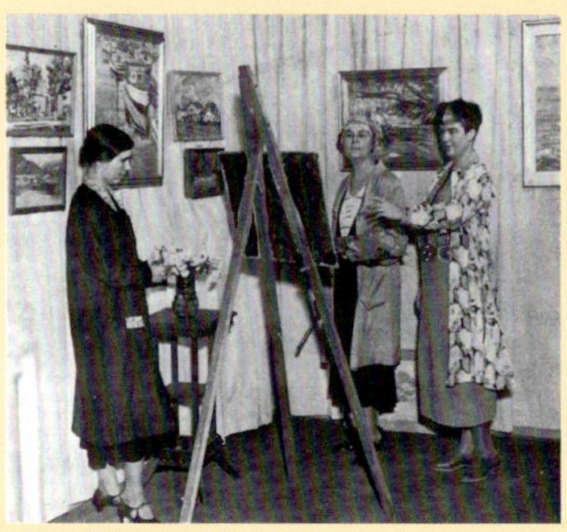

Houston Artists' Gallery, 1931

Houston Artists' Gallery
Grace Spaulding Johns and a group of dedicated women opened the city's first artist-run gallery, the Houston Artists' Gallery, in the basement of the Beaconsfield Hotel on Main Street. The organization sponsored exhibitions, auctions, and lectures.

Contemporary Arts Association*
Houston artists and architects seeking a venue for displaying contemporary art and design founded the volunteer-operated Contemporary Arts Association, initially presenting exhibitions at the Museum of Fine Arts and in 1949 erecting an A-frame museum building on Dallas Street in downtown Houston. The organization gradually gained professional status and curator Jermayne MacAgy was hired as its first full-time director in 1955.

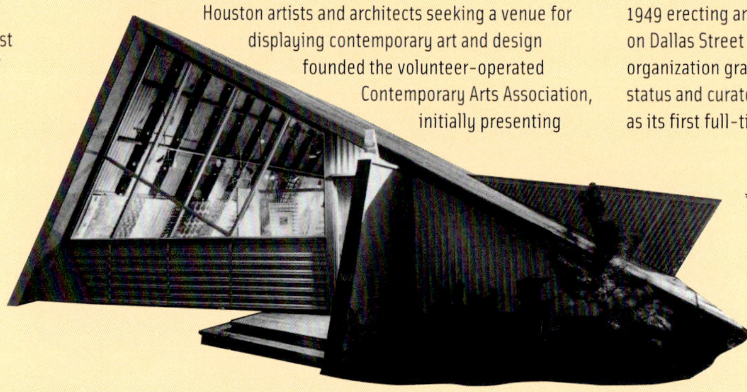

Contemporary Arts Association, Dallas Street, 1950

**The building housing the Contemporary Arts Association (CAA) was from its inception often referred to as the Contemporary Arts Museum (CAM) and the latter name was used almost exclusively from the 1970s to 1990s. In 2002 the institution's name was officially changed to the Contemporary Arts Museum Houston (CAMH).*

Merging Traffic: A Chronology

Caroline Huber and The Art Guys

"Art does not come and lie in beds we make for it. It slips away as soon as its name is uttered: it likes to preserve its incognito. Its best moments are when it forgets its very name."

—Jean Dubuffet

Houston by its very nature—which is open, welcoming, and filled with the sense of possibility—is an ideal incubator for a flourishing range of art activity, sanctioned and unsanctioned. In this friendly climate, artists can experiment and invent as producers and creators. Their own neighborhoods can encapsulate an entire world of day-to-day life, work, and art. Artists are given a kind of psychological license to use ideas, materials, and places fluidly and without limitation. This lack of boundaries, both literally and metaphorically, has made Houston the perfect place for artists to exercise their ingenuity and entrepreneurship.

As we researched this chronology, our process was largely intuitive. The chronology contains somewhat obscure references as well as inclusions that are well known, if not famous. The length of any given reference is not necessarily indicative of its relative importance; in many cases, we felt that some listings simply needed more information. Invariably this type of account will have gaps, omissions, and biases.

In our conversations with as many individuals as we could reach, the common refrain was, "My memory is gone," making catching this information while you can all the more relevant. In response to this disappearing history, this chronology will expand during the course of the exhibition: a Wikipedia page has been set up for participants to make additions and corrections or insert new information. We offer this printed chronology as a place to start.

Wikipedia: http://en.wikipedia.org/wiki/Houston_Alternative_Art

Commerce Street Artists' Warehouse founders: Dan Calhoun, Lee Benner, Robert Campbell, Orson T. Maquelani, Deborah Moore, Virgil Grotfeldt, John Calaway, Rick Lowe, and Wes Hicks, Commerce Street Artists' Warehouse, 1986

ACKNOWLEDGMENTS

Special thanks go to the following individuals for their assistance with this chronology: Mark Allen, Terry Allen, Geri Aramanda, Elia Arce, Chris Ballou, Diane Barber, H. R. Bott, Stephen Bridges, David Brown/DAB Foto, Bernard Brunon, Hiram Butler, Mel Chin, David Cisneros, Frank Davis, Carter Ernst, Helen Winkler Fosdick, Stephen Fox, Elizabeth Frizzell, Scott Gilbert, Wayne Gilbert, Ian Glennie, GONZO247, Merril Greene, Deborah Grotfeldt, James Harithas, Larry Harris, Trish Herrera, George Hixson, Brian Huberman, Fredericka Hunter, The Internet, Terrell James, Mary Jenewein, Patricia Johnson, Paul Kittelson, Paul Kremer, Tom LaFaver, Mary Louise Lopez, Marian Luntz, Laurie McDonald, the Orange Show Center for Visionary Art, Michael Peranteau, Jim Pirtle, Don Quaintance, Bert Samples, Everett Taasivegan, Susanne Theis, Emily Todd, Cleveland Turner, Randy Twaddle, Julia Claire Wallace, Christine Jelson West, Paul Winkler, and Nancy Zastudil.

Note: The chronology continues through page 45 and then resumes on pages 50–118.

1956

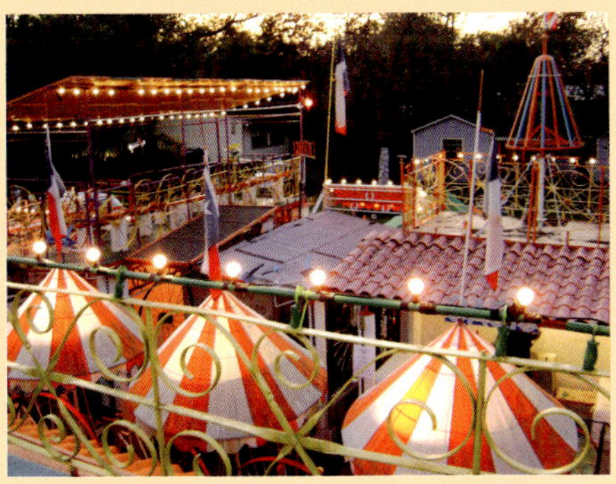

The Orange Show at dusk

The Orange Show

Postman Jeff McKissack began to single-handedly design and build The Orange Show, a brightly colored, carnival-like environment dedicated to the orange and to the virtues of good health and right living. He used concrete, stucco, and found objects—mosaic tiles, wrought iron fencing, wagon wheels, mannequins, and tractor seats—to transform two plots on Munger Street in the East End into a vividly painted architectural maze of walkways, balconies, exhibits, and performance stages. McKissack thought it would be an attraction "bigger than the Astrodome that 90% of the people in the United States will want to see." But when The Orange Show finally opened to the public in 1979, the hordes of visitors he anticipated did not come. McKissack died shortly thereafter. The facility is now preserved by the Orange Show Center for Visionary Art and is the site of numerous events and performances.

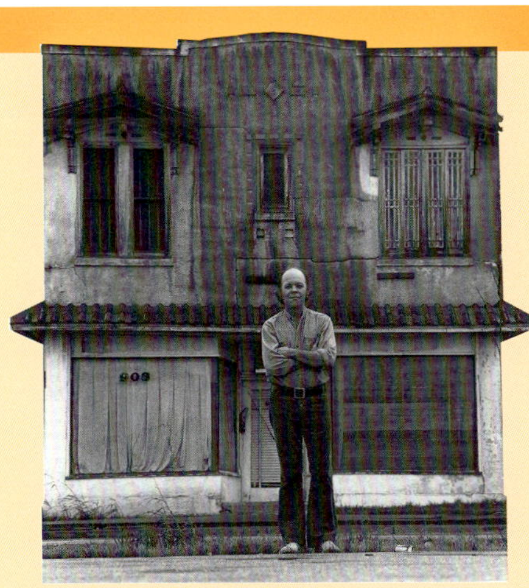

Jim Love in front of his Truxillo Street studio, c. 1972

1963

Jim Love and Roy Fridge Studio

Artists Jim Love and Roy Fridge shared a studio in a two-story derelict storefront on Truxillo Street near West Alabama. It became a meeting place and notorious party site for artists such as Donald Barthelme, Jack Boynton, David McManaway, and Charles T. Williams, along with numerous Houston art patrons and international visitors such as Jean Tinguely and Niki de Saint Phalle.

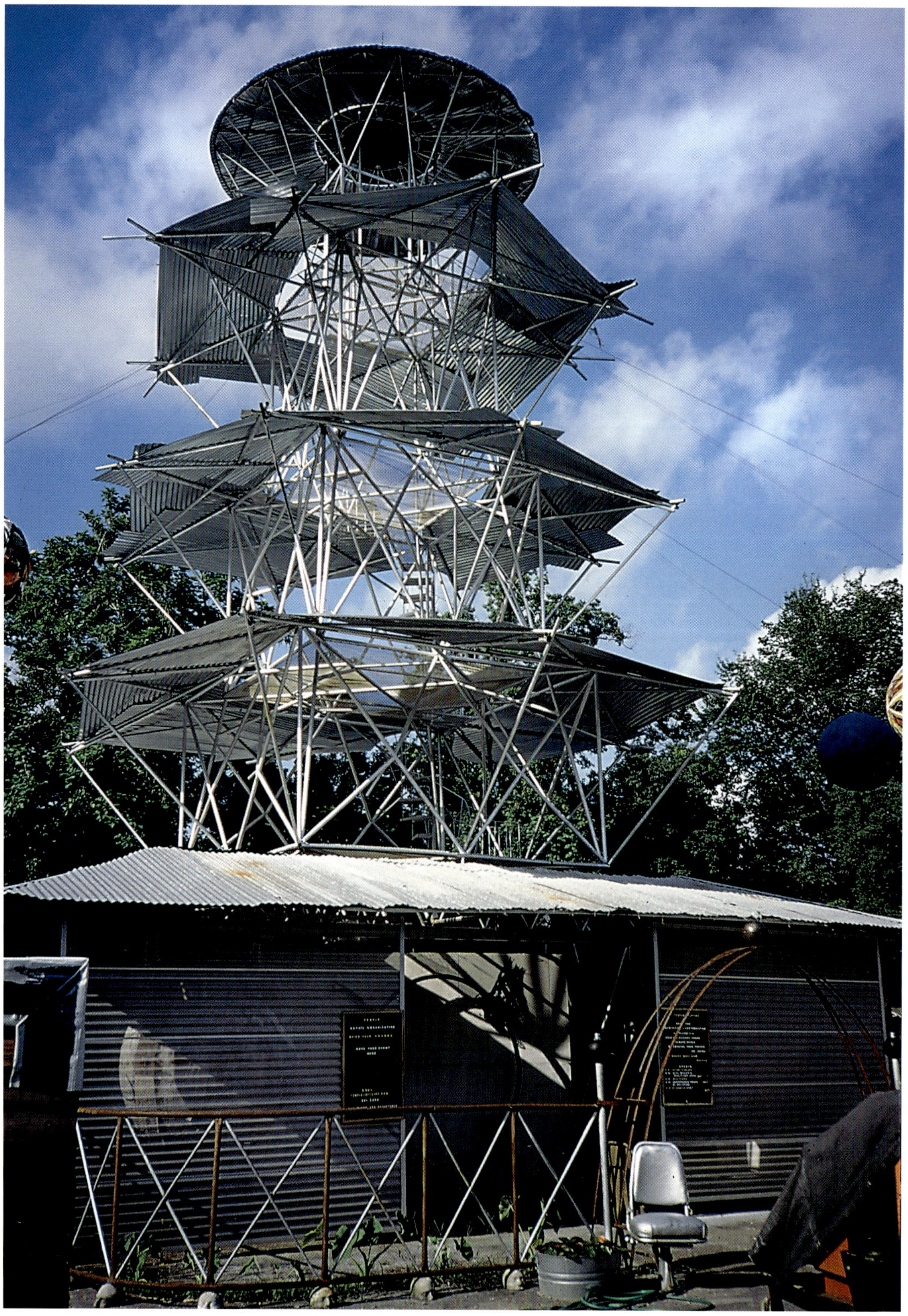

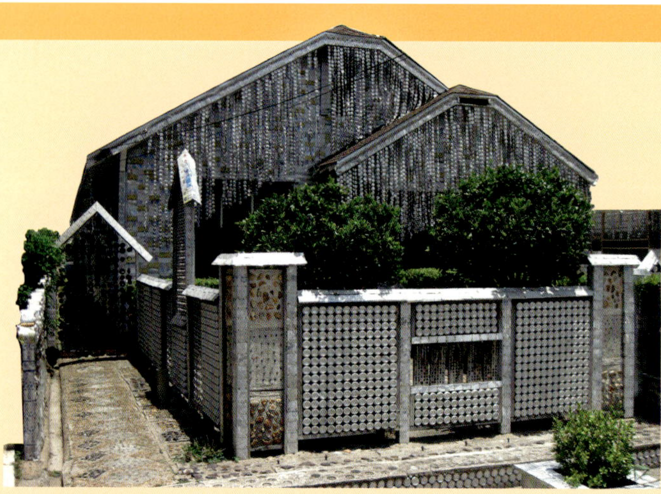

The Beer Can House, 2009

1968

The Beer Can House
John Milkovisch, a retired railroad upholsterer, began to transform an ordinary bungalow in Houston's West End into a kinetic, shimmering environment. Working for twenty years, he covered the entire yard and drive with intricate patterns of concrete studded with marbles, salvaged industrial washers, and stones; decorated the house and trees with garlands made from beer can tops, rims, and pull tabs; and clad the house with thousands of flattened beer cans (he consumed all the beer, with help from his wife, Mary), ensuring that he would never have to paint the house again. "They say every man should leave something to be remembered by," he said. "At least I accomplished that goal." The site is now a revered local monument maintained by the Orange Show Center for Visionary Art.

1969

Daucus Carota
Herschel Berry, Michael Hollis, and Kelly Kirkonnel started Daucus Carota (Latin for "wild carrot") while they were in high school. The group had a shifting membership that included Andy Feehan, Nicky Galmiche, Chris Lesikar, Jim Martin, and Julian Schnabel. Members of Daucus Carota used images and sculptures of carrots in their work, often leaving bunches of real carrots in their wake. They sculpted an oversized painted carrot, which they placed around town, including in front of the Contemporary Arts Museum, in a gesture designed to belittle the art establishment.

No Zoning: Artists Engage Houston

Toby Kamps

Houston is a sprawling behemoth of a city. The fourth largest metropolis in the country, it covers 601.7 square miles, is home to 2.2 million inhabitants, and consists of an agglomeration of discordant neighborhoods and business centers connected by overcrowded roads and highways. Other than its lush canopy of trees, intricate bayou system, and large Memorial and Hermann Parks, the city offers few natural attractions, no obvious center, and little visual charm. It is as flat as a pancake, and its semi-tropical climate is humid and hot. Very hot. Riddled with vacant lots and construction sites, Houston feels like a raw, unfinished place—a mood heightened by the aftereffects of occasional hurricanes and regular floods that sweep though it, knocking out skyscraper windows and snagging plastic bags in treetops. There is little old-world decorum or gentility here. Wealth and poverty, individualism and collectivism, spiritualism and materialism, pollution and nature, progress and the past tangle brazenly on every corner.

Despite its chaotic, car-culture terrain, the city is also an exceptionally art-permeable environment.[1] It supports a large and thriving visual arts ecology, including a glittering archipelago of museums, alternative spaces, public art projects, and commercial galleries, a diverse and vibrant artist and collector community, and a panoply of homegrown folk art sites and events. One of the reasons why culture and commercialism mix so easily in Houston is because it is the only major city in the United States without zoning laws. This policy of laissez-faire land use, combined with Texas's outsized respect for property rights and individual initiative, has allowed countless artists working outside of conventional museums and galleries to weave art directly into the fabric of the city. The exhibition *No Zoning: Artists Engage Houston* uses the concept of unzoned urbanism as a springboard for an investigation of this salient feature of the city's cultural environment—its rich tradition of inspired do-it-yourself public art projects.

Houston is the only principal American city to have resisted the nationwide zoning movement. In 1916 New York City passed the first zoning ordinances in order to protect neighbors from the air- and light-blocking effects of the hulking Equitable Building skyscraper. The laws restricted towers to a percentage of lot size, limited massing at certain heights, and established the concept of setbacks, which determine how much public space must surround a building.[2] In 1926, after many challenges from lower courts across the country, municipal efforts to shape the character of communities by regulating the types of construction that may be built and sequestering different types of developments and businesses in distinct zones were declared constitutional in the Supreme Court decision *Euclid v. Ambler Realty Company* and became national practice. Yet uniquely, despite pro-zoning initiatives, hearings, and referendums in 1927, 1938, 1945, 1947, 1959, 1962, and 1993, Houston voters, politicians, and business interests have remained steadfastly attached to their eccentric mixed-use approach.[3]

Although many point out that contemporary Houston resembles other decentralized Sun Belt cities, having achieved a de facto form of zoning through deed restrictions temporarily limiting development of certain districts, the city is distinct in its radical heterogeneity. In Houston, contrary to popular belief, city ordinances do not allow massage parlors within 1,500 feet of churches, but it *is* possible to have a high-rise in a mansion's backyard, a factory smack in the middle of a bungalow neighborhood, and experimental architecture almost anywhere. This lack of zoning, many believe, stems from Texas's claim to have been founded by mavericks, wildcatters, and self-made moguls—with Houston as its shining beacon of free enterprise.

Nestor Topchy's TemplO, 2000

1969

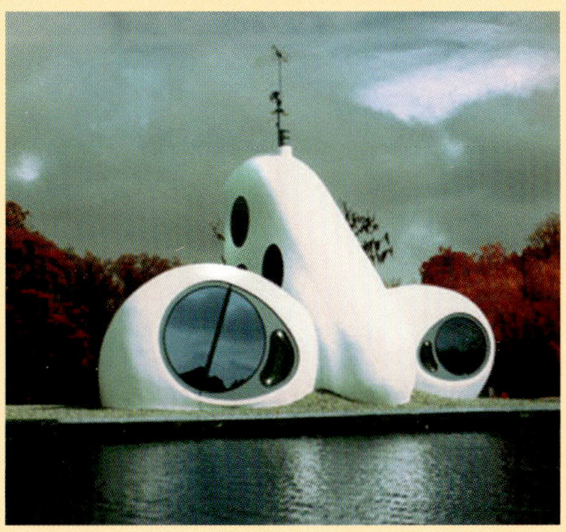

Ant Farm (Richard Jost, Chip Lord, Doug Michels), *The House of The Century*, on the shore of Mojo Lake, 1973

Ant Farm

In 1968 in San Francisco, Chip Lord and Doug Michels founded the architecture and art collective Ant Farm, which later included Douglas Hurr, Hudson Marquez, and Curtis Schreier. In 1969 while Lord and Michels were teaching at the University of Houston College of Architecture, Ant Farm staged a series of free-form architectural performances in the Houston area. Subsequently they worked throughout the United States, but realized some of their important projects in Houston, including *Time Capsule 1972–1984* (1972); a monumental sculpture on Kirby Drive for the Hard Rock Café with an actual 1962 Thunderbird hardtop convertible towering aloft, *STP (Save the Planets)* (1985); and their award-winning project *The House of the Century* (1971–73), a futurist spaceship-like dwelling for Marilyn Oshman Lubetkin located near Angleton, Texas, south of Houston.

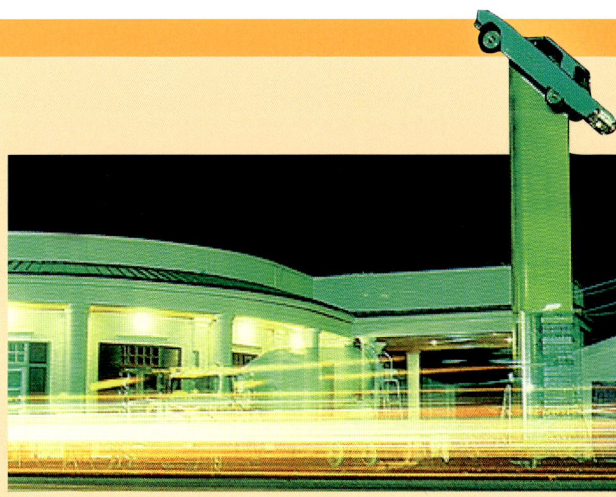

Not Ant Farm (Chip Lord, Hudson Marquez, Doug Michels), *STP (Save the Planets)*, outside of the Hard Rock Café, Kirby Drive, c. 1985

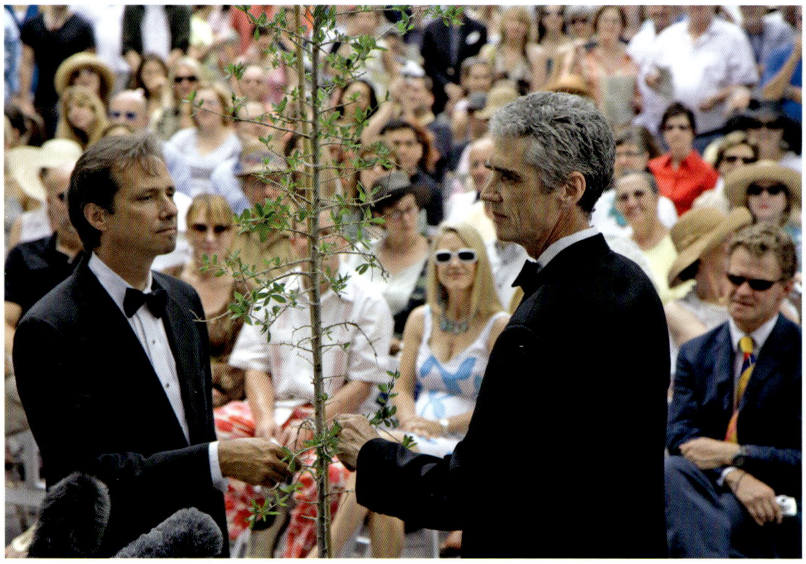

The Art Guys, *The Art Guys Marry A Plant* (performance documentation, Lillie and Hugh Roy Cullen Sculpture Garden, Museum of Fine Arts, Houston), 2009

Although written nearly forty years ago, before a population boom fueled by a massive influx of new residents from elsewhere, the words of sociologist Neal R. Pierce still define the city's stubbornly libertarian spirit: "Houston is populated with people from small towns and farms of the old, rural South. Their salient characteristic is fierce, don't-fence-me-in individualism—the psychology that 'if I want to have a pigpen in my back yard, by God I can!'"[4]

Whether or not Houston's lack of zoning comes from a cowboy mentality or effective lobbying by its business interests is of little importance.[5] Houstonians, for the most part, believe that their city supports and rewards individual initiative, and they take perverse pride in their Darwinian environment.[6] And artists, born entrepreneurs and self-actualizers, have worked hard to earn a place in the city's food chain. Many have built national reputations by showing in Houston's traditional institutions, but many—by choice or necessity—also have taken advantage of the city's rare permeability to inscribe their ideas and efforts directly into the urban fiber. They have offered inspired alternatives to the backyard pigpen with performances, sculptures, exhibition spaces, and urban art environments. As befits a state renowned for its legends, feuds, and sagas, the oral histories of Houston's underground art scene are filled with Texas-size characters and movements—including, to name only a few, the Commerce Street Artists' Warehouse; the Urban Animals' nighttime roller-skating exploits; Bill Steen's Studio One; dancer Farrell Dyde's 3221 Milam; Kirk Farris's McKee Street Bridge project; Paul Kittelson's couch-cushion stegosaurus under a Highway 59 overpass; Mark Larsen's The Artery; I Love You Baby's beer-fueled collective painting projects; exhibitions at Jeff Elrod and Mark Flood's Art of This Century gallery; The Art Guys World Headquarters; Mark Lombardi's On Waugh Gallery; Arena Productions' guerrilla art exhibition on refrigerators at Sears; and Chez Imbecile, Zocalo, notsuoH, Axiom, and many more. Enlightened and powerful patrons of the arts—including, among many others, the de Menils, Hoggs, Laws, Blaffers, Cullens, and the star-chamber civic patriarchs of the Lamar Hotel Suite 8F group—may have opened their wallets like Medicis to build the city's official cultural institutions, but it is the city's artists, laboring like Giottos, who have imprinted their visions on the urban landscape and have made Houston a veritable Florence of funky, extra-institutional art.

In many ways, the twenty-one artists in *No Zoning* have added beauty, social commentary, community, levity, and fascinating texture to Houston's streets and neighborhoods. The artists featured in this exhibition at the Contemporary Arts Museum Houston (CAMH) and at satellite projects throughout the city are The Art Guys (Jack Massing and Michael Galbreth), Mary Ellen Carroll, Mel Chin (of *The Fundred Dollar Bill Project*), Bill Davenport, Ben Tecumseh DeSoto, Sharon Engelstein, "The Flower Man" (Cleveland Turner), Andrea Grover, collaborators Dan Havel and Dean Ruck, George Hixson, Lauren Kelley, Knitta-Please (Magda Sayeg and others), Eric Leshinsky, Lee Littlefield, Rick Lowe, the team of Benjy Mason and Zach Moser, Jim Pirtle, and Nestor Topchy. Some have conventional studios and successful national and international careers. Others prefer to keep it local and shun the embalming effects of museums and galleries.

1970s

1972

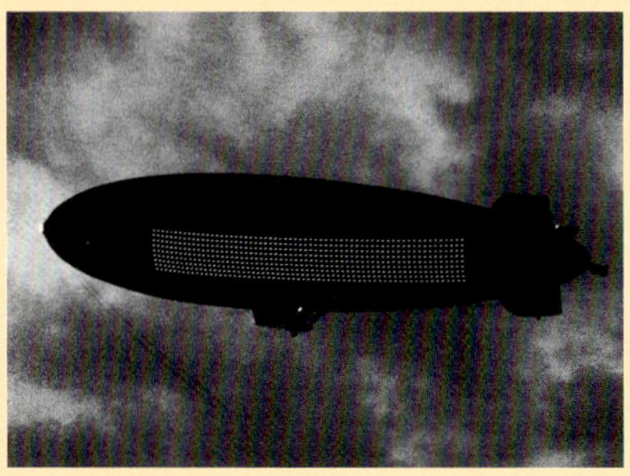

Michael Snow's lightwork on the Goodyear Blimp, 1972

Goodyear Blimp over CAM
During the opening of *Exhibition 10*, curated by Sebastian J. Adler at the Contemporary Arts Museum, artist and experimental filmmaker Michael Snow created an elaborate piece on the advertising light grid of the Goodyear Blimp, which flew over the museum.

Hyde Park Miniature Museum
D. D. Smalley, grandfather of artist and musician Frank Davis, was inspired by his grandson's birth in 1941 and began production of what was eventually called the Hyde Park Miniature Museum. On display in the oversized attic of a house on Hyde Park Street was a range of artifacts, including 250,000 postage stamps wrapped in bundles of 100, dinosaur excrement and bones, Indian skulls, tools, handmade models, over 1,000 clocks, the U.S. Constitution in Braille, wax recordings, a three-toed horse hoof, short wave radio paraphernalia, bee tracking glasses, dressed fleas, and many other curiosities and miscellany, all carefully arranged and catalogued.

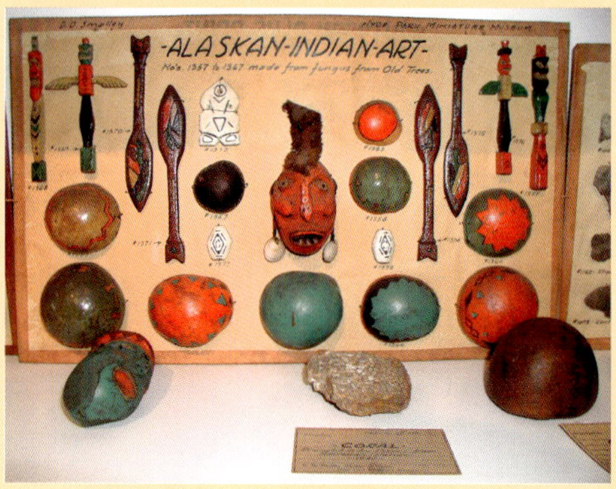

Display from the Hyde Park Miniature Museum, 2005

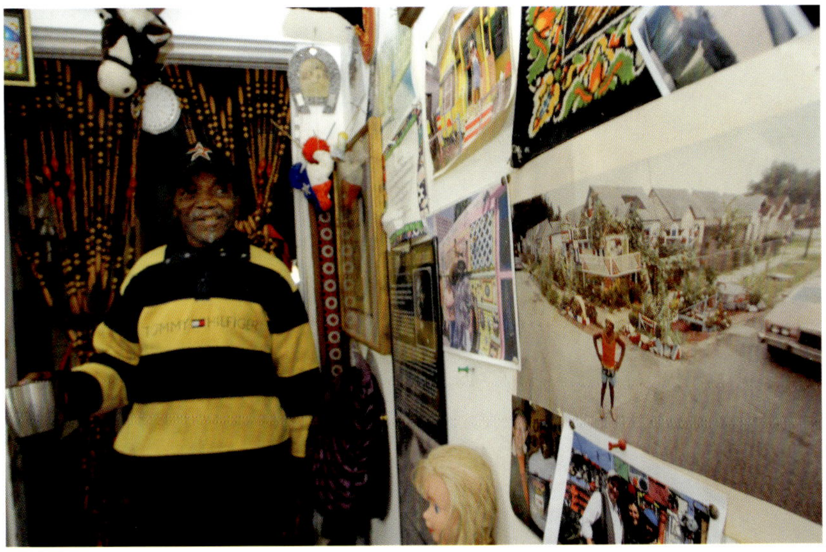

The Flower Man in his home on Francis Street (with photo of his second home on Sampson Street, 1986), 2009

And this group is only the tip of the iceberg: there are countless current practitioners and a long history of do-it-yourself artworks and venues in Houston. Limited gallery space and resources, along with the often difficult logistics of "rezoning" city-based projects by bringing them into the museum, have restricted this exhibition to an incomplete but representative selection of recent and current projects. Telling the larger story of Houston's unzoned art world is left to this catalogue's essays, historical timeline (see "Merging Traffic," page 15), and future historians.

The inspirations for the projects temporarily corralled in the galleries of the CAMH are as diverse as the city itself, where there is no racial majority and where forty-one percent of households speak a language other than English.[7] Two projects—a performance by The Art Guys and an installation by Cleveland Turner, widely known as "The Flower Man"—bookend the broad range of approaches taken by the artists in *No Zoning*.

The Art Guys, collaborators since their days as graduate students at the University of Houston, use humor, philosophy, and all manner of media to reveal mysterious and absurd aspects of life. The final frontier for art, they believe, lies not in the realm of aesthetics, but in the social sphere. Consequently, a focus of their work has long been on inserting art into life by staging performances in public places. *The Art Guys Marry a Plant*, a multipart performance developed for *No Zoning*, consists of a June 13, 2009, wedding ceremony in the Lillie and Hugh Roy Cullen Sculpture Garden of the Museum of Fine Arts, Houston, located across the street from the CAMH, a reception inside CAMH, and a planting party at a public green space to be determined. Is the work an exploration of Germanic lore linking manhood to tree planting, a symbol of our simultaneously loving and destructive relationship to nature, or a provocative test of the slippery-slope "what's next?" argument used by many supporters of California's recently passed Proposition 8 outlawing gay marriage? The Art Guys aren't saying. They have simply organized an all-out, polyandrous, interkingdom hitch-fest, complete with invitations, a minister, and a wedding ring on a branch. The ensuing debate will shape the performance's meaning.

The Flower Man's work is equally engaged in life and nature, but it comes from a searing experience rather than a formal art education. In 1961 Cleveland Turner was traveling by bus from his home in rural Mississippi to Los Angeles to take a job when he became waylaid in Houston by a friend and succumbed to the attractions of alcohol. Eventually he was discovered drunk facedown in a ditch and brought to a hospital by a good Samaritan. While detoxing, he had a vision of a whirlwind of junk swirling in the air above him. If he survived and stayed sober, he resolved, he would devote his life to making beauty out of what others threw away. After more than twenty-five years of keeping this promise, his house and garden on Francis Street in the Third Ward is a riotous explosion of artificial and real flowers, bright paintwork, and inspired assemblages of castaway toys, appliances, and other detritus. Regarded as the premier practitioner of yard art in the United States, The Flower Man has created a sculptural installation on the CAMH's front lawn from found objects and flowers. During regular trips to the museum on his flower-bedecked bicycle, he will update, embellish, and maintain the work, making it a miniature expression of

1973

B. E. & J. Holding Firm
Bob Camblin, Earl Staley, and Joe Tate, all university studio art teachers, used the chance operation of the I Ching to name their collaboration the "B. E. & J. Holding Firm." In the backyard of their shared Montrose-area studio on Garrott Street, they built a large sculptural tower with a payphone on the third floor. It became a meeting place for many artists in the community, including Al Smith, David Folkman, Jack Boynton, and Mark Battista, a former architecture student from Rice University. Their collaboration resulted in three exhibitions at the University of St. Thomas.

Re:Vision
In fall 1973 Ian Glennie, interim director of the Contemporary Arts Museum, organized an exhibition called *Re:Vision,* which included performances, concerts, films, and artworks. One of the projects was a site-based sound portrait of Houston by Robert Whitman, a New York artist known for his theater and technology works. Whitman assembled volunteers and assigned each participant a specific location on a map of Houston and a time to call in. When they reached Whitman, they talked about where they were and what they saw. Using a sound mixing board, Whitman then arranged recordings of the calls into a concertlike sound piece that was broadcast live on Pacifica radio.

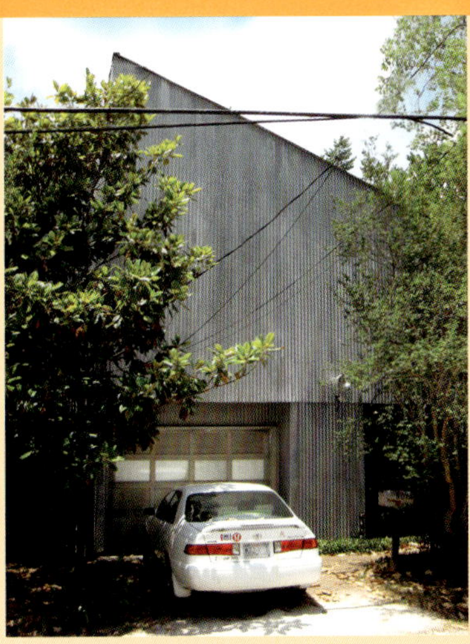

1974

West End* Metal Houses
On Roy Street, a few blocks away from the Beer Can House and mirroring the vernacular metal warehouses scattered throughout the neighborhood, architects Eugene Aubry, Ian Glennie, and Hossein Oskouie designed the first residence using an industrial metal exterior. This residential type has since proliferated in the area (sometimes referred to as "Tin Town") and throughout the city. Glennie and Fredericka Hunter of Texas Gallery were the original inhabitants of the loftlike space, and they presented the first Houston performances of composer Philip Glass and pioneer performance artist Joan Jonas in their home.

*The area informally known as the West End is bounded by Washington Avenue on the north, Memorial on the south, and Durham and Westcott to the east and west, incorporating more formal subdivisions such as Rice Military and Magnolia Grove.

Original West End metal house, Roy at Blossom Streets, 2009

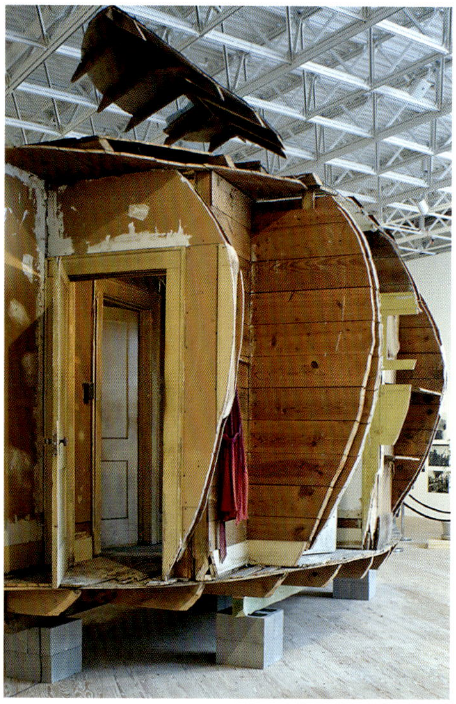

Dan Havel and Dean Ruck, *Give and Take* (detail), 2009. Installation view, Contemporary Arts Museum Houston

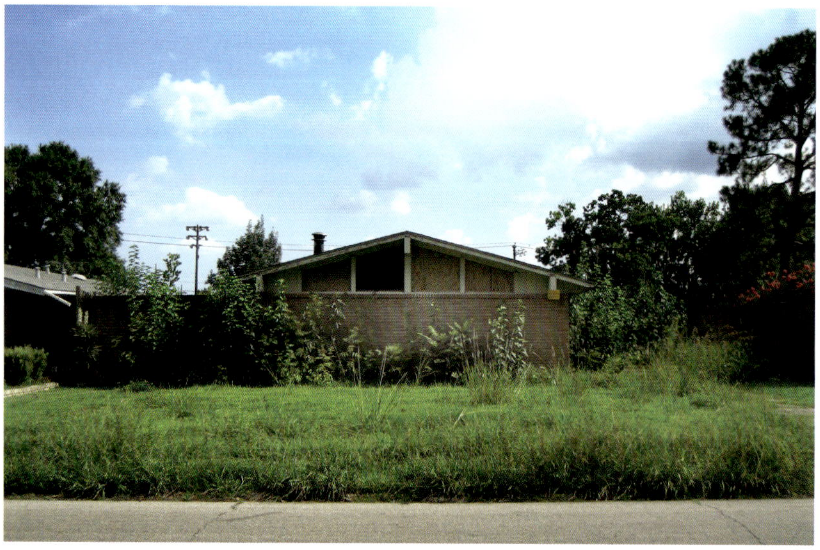

Mary Ellen Carroll, *prototype 180: house*, Sharpstown, 1999–2009

his home-as-*Gesamtkunstwerk*, or total work of art. The other artists in *No Zoning* fall at different points on the spectrum between the tactical conceptualism of The Art Guys and the inspired visions of The Flower Man, but they share the same exuberant drive to make life in Houston a richer, more aesthetic experience.

A number of artists in *No Zoning* employ the city itself—its landscape, architecture, and character—as material and inspiration. Local writer and artist Christa Forster believes that Houston provides fertile soil for all manner of artistic investigations and that its rapid cycles of decay and rebirth, in both the natural and built environment, are catalysts for the creative process.[8] Unearthing and reworking ideas has always been an artist's prerogative, and the continually changing biosphere of Houston, Forster argues, may galvanize artists to realize a concept quickly, before it evanesces like so much of the landscape around them. In a collaboration they jokingly call DD Demo, Dan Havel and Dean Ruck use the city's many condemned houses as sculptural material. Like Gordon Matta-Clark (1943–78), who made sculptural cuts in abandoned buildings in New York and planned an unrealized project along the 610 Loop freeway in Houston (see page 21, top left), they deconstruct abandoned architecture, exploring a broad range of formal and symbolic possibilities. Using handheld power tools, they have made decorative incisions in the skins of wooden buildings, scavenged materials from the exteriors of houses to create funnel-like inverted pathways through their centers, and transformed gutted house interiors into camera obscuras. For *No Zoning*, in a new work titled *Give and Take*, the artists have extracted the core of a small condemned two-story house in Houston's Heights neighborhood and reconstructed it in the Museum's main gallery. Ovoid in outline, as if removed with a giant ice-cream scoop, the core with its intersections of floors, walls, and ceilings—the "give" component—exposes the flimsiness of the structures constituting the idea of home. The "take" component, the hollowed-out house, also on view for a limited period, memorializes lost times and lives.

In another architectural project, located in the master-

1975

The Menil Collection Campus

Facilitated by the lack of zoning in Houston, John and Dominique de Menil discreetly began acquiring thirty acres of property adjacent to the University of St. Thomas, at first intended for potential university expansion. They later decided to build their museum there and to maintain the residential properties against the incursion of unwanted architecture and businesses. In 1974, under the direction of architect Howard Barnstone, the many bungalows comprising the neighborhood were all painted gray with white trim, inspired in part by Dominique de Menil's Rice Museum exhibition of grisaille painting *Gray is the Color*. This gray theme informed the look of the Renzo Piano–designed Menil Collection, which opened in June 1987 on part of the site where some houses had been demolished or moved. The remaining bungalows today are art administrative offices, arts spaces, and homes—a unique and homogeneous neighborhood-within-a-neighborhood.

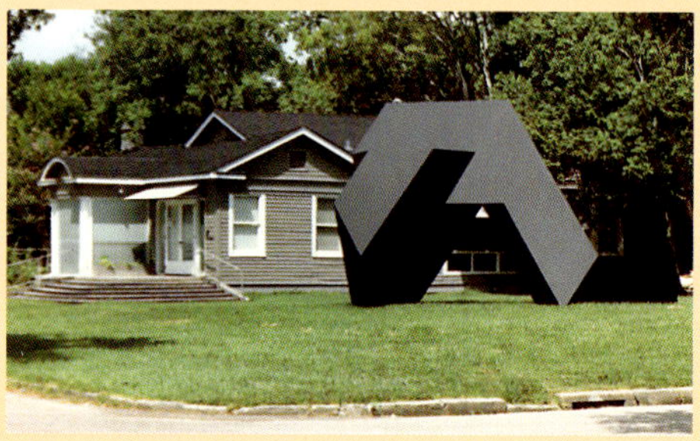

Menil Foundation office located on future site of the Menil Collection, Branard at Mulberry Streets, c. 1974

1976

See Saw

As part of the Main Street Festival, artist Mel Chin created an earthwork called *See Saw* in Hermann Park with funds he raised from GeoSource, an oil company. Chin and GeoSource worked closely to build the work, which consisted of two six-by-six-foot "planter boxes" set sixty inches apart and linked by a hydraulic system, so that they ascended and descended in opposition to each other when visitors stood on them.

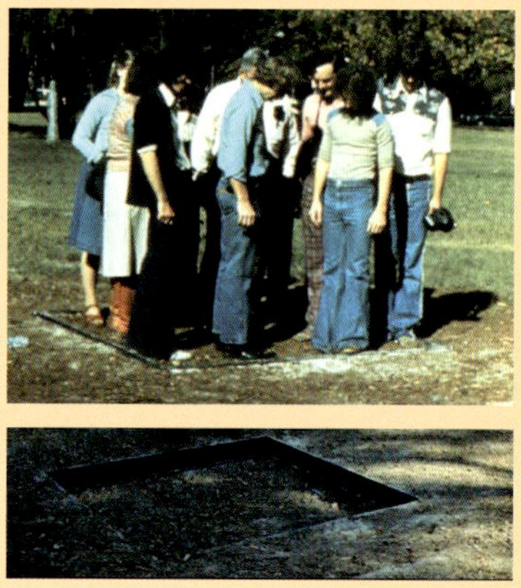

Mel Chin, *See Saw*, 1976

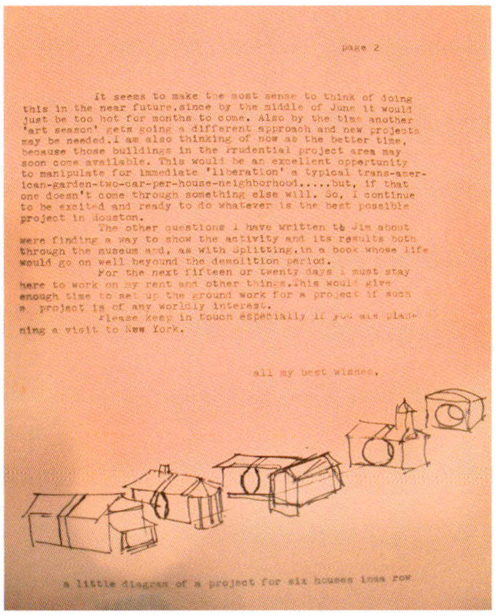

page 2

It seems to make the most sense to think of doing this in the near future, since by the middle of June it would just be too hot for months to come. Also by the time another 'art season' gets going a different approach and new projects may be needed. I am also thinking of now as the better time, because those buildings in the Prudential project area may soon come available. This would be an excellent opportunity to manipulate for immediate 'liberation' a typical trans-american-garden-two-car-per-house-neighborhood.....but, if that one doesn't come through something else will. So, I continue to be excited and ready to do whatever is the best possible project in Houston.

The other questions I have written to Jim about were finding a way to show the activity and its results both through the museum and, as with Splitting, in a book whose life would go on well beyound the demolition period.

For the next fifteen or twenty days I must stay here to work on my rent and other things. This would give enough time to set up the ground work for a project if such a project is of any worldly interest.

Please keep in touch especially if you are planning a visit to New York.

all my best wishes.

a little diagram of a project for six houses in a row

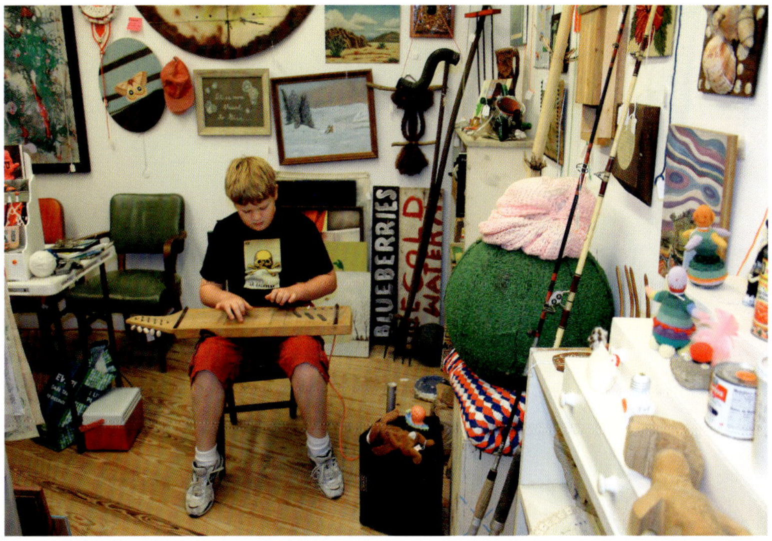

Gordon Matta-Clark, *Letter from Gordon Matta-Clark to Marilyn Oshman Lubetkin* (with sketch of proposed Houston project), May 15, 1975. Estate of Gordon Matta-Clark on deposit at the Canadian Centre for Architecture, Montréal

right:
Bill Davenport, *Bill's Junk* (interior detail with shopper), 2009. Installation view, Contemporary Arts Museum

planned community of Sharpstown in southwest Houston, artist Mary Ellen Carroll, who divides her time between New York and Houston, where she teaches in Rice University's School of Architecture, takes a more Duchampian approach to intervening in the city's built environment. She has purchased an abandoned ranch-style tract house in Sharpstown, which was founded in 1955 by developer Frank Sharp and became a national model for car-centric subdivisions, and intends—with the help of a house-moving company—to pivot the house 180 degrees, keeping the original lot proportions so that the rear of the house and its spacious backyard face the street, which otherwise consists entirely of uniform facades and small front yards. Obviously, this humorous form of culture jamming (which is only possible because the house abuts a park, freeing her from the yard setbacks stipulated by community deed restrictions) will disrupt the monotony of a well-loved yet cookie-cutter neighborhood. But the rotation also will highlight the myriad expectations, tacit and explicit, to which all city dwellers unconsciously conform. Carroll hopes her house, which will be used as a creative conference center (and whose floorboards provided the inspiration for the multipurpose table-cum-podium serving as a platform for performances, symposia, and artists' talks in the exhibition), will inspire others to see the potential in the ordinary as well as to think outside the box, the plat, the city grid.

Along with suburban sprawl, Houston also is a playful place full of the handmade: jury-rigged houses, honky-tonks, barbeque joints, tire repair shops, and icehouse bars throughout the city appear to have been thrown together over the course of a few afternoon beers. This loose, impromptu spirit inspires a number of exhibition artists. *Bill's Junk*, a storefront operated by Bill Davenport on the ground floor of the building he occupies with his wife, the painter Francesca Fuchs, is part meta-thrift shop, part engulfing art installation. It is filled with all manner of curios, but it specializes in amateur art objects—what Davenport offhandedly refers to as "the things people made but then don't want anymore."[9] Collected over years of haunting resale shops and rummage and estate sales, the paintings, ceramic pots, and craft-shop woodworking projects in *Bill's Junk* reflect the good, the bad, and the ugly sides of self-taught art making. A penciled price tag with a description dangles from every item, adding humorous layers of meaning

1977

Mayhem at CAM
The Kilgore Rangerettes, a renowned women's synchronized drill team dressed as miniskirted cowgirls, performed during the opening night of an exhibition at CAM organized by James Harithas featuring the work of Antoni Miralda, a sculptor whose medium is food and its attendant ceremonies. In a nod to the local Rainbow Bread Company, the artwork on view was an installation of bread dyed all the colors of the spectrum. Perhaps stirred by the high-kicking Rangerettes, the opening night crowd erupted in mayhem and tore the bread apart in a food fight that spilled into the streets.

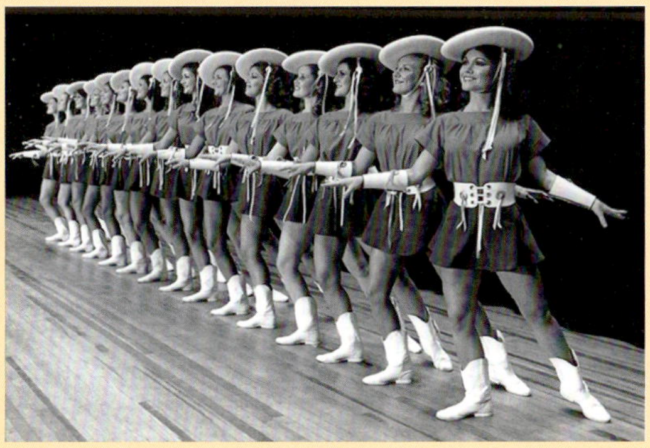

The Kilgore Rangerettes, mid-1970s

SWAMP
A community-wide offshoot of the Rice University Media Center, the Southwest Alternate Media Project (SWAMP) was founded as a Texas-based nonprofit organization to promote the creation and appreciation of film, video, and new media, as well as, originally, to provide low-cost access to media production facilities.

1978

Christ Church Gallery
Artist Terrell James opened and operated a gallery for several years on the premises of the downtown Christ Church Cathedral, an Episcopal church founded in 1839.

Women's Caucus for Art
The Houston Women's Caucus for Art was founded to actively support equal opportunity and visibility for work by women. Participants included such individuals as MaryRoss Taylor, Gertrude Barnstone, Lynn Randolph, Toby Topek, Suzanne Bloom, and Roberta Graham Harris.

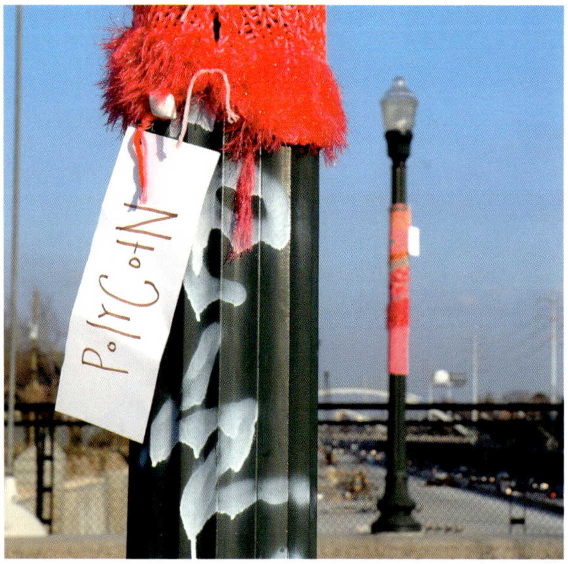

KnittaPlease, tagged streetlights over Highway 59, Houston, 2006

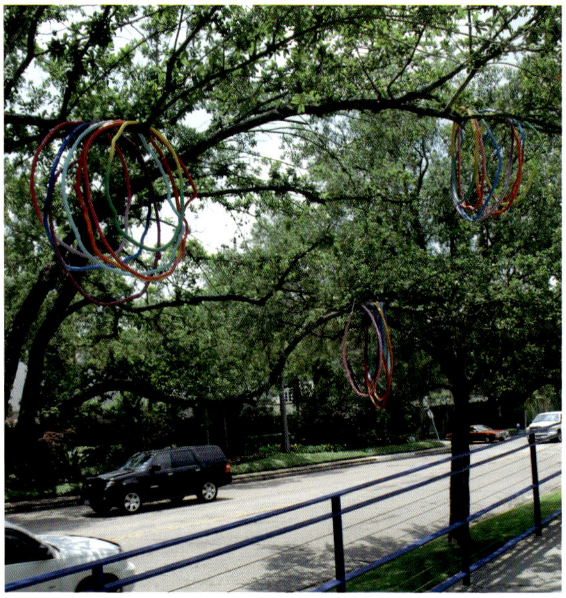

Lee Littlefield, *Rings on Bissonnet*, 2009. Installation view, Contemporary Arts Museum Houston

and value. The artist's undergraduate diploma is $32,000, the price of tuition; a mud dauber's nest is 75¢, or "25 cents a hole"; and *Island of Tears*, a painting depicting surfers frolicking in an ocean of Christ's tears, is $300, simply because it is such an outrageously nutty image. For the exhibition, Davenport has installed within the museum a satellite branch of his shop, where he regularly oversees its operation.

Taking the populist-conceptualist approach of *Bill's Junk* even more to a street level, the collective KnittaPlease, a group of "guerilla knitters" led by Magda Sayeg, has been applying graffiti strategies to aspects of the city since 2006. They have "tagged" signposts, door handles, and car antennae across Houston with colorful knit cozies, making countless urban corners warmer and fuzzier. Members of the collaborative, with nom-de-knit monikers like "PolyCotN" and "MascuKnitity," have recently increased the scale and ambition of their projects, recycling thrift-store afghans to wrap a bus in Mexico City. For *No Zoning*, KnittaPlease has swaddled the large front desk in the CAMH's Brown Foundation Gallery as well as the 194-foot Bissonnet Street terrace railing, adding an inviting layer of the homespun to the museum's angular modernist design.

Sculptor Lee Littlefield also takes a commando-like approach to infiltrating his three-dimensional art into the city. Since 1998, he has been installing eye-catching sculptures he calls "Pop-Ups" along Houston freeways. Made from reshaped vines and wood he collects from various Houston locales, Littlefield's Pop-Ups resemble vegetation from the alien planets of sci-fi movies. They seem to appear without warning like exotic weeds in underpasses and embankments along Interstates 10 and 45 where, he says, they can "burst, dazzle, and wink at those that pass by."[10] At first, the sculptures, which are painted in a distinctive scheme of graduated brilliant colors, were routinely removed by the agencies responsible for the public right-of-ways, depending on when they were first noticed. Gradually, however, Littlefield began negotiating with the Texas Department of Transportation and Harris County Flood Control.

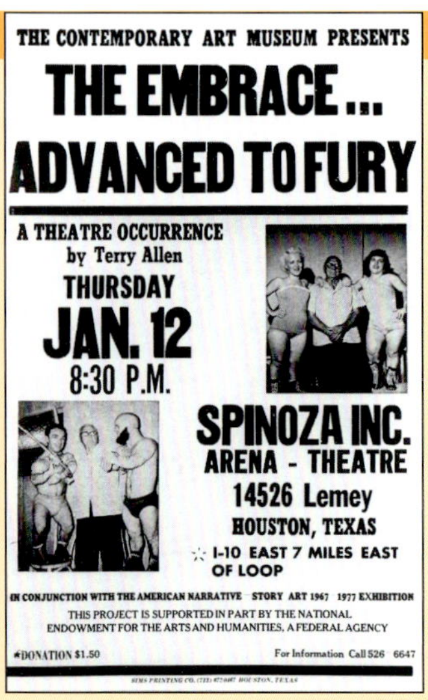

1978

Ring II: The Embrace ... Advanced to Fury
Terry Allen presented his music-theater piece *The Ring* in a full-scale wrestling ring erected in Spinoza, Inc., the industrial warehouse of Max Miller's railroad track company near Channelview. In the ring, a couple verbally recounted their relationship as a male and a female wrestler violently acted out their roles while random audience members stood and recited parts of the narrative. This was one of the first public performances of actress/performance artist Jo Harvey Allen.

Poster for Terry Allen's *The Embrace...*, 1978

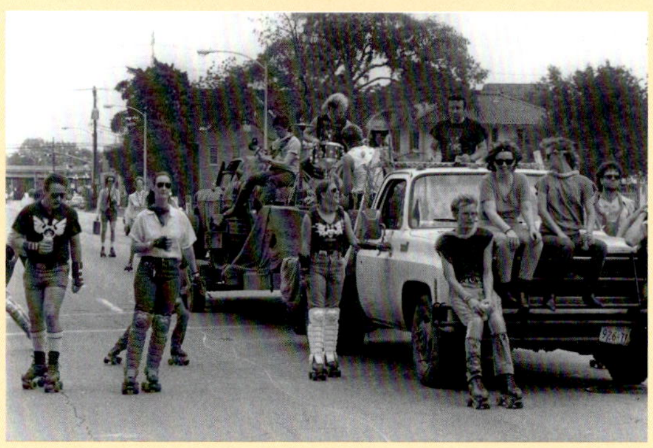

Urban Animals, New Music Parade, Montrose Boulevard, 1986

1979

Urban Animals
The Urban Animals, a loose-knit group of street skaters, was formed by Edie Scott and Scott Prescott. Their activities included roller hockey, parking garage surfing, midnight crosstown skating, bar hopping, roller jousting, and graffiti art. At their zenith in the late 1980s, they numbered several hundred and included skating filmmakers, artists, mechanics, lawyers, electricians, topless dancers, bartenders, and even a Harris County deputy. The Animals became notorious among the press, city government, and local police, but the group's creative output was large and its charitable efforts at local shelters and community centers were generous.

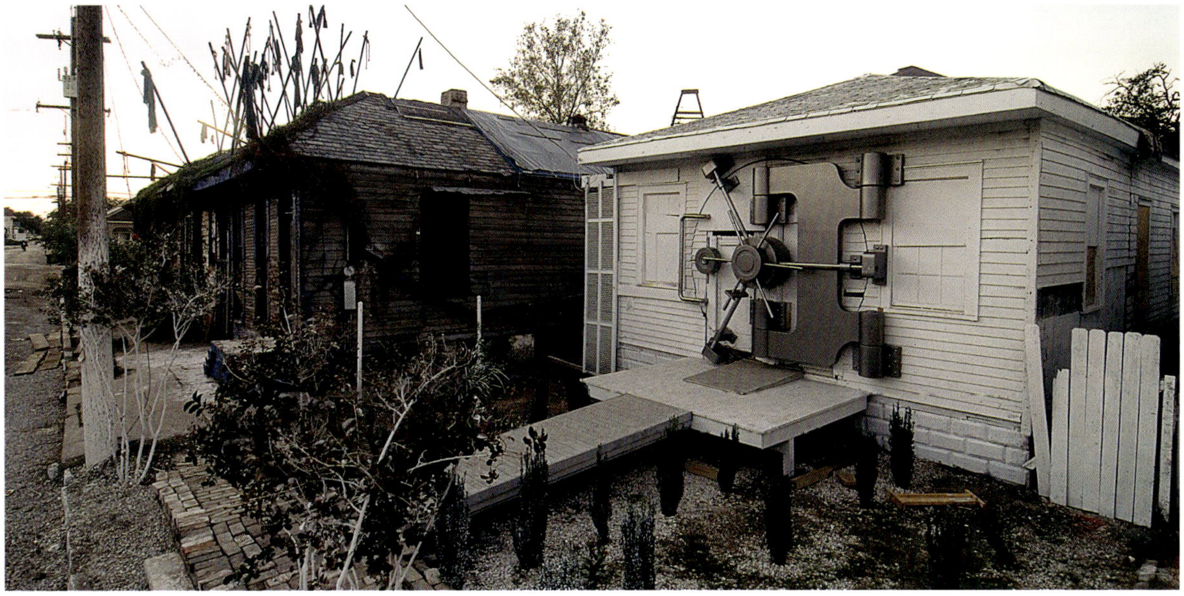

Mel Chin, *SAFEHOUSE*, 2008.
North Villere Street, St. Roch neighborhood, New Orleans

Littlefield now has reached agreements that allow allow him to place his sculptures according to specific rules. Found everywhere from Houston to New York, Littlefield's biomorphic abstractions serve as protagonists in a larger narrative: the artist's dream of being a Johnny Appleseed of a nationwide crop of Pop-Ups glorifying the country's urban areas and thoroughfares.

Other artists in the exhibition grapple critically with daily life in Houston, seeking to fix problems and realize potentials. Mel Chin, a native Houstonian now living and working in North Carolina, is universally regarded as the George Washington of socially engaged art in the city. Throughout his career, he has sought to develop community-based art projects, fusing what he calls "science and poetry" in a positive form of protest to provide an inspirational spark for community organization.[11] Debuting in fall 2008 during the new Prospect.1 New Orleans biennial exhibition of contemporary art with an abandoned house reconfigured to resemble a bank vault, his collaborative work *The Fundred Dollar Bill Project* is a multipart, community-based initiative to draw attention to the widespread problem of lead contamination in the urban environment. Due to careless paint scraping and pollution from nearby highways built when gasoline contained lead additives, areas of New Orleans and Houston have the most lead-saturated topsoil in the country. Lead, which is known to cause learning disabilities in children, is increasingly linked to violent behavior and cycles of poverty and crime in cities.[12] In New Orleans and at the CAMH, Chin has asked community members to draw their own portraits and denominations on blank currency patterns, which are then cut out and pinned to gallery walls. He plans to amass six thousand pounds of these notes—the weight of the $300 million in one-dollar bills it will take to ameliorate this problem in one city by using calcium phosphate to form unbreakable, neutralizing molecular bonds with the toxin. Collected from citizens across the country, the notes will then be delivered to Congress in Washington, D.C., in a customized, vegetable-oil-powered armored truck as a grassroots plea for a solution to a crippling problem.

The Red House
Placing a classified ad in the *Houston Chronicle*, artist Mel Ziegler offered to paint any house for free as long as the owner accepted his conditions that the entire edifice, inside and out, be painted boldly in red and left that way for three months. The house remained a compelling architectural quirk on Bomar Street in the Montrose neighborhood for fifteen years because the owners kept repainting the house as Ziegler had originally instructed. The structure still exists but is no longer painted red.

Square One
Mark Lombardi moved to Houston in 1975 to become an assistant curator under Director James Harithas at the Contemporary Arts Museum. In 1979 in an attempt to support himself and other local artists such as James Bettison, Ibsen Espada, Andy Feehan, and Andy Mann, he opened the gallery Square One on Bissonnet Street. Later in 1994, Lombardi began an art practice of tracking various political, energy, and military-industrial complex conspiracies on thousands of index cards, then mapping the connections on elaborate flow chart-like drawings.

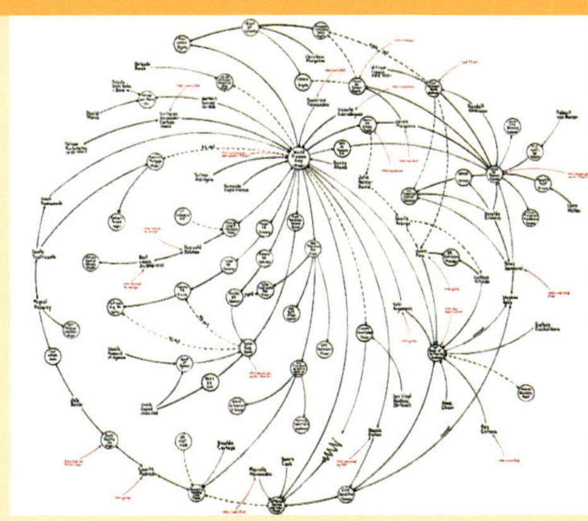

Mark Lombardi, *World Finance Corporation, Miami, Florida, c. 1970–79 (6th Version)* (detail), 1999

120 Portland
Michael Peranteau and artist Max Pruneda began monthly exhibitions of area artists at 120 Portland, a restaurant where Pruneda was chef. The openings were held on Sundays, when the restaurant was closed.

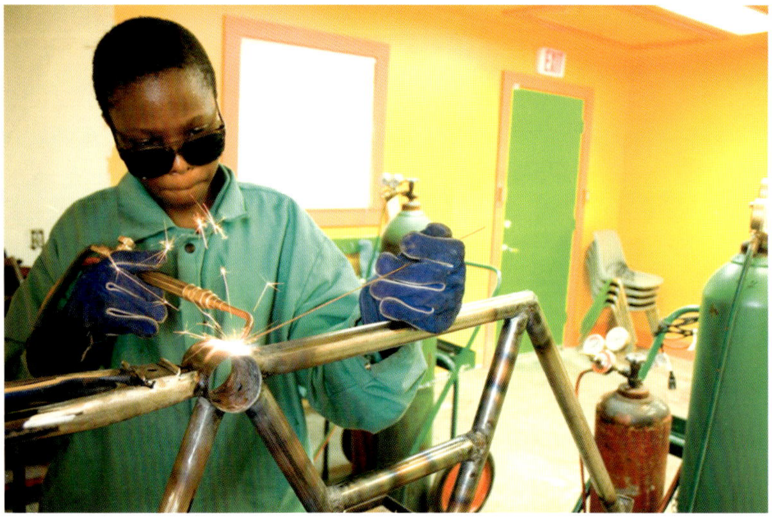

Welding at Workshop Houston, 2007

right:
Eric Leshinsky, *Museum for Missing Places* (*Exhibit 3: Valuing Vacancy*) (detail from website), 2005–06

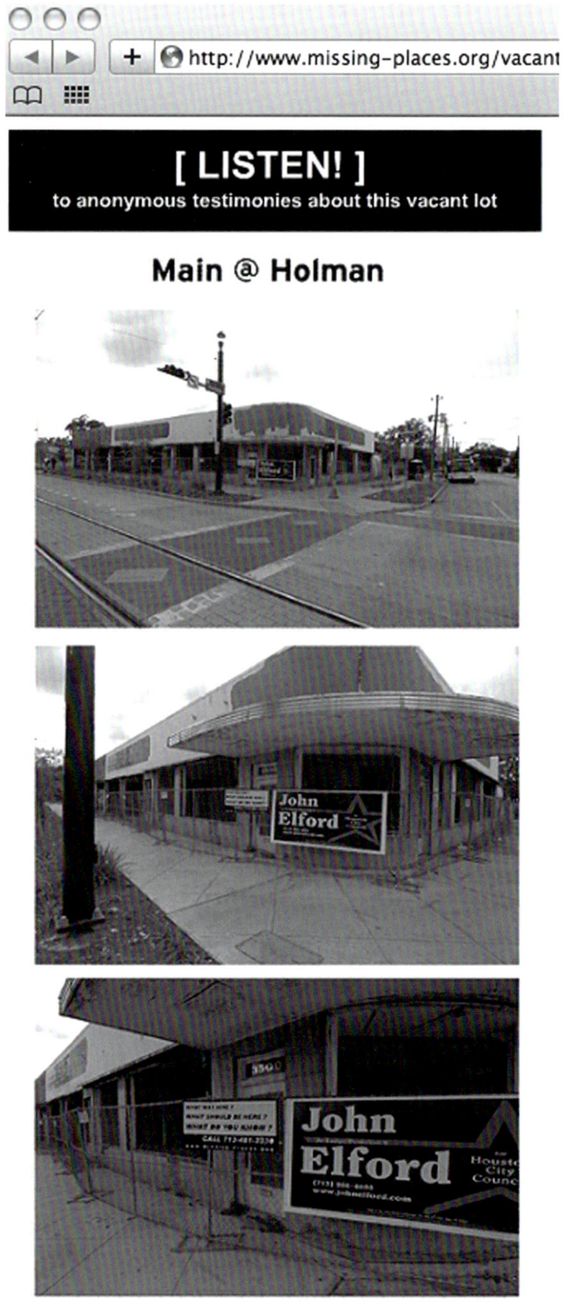

Founded by Benjy Mason, Zach Moser, Katy Goodman, and Seth Capron in 2003, Workshop Houston is an after-school neighborhood center based in Houston's historically black and poor Third Ward. Equipped with welding equipment, sewing machines, and computer recording technology, its Bike Shop, Style Shop, Chop Shop, Beat Shop, and Scholar Shop get kids working on fun, creative, and practical projects. Begun as a means for a group of artist friends to live and work communally and constructively, Workshop Houston has become a resource center and think tank—an art school providing practical skills to neighborhood kids and helping them produce original designs. For *No Zoning*, Mason and Moser employ Workshop Houston's community-organization model for their own artistic project: the *Yacht Shop*. Each weekend, as if in a living-history museum, Mason, Moser, and a group of volunteers are building a nineteen-foot wooden sailing skiff in the galleries. When the boat is finished, Mason and Moser plan to burn it at sea, evoking a Viking funeral—a gesture that echoes their emphasis on group process over precious product.

The *Museum for Missing Places*, a Web-based institution developed by architect Eric Leshinsky in 2005

1979

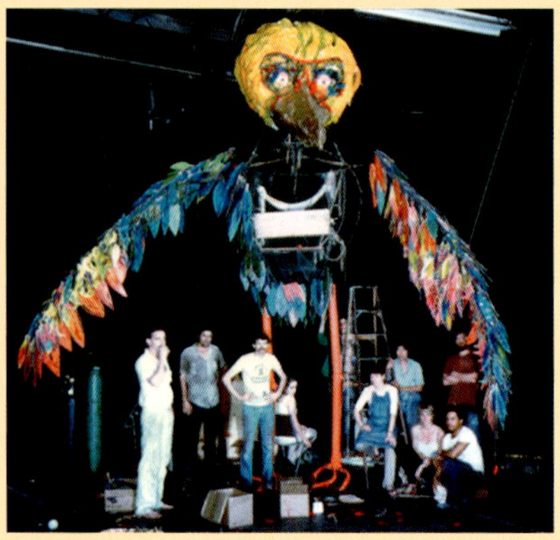

Robert Shuttlesworth, Mark Coughlin, Ed Wilson, Judy Long, Jack Massing, Kathy Wilson, Mary Jenewein, Kelly Alison, Bert Samples, and Jim Poag, *SUMfest*, Lawndale Art and Performance Center, Hillman Street, 1982

Lawndale Art and Performance Center

Lawndale Art and Performance Center (now Lawndale Art Center) began in a warehouse located on Hillman Street near Lawndale in the East End of Houston after a fire displaced the painting and sculpture department of the University of Houston. Under the direction of artist and sculpture professor James Surls with programming implemented independently from the university, the cavernous former cable factory grew into a freewheeling laboratory environment that served as classroom, studio, and exhibition and performance space for students and artists in the community. One of the earliest exhibitions was *Pow Wow: Contemporary Artists & Models Ball, Miniatures Exhibition*, an exhibition of work by over five hundred artists. In 1993, Lawndale moved to its current location on Main Street in the Museum District.

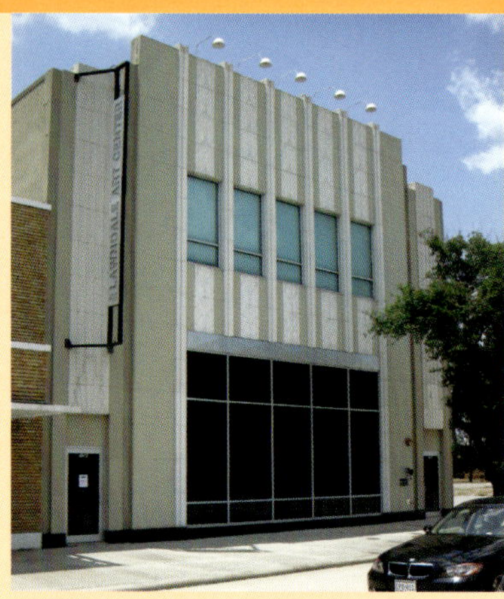

Lawndale Art Center, Main Street, 2009

Smithsonian Archives of American Art

As part of a national initiative the Smithsonian Archives of American Art began a pilot project, the first privately funded archive documenting Texas artists. Originally scheduled to function for two years, it continued through 1985 because of the scale of the work. This statewide archive was run locally by Sandra Curtis Levy and Terrell James, with Liz Ward and Maggie Olvey assisting. A duplicate of this archive, which is part of the National Archives of American Art, is kept on microfilm at the Museum of Fine Arts, Houston.

(http://www.missing-places.org), examines the rapid cycles of redevelopment occurring around the CAMH in Houston's Museum District. Initially a response to the dismantling of the district's residential neighborhood by developers looking to replace single-family dwellings with high-density, high-profit townhouses, the *Museum for Missing Places* became a study of the city and its relentless evolution. Houston, Leshinsky argues, is unusual among American cities because its "historical continuity has long been defined strangely by the impermanence of its built landscape rather than its fixity."[13] What Houston needs, he believes, is an institution dedicated to studying its change. After all, this is a place where longtime residents can get lost because familiar landmarks vanish overnight. Originally the project featured online maps on which website visitors could "tag" changing places with comments and photographs, as well as physical questionnaires located at the places in flux for passersby to fill out. In this way, it operated as a "feedback loop" through which Houstonians could add ever more layers of information about their city.[14] In *No Zoning*, the *Museum for Missing Places* is accessible only as a website. By fixing empty, oddball, and transitory urban "non-places" and public observations about them in online amber, it provides a rare opportunity to step outside the continuous flow of city life in Houston and consider the sum of its losses and gains.

As Leshinsky's virtual museum points out, Houston has an exceptionally large and diverse constellation of institutions dedicated to preserving and presenting visual art. Aside from its commercial galleries and alternative spaces, it has the encyclopedic Museum of Fine Arts, Houston, the non-collecting CAMH, and the Blaffer Gallery at the University of Houston, which also presents contemporary art and does not collect. It is home to the Menil Collection and the Station Museum, established as private foundations through which individual Houstonians have shared their collections and passions with the city. In addition, it has the Orange Show Center for Visionary Art, an organization responsible for preserving two folk art environments—Jeff McKissack's shrine to citrus fruit and John Milkovisch's Beer Can House—as well as organizing the Art Car Parade, an annual citywide event now held downtown that began in 1986 when a group of artists paraded their customized and decorated cars down Montrose Boulevard.

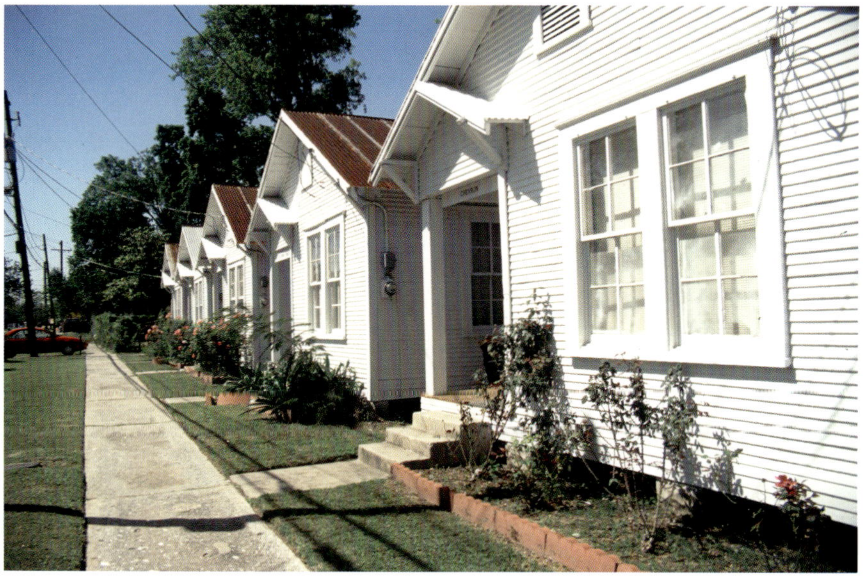

Project Row Houses, Houston, c. 2000

As diverse as these institutions may be, they are still limited by their spaces, budgets, and missions. Several artists in *No Zoning* offer alternatives to the city's established institutions. In 1993 Rick Lowe, trained as an artist, started a new institution that uniquely blends art and real life when he founded Project Row Houses in the Third Ward. Lowe and volunteers from across Houston transformed a block of abandoned shotgun shacks into art exhibition spaces and, later, housing for single mothers. Not only does Project Row Houses present changing exhibitions by regional and international artists and preserve an endangered form of vernacular architecture, but, as Lowe points out, it also creates "social sculpture," an art form pioneered by German artist Josef Beuys (1921–86) that defines collective activity as a form of art. In this sense, Project Row Houses, with its ongoing mission of creating "community through the celebration of art,

1980

1980s

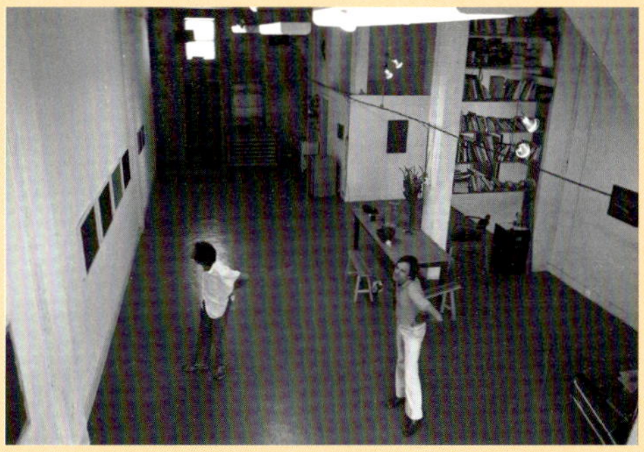

Mel Chin and Joe Dugan, interior of Studio One, 1981

Studio One
William Steen founded Studio One in a storefront studio space he shared with Mel Chin on Congress Street in a derelict area east of downtown Houston. For several years, it was one of the most influential art spaces in the city. Art exhibitions, readings, lectures, films, and performances were staged there, including works by experimental punk band Culturcide, improvisational musician Richard Landry, avant-garde filmmaker Kurt Kren, The Art Guys, and actor/artist Dennis Hopper. Steen also became a liaison to various outsider and prison artists such as Henry Ray "Pretty Boy" Clark.

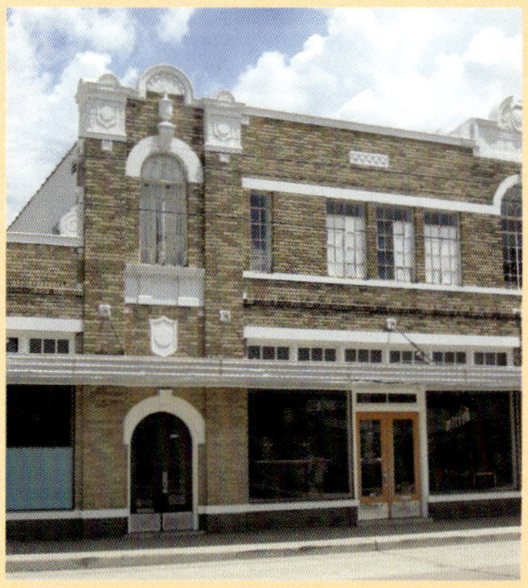

3221 Milam, 2009

3221 Milam
Dancer and choreographer Farrell Dyde founded the alternative space 3221 Milam, which presented art exhibitions, performances, dance, and music.

Rock Extension
Artist Kate Ericson's *Rock Extension* was a row of rocks that extended from the front porch and down the walkway of a house in the Montrose area. Ericson went on to create several other important works in Houston in collaboration with her husband, Mel Ziegler.

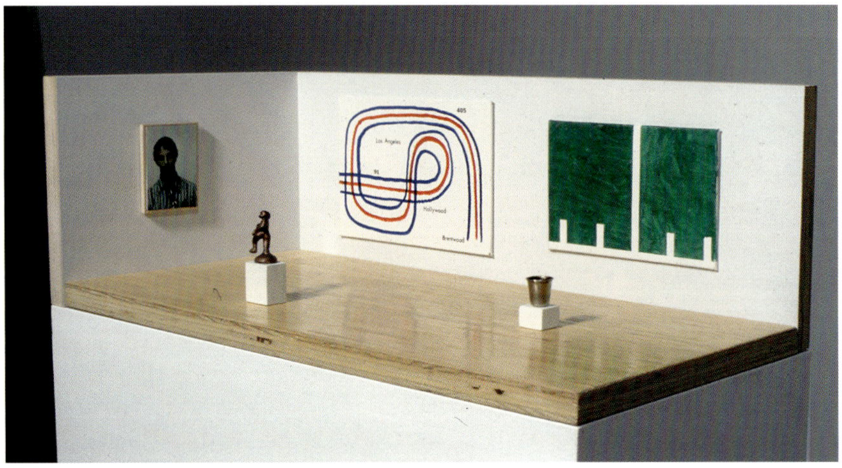

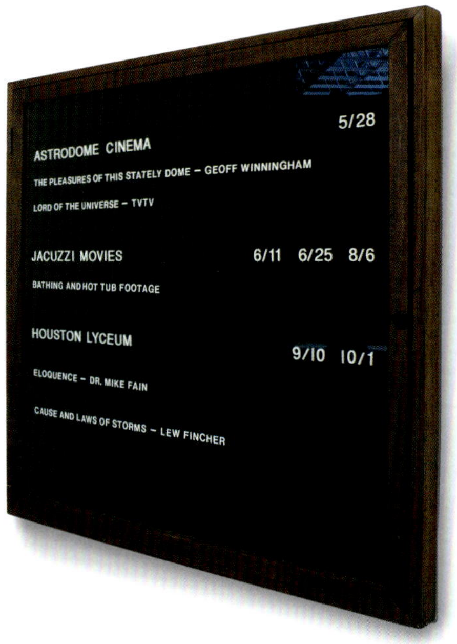

Sharon Engelstein, *Gallery One Three Seven* (Jeff Elrod exhibition, *Killer Paintings*), 1994

Andrea Grover, *Astrodome Cinema*, *Jacuzzi Movies*, and *Houston Lyceum* (marquee displaying screening and lecture events and times), 2009. Installation view, Contemporary Arts Museum Houston

African American culture, and history," is itself a work of art.[15] For *No Zoning*, Lowe steps back into his artist shoes by contributing a series of photographic portraits celebrating the residents of the Third Ward. Presented as transparencies in illuminated light boxes, as a diptych of photographs laminated on aluminum, as a stylized banner, and as a billboard in a park adjacent to Project Row Houses, the carefully composed and digitally edited photographs not only depict individual residents, but also describe their livelihoods in text captions. For example, Brother-N-Law poses with the tools of his catering trade above the words "Every Neighborhood Needs One," and Kenya Shabazz, a self-appointed guardian of neighborhood children, is dressed in his Black Panther's uniform and accompanied by the phrase "Power of Peace." Lowe realizes that the white-painted shotgun shacks of Project Row Houses have become positive emblems for the neighborhood and for Houston. Of these promotional portraits, he says, "I wanted to use some of the same marketing and branding strategies that made the architecture so well known to celebrate the real icons of the Third Ward—its residents."[16]

In *Gallery One Three Seven*, a miniature 1.37-square-foot exhibition space, artist Sharon Engelstein responds with humor and ingenuity to the constraints of exhibition making by displaying very small works, small enough to be shipped in envelopes. The project began on a whim in 1994 when Engelstein decided to transform a $7\frac{1}{2} \times 10\frac{3}{4} \times 20\frac{3}{4}$-inch model of Houston's Texas Gallery, which she first had made to test an idea for a full-scale sculpture, into a functioning exhibition space. Since its inception, *Gallery One Three Seven* has presented exhibitions of miniature work by Jeff Elrod, Mark Flood, and Nicola Thompson. Engelstein, who also has built a highly detailed replica of one of the Project Row Houses galleries, understands the way miniaturization can intensify an idea. Exhibitions for her *Gallery One Three Seven*, she jokes, are similar in quality, design, and impact to their full-scale endeavors, "but much smaller."[17] During *No Zoning*, Engelstein will organize seven mini-exhibitions of work by various artists, including Andrea Corson, David McGee, Hills Snyder, Amber Eagle, and Alexander Kvares. Begun at the end of a local recession in the nineties, *Gallery One Three Seven* once served as a low-cost means for

1980

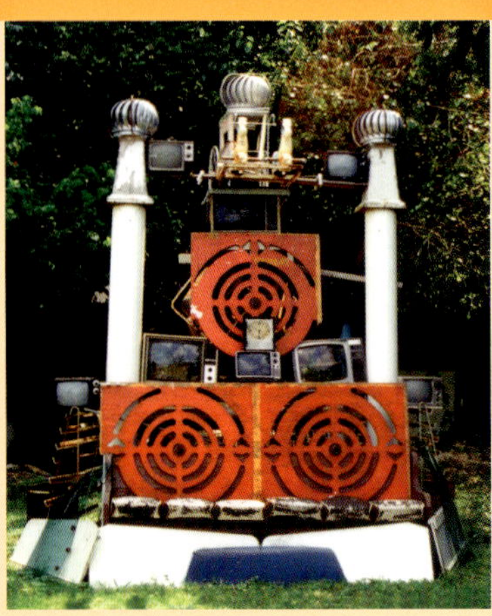

Sculpture in the yard of the Fan Man, c. 1995

The Fan Man

Bob Harper, the Fan Man, began to build an environment in the Third Ward that he called the "Third World." Assembling found materials like abandoned TVs, water skis, mannequins, bottles, and numerous electric fan blades, he said, "I build for the Lord. Everybody can look at what I build and know that there is a God up above because I get my ideas from the blue sky." The project grew until it covered the house and yard. In 1992 the house burned down when a gas heater exploded; Harper's mother died from injuries sustained in the fire. The Fan Man then moved to a property owned by his brother and began to rebuild his environment, working on it until his death in 1995.

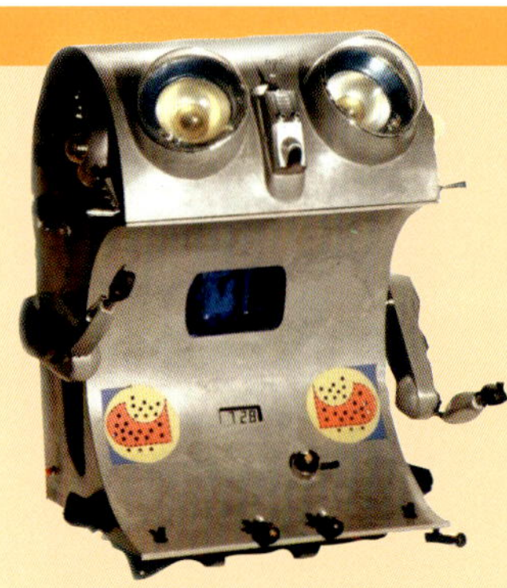

H. J. Bott, *ROWE™* and *ART-BARF™* ROBOTTs, both 1980

1981

DoV-z ROBOTTs

After making a series of sculptural radio-controlled robots, artist H. J. Bott staged eight biweekly robot performances in his studio in the Heights, which were highly attended by local Houston artists.

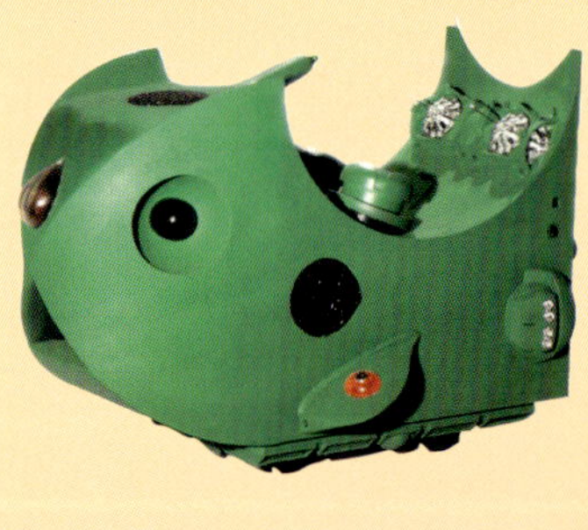

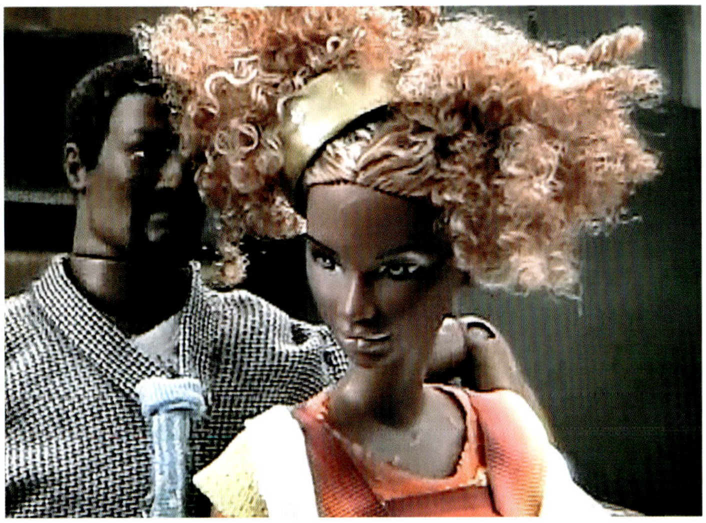

Lauren Kelley, video still from *Big Gurl*, 2006

artists to create the aesthetic and communal experience of an art exhibition. Today, as the country downsizes during a global financial crisis, this pocket project is a feisty reminder that art and artists will persevere.

Many believe Houston's social sphere shares some of the malleability of its urban landscape. Perhaps because it is a young place, which only boomed after air conditioning became widespread in the 1950s, and because, as a resident raconteur puts it, "there's no reason to live here unless you want to make something happen," the city is known for being a place where it is easy to meet like-minded individuals and where efforts to start something new often find moral or financial support. As evidenced by the alternative spaces Lawndale Art Center, founded by artist James Surls in 1979, and DiverseWorks, founded by artist Charles Gallagher in 1982, creative Houstonians have long been successful at marshaling resources, colleagues, and audiences. Two artists in *No Zoning*, Andrea Grover and Lauren Kelley, work as artist-impresarios, either building support systems for media that interest them or finding alternative means of broadcasting their visions.

Andrea Grover, who began her career as an artist making, among other things, installations, sound art, and digital photographs, came to Houston as a Core Fellow at the Glassell School of Art at the Museum of Fine Arts, Houston, which every year invites a small group of accomplished emerging artists and critical writers to work in the school's studios. During her two-year residency, Grover started making a 16mm film entitled *Rubbernecking* set in the city's East End neighborhood, and after her residency ended, she moved into an old church on Aurora Street in the Heights neighborhood, where she started screening films and videos by peers. Eventually this home theater became the Aurora Picture Show, a public micro-cinema with Grover as its creative director. Earlier this year, Grover retired from Aurora to expand her work as a "platformist," a term coined by artist David Robbins to mean "one who invents a platform and works actively with it as a medium for the presentation of others ... an artist at presenting others."[18] During the run of *No Zoning*, Grover is organizing and hosting a number of projects, including screening historic films such as Geoff Winningham's *The Pleasures of This Stately Dome* (1975) and Top Value Television's *The Lord of the Universe* (1974) on the construction and history of the Astrodome (the first domed stadium, nicknamed "The Eighth Wonder of the World," it opened in 1965); reprises of lectures entitled "The Cause and Laws of Storms" and "Eloquence" given at the Houston Lyceum (1854–1904), a precursor to the public library; and a series of "Jacuzzi movies" screened with audience members in portable pools on the CAMH's Bayard Lane backyard lawn.

The search for new platforms also inspires video artist Lauren Kelley. Her video *Prototypical Obsession/Oppression* is a work of art intended to be broadcast on public-access cable television as a pilot episode for a series she is developing titled *Limited Edition Logic*. Shot in stop-motion animation on miniature handmade sets using dolls and action figures, the work is a comedy of cultural tensions. Like all of Kelley's art, it addresses contemporary manners and mores through a delirious mix of outrageous humor, sincere engagement with social problems, and compelling visual effects. Among the topics it addresses

1982

Dark Continence
William Steen was commissioned to create a performance in front of the downtown library. Called *Dark Continence,* the performance included projected imagery, elaborate scaffolding, and dancer Margaret Boswell with music by Culturcide.

Houston Center for Photography
The Houston Center for Photography was founded as a member-run cooperative and was eventually incorporated as a nonprofit visual arts organization devoted exclusively to photography and related media.

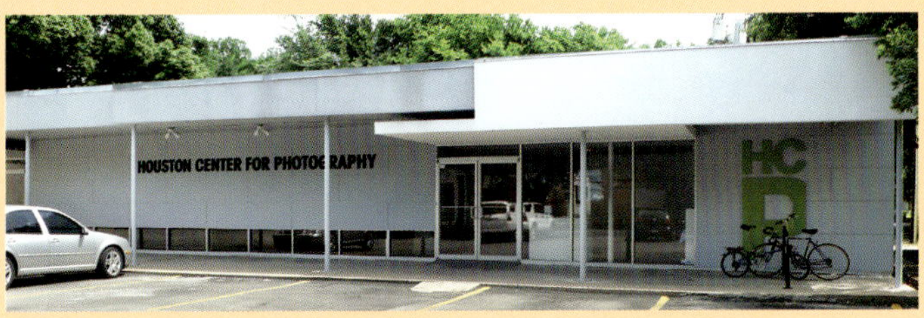

Houston Center for Photography, c. 2006

McKee Street Bridge
The McKee Street Bridge, which spans Buffalo Bayou in the northeast corner of downtown Houston, was regularly trashed with vandalism and graffiti up until the early 1980s. Artist/environmentalist Kirk Farris and photographer Paul Judice created an exhibition called *Bridges over Buffalo Bayou* that appeared at the Houston Public Library's downtown branch. Farris then acquired donations of paint and lighting supplies, as well as approval from the City of Houston, and went on to single-handedly revitalize the bridge. He continued the project with the acquisition of nearby property and added park space, which has become a source of civic pride.

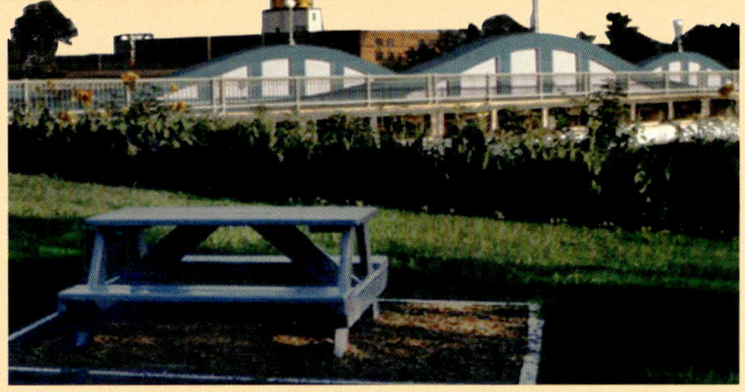

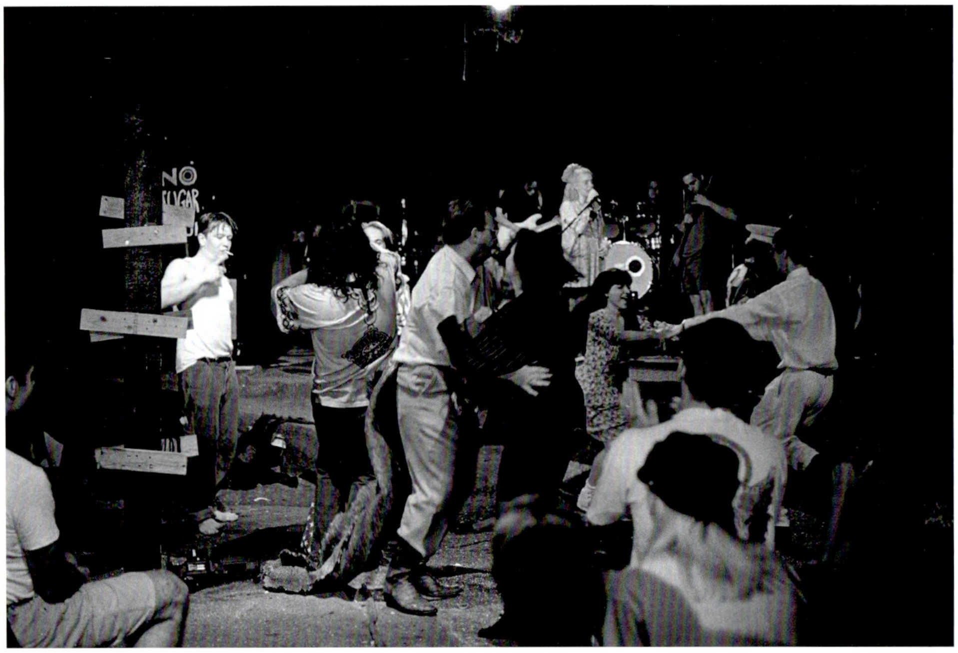

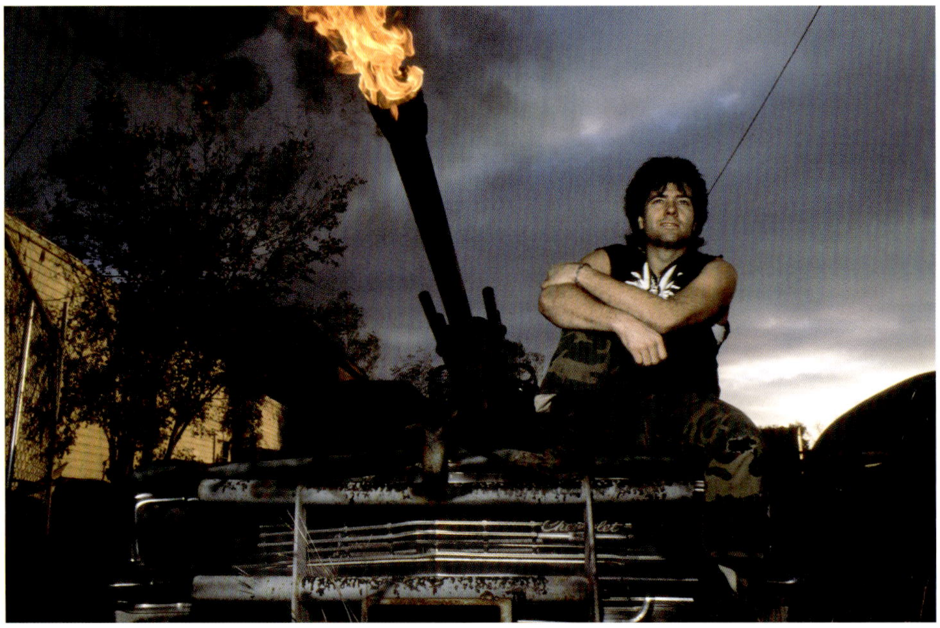

top:
George Hixson, Jason Nodler's *In the Underthunderloo*, 1993

right:
Ben Tecumseh DeSoto, *Scott Prescott*, 1987

1982

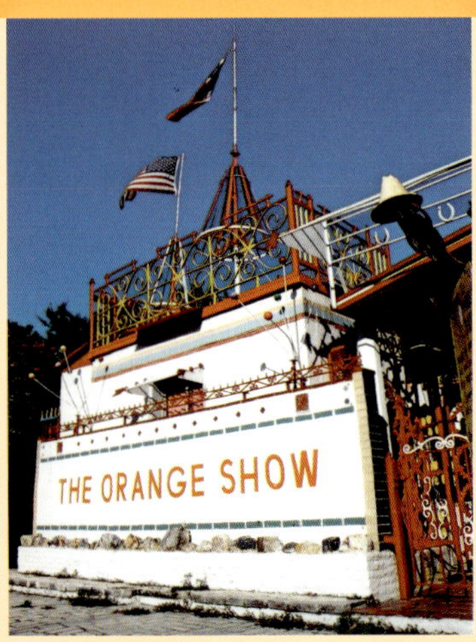

Facade of The Orange Show, c. 2000

The Orange Show Re-Opening
The Orange Show re-opened to the public after its restoration by the Orange Show Foundation (now the Orange Show Center for Visionary Art).
In 1983 the Orange Show Foundation began its stewardship of other visionary art sites and programming inspired by these sites.

Kuumba House
South African native Lindi Yeni founded Kuumba House to create, teach, perform, and preserve African art forms of dance, theater, music, and other creative expressions.

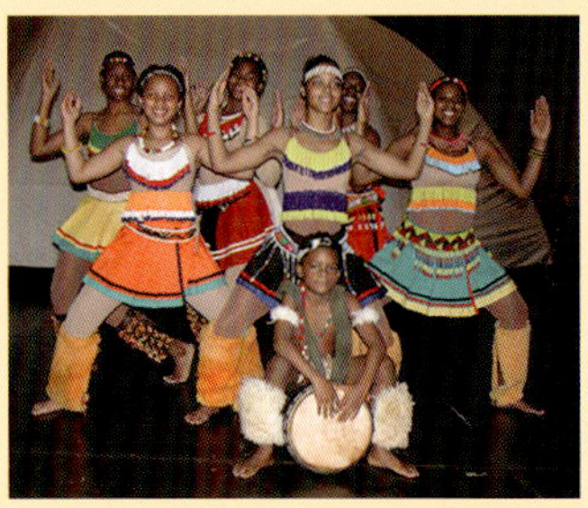

Kuumba House's dance troupe The Kuumba Kids, c. 2008

Midtown Art Center
The Midtown Art Center was founded at LaBranch and Holman Streets in 1982 as a multidisciplinary arts complex with music, visual art, performance, and literary programs. It continues as a community outreach organization.

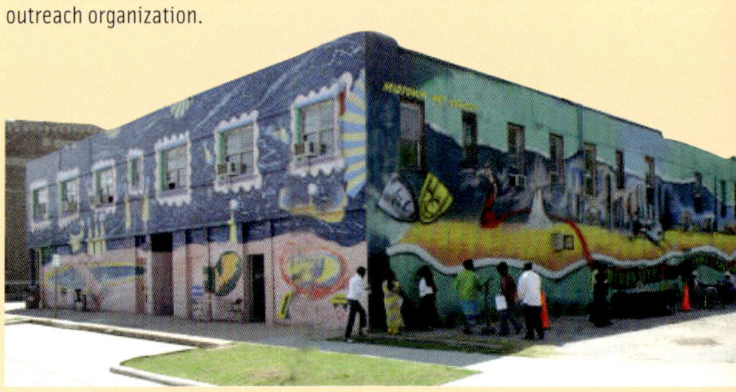

are racial and gender inequalities, manipulative relationships, and the problems of materialist societies. Although it is scheduled to be broadcast fifteen times on cable television in Houston during the run of *No Zoning*, the work also is being screened in the CAMH's galleries alongside its sets and props. *Prototypical Obsession/Oppression* aims to break out of the bubble of the contemporary art world and reach the widest possible audience through television. Subverting the medium responsible for shilling the goods and attitudes it satirizes, the pilot episode is an entertaining rallying cry for individuals to assume leading roles in their own lives and entertainments.

Of course, every scene and epoch needs its chroniclers, and photographers George Hixson and Ben Tecumseh DeSoto have been important participant-observers of Houston's institutional and extra-institutional art worlds for over twenty years. Hixson's approach is that of street photographer. Shooting with a handheld camera, he has made a specialty of placing himself in the middle of the action to chronicle the energies, emotions, and puzzling juxtapositions that happen when artists are let loose in a city. Whether shooting the Urban Animals, a "roller-skating band of artists ... dedicated to sex, drugs, and rock 'n' roll";[19] documenting early Art Car Parades and events at the Commerce Street Artists' Warehouse, an important artist-run studio and exhibition space that closed in 2007; or taking a road trip to a busking festival in New York with fellow *No Zoning* artists Jim Pirtle and Nestor Topchy, Hixson finds candid images that convey energies, personalities, and milieus.

DeSoto, a longtime photographer for the *Houston Chronicle* newspaper, takes a more photo-documentary approach. Keeping a critical distance, he reports on personalities and events. His contribution to *No Zoning* consists of a grid of thirty-two photographs of Houston artists—both well known and more obscure—shown in their studios from the early 1980s to the present. Carefully staged and composed in collaboration with his subjects, DeSoto's portraits are often of artists presenting themselves for posterity. DeSoto's images, several of which portray the same artists decades apart and include legends of the Houston art scene like Jesse Lott, James Surls, Toby Topek, and Beth Secor, provide a rare insight into the usually private space of art making and a sympathetic opportunity to consider the arcs of lives and careers.

As architect Cameron Armstrong notes in his essay in this catalogue (pages 32–37), although Houston is far from a paradisiacal place, it contains many utopian pockets. Jim Pirtle and Nestor Topchy, denizens of the city's alternative art and performance scenes, have each in his own way worked to produce more perfect and personalized worlds within the city. Pirtle, a painter and performance artist, is creator of the famed downtown space notsuoH (Houston spelled backwards). Housed in a defunct shoe store, which Pirtle purchased in 1995 along with thousands of pairs of outdated women's shoes, this bar and social hall was created to serve as a kind of adult playground, a place where art and life could blend late into the night. At various times, with simple but effective modifications, notsuoH has housed an active dance studio, concert halls, and performance venues. For *No Zoning,* Pirtle has constructed a bar that chronicles his life within the Museum. Serving drinks at the exhibition's opening and during special events, *Ghost Bar* will contain relics from performances like his multiyear commitment to wearing only polyester clothing as well as his life as a bartender at notsuoH. A homegrown variant of the infamous (and self-descriptive) participatory bar and art installation *Free Beer (The Act of Drinking Beer with Friends Is the Highest Form of Art)* (1970–79) by San Francisco Zen-conceptual artist Tom Marioni, Pirtle's scrapbook-bar is made of vitrines containing materials salvaged from his art and time-capsule building projects that memorialize his lifelong investigation of improvised art, communal celebration, and other intoxicants.

Nestor Topchy takes a more social-engineering approach to utopia, building and planning communal spaces for artists and creative individuals. In 1989 he and a group of artists, including Rick Lowe and Dean Ruck, rented a two-acre plot of land in the West End containing a defunct truck-washing station, which they gradually converted into Zocalo, an artist-run exhi-

1983

Core Program of the Glassell School
A postgraduate fellowship program was founded at the Glassell School of Art at the Museum of Fine Arts, Houston. It continues to thrive today providing recipients with studio space, facility use, a stipend, seminars with visiting artists and scholars, and an annual exhibition. Numerous artists from the program have contributed to the development of the Houston art scene and continue to reside in the city.

Center for Art and Performance
In 1982, Michael Peranteau and artist Max Pruneda founded the Center for Art and Performance (CAP), a gallery/alternative art space on Almeda Road.

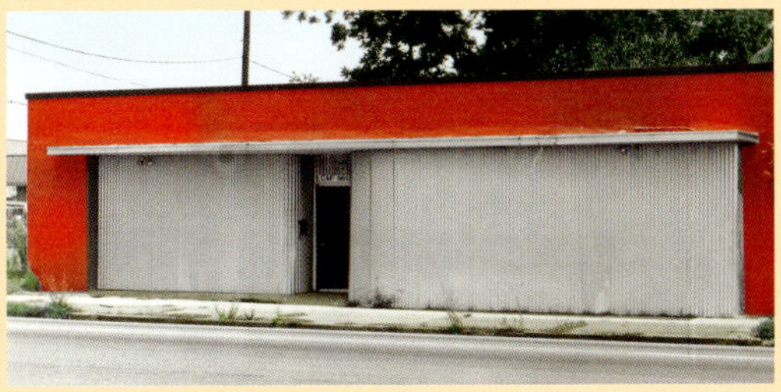

Center for Art and Performance, c. 1983

DiverseWorks
Artist Charles Gallagher founded DiverseWorks in an historic Civil War-era armory and dry goods store on Travis Street in downtown Houston. It included studios and an artist-in-residence program with James Bettison, Billy Hassell, Doug Laguarda, Don Redmond, Lisa Schoyer, and Beth Secor as early participants. In 1989 a fire forced DiverseWorks to move to its current location near the East Freeway, a warehouse complex where some artists also maintain studios privately. DiverseWorks Artspace continues as a vital laboratory where programming includes the visual, performing, and literary arts.

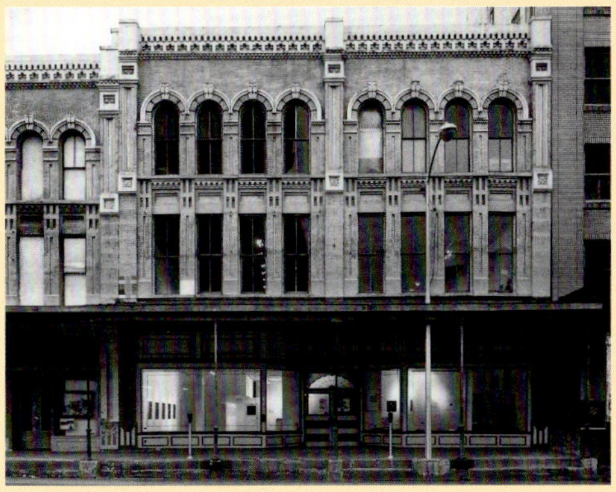

DiverseWorks, original Travis Street location, c. 1983

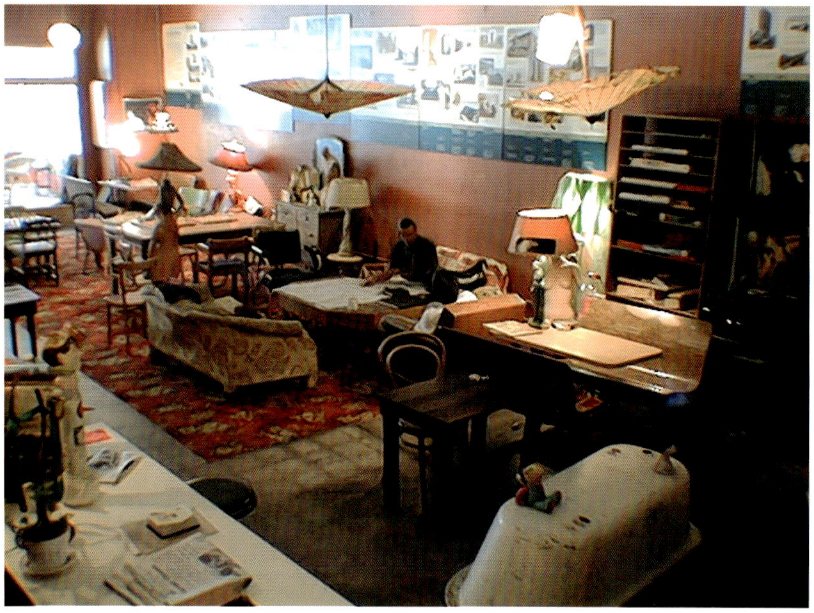

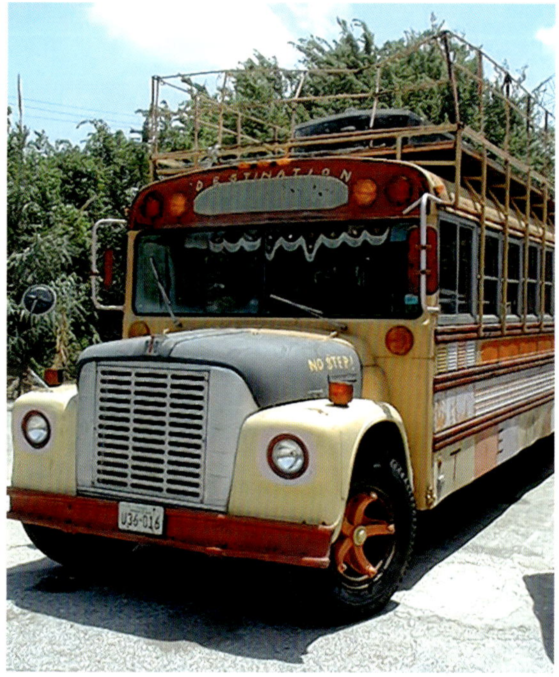

Jim Pirtle's notsuoH (interior), c. 2000

right:
"Zocalo Mobile Village" performance art bus, 2000

bition, performance, and residential space named for the main square in Mexico City. Eventually, Topchy took sole control of the site, renaming it Templ0 after the five-story pagoda-like structure he had constructed out of rebar atop a building. By the time he lost his lease in 2001, Topchy and his collaborators had equipped Templ0 with a drive-in movie theater, a bar, a café, artists' studios, offices, and a fountain and pond constructed of beer bottles. *No Zoning* features photographs, drawings, models, and blueprints documenting the history of Topchy's enterprises, including proposals for Organ, a new domelike structure of 148 stacked shipping containers ringed by a square of 288 containers, that will serve as a not-for-profit community of artists' studios, galleries, and creative-economy businesses, all built around ecologically friendly ponds and amphitheaters. When Organ (which like its predecessors has an "0" in its name to represent what Topchy calls "a calm, abiding situation"[20]) is realized—as its designer's persistence and track record suggest it will—it will be an oasis of collective creativity in capitalist Houston.

Although they work independently and without a unifying ideology, the artists featured in *No Zoning* share their irreverent and utopian approach to art and urban life with the Situationist International movement of the 1960s and 1970s. Active primarily in Paris, the Situationists combined elements of Marxism and Surrealism in art, performance, architecture, and design projects intended to liberate city dwellers from the restrictions of capitalist societies.[21] They developed a broad range of subversive projects, including agitprop posters and comic books; analytical, against-the-grain tours, or "drifts," through cities; and graffiti maxims like "Beneath the paving stones—the beach!"[22] Of course, for the many reasons laid out in this essay, Houston in 2009 has little in common with Paris in 1968. However, the artists featured in *No Zoning*, like their Situationist

1983

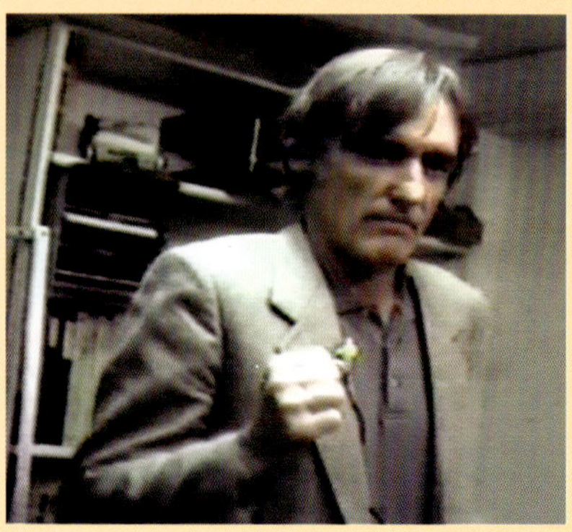

Dennis Hopper at the Rice University Media Center, video still from a documentary film about his appearance, 1983

Dennis Hopper in Houston
In May at Studio One, William Steen presented *Paintings and Assemblages* by Dennis Hopper, with a related screening at the Rice University Media Center of a film (*Out of the Blue*, 1980, directed by and starring Hopper) involving a school bus accident. The entire audience was then transported via school buses to the Big H Speedway stock car race track for the "Russian Dynamite Death Chair Act." In the infield, Hopper sat in a chair rigged with six sticks of dynamite and safely blew himself up.

Consolidated Arts Warehouse
In the summer, artist Lee Benner renovated the old Consolidated Meats Warehouse on Montrose just south of the Highway 59 overpass. The first event, "Dance with Live Artists," was a huge blowout with five bands, multiple happenings, and artwork on display. The venue remained open periodically for the next couple of years, catering to punk music and exhibitions of young artists in Houston's burgeoning art scene.

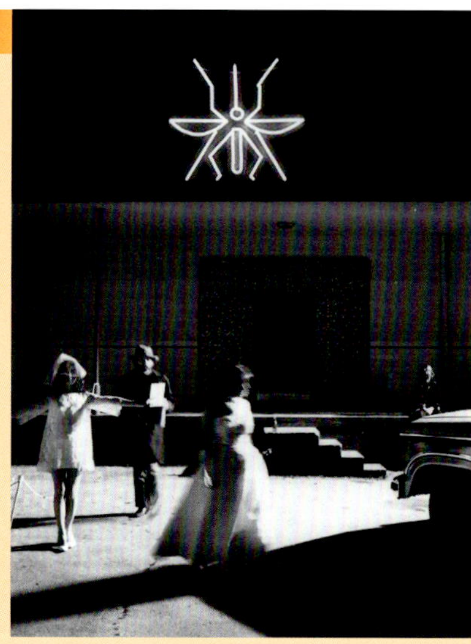

Exterior of the Consolidated Arts Warehouse, c. 1983

predecessors, deploy humor, play, and critical thinking strategies to constructively disrupt limiting or wrongheaded patterns of life in their own metropolis.

The artists of architecture, neighborhood, cable television, photography, performance, platform, workshop, found wood, and yarn in *No Zoning* have been able to carve out measures of freedom for their work in Houston itself because their city, for better or worse, is so unrestrictive. Unlike their continental counterparts who attacked the shibboleths of their cultures, these Houston artists instead have focused on developing their individual spheres. In this way, they have been able to create and share, often in their own backyards, versions of the more perfect worlds the Situationists could only imagine. Equipped primarily with their own creativity and labor, they have permeated their city's urban fabric to beautify its bleak corners, celebrate its idiosyncrasies, heal its ills, challenge its weak points, and offer alternative aesthetic experiences that transcend conventional venues, mediums, and expectations. It is fair to say that the artists in *No Zoning* love Houston and that the place—just by being its unzoned self—loves them back. By so openly, if often obliviously, incorporating these artists' affectionately subversive endeavors in its precincts, the city of Houston is itself an extraordinary partner in their attempts to shatter long-standing ordinances separating art and life.

Notes

1. For the idea of art permeability and much brainstorming on this exhibition, I am indebted to Alison de Lima Greene, curator of contemporary art and special projects at the Museum of Fine Arts, Houston. Rainey Knudson, founder and executive director of the online Texas art blog Glasstire (www.glasstire.com) also provided important early input.

2. Brendan O'Flaherty, *City Economics* (Cambridge, MA, and London: Harvard University Press, 2005), 173.

3. For a succinct history of zoning initiatives in Houston, see Joe R. Feagin, *Free Enterprise City: Houston in Political and Economic Perspective* (New Brunswick, NJ: Rutgers University Press, 1988), 157–58.

4. Neal R. Pierce, *The Megastates of America* (New York: Norton, 1972), 531, quoted in Feagin, *Free Enterprise City*, 158–59.

5. In *Free Enterprise City*, Feagin makes a strong case that Houston has benefited tremendously from federal spending (e.g., dredging the Ship Channel and NASA) and that the city's low tax rates and associated deficits in infrastructure and social services place a disproportionate burden on the poor.

6. In fact, the public relations campaign "Houston. It's Worth It." and the publication *HIWI* (Houston: It's Worth It./ttweak LLC, 2007), developed by ttweak (Dave Thompson and Randy Twaddle), turn the city's vices into virtues and say that it is an easy town to love despite its many disadvantages.

7. U.S. Census Bureau, "State and County QuickFacts: Houston, Texas," http://quickfacts.census.gov/qfd/states/48/4835000.html (accessed February 28, 2009).

8. Christa Forster, telephone conversation with the author, October 16, 2008.

9. Bill Davenport, unpublished curriculum vitae, March 2009.

10. Lee Littlefield, "Artist's Statement," n.d.

11. Mel Chin, conversation with the author, February 19, 2009.

12. PLoS Medicine, "Association of Prenatal and Childhood Blood Lead Concentrations with Criminal Arrests in Early Adulthood," http://medicine.plosjournals.org/perlserv/?request=get-document&doi=10.1371/journal.pmed.0050101&ct=1 (accessed March 11, 2009).

13. Eric Leshinsky, *Museum for Missing Places*, http://www.missing-places.org (accessed August 1, 2009).

14. Ibid.

15. Project Row Houses, "home/history," http://projectrowhouses.org/history/ (accessed February 19, 2009).

16. Rick Lowe, conversation with the author, November 2008.

17. Patricia C. Johnson, "One Three Seven: Hey, let's get small," *Houston Chronicle*, July 17, 1994.

18. David Robbins, "High Entertainment," *Art Lies*, no. 57 (Spring 2008), http://www.artlies.org/article.php?id=1585&issue=57&s=1 (accessed March 9, 2009).

19. Scott Prescott, conversation with the author, December 18, 2008.

20. Nestor Topchy, conversation with the author, January 29, 2009.

21. See Simon Sadler, *The Situationist City* (Cambridge, MA: MIT Press, 1999).

22. See Greil Marcus, *Lipstick Traces: A Secret History of the Twentieth Century* (Cambridge, MA: Harvard University Press, 1990).

1984

The Flower Man
Cleveland Turner found himself homeless and living on skid row until he had a vision in 1983 of a whirlwind that deposited colorful junk onto a long wall. Since then, he has transformed his homes in Houston's Third Ward with massive amounts of colorful debris, handmade sculptures, and flower gardens.

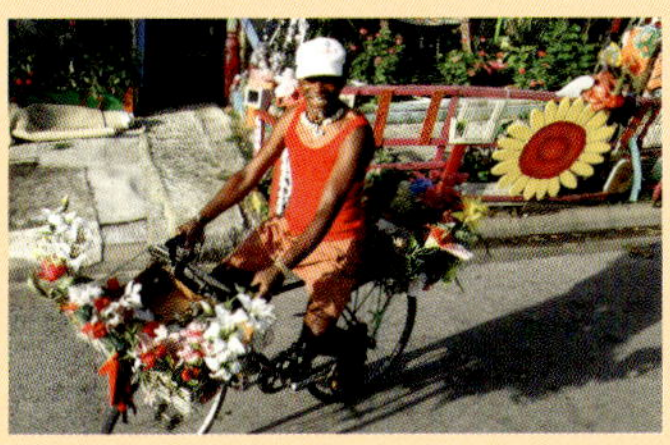

The Flower Man, 2007

FotoFest
FotoFest was founded by photographers Fred Baldwin and Wendy Watriss and European gallery dealer Petra Benteler as the first international biennial of photography and related art in the U.S. In March 1986, FotoFest presented its first biennial of photography in sixty-four sites around Houston.

Firehouse Gallery
The Houston Women's Caucus for Art opened an exhibition space, the Firehouse Gallery, in former Houston Fire Station #16 on Westheimer Street in Montrose.

Fruitmobile
The Orange Show Foundation commissioned artist Jackie Harris to create the *Fruitmobile*, a decorated art car that has become an endurring symbol for the form.

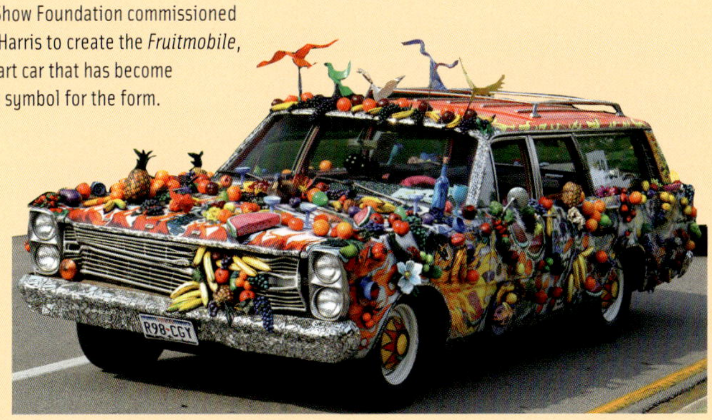

Jackie Harris's *Fruitmobile* in the Houston Art Car Parade, 2005

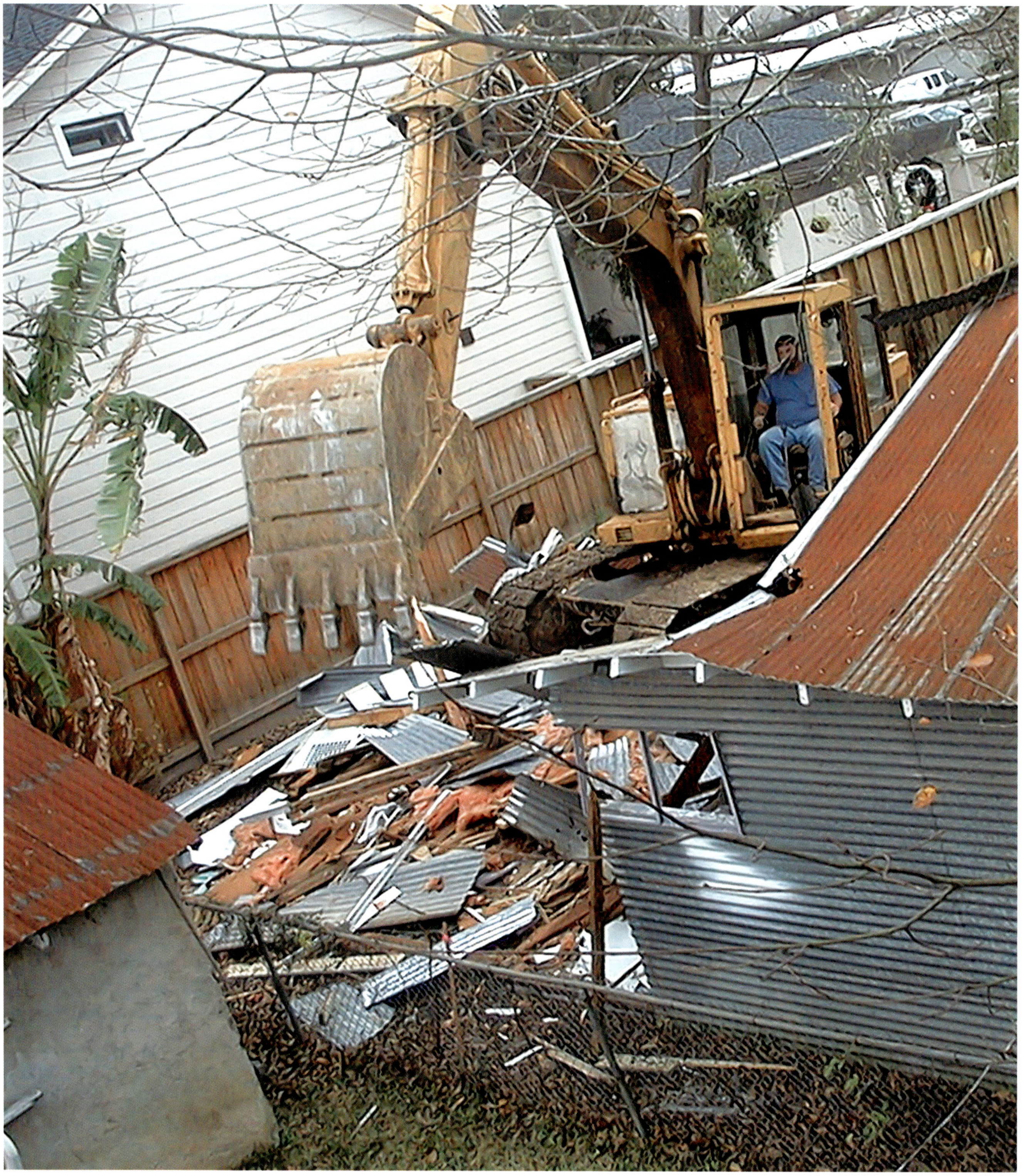

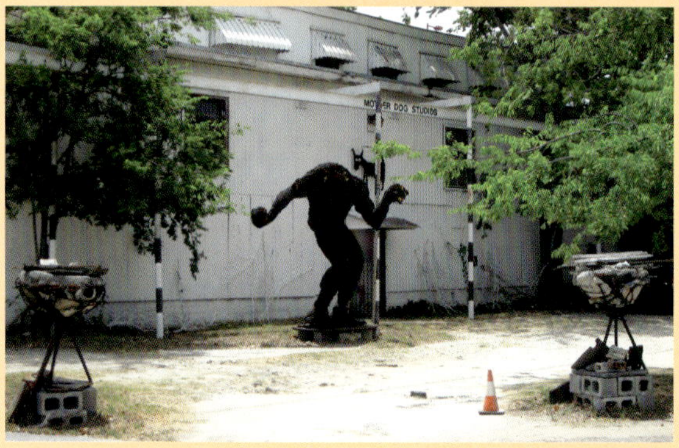

MotherDogStudios with one of the figures from Paul Kittelson's *Mindless Competition* (1988), 2009

1984

MotherDogStudios
MotherDogStudios was organized on Walnut Street on the eastern edge of downtown by artists Charlie Sartwelle and John Runnells to provide sixteen studio spaces for artists and present exhibitions in the Mother Dog Museum of Modern Art.

Transco Tower Gallery
Transco Tower opened an exhibition space in its lobby, regularly showing artists from the city and region. It continues today as Williams Tower Gallery, curated by Sally Sprout.

1985

NAAO Conference
DiverseWorks hosted the National Association of Artists' Organizations (NAAO) conference on April 24–27. Panels, lectures, and performance and video events with artists, curators, and arts administrators from across the United States occurred at a number of locations, including DiverseWorks, Lawndale Art and Performance Center, Square One, and Republic Bank. Joan Mondale gave the keynote address and Frank Hodsoll, Chairman of the National Endowment for the Arts, was a speaker. Events included the Performance Rodeo at Lawndale Art and Performance Center.

Speed Street
In 1981 Patrick Waugh began work on *Speed Street*, a teaser for an unrealized feature film on Houston's roller-skating gang the Urban Animals. Conceived and directed by Waugh, with production and art direction by Scott Prescott, the 18-minute 1985 film features gritty nighttime skating footage shot at daredevil speed, roller joustings, and a high-energy music soundtrack.

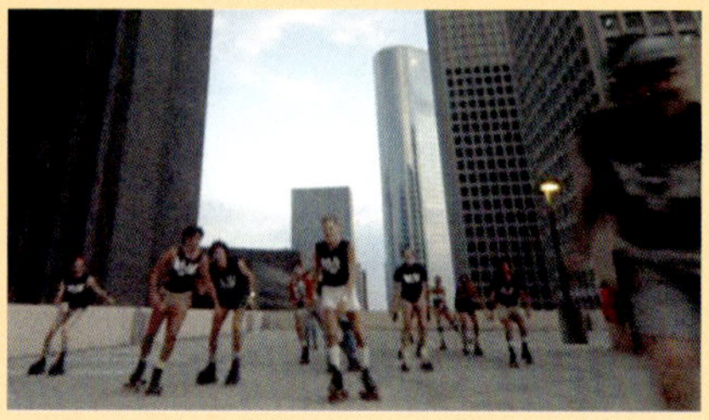

Un-Zoned: A Memoir

Cameron Armstrong

At the beginning of 1993, by what seemed a series of accidents, I found myself in the middle of the latest (and probably last) of Houston's five attempts to impose a top-down, legislated order on its famously unruly urbanism. At the time, the city had only just begun to recover from the decade-long depression following the oil economy's collapse. For a variety of reasons, including dissatisfaction with previous development and fears of chaos should construction resume, a comprehensive land use ordinance, a.k.a. zoning, seemed a strong possibility. As a commercial real estate broker, a sometime expert on zoning elsewhere (New York), an architect, a property owner in a neighborhood deemed by the City of Houston to be "un-zonable," and someone related by marriage to die-hard zoning critics, I found myself ringside at the heated debate over the new law. More than that, by the end of January I had been cajoled into helping my little neighborhood write its own "special district ordinance" to be enacted under the aegis of the overall plan.

The West End, named for the trolley line once connecting it with downtown, is bounded by Washington Avenue on the north, Memorial on the south, and Durham and Westcott to the east and west. Much of it had originally been part of the village of Brunner, the first area platted outside Houston's ward system. Early residents, often newly arrived from Central Europe, had built ranks of dignified cottages in a patchwork of small subdivisions between 1900 and 1930 (including "Rice Military," as the area is now often called). Later, as Houston grew and their children relocated to the suburbs, the West End welcomed new immigrant communities, mostly Hispanic. A cluster of African American families, whose tenure predated most others, remained in its heart. By 1995 the neighborhood's low rents and exotic charm had also attracted museum directors Walter Hopps and Linda Cathcart, curators Caroline Huber, Janet Landay, Bertrand Davezac, and Cecily Horton, and artists such as Terry Andrews, Bobbie Bennett, John Berry, Sharon Berryman, Karin Broker, Dick Craig, Roy Fridge, Jim Groff, Dan Havel, Terrell James, Jim Love, Rick Lowe, Andy Mann, Kirk McCarthy, D. A. McNulty, Kathleen Packlick (and her West End Gallery), Kate Petley, Dean Ruck, Trudy Sween, Jackie Tileston, Nestor Topchy, Tricia Tusa, Randy Twaddle, Sharon Wilcutts, Dick Wray, Peter Yenne, and Frank Zeni. Nearby were other artists, like The Art Guys and Frank Martin, and the art galleries of Hiram Butler (now Devin Borden Hiram Butler Gallery) and Fredericka Hunter and Ian Glennie (Texas Gallery).

Demolition of metal building in West End neighborhood

But whatever its artist and gallery density, the West End was in most respects typical of nearby inner city neighborhoods. Sandwiched between major business centers, established residential areas, and tracts primed for large-scale development, few such areas had seen much of Houston's postwar prosperity. As backwaters in the city's boom, they had become host to numerous marginal business and residential communities. Nor did they conform in any obvious way to the future imagined by the new zoning ordinance. The West End Special District Ordinance and similar attempts to customize the new law emerged from this misfit. These initiatives inevitably created disagreement and tension as planners tried for regulations that would balance differences rather than enforce conventions. Some in the contentious process of crafting the West End's specialized regulations demanded unfettered rights for business, while others wanted new construction limited to single-family homes. Yet others fought to protect historic architecture or assure cheap property for immigrant homesteads. The artists found their own voice in visions of studios and art parks. All feared the massed subdivisions and malls of developers' dreams, but few wanted to stop construction outright. Hopes for change (and redevelopment) were explicitly opposed to fantasies of preservation. As might be expected in a city riven by extremes of stability and growth, yet dedicated to both, the debates were fought on implicitly cultural grounds, touching deep expectations

Commerce Street Artists' Warehouse (CSAW)
Commerce Street Artists' Warehouse, located in a warehouse on the far eastern edge of downtown, was founded as an inexpensive home and studio for Houston artists, with exhibition space and a large performance area. Despite ownership changes and internal leadership struggles, the facility served for over two decades as living and studio space for up to forty visual artists at a time, and housed many different communal galleries. Artists who have had studios at CSAW include Wes Hicks, Virgil Grotfeldt, Deborah Moore, Orson Maquelani, Kevin Cunningham, John Calaway, Robert Campbell, Jack Massing, Rick Lowe, John Peters, James Bettison, Jim Pirtle, Nestor Topchy, Steve Wellman, George Hixson, Rodney Elliott, Daniel Adame, Teresa O'Connor, Elaine Bradford, Ben DeSoto, Cynthia Cupach, Y. E. Torres (Yet), Betsy Odom, and I Love You Baby, among many more.

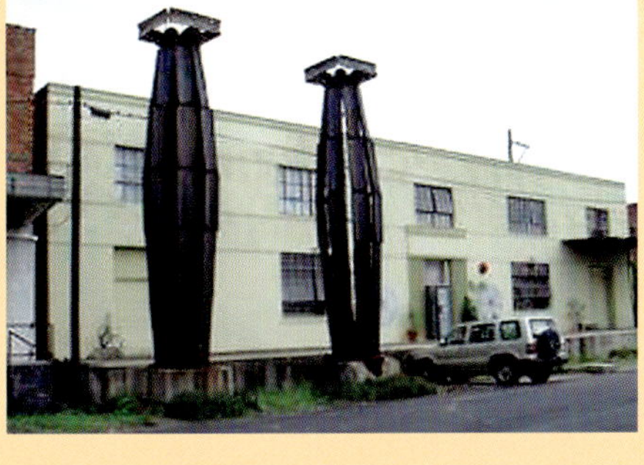

Commerce Street Artists' Warehouse, c. 2000

The Mule Men
The Mule Men were Jim Kanan and Steve Paulk, whose collaboration grew out of their shared construction company. Together they made several large-scale mobile works including *Texan Mexan Drive-In* and *Paging Oral Roberts*, which were part trailer home and part outdoor movie theater.

Fresh Paint
The exhibition *Fresh Paint: The Houston School*, curated by Barbara Rose and Susie Kalil, was presented at the Museum of Fine Arts, Houston. Sparking heated debate about inclusions versus exclusions and the true definition of the "Houston School," the exhibition nevertheless was a watershed moment in the maturation of the Houston art scene.

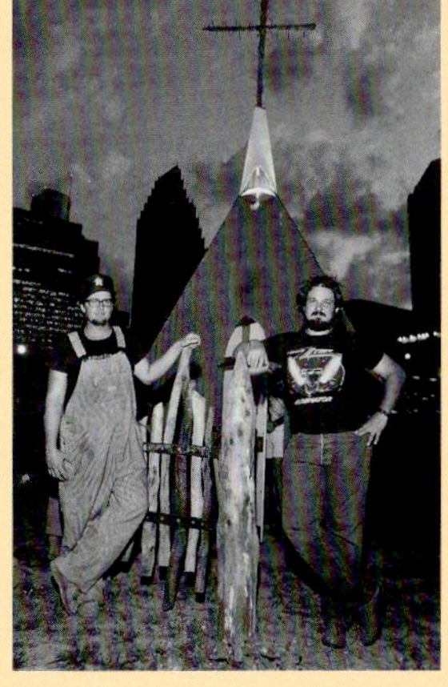

The Mule Men (Jim Kanan and Steve Paulk), *Texan Mexan Drive-In*, 1987

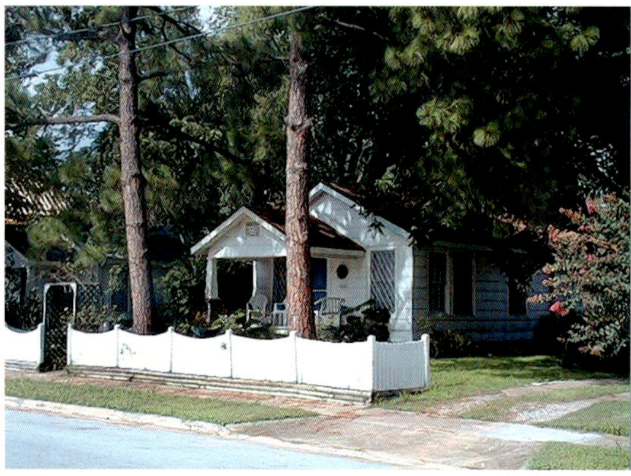

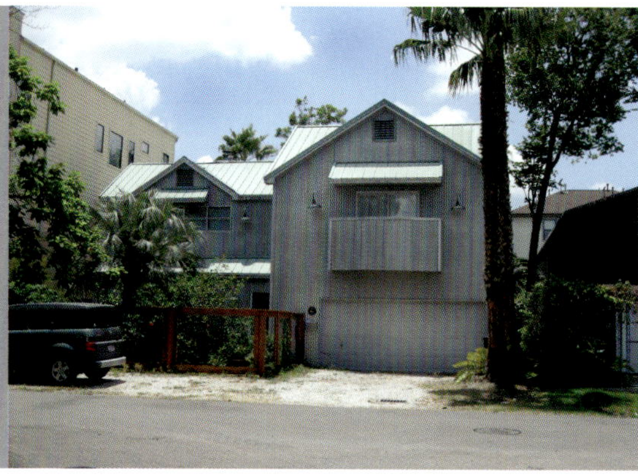

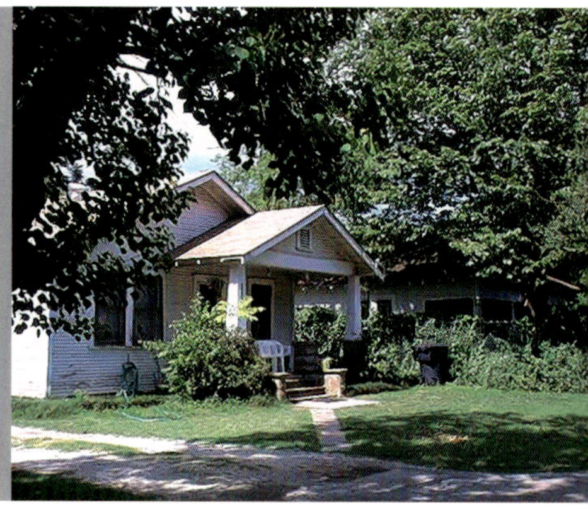

Various housing types including original bungalows and new metal-clad structures in the West End neighborhood, 2000–2009

about home and community. Passions ran high. Although zoning ultimately failed by referendum, its microcosm in such debates was a crucible of self-consciousness throughout the inner city. In the minds of some artists, these neighborhoods and their small buildings must suddenly have appeared in a new light, as art materials in themselves. What remained was to put those materials to use.

Such ideas were not entirely new and certainly not to 1990s Houston. Nationally, site-specific sculpture was well established: artists like Gordon Matta-Clark, Michael Heizer, and Richard Serra had long since pushed deep into the landscape. As early as the 1960s, local folk artists like Jeff McKissack with The Orange Show and John Milkovisch with the Beer Can House had launched paradigms of expressive shelter. During the 1970s and '80s, this tradition was carried forward by Cleveland Turner ("The Flower Man"), among others. The appearance of Dan Havel's *Alchemy House* (1993–94), Jim Pirtle's notsuoH (1996–ongoing), and other site works echoed this individualist spirit, but also addressed the paradoxes attending communal memory in a place radically devoted to dynamic growth and civic reinvention. Unlike either the folk monuments or previous artistic works, these projects did not simply memorialize extraordinary visions. Instead, moved by a do-it-yourself spirit, their authors dedicated a synergism of sculpture, architecture, and performance to social construction. Exploiting disused properties, low property values, and the boundless permissions of a city unzoned by either laws or proprieties, they engaged Houston on its own terms and at its own scale.

This migration to neglected areas carried strong echoes of regional history. Like the pioneers, the artists often co-operated in clearing each other's property and erecting rustic shelters—although now in disused warehouses rather than wilderness clearings. Like the builders of Houston's railways, ship channels, and airports, they sought large government grants. But their approach to "undeveloped" land (and neighborhoods) was new and quite different. The little villages along Washington Avenue, parts of Houston Heights, and areas to the east and south of downtown, having generally fallen into disuse and disrepair, had long been overlooked by mainstream entrepreneurs and were up for grabs. To the artists, these voids in the economic geography offered an inverted, looking-glass version of the homogenized desires and products of conventional development. With an ethos echoing land brokerage as much as art, they saw raw material for large-scale works in these neighborhoods' undervalued properties and improvised infrastructures of casual industry and familial networks. Borrowing and squatting their way toward legal tenure, they turned warehouses and humble dwellings first into cooperative studios, and then into spaces for theatrical and artistic performance. Vacant tracts and old houses were transformed from scenes of abandonment into venues for new symbolic geographies. Any step in constructing a site work could take on ritualized significance—even the processes of negotiating ways through (and around) the building codes could fulfill a Duchampian aesthetic of performance. With a vivid sense of being "unzoned," the artists recast close-knit neighborhoods of

1986

Architecture & Culture: The Fourth Ward

This exhibition featuring archival and contemporary photographs, architectural models, maps, sculpture, paintings, documentary videos, and oral histories about the historic neighborhood of Freedman's Town opened at DiverseWorks, co-sponsored by the City of Houston Archaeological and Historical Commission and the Greater Houston Preservation Alliance. Accompanying events included "A Celebration of the Churches" with gospel singing; Ed Hugetz and Brian Huberman's video *Who Will Stand with the Fourth Ward*, produced by SWAMP; a University of Houston College of Architecture design charette; and a roundtable discussion with architects V. Nia Dorian Becnel, William Neuhaus, and Renzo Piano, and community organizer Lenwood Johnson.

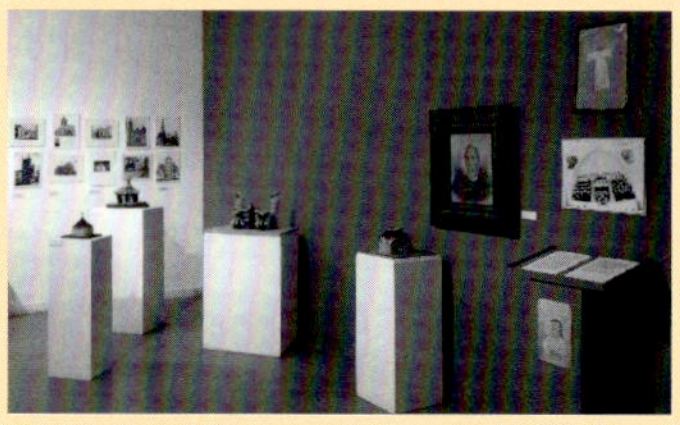

Installation view of *Architecture & Culture: The Fourth Ward*, 1986

Rendez-Vous Houston

As part of the Sesquicentennial celebrations of Houston, the Houston Festival produced an outdoor concert/spectacle by French composer Jean Michel Jarre. Using the entire west side of downtown Houston as a skyline backdrop, the event included music, laser lights, and gigantic projected images on the buildings. An estimated 1.3 million people attended the event, making it one of the largest concerts in history up to that time.

New Music America 1986

The Houston Festival presented New Music America 1986 as part of the city's Sesquicentennial celebrations. The world's largest festival of experimental music, which showcased renowned musicians and artists working with sound, was inaugurated in New York at The Kitchen in 1980. It was presented yearly in different cities in the United States until 1990. The festival in Houston exploited the city's special qualities and spaces, including the Astrodome, the underground tunnel system of downtown, various office lobbies, a YWCA pool, and incoming airline flights.

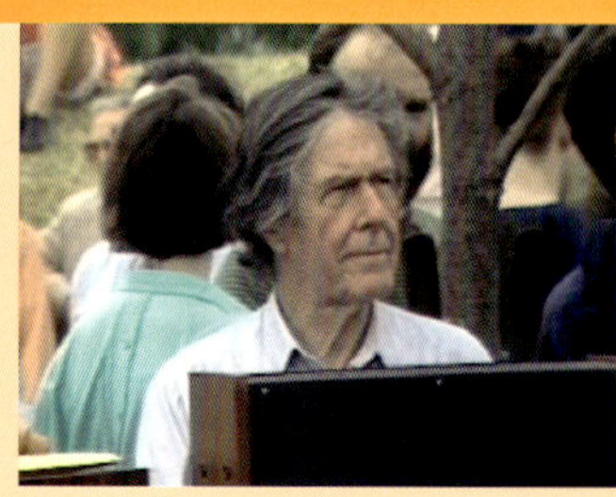

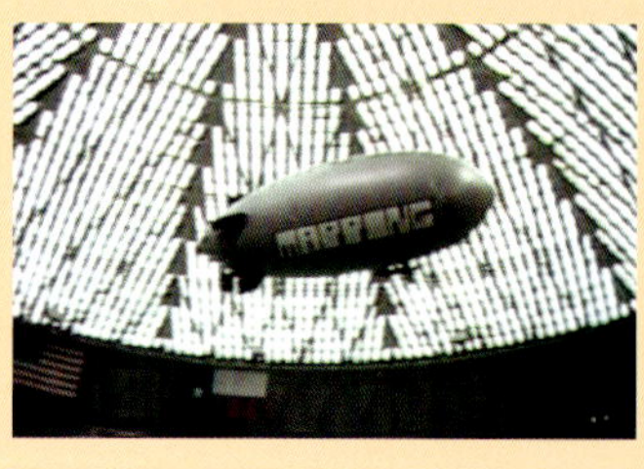

John Cage at the world premiere of "Ryoanji," 1986
Blimp balloon in the Houston Astrodome, New Music America 1986

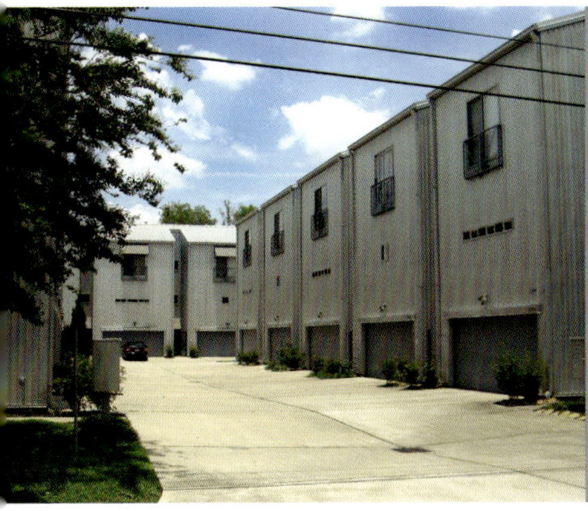
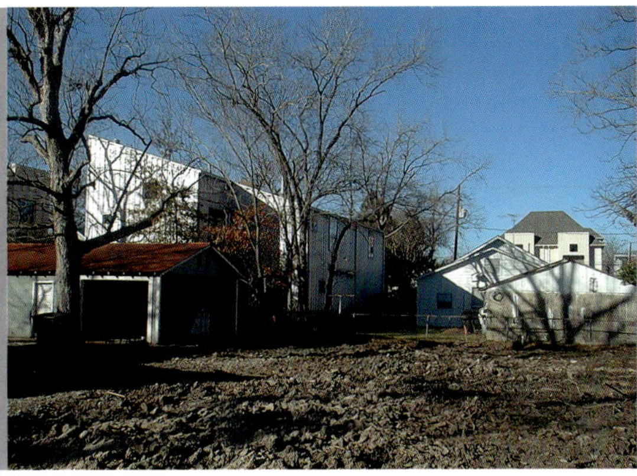
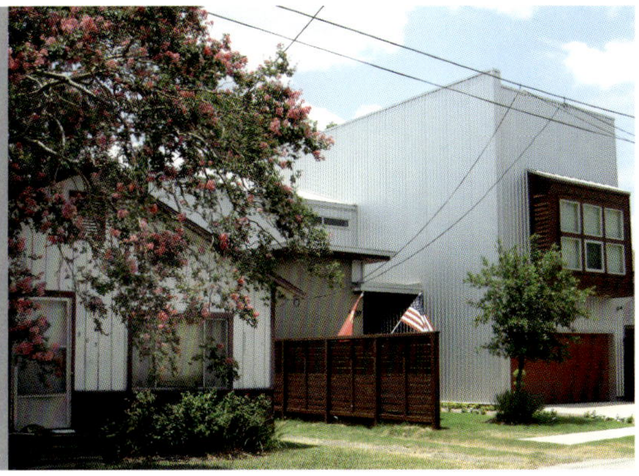

small churches, corner stores, shared gardens, and family ties into the means by which authentic community could be recovered and celebrated as social sculpture.

The range of this work was as broad and deep as the cultural and spiritual voids it symbolically reversed. At Main Street's notsuoH, Jim Pirtle had recognized a human-scale apotheosis of the Cornellian box in a fossilized, defunct retail space (complete with sales slips and thousands of shoes). The bar, coffee shop, and performance spaces that emerged were soon colonized by artists, misfits, and business people, their drinking and chess serenaded by the in-house band Free Radicals. In celebratory parades and performances like *The Art Guys Blow Through Town* (1995)—with leaf blowers!—and in ritualized deconstructions like Dan Havel's *Alchemy House*, others claimed the entirety of the city as both site and medium. In a Third Ward block of shotgun houses, Project Row Houses transformed artist collaborations and an emergent venue for installation into a progressive model of community. These works expressed the conflict between the corrosive reality of Houston's dehumanizing scale and hectic redevelopment, and human needs for stability and meaning. Nested in the tensions between solid object and ephemeral performance, they created an art of place in which an aesthetic of community could supersede the soulless economics driving their mainstream twins, the "complexes," "plazas," and "mansions" of conventional success.

It's easy to see why the proposed zoning ordinance was equally toxic to certain artists and developers. The commitment to a deregulated imagination that led West End artists like Jim Love and Karin Broker to oppose rules mandating the construction of suburban-style "starter homes" was not so different from the spirit that inspired Meredith James, co-founder of the ordinance-slaying Houston Property Rights Association (and my cousin by marriage), to declare, "Zoning … a Mortal Sin ('Thou Shalt Not Covet Thy Neighbor's Property')." Developers and artists alike reveled in the city's tacit and explicit permissions to destroy or appropriate whatever value they could identify. But the politics of this common cause also had a "through-the-looking-glass" quality, since with the Special District Ordinance the artists hoped to preserve rather than overcome what Walter Hopps had called the West End's "funky reality." In the end, neither artists nor developers got to see whether zoning would sustain or destroy the liberties they imagined. Certainly, with its defeat, chances for preserving the area's diverse complexity were doomed, along with its historical assemblage of wooden cottages. But so were opposing hopes for suburban subdivisions. Ultimately, a strong market for medium-density "town houses" would sweep through the neighborhood and literally carry it off: hundreds of little houses were trailered away or destroyed in the ensuing decade, as were the last remains of 1917's mutinous Camp Logan and ultimately some of the West End's key site works, including Nestor Topchy's TemplO (1996–2001) and *O House* (1995) by Dan Havel, Kate Petley, and Dean Ruck.

The debates over zoning and the ordinance's defeat had preserved the developers' unrestrained license, awakened the artists, and pushed into sharp relief the absences embedded in

1987

New Music Parade
New Music Parade by New York musician/composer Tom Cora, noted for his improvisational work in jazz and rock, launched New Music America 1986 in Houston. Cora collaborated with local artists Trish Herrera and Rachel Hecker on the organization of the parade, which included a hodge-podge of Houston's art community, including the Urban Animals, sculptural cars by Jackie Harris and Paul Kittelson, belly dancers, and more. The New Music Parade proceeded south on Montrose to the Museum of Fine Arts, Houston sculpture garden, which opened that same day with an event featuring the world premiere of John Cage's "Ryoanji." Inspired by the success of the New Music Parade, The Orange Show organized the first Art Car Parade in 1988.

Stegosaurus by Paul Kittelson
DiverseWorks sponsored public artworks placed throughout Houston. Paul Kittelson received one of these modest $500 grants and created his *Stegosaurus*, a life-size dinosaur made of foam cushions over a metal armature, which he installed under the Highway 59 overpass (later demolished) at Montrose Boulevard. The sculpture became a public phenomenon during its nine-month installation. It met its demise when it was set on fire by anonymous arsonists. (*see photo p. 65*)

On Waugh Gallery
Artist Ted Brown, with artist Mark Lombardi and photographer Frank Martin, opened an exhibition space in a building on Waugh Drive. Over two years, shows included work by such artists as Steve Brudniak, Mary Long, Paul Kittelson, and Ed Wilson.

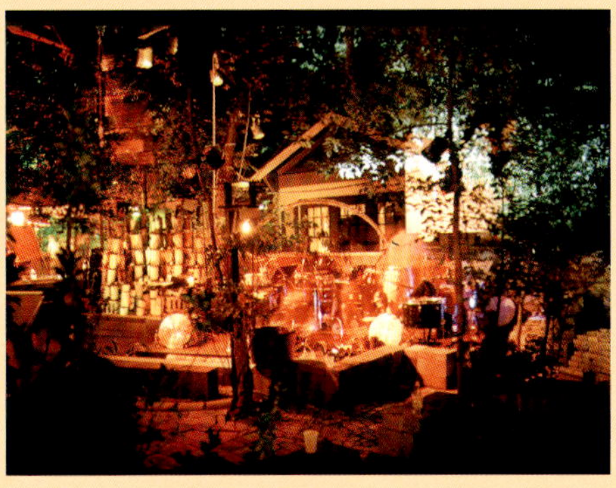
The Artery sculpture garden at night

The Artery
Artist Mark Larsen founded The Artery, an art and performance space that was part art school, part arboretum, and part center for political activism. Located in a house on Jackson Street in the Museum District, The Artery today serves a large group of Houston's artists, actors, musicians, and social activists.

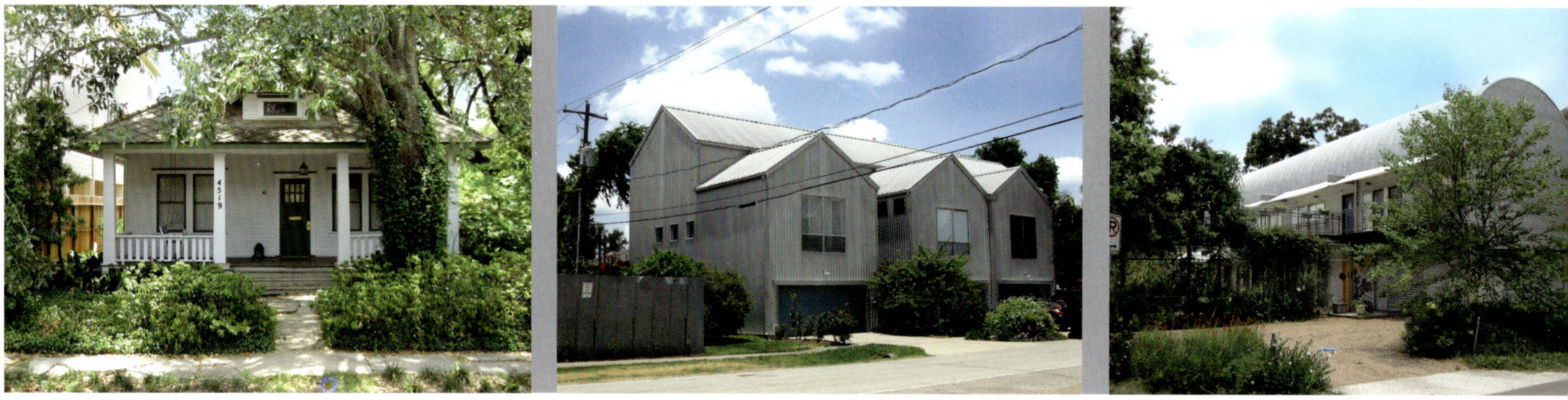

Various housing types including original bungalows and new metal-clad structures in the West End neighborhood, 2000–2009

Houston's sprawling approach to city-building. These voids had emerged not only in its economic geography, but throughout the fabric of urban life. Awash in speeding automobiles, parks and city streets had lost their power to anchor personal symbologies. Dwarfed by freeways and massive towers, the axes and squares of old-fashioned city planning could have little impact on visual order or much grip on civic experience. Traditionally scaled mainstays of civic memory, whether bronze figures raised on pedestals, men on parade, or site-specific messages inscribed in building facades, were literally lost amongst vast expanses of subdivisions and strip malls; only in epic form could human scale claim the foreground, as with the ritual pilgrimage of cowboys, horses, and wagon trains from across the state to Houston's annual rodeo. But the defeat of time-honored ways of joining people to their city pointed neither to inherent flaws nor to the obsolescence of underlying human needs. The very success of Houston's culture of rampant growth had itself created this failure, by denuding the landscape of the intimacy in which these methods could function. Only in forgotten backwaters like the West End was memory still embedded in buildings, society still engaged with place.

Echoing the auto industry's use of identical chassis for multiple models, Houston's real estate developers typically erect similar buildings and combinations of buildings, differentiated only by "design themes," for the sake of common architectural, infrastructure, and cost-effective designs. They have come to depend on the ability to achieve a simple, seamless integration of financial capital with large tracts of readily accessible land, all structured around predictable patterns of market demand and economic concentration. Therefore, whether working as a single huge enterprise or as many small players, they were unable to easily extract value from poor, complex neighborhoods like the West End. Uncertain land titles, improvised utilities, and persistent social problems put these otherwise available and well-located areas out of operational reach. As a result, the West End and its cousins were systematically neglected during the the boom years of the 1960s and '70s, and ultimately subjected to extreme stresses of poverty and decay. However, for the artists, this impoverishment had the perversely positive effect of maintaining the low land costs needed by big art projects, and preserving the communities that served them as both sites and subject matter. Investment-starved but rich in history, these areas begged comparison with the cultural voids of successful mainstream "complex" and "strip" developments. The very strangeness of their use as venues for recovering an active, civil urbanity commanded a powerful foreground for the works they came to host. Paradoxically, the magnitude of the mainstream's success (of which its inability to assimilate small, depressed backwaters was the flip side) had produced in them a parallel, marginal world, where the spiritual emptiness of the city's urbanism could be ritually exorcised.

The usual response of land men to forgotten remnants of previous booms—that is, to "bottom feed" and assemble likely properties, and then spin them into new rounds of speculation—can seem cannibalistic when considered in terms of the greater

1987

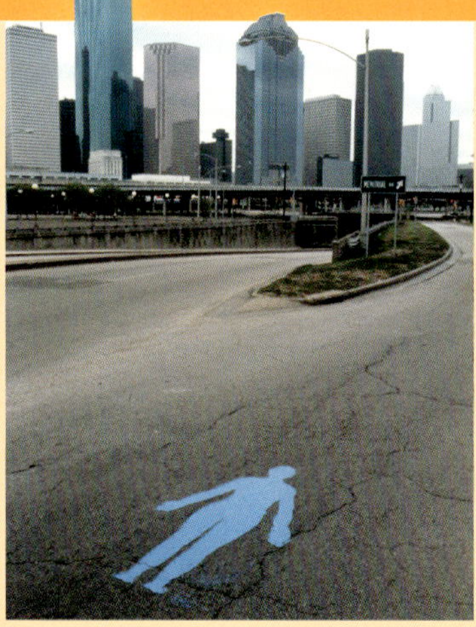

Painted figure marking part of *The Human Tour*, Houston Avenue, 1987

The Human Tour
Michael Galbreth dedicated the project *The Human Tour: An Anthropomorphic Route through the City of Houston* "to a more human city." He created a human figure that was thirty-four and a half miles long, superimposing it over the streets of Houston to connect six disparate neighborhoods. He placed slow-scan video cameras and permanent markers at the figure's head, hands, and feet. The monitors receiving the video images, the project's working drawings, and its maps were installed at DiverseWorks.

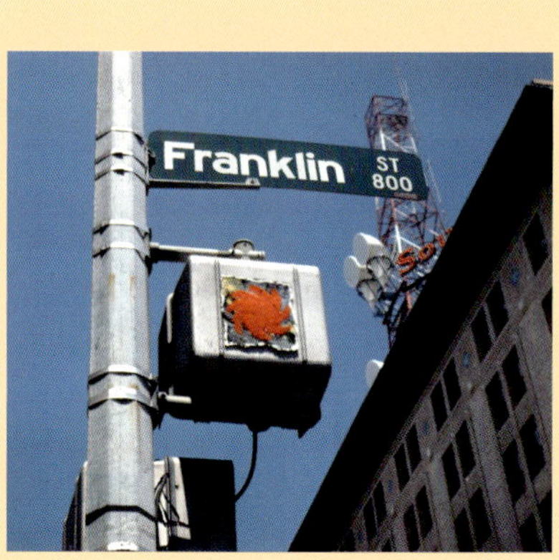

One of the *Tar Babies* on a street post in downtown Houston, 1987

Tar Babies
In April Los Angeles artist Michael McCall tarred telephone poles and switching boxes throughout Houston with his nine-inch-square *Tar Baby* paintings, which were mixed-media paintings on roofing tar paper.

Community Artists' Collective
The organization was conceived by artists and art educators Michelle Barnes and Dr. Sarah Trotty (Texas Southern University) to assist African American artists with a special sensitivity to women artists. In 1989 its headquarters was established in midtown. The Collective has sponsored numerous exhibitions and educational programs, many aimed at making cultural experiences more accessible to inner-city youth.

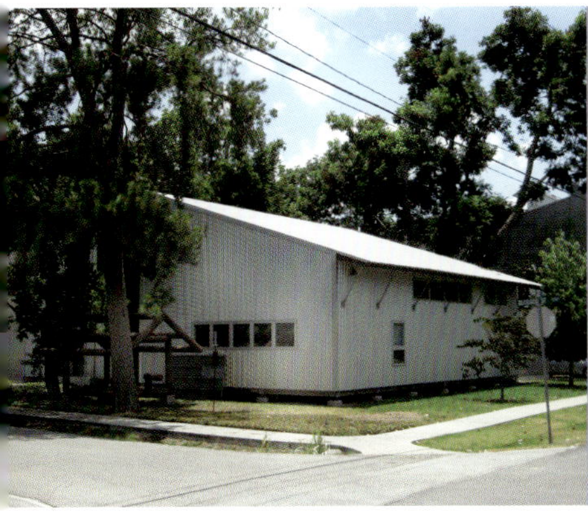
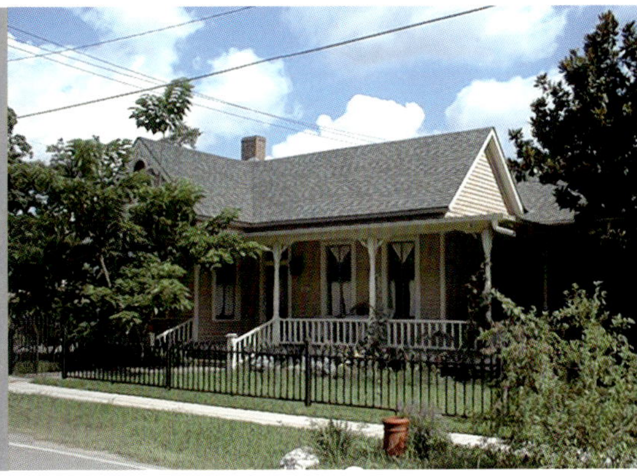
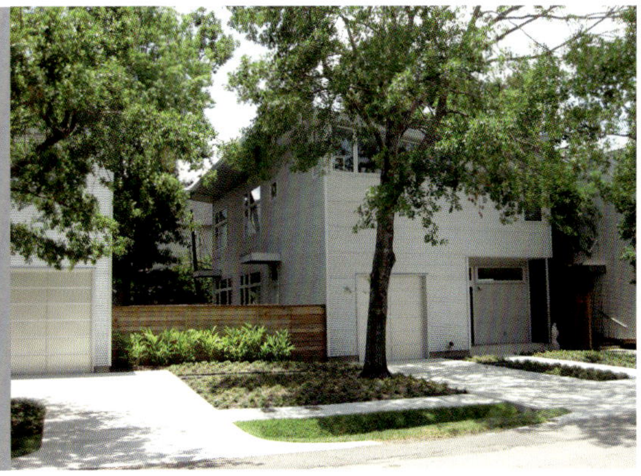

civic good: it's not intuitively obvious that destroying established communities for the sake of short-term (re)development is a good thing. Destruction was also part of the artists' vocabulary, and there is a parasitic element in works piggybacked on neighborhoods' dissolution, such as the serial appropriation of soon-to-be-demolished buildings by Dan Havel and Dean Ruck. In principle, the artists' exploitation of the city's broad freedoms in their transformation of cheap, available properties, and even whole neighborhoods, can seem little different from the workings of the official real estate economy. Certainly, their libertarian ethos was no less rooted in Houston's myth of the entrepreneurial pioneer. Sifting through the detritus of cycle after cycle of boom and bust, both artists and developers instinctively saw in these debris the foundations of new value.

The process of negotiating the West End Special District Ordinance forced the entire neighborhood to confront its prospective redevelopment, recognized as inevitable with or without zoning. My role as interpreter was predicated on competence with such regulation, belief in its positive potential, and a position astride the stake-holding communities. However, as I discovered the ways in which the new law would constrain unconventional uses and new site works, to say nothing of my own hopes for contemporary architecture, I came to respect Houston's traditional liberties. Like everyone in the neighborhood, I was compelled to rethink my work (in design and real estate), my loyalties (to artists, neighbors, and realtors), and my agreement (or disagreement) with family advocates of the free market. Professionally, I was thoroughly implicated in the machine of redevelopment, yet personally I was drawn to the consolations provided by art's deeper focus. The differences refracted in the prism of zoning politics were divisions also emerging naturally within my own view of Houston and its future. Certainly, there was much to dislike about the city's disordered state: the mishmash of uses and scales, the jarring breaks in landscape and utility. But by the peak of zoning's political campaign, consistency had begun to seem a poor trade for liberty and the vitality it guarantees. The tragedy of the West End was that the freedoms necessary for its site works would also assure their destruction in the next round of speculation. Since then, events have shown mainstream development to be as corrosive as ever to the social, spiritual, and cultural needs of urban life. Negatively, one could point to a never-ending circle of decay and demolition, producing little of lasting value. An optimistic view is that, unzoned, Houston will continue to cast up doppelgangers of its formless growth, reverse self-images performing its deeper necessities. Regardless, like my own involvement in the zoning struggle, the city's future seems foretold in past relations. Nowadays, our way of making and re-making it seems to me simply an exhaustive research into what can be removed and what added. The results, whether suburban tracts or soulful artworks, seem not accidental at all, but rather the inevitable lifework of Houston, the emergent city, a place where anything can happen, and everything eventually will.

Robbie Conal Posters
DiverseWorks brought Los Angeles artist Robbie Conal to Houston to install his posters of politicians and celebrities guerilla-style throughout the city, including images from his *Men With No Lips* and *Women With Teeth* series.

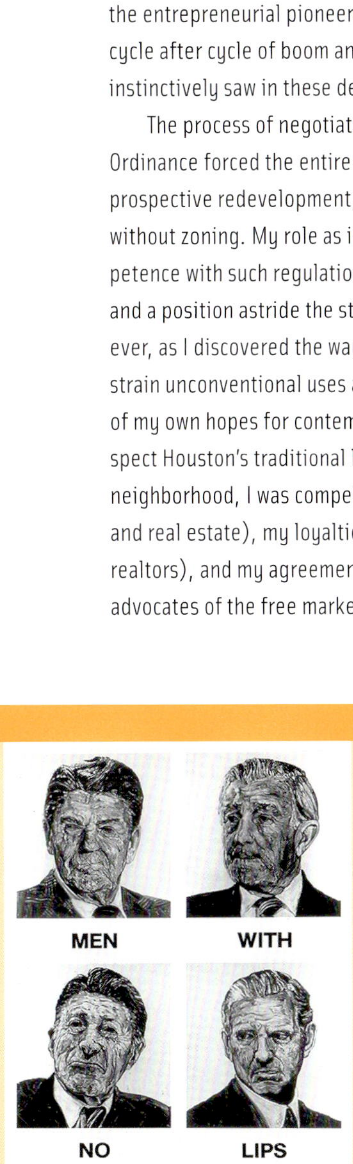

Robbie Conal's *Men With No Lips* poster, 1987

Houston Gorilla Girls
Inspired by the activities of the New York and Chicago Guerrilla Girls who offered a critique of male-dominated art world activities, a small group of steadfastly anonymous women artists formed the Houston Gorilla Girls. Dressed in gorilla masks and costumes to hide their identities and to foment a satirical counterpoint at art openings, they carried signs, targeted art events, and distributed handouts with statistics about the poor representation of women in the arts.

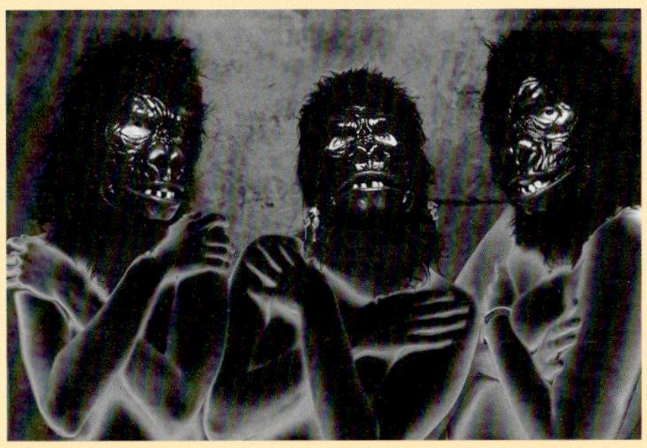
Houston Gorilla Girls, 1987

Super Canvas
Patrick Media began its sponsorship of the Super Canvas Project in which a panel selected artists to design billboards, which were then produced and displayed throughout Houston. This project continued for a few years.

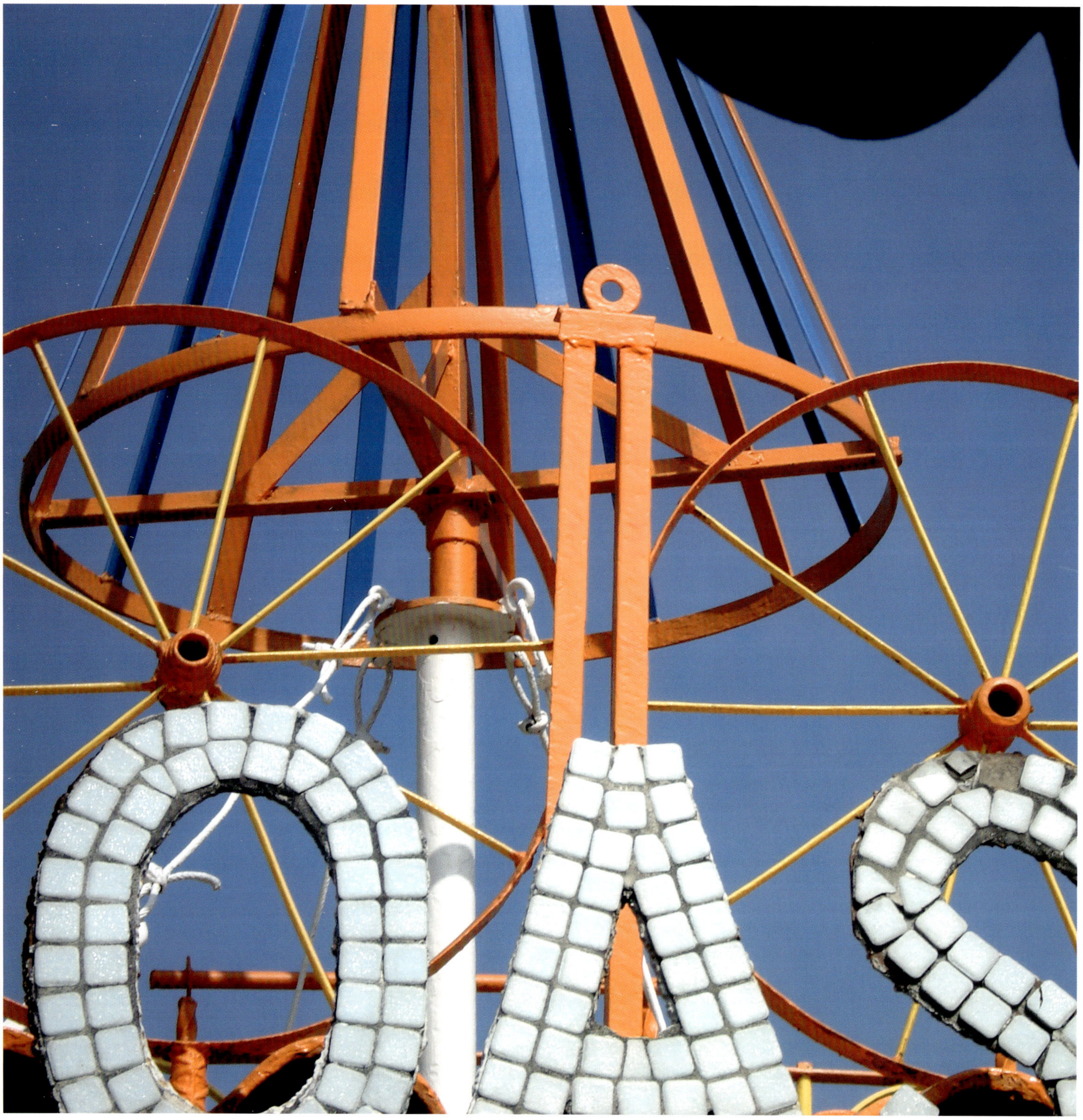

1987

Watermelon Flats
Local artists banded together to organize their own temporary outdoor sculpture show called *Watermelon Flats* set along Buffalo Bayou in a location across from the Wortham Center, an area that was once an outdoor farmers' market. Included in this inaugural exhibition were works by Paul Kittelson, Noah Edmundson, Jackie Harris, The Art Guys, Dean Ruck, Olin Calk, Carter Ernst, and Tim Glover, among many others. *Watermelon Flats* eventually became what is today Buffalo Bayou Art Park.

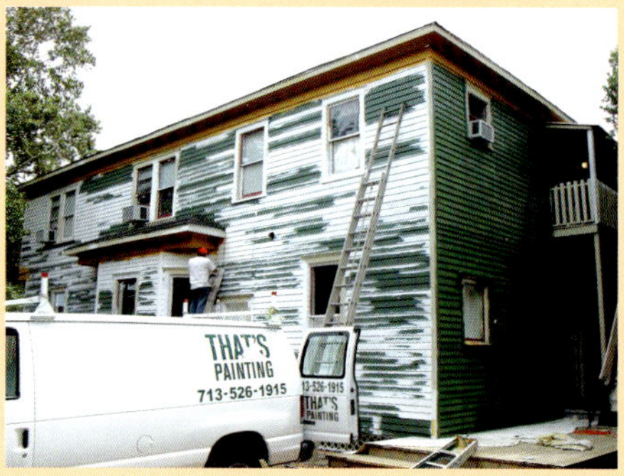

Bernard Brunon, *Pearl Green, Caramel Corn, Cottage Red, 09/2006*, installation view of a private residence, Houston, 2006

1988

That's Painting Productions
French-born conceptual artist Bernard Brunon began a high-concept art project in Houston that consisted of painting rooms, walls, or exteriors in a manner that was indistinguishable from typically painted rooms, walls, or exteriors. He considers these "jobs" as his artwork and signs, dates, and catalogues his efforts.

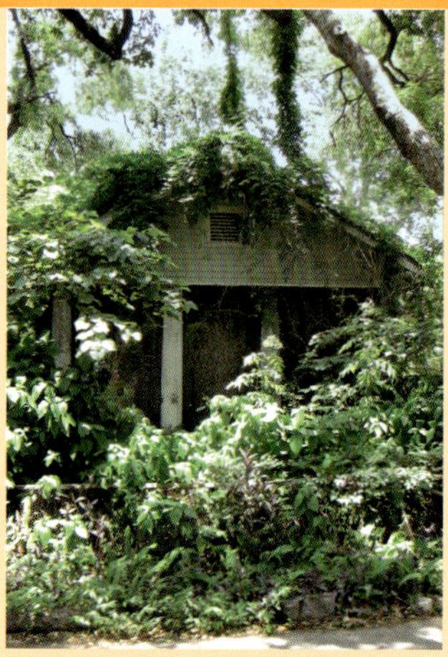

Magnolia Grove Neighborhood
Painter Salle Werner Vaughn began to acquire neighboring bungalows and transform them into environments evocative of another time and place; the houses hovered somewhere between artwork and home. To create the neighborhood, Vaughn purchased her property in tandem with Hiram Butler, who bought the block adjacent to hers to build his gallery and sculpture garden, retaining one of the modest houses on the property for his home.

Salle Werner Vaughn's bungalow, 2009

Handmade Personal Spaces in Houston

Susanne Theis

This essay first appeared in Good, *a book commissioned by Toni and Jeff Beauchamp to commemorate the new millennium in 2000, and has been revised and updated for this catalogue.*

opposite:
Detail of roof ornaments on Jeff McKissack's The Orange Show, Munger Street, c. 2004

One person—using common discarded objects, simple tools, and a lifetime of wisdom and technical knowledge—dedicates years of solitary labor to giving material form to a private vision, transforming a home, garden, or place of business into a monumental work of art. This is essentially the story of the hundreds of handmade personal spaces found all over the world. Houston is home to an unusually large number of these sites, and the way that our buttoned-down, no-nonsense city and the creators of these improbable art environments interact with and affect each other is one of the most interesting things about Houston. It's what helps keep me here from one August to the next.

For nearly twenty-five years, I was a part of The Orange Show Foundation, which has worked to identify more than a dozen of these handmade personal spaces within Houston's expansive city limits. Located within a two-mile radius of downtown are three of the most highly regarded examples of the art form in the country. The Beer Can House is covered with flattened beer cans, the surrounding trees draped in hanging garlands of pop-tops and lids that clink like wind chimes. The original Flower Man's Garden, embellished with childhood relics and found objects from Cleveland Turner's bicycle travels around Houston, turned his shotgun house into a neighborhood landmark. And the Orange Show, a huge, mazelike monument of concrete, brick, steel, and anything from gears and tractor seats to statuettes, extols the virtue of the orange.

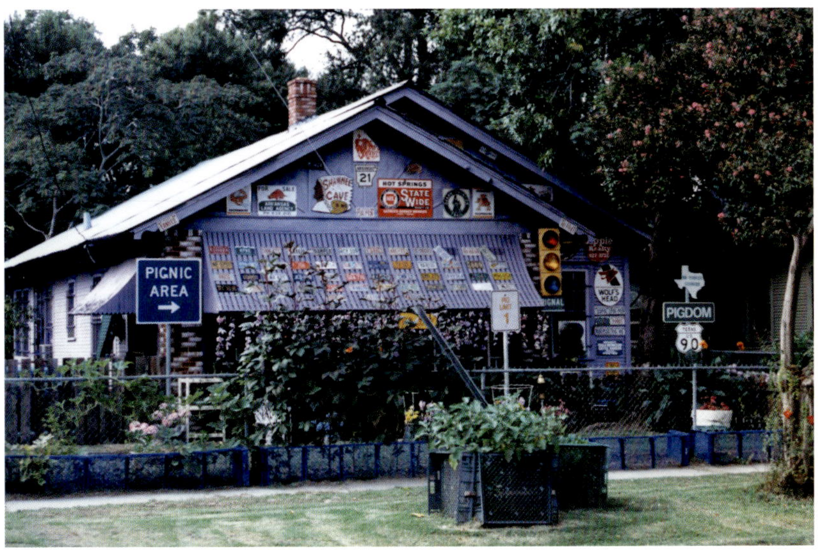

below:
Victoria Herberta's Pigdom, Crawford Street, 1987

A few years ago, there were even more. Wonderful places, like the Fan Man's Third World, a major construction of toys, mannequins, television sets, and endless other items, have been lost upon the death of their creators. Still others, like Victoria Herberta's Pigdom (a bright purple homage to the pig and once home of the pigs Jerome and Priscilla), Sylvester Williams's Eagle's Nest (a yard filled with thousands of history-laden objects from hundred-year-old farm tools to pre-electric irons and books of news clippings documenting the achievements of contemporary black Americans), and Howard Porter's OK Corral (dominated by brightly colored tables, chairs, umbrellas, and yard art, including a fence of found objects in a western motif), remained a part of the landscape in 2000, but in a less vivid form because their creators were no longer able, for one reason or another, to spend quite as much time on their environments as they had previously.

These sites are sometimes called "folk art environments," although that is not a strictly accurate label. Many of these spaces celebrate self rather than community and depict personal experiences, struggles, and values rather than shared traditions. By transforming the junk of our culture into vessels (or vehicles, but that's another story) for personal expression, the people who create these handmade personal spaces are communicating private realities in a most public way.

The Art Car Parade
In 1988 The Orange Show, in conjunction with the Houston International Festival, organized and presented the first Art Car Parade in downtown Houston as a tribute to the burgeoning phenomenon of "art cars." The parade continues annually under the auspices of the Orange Show Center for Visionary Art and has become an internationally recognized focus of the art car movement.

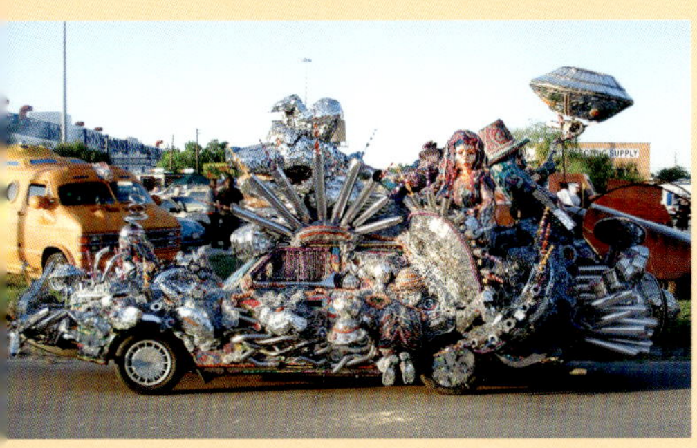

ltrip High School's *Atomic Dog*

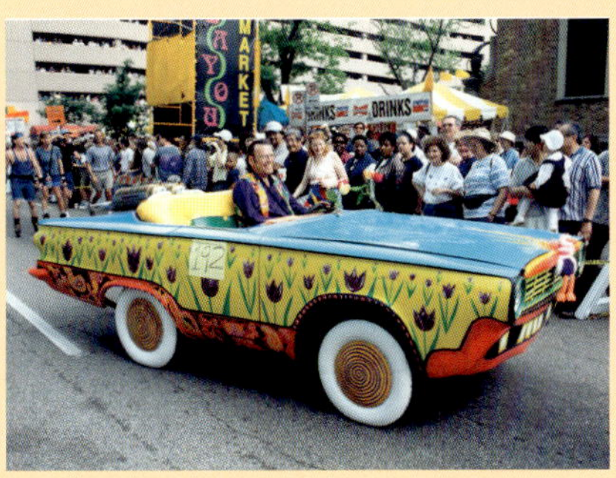

Dean Pauley's *Miss Vicky*

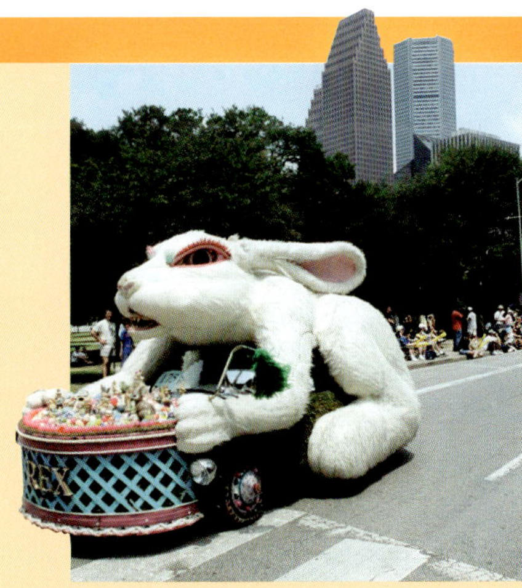

Larry Fuente's *Rex Rabbit*

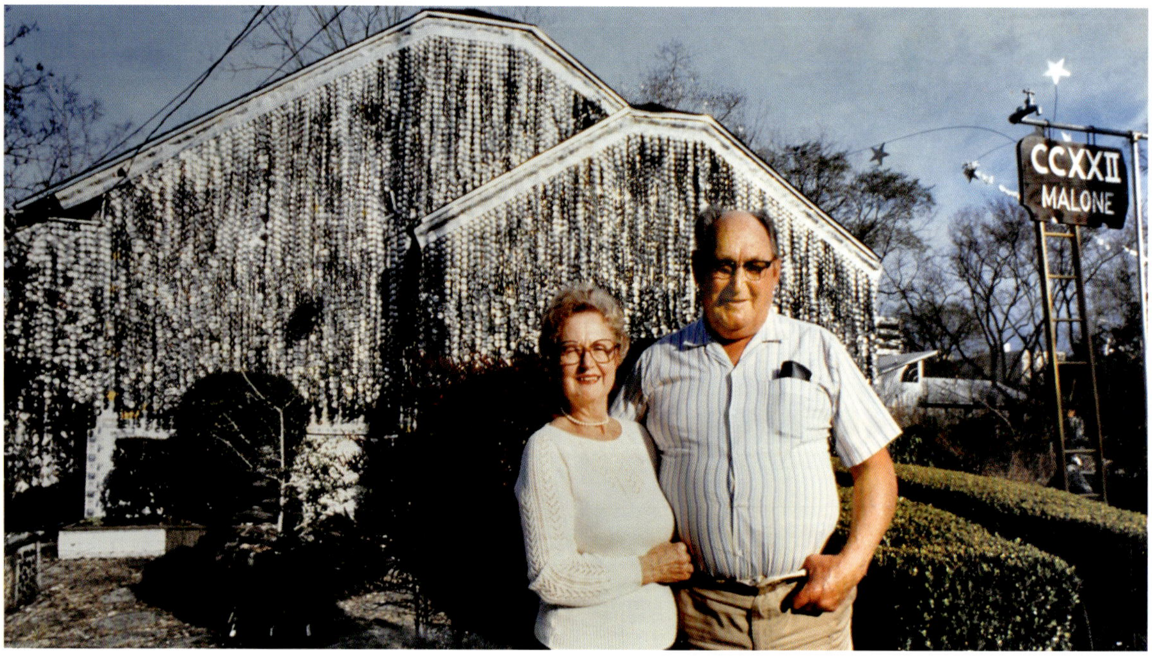

Mary and John Milkovisch in front of the Beer Can House, Malone Street, 1984 (with detail of the front fence, 2009, below). Now owned, restored, and conserved by The Orange Show Center for Visionary Art

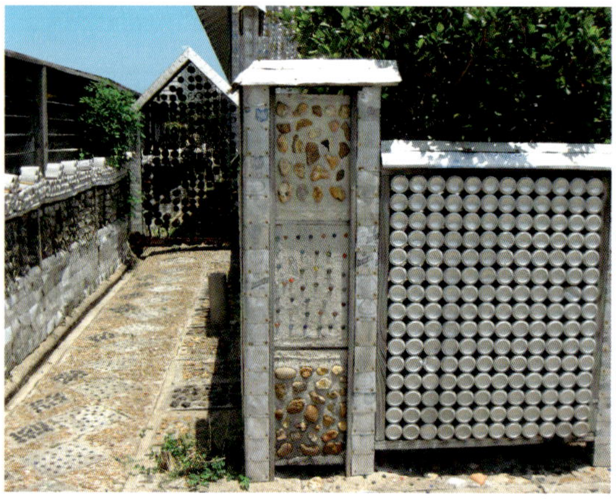

Why Houston? Lack of zoning and yearlong temperate weather help explain some of this creative activity, but more important is a shared attitude among Houstonians that permits and perhaps even encourages eccentric and visionary feats. This attitude was evident in the very founding of the city on the mosquito-infested banks of Buffalo Bayou and finds expression in the figures that we use to identify ourselves: the cowboy, oil wildcatter, and astronaut. It has evolved through the clash of cultures wrought by geography and history, drawing on the intellectual and aesthetic traditions of the Deep South, the frontier West, and Mexico.

Once known as the "Magnolia City" before air pollution reduced the numbers of magnolia trees, Houston is, in part, a southern city. The Civil War, slavery, and Reconstruction are parts of our past, and we share the South's cultural stereotypes. Jeff McKissack—postman, traveler, nutritionist, and builder of The Orange Show—could have been an eccentric character in a Eudora Welty story. Turner, "The Flower Man," has told me

1989

Buffalo Bayou ArtPark
The Buffalo Bayou ArtPark was founded as a continuation of the *Watermelon Flats* show. Today it is an artist-run organization that features a constantly rotating collection of public art below the Sabine Street Bridge between Allen Parkway and Memorial Drive. Twenty to twenty-five works of art are displayed at the park at any one time.

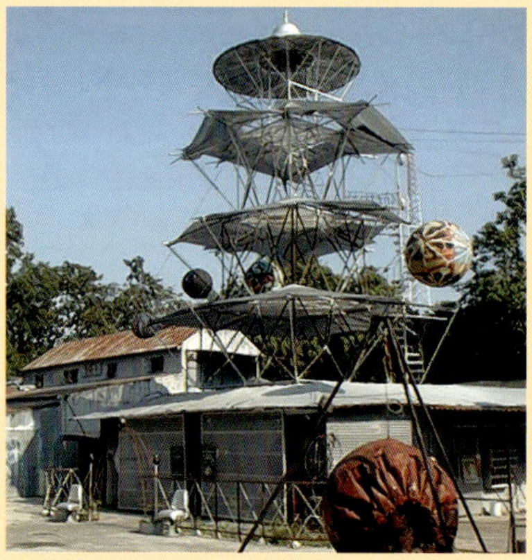

Nestor Topchy's TemplO, 2000

Meaux's Bayou/ Zocalo/ TemplO
Nestor Topchy, Rick Lowe, and Dean Ruck moved to a six-acre site on Feagan Street in the West End to fashion one of the most energetic communal art projects in the city. The site included several living spaces, a theater, a communal kitchen, gardens, several warehouse spaces for studios, and an outdoor stage and canopy used as a drive-in movie theater for up to thirty-five cars. Many artists lived and worked there, including Jim Pirtle, Andy Mann, Michael Battey, Fritz Welch, Mario Perez, and Giles Lyon. Initially called Meaux's Bayou, Topchy changed the compound's name to Zocalo, and then to TemplO as it grew and transformed.

Rubber–An Art Mob
Begun by artists Wayne Gilbert and Bill Hailey and filmmaker Ramzy Telley, Rubber–An Art Mob mounted twenty-five to thirty exhibitions in Texas. For a few years, the group ran 101 Space, located near downtown, as their home base. Their projects included film, video, performance art, and visual and sculptural exhibitions.

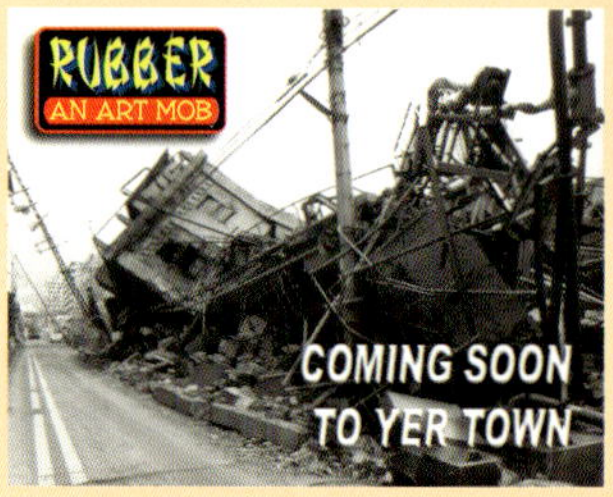

Social Bodies
Social Bodies, a one-night exhibition of the work of John Peters, occupied two sites: Homage, a downtown club, and 3221 Milam. To serve as his stand-in at one site, Peters hired a male model, who signed his own eight-by-ten headshots as "John Peters." On his new canvases, Peters sold advertising space by the square inch.

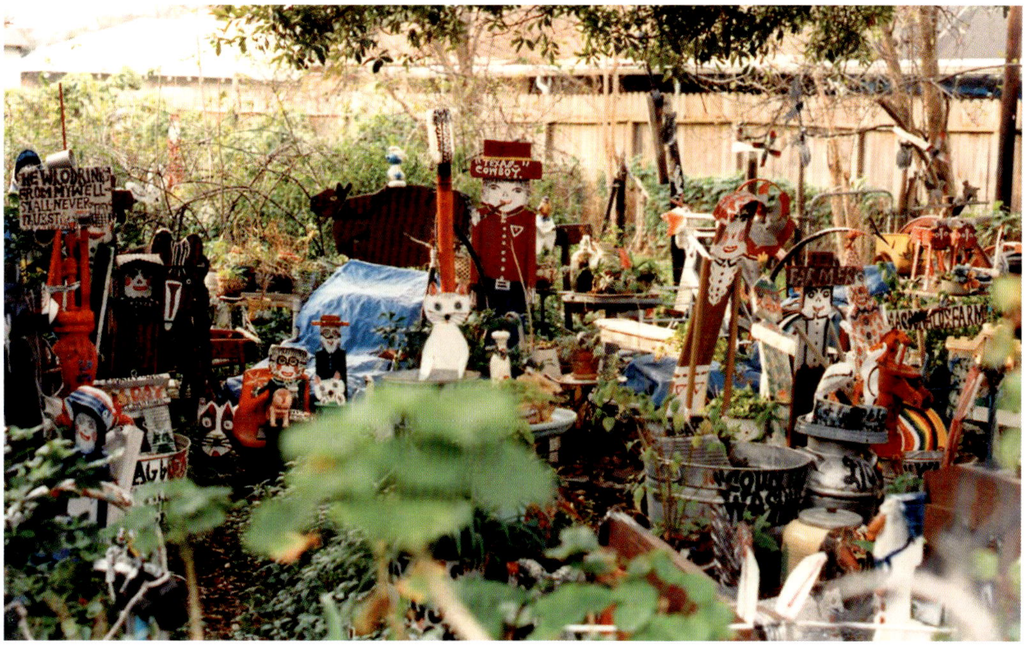

Ida Mae Kingsbury's yard, Pasadena, Texas, 1989. The handmade environment is lost but numerous individual pieces have been saved

tales of gardening with his mother and aunt in Mississippi that sound like the stories of strong and loving women in Alice Walker's novels.

And the life of Ida Mae Kingsbury sounds like a William Faulkner story, revealing the South as a place of tangible memories. In the years following the death of her husband, lonely and estranged from her family, Kingsbury found solace in the accumulation of objects—outgrown dresses, dolls no one would play with, and shirts that her late husband would never wear. They crowded her Pasadena home so much that she was forced to sleep in her car. She also populated her garden with figures constructed from fence posts, tin cutouts, and found objects—a sheriff, a postman, dogs, cats, happy ladies, loving couples—her own community to replace the one she had lost.

A distinctly vital part of our southern legacy is the presence of an African aesthetic that survived centuries of forced enslavement, many of these art forms rooted in the strong visual and cultural traditions of the ancient African kingdom of Kongo.

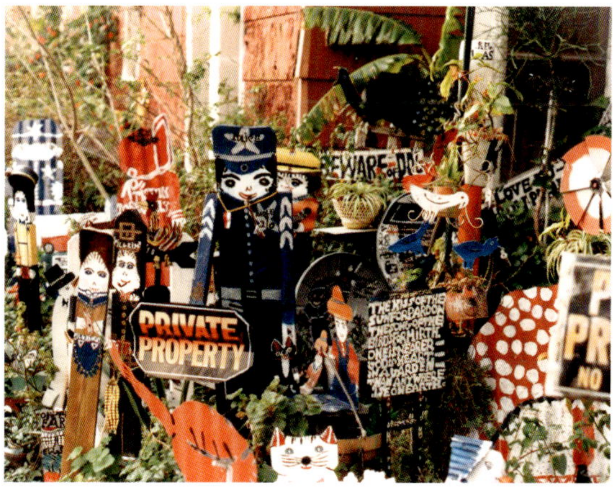

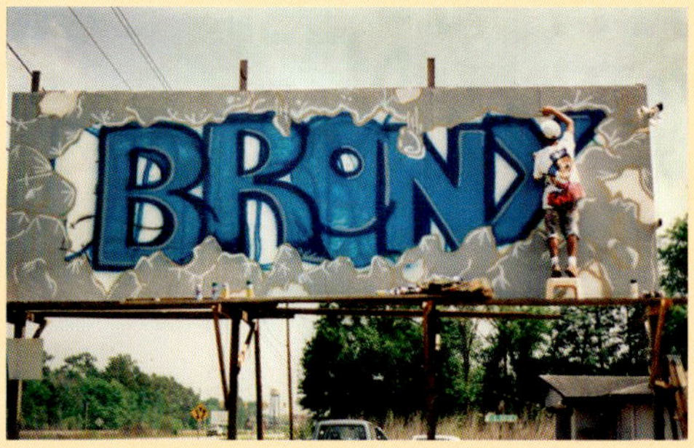

GONZO247 tagging a billboard on the east side of downtown Houston, 1990

Aerosol Warfare

Graffiti artists GONZO247 and MERGE360 began to document on video what they were doing both legally and illegally. They established a pen pal system with graffiti artists in other cities, exchanging videos of their work. They then compiled these videos from all over the world under the name Aerosol Warfare to create a video magazine covering all aspects of emerging hip-hop culture; centered on graffiti, the magazine is now sold worldwide. In 1992 they established Houston's first "wall of fame," a legal spot for artists to graffiti, which is still running today at Palmer and McKinney Streets. In 1994 Christian Azul joined Aerosol Warfare.

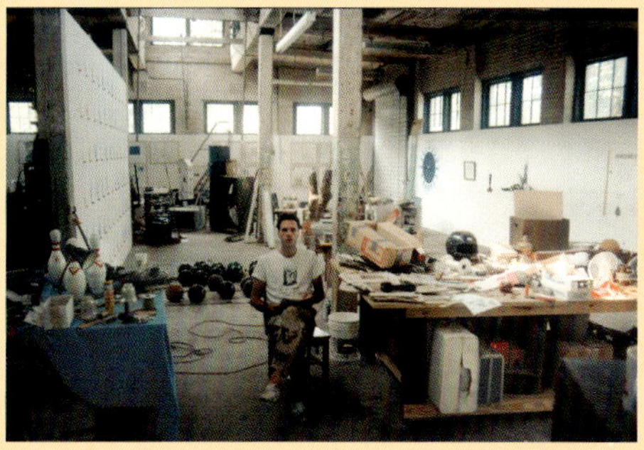

Jack Massing in the Art Guise World Headquarters, 1990

Art Guise World Headquarters

In 1989 The Art Guys renovated and moved into a nineteenth-century warehouse on the northern edge of Houston's Heights neighborhood. This became their studio as well as an alternative art space, where they presented and staged exhibitions and performances of their own work and the work of other artists. For more than fifteen years while at this location, The Art Guys Museum (its name changed frequently) was a Houston hot spot for unusual and sometimes seminal exhibitions, performances, and events.

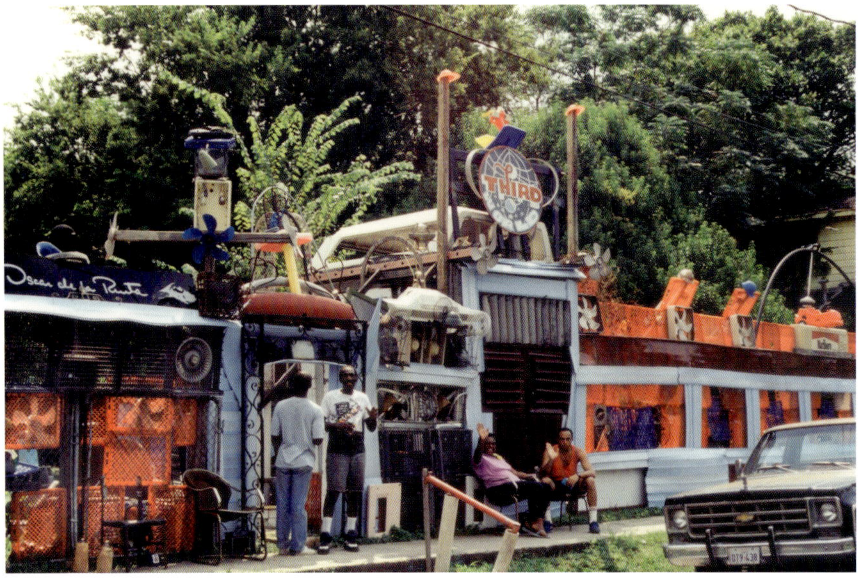

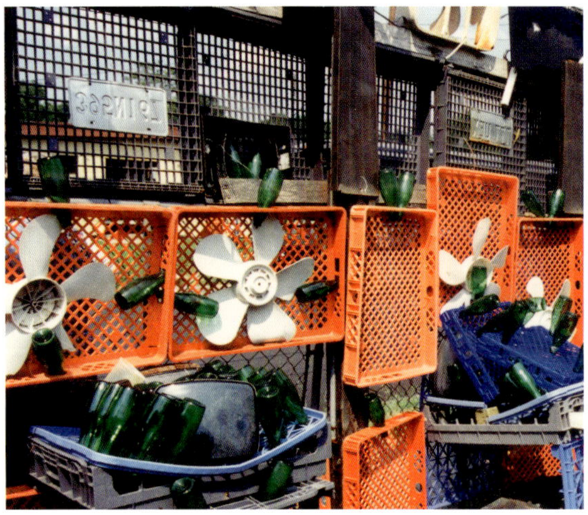

Facade and detail of Bob Harper's (the "Fan Man") Third World environment, 1989

You have only to visit the sites created by African American artists in Houston to find elements traditionally expressive of motion (wheels, tires, and other round objects), containment (jars, jugs, and other vessels), figuration (icons, dolls, roots, and sculptures), and the presence of medicine (healing herbs). A walk through "Fan Man" Bob Harper's Third World on a windy day once brilliantly illustrated all these elements at work. Hundreds of fans, freed from their steel encasements and placed throughout the garden, spun in the wind. The walkway was lined with bottles carried home from his job at the convenience store a block away. In the center of the yard, a tower was constructed of discarded televisions and oven tops, on top of which perched a blonde mannequin.

Houston is part of the pioneer West as well, where the language, religion, food, and cultural traditions brought by newly arrived settlers, attracted to the promise of freedom from the past, have survived to various degrees. Certainly some of Texas's best cultural contributions come from this mixture, such as conjunto music, born when Norteño Mexican Musica met the German-Czech polkas of central Texas. Emblems of the old West—a lost boot, castoff cowboy hat, broken toy rifles—decorated the fence around Howard Porter's OK Corral, which by 2000 was being surrounded by the new town houses of the Fourth Ward, one of only nine remaining shotgun houses (a modest dwelling containing adjoining rooms in a narrow plan) within a ten-block radius. Porter himself, a house painter by trade, had painted more than four hundred of these vernacular dwellings over the last forty-five years. The OK Corral had become a gathering place where forty or so of his close friends could sit on derelict furniture resurrected with an inventive coat of paint and could eat Porter's famous barbecue while taking in one of the most sublime views of downtown Houston around.

Finally, we were also once part of Mexico. Remnants of Mexican aesthetics and spirituality are entwined in our mongrel experience, including the idea that art is a healing experience open to all and not solely a commodity created by the educated for the elite. In the retablos and ex votos (shrines and devotional

1989

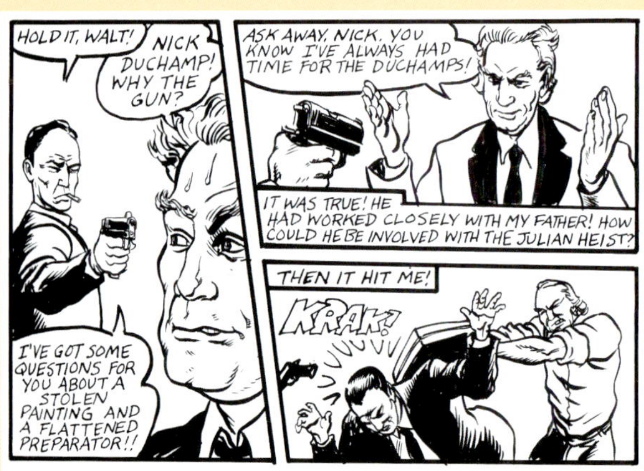

Detective Nick Duchamp and a character based on curator Walter Hopps from Scott Gilbert's *True Artist Tales*, 1989

True Artist Tales

Artist Scott Gilbert began his art comic strip in *Public News*, which was then Houston's leading alternative newspaper weekly. *True Artist Tales* was a make-believe comic soap opera in which Gilbert sprinkled recognizable characters with pseudonyms to present a semi-fictitious rendering of the Houston art scene.

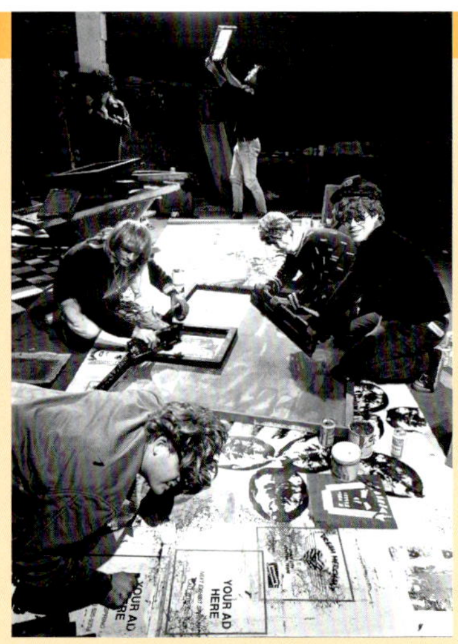

Silk-screening for *Primal Screen*, 1989

Primal Screen

Primal Screen: A Fake Art Movement, an exhibition organized by artist John Peters for Treebeard's Restaurant on Market Square, included work by Jane Addison, Jose Cipriano Aquirre, James Bettison, Mel Chin, Randy Cole, Jeff Cowie, Ramona Fabregas, Wes Hicks, John Kaiser, Jack Massing, Joel Orr, John Peters, and Santiago Pretence, with opening night music by Jim Pirtle.

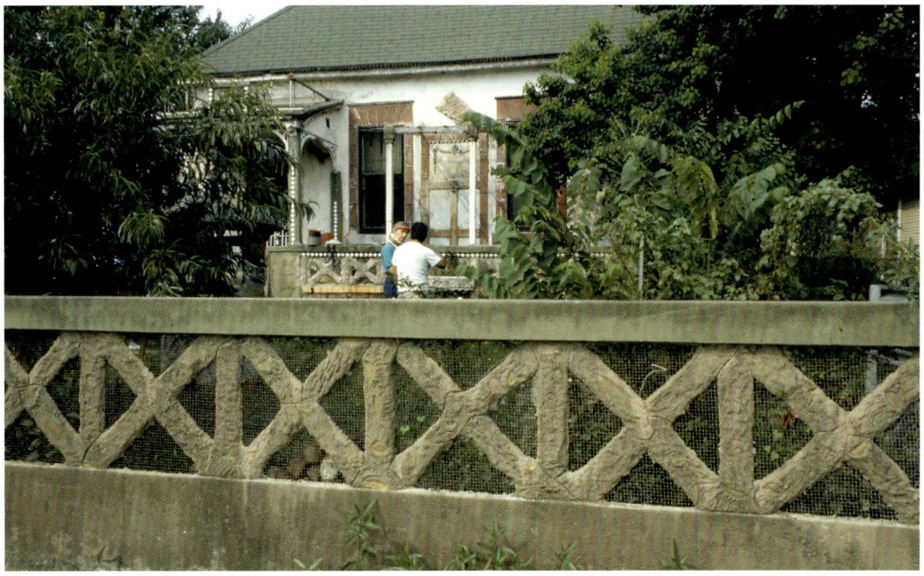

El trabajo rustico (concrete simulated logs) fence in front of Timiteo Martinez's home in the East End, c. 1985

items) made in gratitude for miracles performed and prayers answered, no object is too ordinary to be decorative; no material, too humble; no color, too bright; and no mixture of textures, lines, and shapes, too varied. A house constructed by the late Timiteo Martinez in old Second Ward was one of my favorites in Houston. It couldn't have been more than four hundred square feet, made of the most inexpensive building materials, but it showed a wealth of wit and flair. It boasted a trompe l'oeil door, a beautiful religious grotto, and a fence in the style of *el trabajo rustico* (the craft of scoring concrete to look as though it were wood logs).

For all the historical influences that help to explain why there are so many handmade personal spaces in Houston, the most important clue may be Houston's lack of a coherent center, both literally and metaphorically. Many of us are immigrant Houstonians, which means that the city is constantly being reinvented. In traditional communities, shared memories, values, perceptions, and beliefs make up a cohesive whole and provide boundaries for acceptable behavior and group expression. The blithe abandonment of centers and boundaries that is characteristic of Houston allows its more free-spirited artists to communicate personal experiences in ways that open up possibilities for others: it is the clearest demonstration of the power of the human drive to create. In a place where your neighbor can cover his house with beer cans or make a monument to the fruit he loves most, are your dreams too improbable?

Update: 2009

Much has happened in the world, in Houston, and in the lives of the people and their handmade sites since this essay appeared in 2000. That the curators of *No Zoning* thought this essay still seems relevant in 2009 gives me a welcome opportunity to revisit and update the artists and their spaces.

Jeff McKissack's Orange Show was listed on the National Register for Historic Places in 2007. It continues to be the location and inspiration for events that celebrate the human gift for personal expression. Recognizing that its mission had expanded, the organization that owns and maintains the site became the

1990s

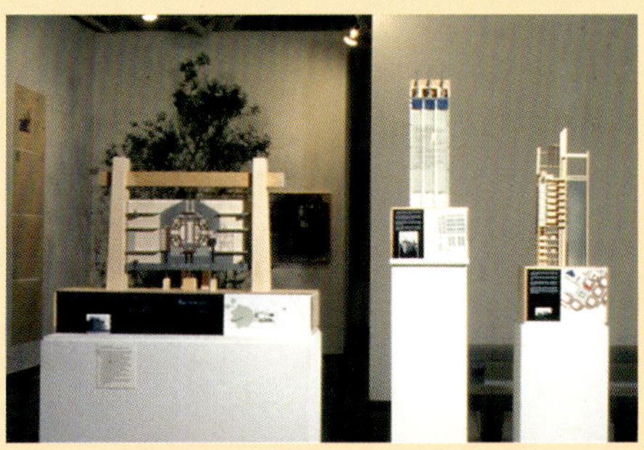

Project Houston, installation view, DiverseWorks, 1990

1990

Project Houston
Organized by Deborah Brauer for DiverseWorks, *Project Houston* was a collaborative exhibition presenting designs for Houston's future by artists, architects, engineers, scientists, a choreographer, and a composer, working both individually and in teams. Held May 2–July 29, the exhibition addressed urban and sociological issues facing Houston, such as housing preservation and reuse, transportation, environmental responsibility, and urban revitalization. The collaborations were documented in a catalogue.

Summer Street Studios
Keith Hollingsworth, who lived and worked in a studio on Summer Street during the nineties, held annual Erotic Art Shows as well as other sporadic exhibitions and performances.

S.H.A.P.E. Protest Installation
After the 1989 shooting death of Ida Delaney at the hands of a drunk, off-duty police officer, Rick Lowe presented an exhibition in the playground of the S.H.A.P.E. Community Center as part of his Victims series. The exhibition featured life-size figures of painted plywood representing those killed by violence installed in a large-scale tableau.

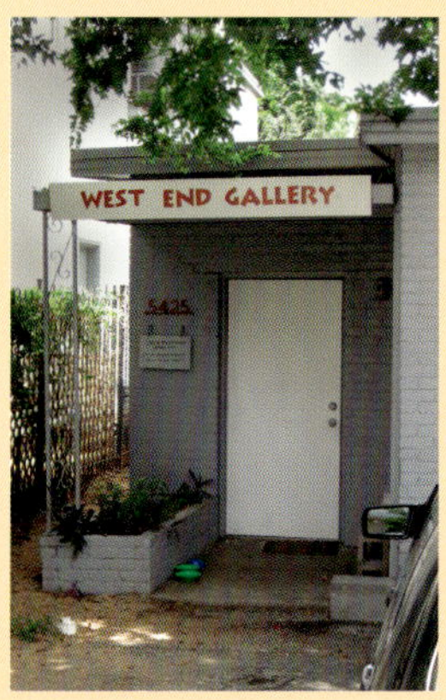

West End Gallery, 2009

1991

West End Gallery
Artist Kathleen Packlick opened the West End Gallery on Blossom Street, occupying a small space adjacent to the West End Bike Shop.

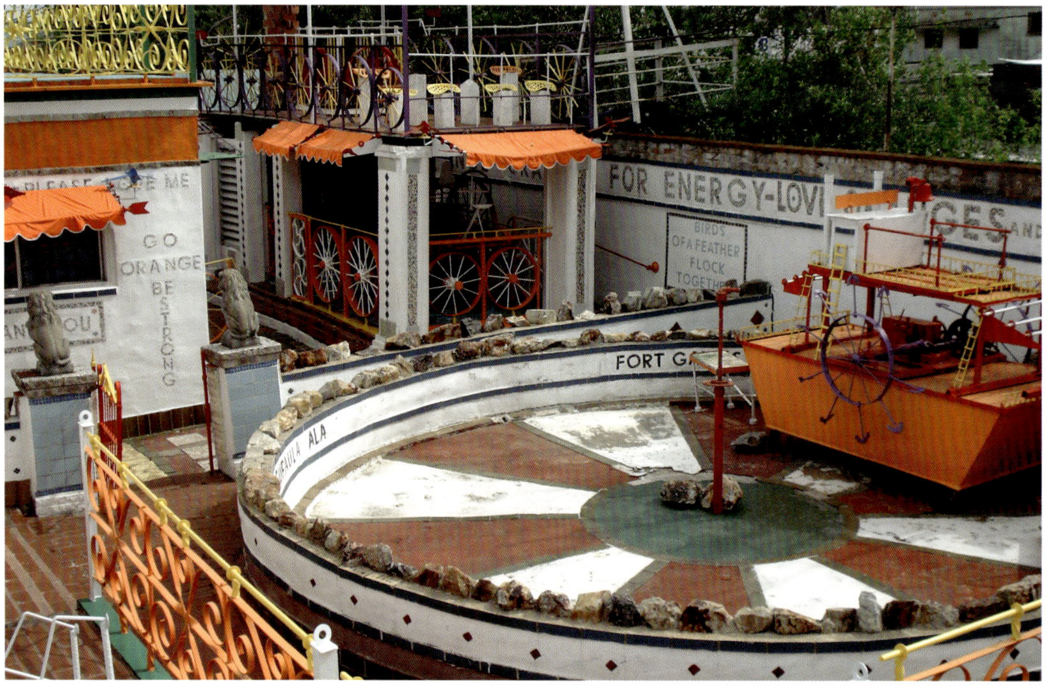

Performance arena of Jeff McKissack's The Orange Show, Munger Street, c. 2004

Orange Show Center for Visionary Art in 2003. The largest of The Orange Show's programs, the Art Car Parade, now twenty-two years old, is known around the world as a spectacular festival of creativity on wheels. Other programs, such as mural projects with at-risk youth, are less well known but have profound impact on the lives of those involved.

The Beer Can House was acquired by The Orange Show Foundation in late 2001 after ill health forced Mary Milkovisch—whose late husband, John, had created the house from his daily six-packs—to enter an extended care facility, where she passed away in 2002. Generous gifts from The Brown Foundation and Houston Endowment, along with the support of many others, led the way for a monumental effort to transform what had once been a private home into a public treasure. The house, the interior of which now contains an exhibition about its creation, was memorably dedicated by Mayor Bill White on March 6, 2008. Milkovisch's creation has assumed a revered place as an icon of Houston's freewheeling culture.

The OK Corral in Houston's Fourth Ward, where Howard Porter practiced his painting on every surface of his house, using a feather duster to apply finishes of contrasting colors, was sold to developers in spring 2004. Friends who once sat in his yard, filled with Western memorabilia and enough tables and chairs to entertain a crowd, have not seen Porter since the completion of the Fourth Ward's conversion to a middle-class urban neighborhood. In September after its sale, the vacant house was destroyed by fire of an unknown origin.

The Flower Man survived two hurricanes and a Molotov cocktail after this essay first appeared, then a fire set by vandals in early 2003 caused Cleveland Turner to leave the house on Sampson Street. With help from Project Row Houses, he purchased a house with a large yard a mile away, and he has

1991

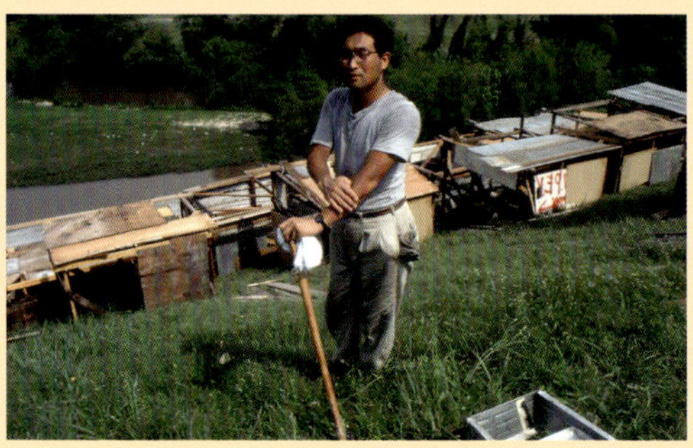

Tadashi Kawamata installing *Favela in Houston*, Buffalo Bayou, 1991

Favela in Houston
As part of its *Landscapes* public sculpture exhibition, DiverseWorks and the Houston International Festival commissioned a work by Japanese artist Tadashi Kawamata, known for his installations, or "displacements," that construct chaotic architectural growths around existing aspects of the urban landscape. Kawamata created *Favela in Houston*, an elaborate series of rooms made from scrap lumber and installed along the banks of Buffalo Bayou.

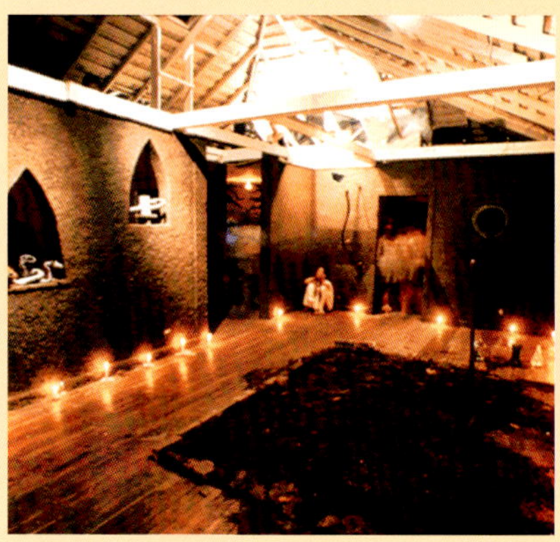

Alchemy House, installation view, 1991

Alchemy House
Dan Havel created *Alchemy House* from an existing bungalow on Blossom Street as part studio, part sculpture, and part performance space, with performances by Kelli Scott Kelley and sound design by William D. Kelley. It was a center of activity for many members of the art community in the months prior to its expected demolition.

since transformed the house and gardens into a riot of color. Inside, dense installations of thousands of seemingly random objects fill the entire house, leaving only narrow paths to walk from room to room. Since 2005 a school bus-sized tribute to The Flower Man has appeared in the Art Car Parade.

When a salvage company was hired to clear Ida Mae Kingsbury's house in 1990, hundreds of her sculptures were transported by volunteers to The Orange Show's garage. Since then the Friends of Ida Kingsbury have organized exhibitions of her art and donated a substantial portion of the work to the Grassroots Art Center in Lucas, Kansas, where it is currently on exhibit.

Timiteo Martinez's house in Houston's Second Ward still stands, though the original colors and scored concrete surface have been painted white. Only subtle remnants of the original vision and craft remain. The loss of many of the unique features of this handmade wonder is partially compensated for by the lively new generation of the Martinez family that has come to occupy the house.

In 2007 I became programming director at Discovery Green, Houston's new downtown park. As part of a team working to create a vibrant urban park on land that was once a surface parking lot, I have gained a new perspective on "Handmade Personal Spaces." Houston provides fertile ground for the creation of these sites for the reasons I gave in 2000, but also because artists, patrons, and institutions are on hand to recognize art in unexpected places. My original essay did not give credit enough to the art community itself for its wisdom, generosity, and courage in supporting these sites. *No Zoning* is an important development in telling this story.

Creating a sense of place is remarkably difficult; the landscape is literally littered with failed attempts. Yet without sophisticated tools or many resources beyond their own vision and labor, Jeff McKissack, John Milkovisch, and others created spaces that continue to engage new audiences and help define the city that has embraced their creations.

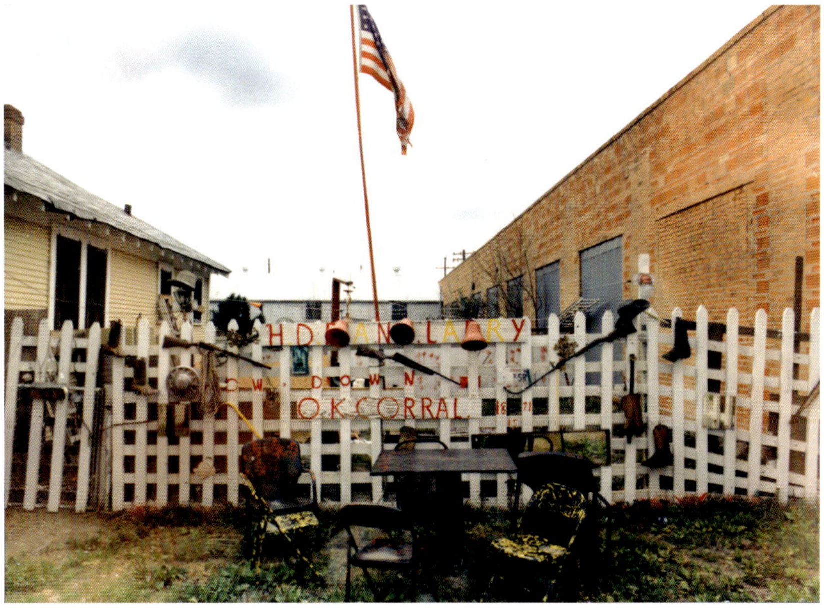

Howard Porter's OK Corral, 1994

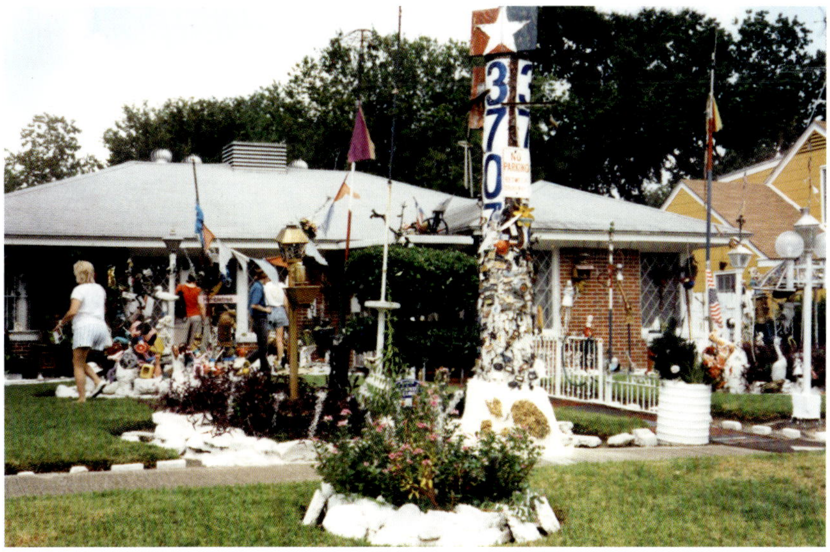

Front yard of Sylvester Williams's Eagle's Nest, 1995

1992

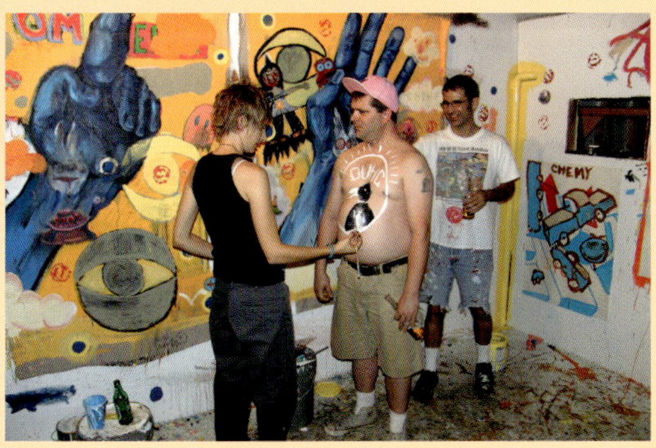

Betsy Odom and Chris Olivier paint Rodney Elliott during I Love You Baby's *Shirts and Skins*, Commerce Street Artists' Warehouse (CSAW), 2002

I Love You Baby
Paul Kremer, Will Bentsen, and Rodney Elliott, began meeting and painting communally. Soon an art collective was launched with these three artists as core founders, followed by continuously changing members. In 2002 the group began meeting regularly at CSAW and adopted the name I Love You Baby (ILYB). Today it works on paintings, sculptures, and plans for street art and conceptual projects—all while drinking beer. Their website iloveyoubaby.org acts as their primary exhibition space.

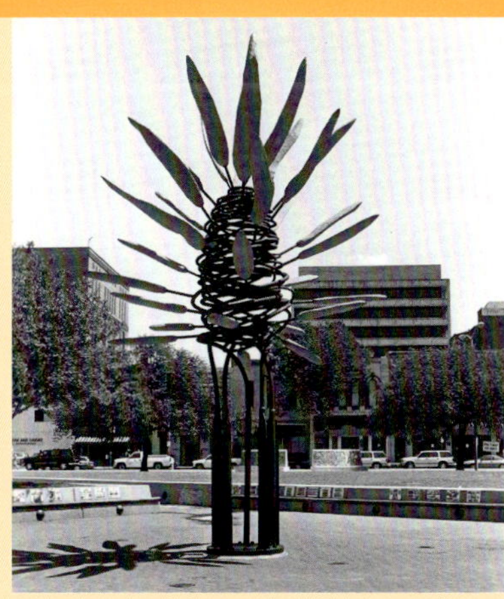

James Surls's sculpture *Points of View*, Market Square Park, 1992

Market Square Park
Soon after DiverseWorks began programming in its building next to Market Square, it initiated a plan for an artist-designed park. Participating in this landmark park project, one of the first artist-designed parks in the country, were Malou Flato, Paul Hester, Douglas Hollis, James Surls, and Richard Turner. They worked collaboratively to design the park in cooperation with the Houston Parks and Recreation Department. It was dedicated in 1992.

Note: The chronology resumes on page 50.

Because It Is Houston,

the streetlights have to take the place
usually reserved for the moon in the poem

and the traffic in the background with its roar and surge
stands in for the ocean
                    tossing wrecks like driftwood on the shore.

Because it is Houston the
tight little blond talking on her cell phone

while backing her SUV at high speed through the parking lot
is a respected citizen

and the gnarled, serpentine, stretched out limbs of oaks
above certain shady boulevards

suggest that even ugly can be beautiful.

Because it is Houston,
a moist wind from the south at dawn

carries the faint petrochemical bouquet
                    from the landfills of our fathers
                                    and the landfills of their fathers.
So sweet it smells!

A morning shower
has knocked down blossoms from the honeysuckle bush
                                                into the grass
like little ivory trumpets.

Because there is no one better qualified around,
                because it is Houston,

you are the one who gets to kneel
beside the broken sidewalk

and look at them in silence.

—Tony Hoagland, 2009

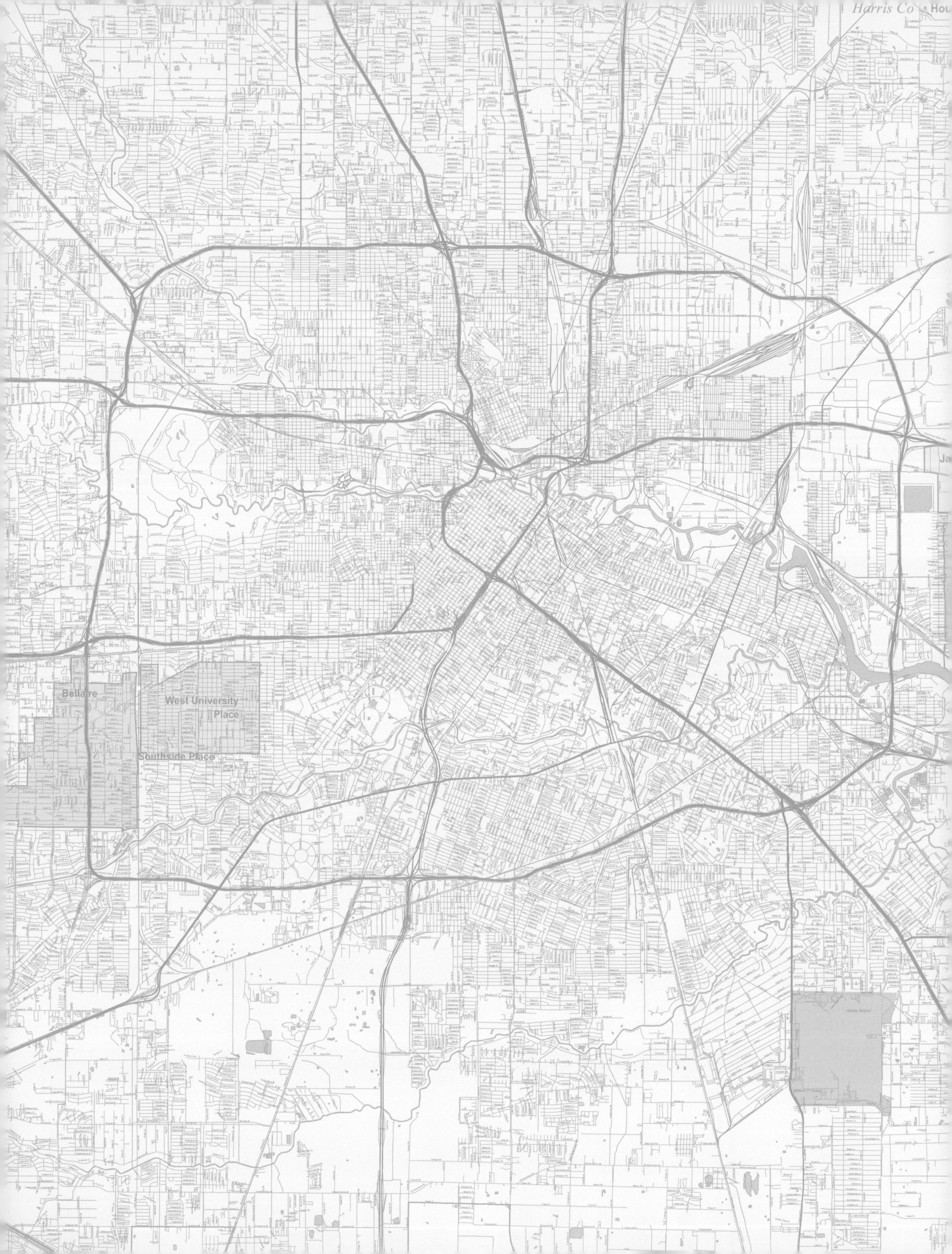
Harris Co
Bellaire
West University
Place
Southside Place

Artists and Works in the Exhibition

Catalogue Entries by
Meredith Goldsmith

The Art Guys

The Art Guys (Michael Galbreth and Jack Massing) have been making art and performing collaboratively since they met at the University of Houston in 1982. Conceptual artists who explore social and artistic conventions, The Art Guys work in performance, sculpture, installations, drawings, videos, and anything else that suits their aim of making visible the usually unconsidered patterns of behavior, thought, and life in general.

Although they exhibit in museums and galleries across the country, The Art Guys have regularly used the city of Houston as a setting for their performances and sculptures. In *Bucket Feet* (1994), they dressed in suits and walked ten miles through downtown with buckets of water attached to their feet; in *The Golden Dumpster (After)* (1995), they coated an outdoor dumpster with gold paint; in *The Giant Art Guys* (1998), they created fourteen-foot statues of themselves and placed them in front of a used-car dealership; and in *Yard Crew* (1990), they donned dungarees, carried a weed trimmer and a lawn mower onto the back lawn of the CAMH, and, without permission, "lowered the grass in an even manner."[1]

Recently, they have produced works that explore life-cycle events. In 2008 they performed *The Art Guys Lie in State*, in which they presented themselves—eyes closed in mock death and bodies clad in black suits on black-draped tables—in the rotunda of Houston's City Hall and invited the public to view them for one hour. In *Forever Yours* (2007–2008), The Art Guys have sought (so far unsuccessfully) to sell their cremated remains after they die, with their ashes to be contained in bronze urns in the shape of self-portrait busts.

For *No Zoning*, The Art Guys present a new performance titled *The Art Guys Marry a Plant*. On June 13, 2009, at 11:00 in the morning, The Art Guys married a live oak sapling in a public ceremony at the Lillie and Hugh Roy Cullen Sculpture Garden of the Museum of Fine Arts, Houston, with a reception immediately following in the Contemporary Arts Museum Houston. The tree will be planted and a bronze plaque commemorating the event will be installed alongside it at a site to be determined. Every measure was taken to ensure that this was a traditional wedding—albeit a polygamous one that spans biological kingdoms and stirs up all manner of current ecological and civil rights issues. The Art Guys, however, are not themselves commenting on the work's environmental or social aspects. They hope their wedding guests will shape the meaning of this provocative union.

1. http://theartguys.com/IMAGES/Works/Performance/YardCrew.jpg (accessed July 22, 2009).

1992

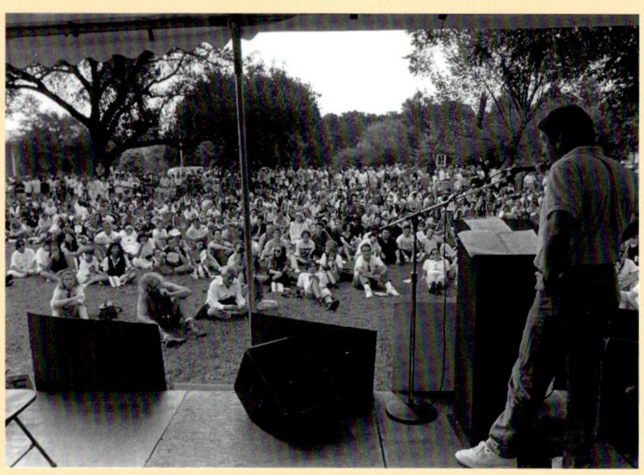

"Don't GAG the Arts" rally on the Menil Collection campus, 1992

Don't GAG the Arts

The rally "Don't GAG the Arts," held in the park on the Menil campus to protest censorship of grants by the National Endowment for the Arts (NEA) and to support freedom of expression, drew a large and vocal crowd. The NEA had rescinded grants awarded to four artists, Karen Finley, John Fleck, Holly Hughes, and Tim Miller, because of their works' provocative content. Rally speakers included Walter Hopps, Peter Marzio, Michael Peranteau, Tim Miller, and Paul Winkler. Artists made "Don't Gag the Arts" posters, placards, and fans. The "NEA Four" took their case to the Supreme Court and in 1998 the Court upheld the grant awards.

1993

ARTCRAWL

ARTCRAWL Houston was inaugurated, an annual downtown event that invites the public to tour artists' studios in the downtown area.

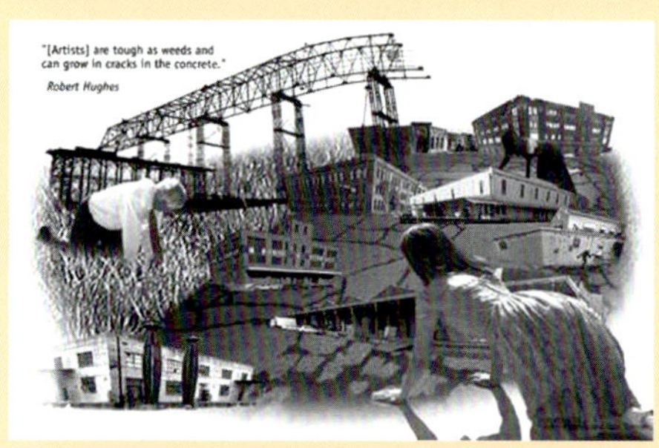

Invitation for the 6th Annual ARTCRAWL, 1998

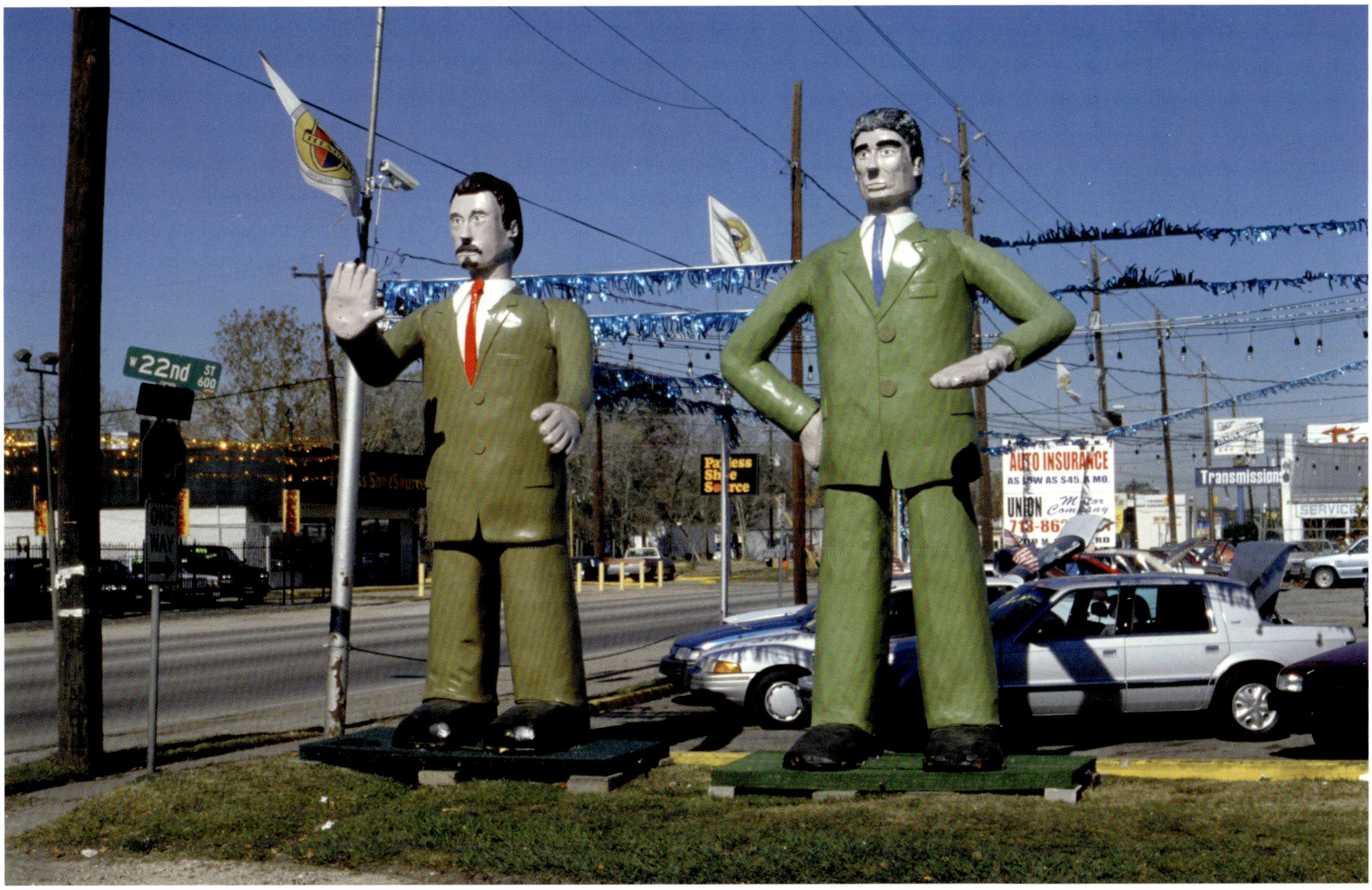

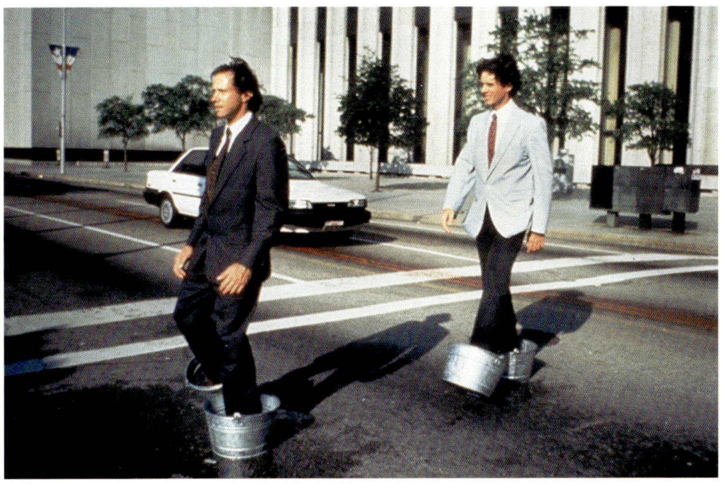

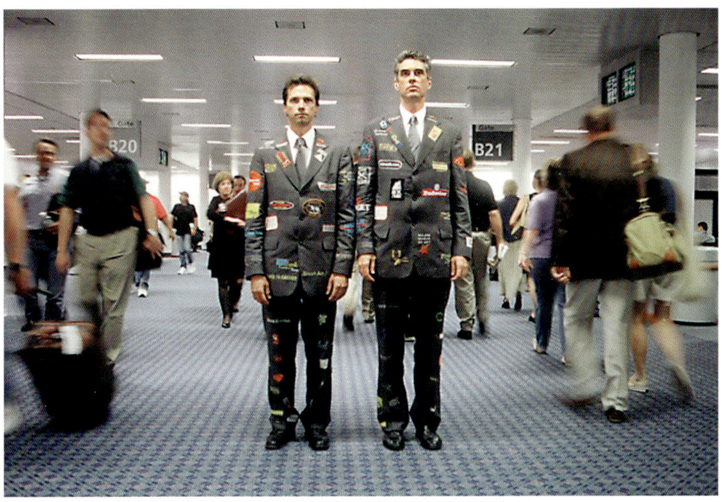

The Art Guys
top:
The Giant Art Guys, 1998
Metal, wood, polyurethane, paint
14 feet, height

center:
Bucket Feet (performance documentation, downtown Houston), 1994
Galvanized buckets, water

bottom:
SUITS: The Clothes Make the Man (performance documentation, George Bush Intercontinental Airport, Houston; The Art Guys leased advertising space on suits designed by Todd Oldham and wore them for a year throughout the U.S.), 1998–99
Nylon, rayon, on wool and silk suits
All courtesy The Art Guys

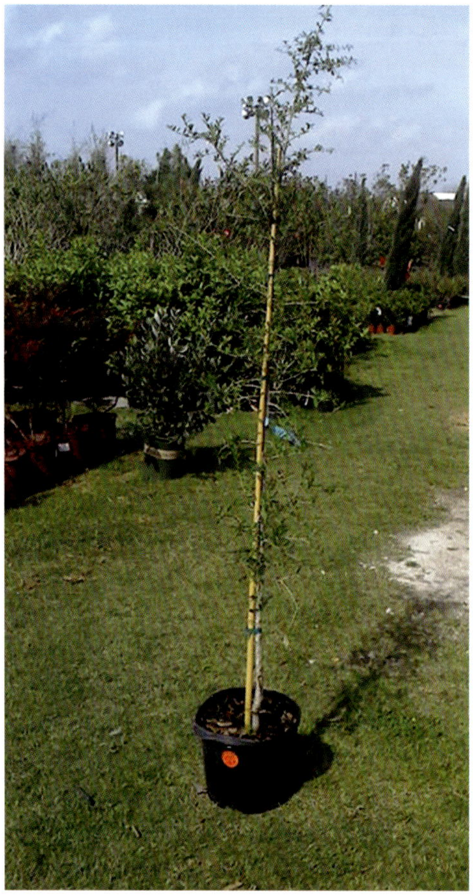

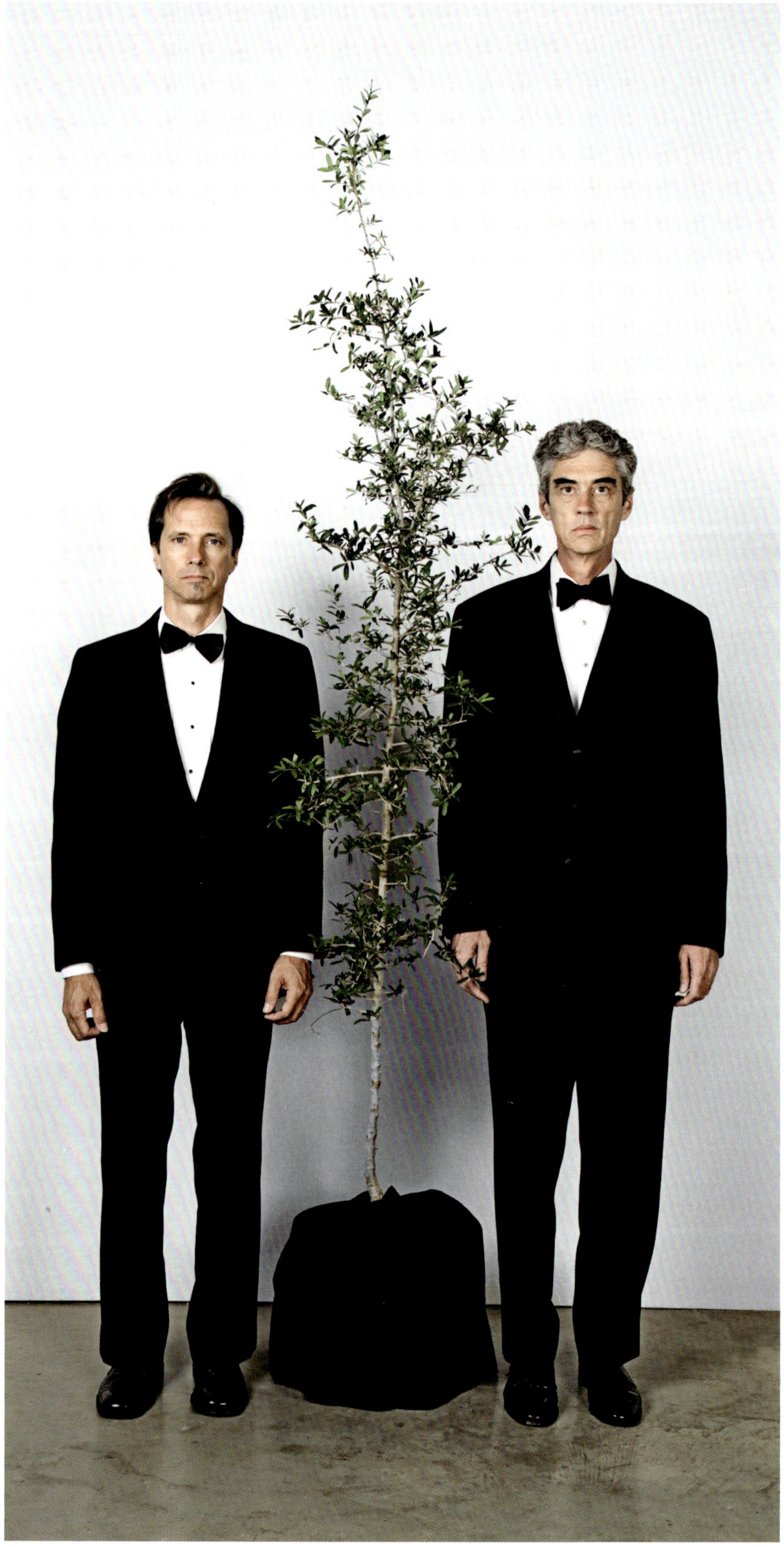

The Art Guys
The Art Guys Marry A Plant (live oak tree at plant nursery), 2009
Live oak tree, dirt, clay pot

The Art Guys Marry A Plant (engagement photograph), 2009
Live oak tree, dirt, clay pot
Both courtesy The Art Guys

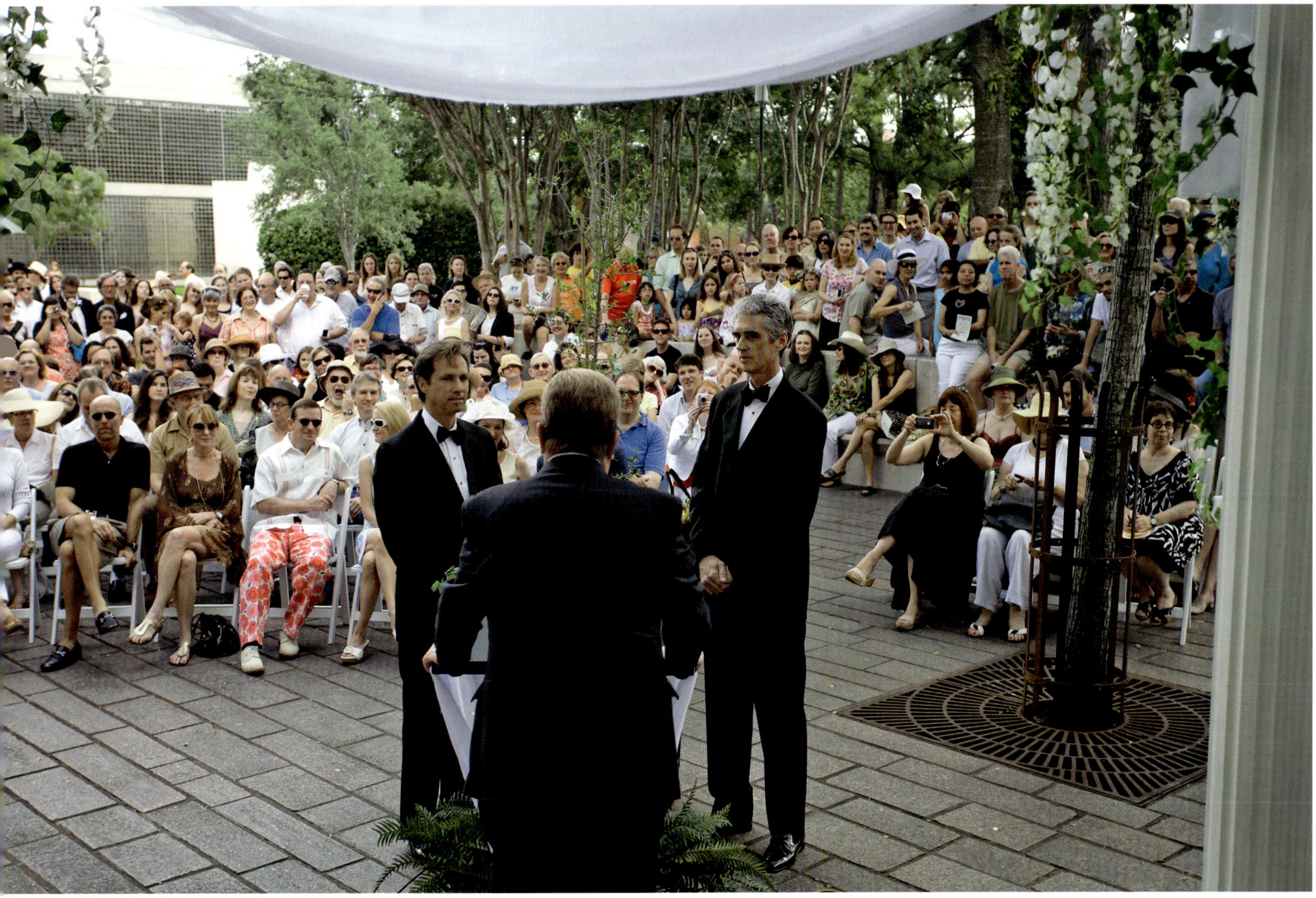

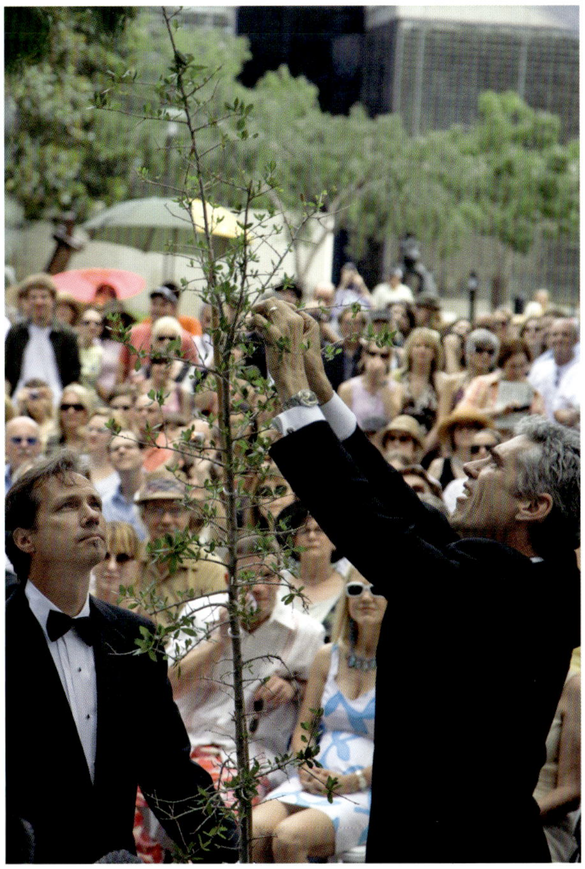

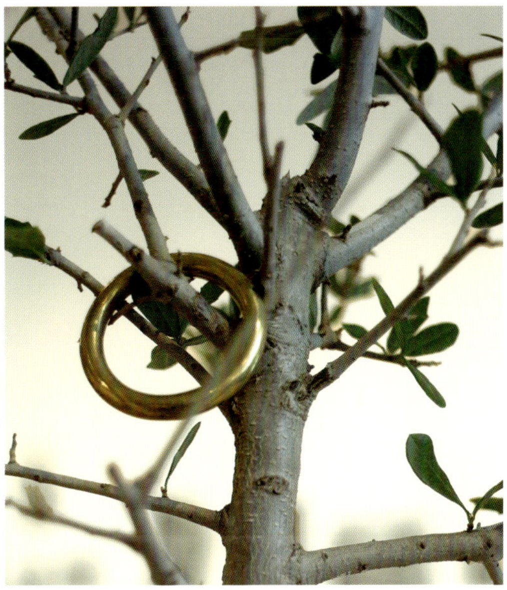

The Art Guys

top and bottom left:

The Art Guys Marry A Plant (performance documentation, Lillie and Hugh Roy Cullen Sculpture Garden, Museum of Fine Arts, Houston), 2009

Live oak tree, dirt, clay pot

bottom right:

The Art Guys Marry A Plant (wedding ring), 2009

Live oak tree, dirt, clay pot, gold ring

Tree: 104 x 18 1/2 x 18 1/2 inches

Both courtesy The Art Guys

Mary Ellen Carroll

Mary Ellen Carroll juggles the roles of urban planner, designer/architect, filmmaker, linguist, trickster, photographer, and sculptor in her wryly humorous conceptual art, working in performance, neon, photography, public art, ceramics, published books, and even trademarks, patents, and intellectual property. Carroll's practice is intentionally without a signature style, and her projects can be enigmatic, highlighting broad concepts that investigate ideas of the double or copy and the fundamental question of what is a work of art.

She begins her process by writing, or, as she calls it, "drawing in language," to identify paradoxical intersections of power relations and structures, and then makes work that subtly challenges audiences to think about these cultural constructions in new ways. Past projects include *All of the Men Who Think They Can Be Me* (2001), during which she collected résumés, headshots, and physical descriptions sent to her in response to an ad soliciting people to "be her"; *The Toni Negri (drinking from the same glass)* (2001), a drinking fountain that allows five people to drink simultaneously yet can only be activated by the drinker in the center position; and *Federal* (2003), a series of photographs and a twenty-four-hour video portrait of the Federal Building in Los Angeles, which explores post-9/11 themes of watching and being watched.

Dividing her time between New York and Houston, Carroll teaches at Rice University's School of Architecture and collaborates with Charles Renfro on a traveling studio course. For their graduate class, they took the participants to Houston landmarks, including Joel Osteen's Lakewood mega-church, former boxer George Foreman's church, and the Houston Ship Channel, for a critical examination of how industry and ideology affect building typology.

The lack of zoning laws in Houston, Carroll posits, creates an urban analogue to the large amount of acreage employed in the Land Art movement of the 1960s and 1970s. In both cases, artists, architects, and creative thinkers have tremendous freedom to realize their ideas. Houston's distinction as the largest metropolitan area in the United States without a formal zoning code is the sole reason that her current multipart project *prototype 180* (1999–2009) is located in the city. For the project, she is working with engineers to rotate a house and its lot 180 degrees. One of thousands of nearly identical homes built during the 1950s in the master-planned Sharpstown subdivision in Houston, this house, once turned, will intentionally alter the unity of its neighborhood. As this project continues, Carroll intends to make the house eventually "disappear"[1] as she removes it from the power grid and equips it with renewable energy technologies. She also intends to integrate high-definition video cameras in the eaves of the house to simultaneously capture the neighboring reaction to the transformation of the lot. The footage from these cameras is from the house's point of view and will be streamed through the Internet from Google Earth. The neighbors will be able to "talk back" to *prototype 180* through a wifi cloud that will be installed over the neighborhood, Sharpstown I. "The house becomes the protagonist in the narrative," Carroll says. "Making architecture perform as a work of art is the conceptual framework for *prototype 180*."

In the CAMH's galleries, Carroll has installed a sixteen-foot diameter combination stage/table replicating the dimensions and hardwood floor of the *prototype 180* house's living room. Carroll's circular platform functions as a site for meetings and symposia—including a debate on land use in Houston by mayoral candidates—and as a stage for performances. After the exhibition, a similar structure will be the central architectural feature in Carroll's *prototype 180*, which she intends to transform into an institute concentrating on the study of neighborhoods.

1. This and subsequent quotes by Mary Ellen Carroll are from conversations with the author, November 2008.

Mary Ellen Carroll
opposite top:
The Center and the Scoff (or how to make things disappear)
(a stolen, red, 1980s American sedan placed by crane in the middle of the forest as part of a commission for the Fields Sculpture Park at Art Omi, Ghent, New York), 2001
C-print
30 x 40 inches
Courtesy the artist and Galerie Hubert Winter, Vienna

1993

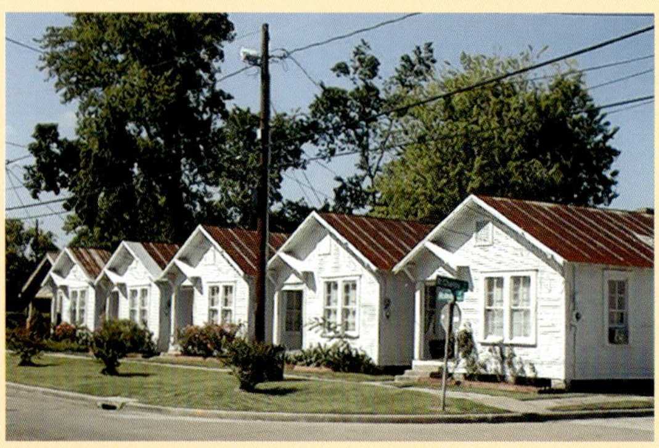

Project Row Houses, c. 2000

Project Row Houses
Project Row Houses, conceived and founded by artist Rick Lowe, rescued and rehabilitated a series of shotgun-style houses in Houston's Third Ward, one of the city's oldest African American communities. Installations, exhibitions, and performances were programmed in the houses, some of which also became community-based living facilities.
The opening of Project Row Houses was preceded by the *Drive-By Show*, which invited artists to paint on the plywood temporarily covering the windows of the row houses facing Holman Street.

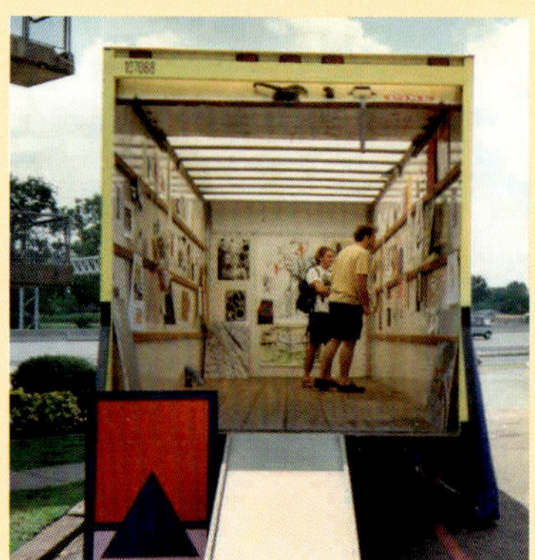

Arena Production's *Cross-City Blowout* art mobile, 1993

Arena Productions
Curator Chris Ballou and artist Sean Thornton staged a series of interactive public art exhibitions in response to what they saw as inadequate art-presentation strategies by galleries and museums. Unusual in format, these exhibitions appeared in unlikely places: *Frost Free* was held in the appliance department of a Sears store; *Potlatch* occurred in a local warehouse as part of *Rolywholyover—A Circus for Museum by John Cage*, presented at the Menil Collection; and *Cross-City Blowout* was a traveling "art mobile" stuffed full of artworks from Houston artists.

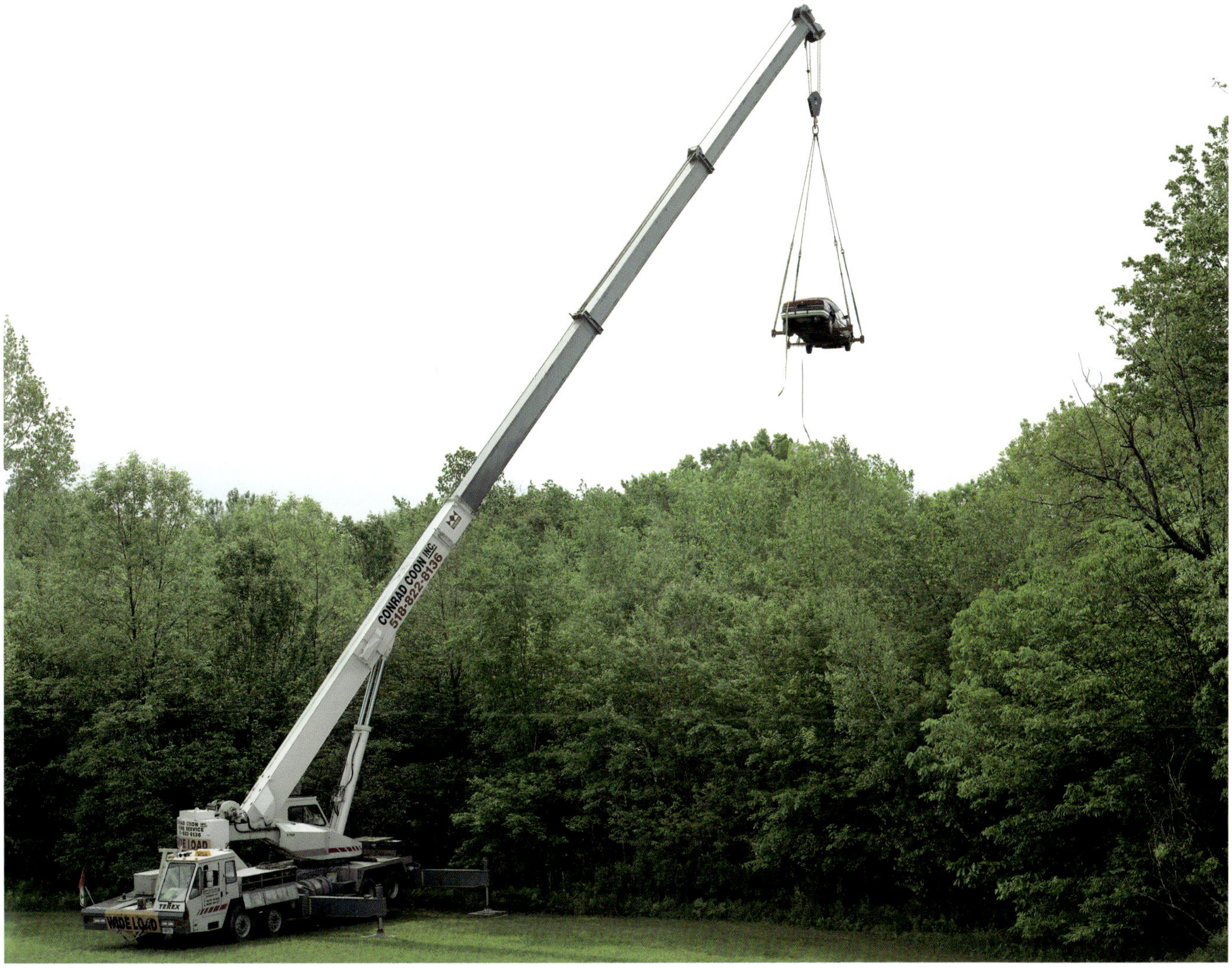

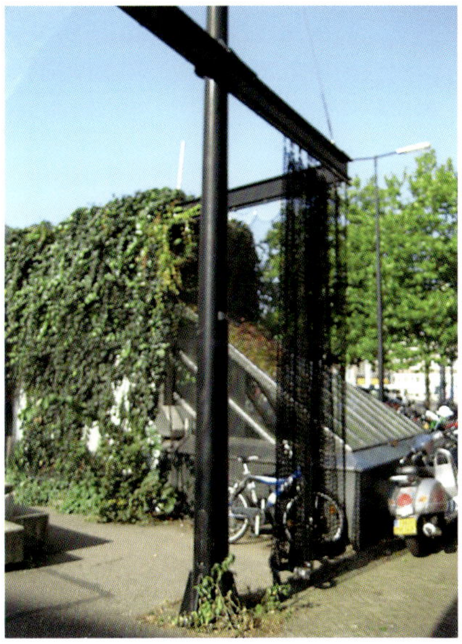

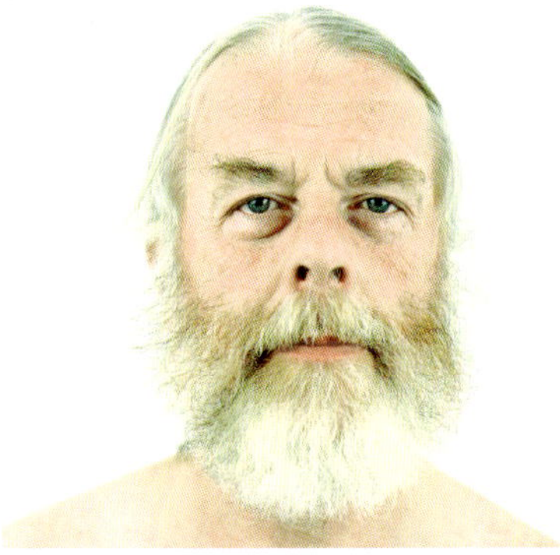

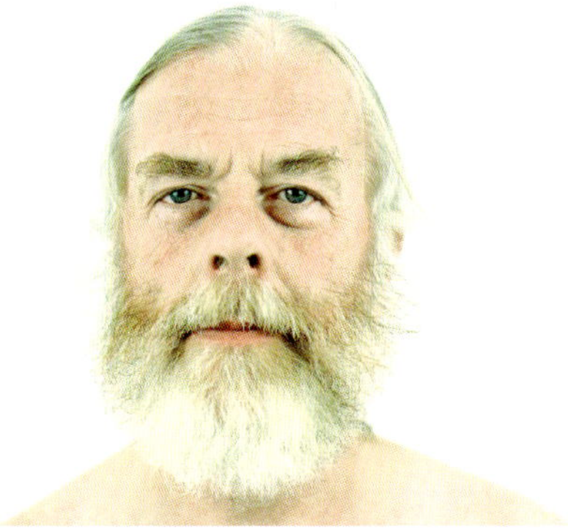

Mary Ellen Carroll
bottom left:
Study for hydroponic curtain wall (a plant-friendly playing field barrier), 2008
C-print
8 x 10 inches

bottom center and right:
You and We (Fred Sandback), 1999
Two C-prints (diptych)
27 x 27 inches each
All courtesy the artist and Galerie Hubert Winter, Vienna

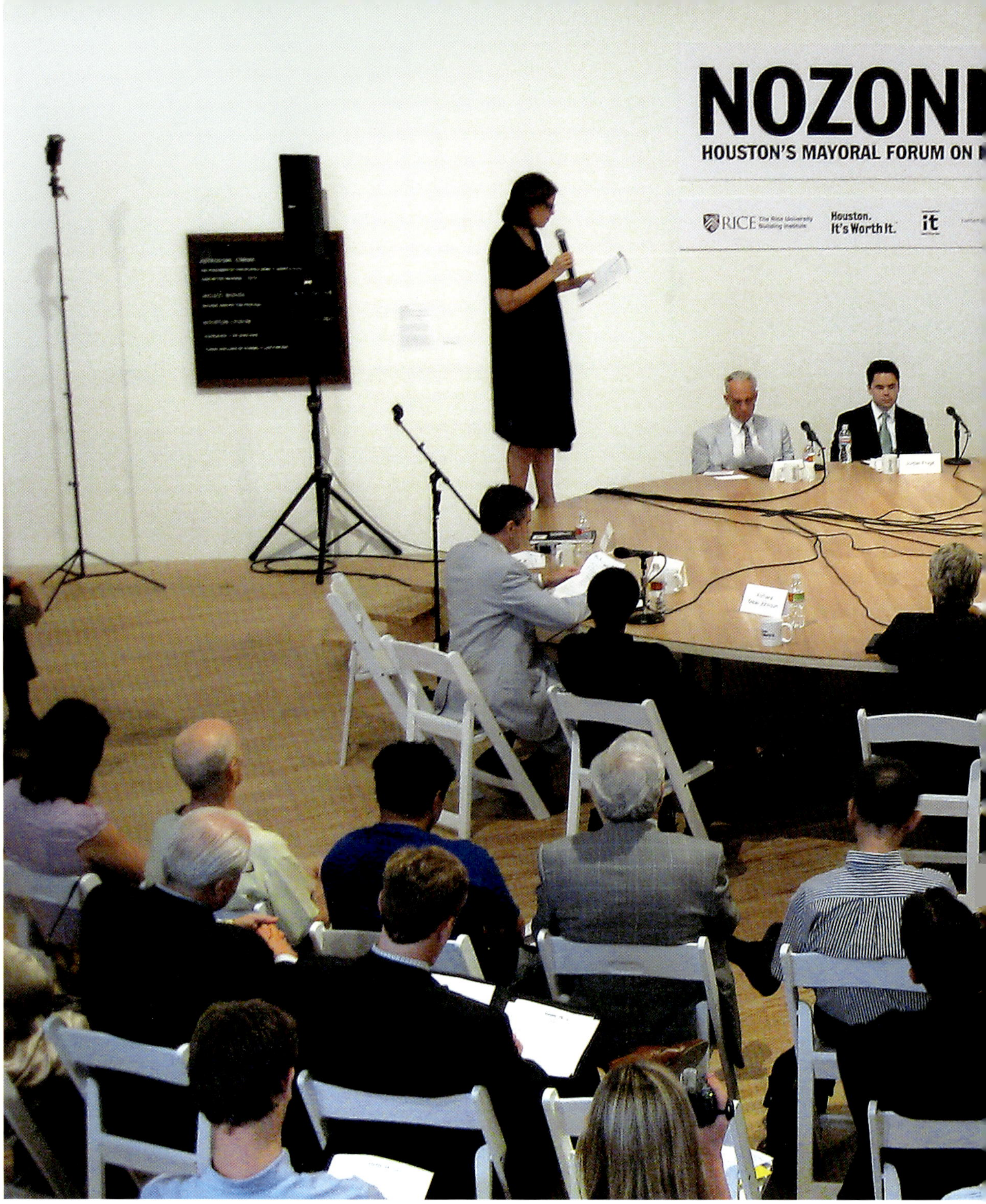

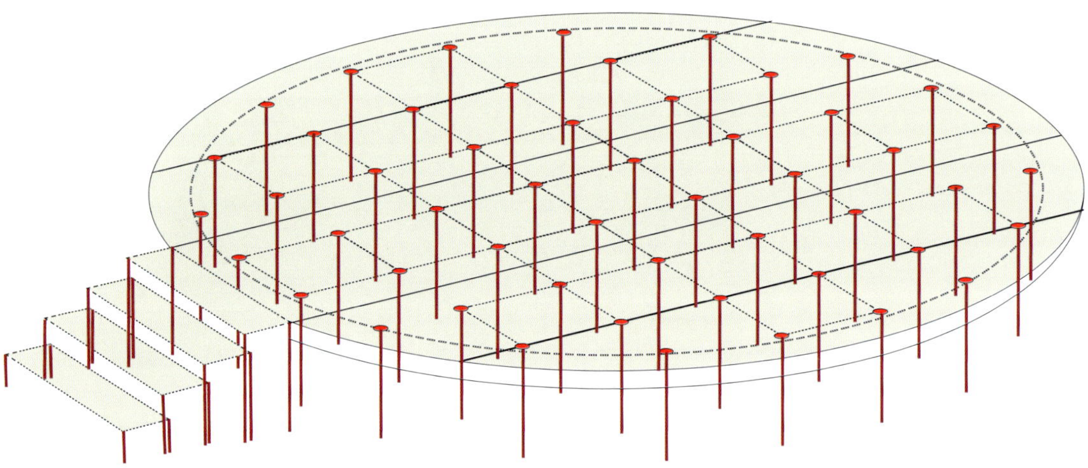

Mary Ellen Carroll
prototype 180: table, 2009
Digital rendering
Courtesy the artist and Galerie Hubert Winter, Vienna

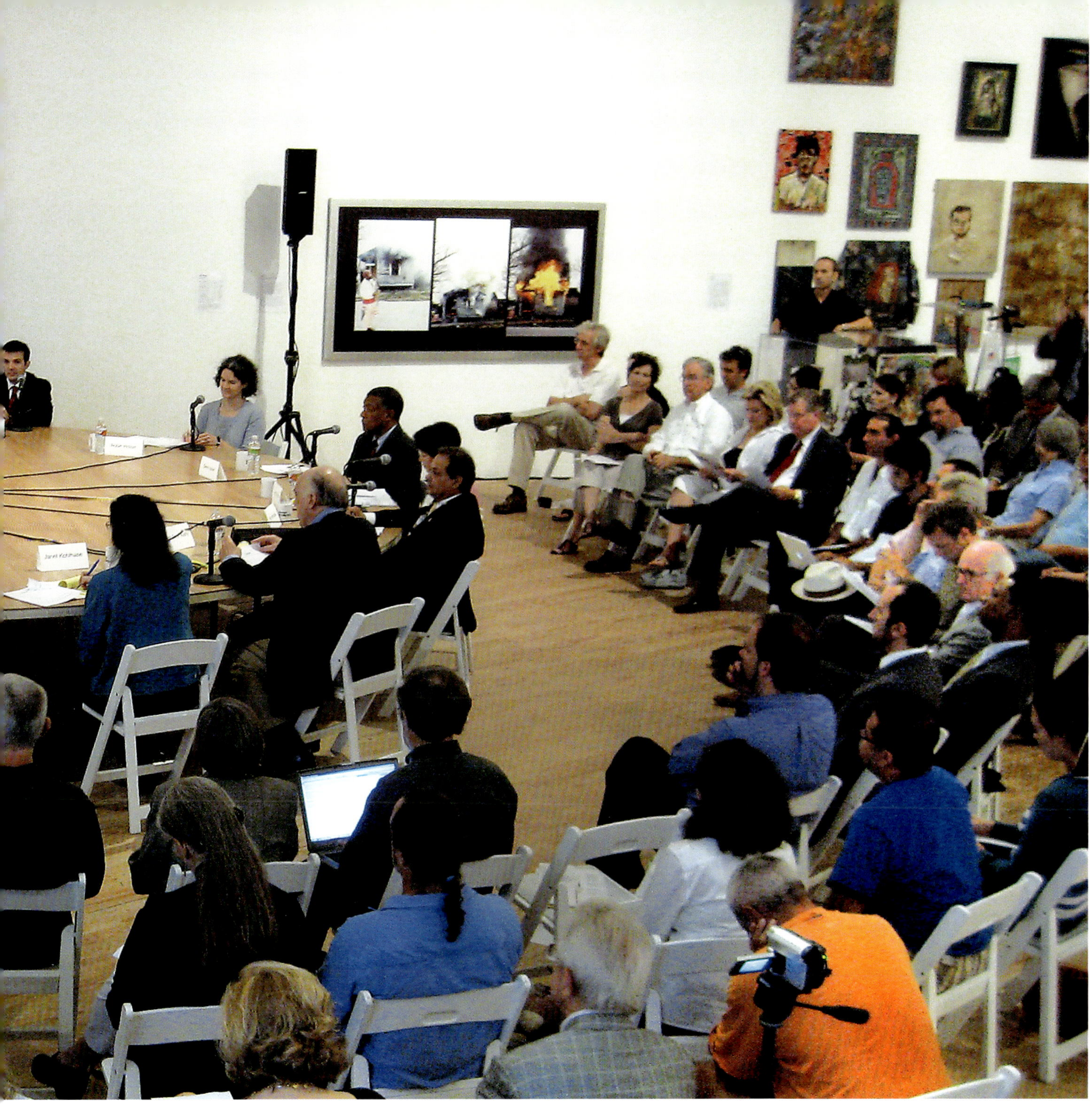

Mary Ellen Carroll
prototype 180: table, 2009
Wood, laminate flooring, pipe, stools
32 5/8 inches, height x 192 inches, diameter
Installation view during candidate debate "NOZONE: Houston's Mayoral Forum on Land Use," Contemporary Arts Museum Houston, July 9, 2009
Courtesy the artist and Galerie Hubert Winter, Vienna

Bill Davenport

Bill Davenport arrived in Houston in 1990 as a Core Fellow artist-in-residence at the Museum of Fine Arts, Houston. He is known for making sculptures from banal and low-tech materials that often fool the eye and challenge notions of value and authenticity. These include a giant wagon wheel fabricated from Styrofoam and painted to look like wood, multicolored yarn balls of various diameters, and logs hewn and painted in a sloppy Pop Art style to imitate canned foods. In addition, Davenport has produced and staged a number of public events in Houston. In 1993 he painted chunks of concrete, dubbed *Dubuffet Rocks,* and scattered them across the Art League of Houston's sculpture court; in 2004 he presented *Honest Abe's Art Corral*, an outdoor exhibition of thrift-store paintings, at the annual Houston Heights Festival; and in 2006, at the Westheimer Street Festival, he fenced off part of a public parking lot for *Timberland Art Corral*, an outdoor sculpture display featuring pineapple tops and other detritus salvaged from a nearby dumpster.

His latest endeavor, *Bill's Junk*, which opened in November 2008, is a storefront at 1125 East 11th Street in Houston's Heights neighborhood. Brimming with household objects, natural curiosities, and handmade knickknacks, his junk store is an extension of the tongue-in-cheek and trickster aspects of his work. It specializes in amateur paintings, ceramics, and woodworking projects—what Davenport calls "stuff people made then didn't want anymore"[1]—that he has collected over years of haunting garage sales and other thrift stores. Almost better than the items themselves are their price tags, attached with string and containing deadpan descriptions and prices that Davenport makes up: "Burst heater hose, Toyota Celica, $18," "Cumberlandite: the magnetic mineral of Rhode Island, $13," or "Dead Bee, $.35." By tagging these objects with his own descriptions and prices, Davenport gives them a new context and throws into question the conventions of value in the art market. The fact that he displays his own sculptures for sale alongside these objects also begs the question: Is *Bill's Junk* a curio shop or an art installation? The store's playful premise and accessible prices can transform initially detached observers into amused and engaged shoppers.

For *No Zoning*, Davenport has installed a fully functional satellite of *Bill's Junk* in the CAMH. Houston has hundreds of junk shops and thrift stores, but Davenport's is the only one that features so prominently the wide-ranging art of anonymous individuals. His assignment of prices to these works of art according to their curiosity and eccentricity rather than virtuosity or name recognition is a lighthearted reminder of the highly subjective economic forces influencing the lives and livelihoods of artists.

1. Artist's unpublished curriculum vitae, March 2009.

Bill Davenport
Bill's Junk (interior and exterior), 2008–ongoing
1125 E. 11th Street, Houston
Store selling handmade furniture, pottery, art, gifts, curios
All courtesy the artist

1994

Museum of the Weird
Dolan Smith founded the Museum of the Weird in his two-bedroom house in Houston's Heights. Attending by appointment, visitors could view a pet columbarium where Smith entombed the ashes of people's pets, a homemade "Bed of Nails," twelve-foot long tusks, a giant model of a heart, an oversized papier-mâché wasps' nest, and the "Dome of Silence," as well as Smith's paintings. The Museum of the Weird also included the "Scar Room," where Smith documented every scar on his own body and urged visitors to add scar stories of their own.

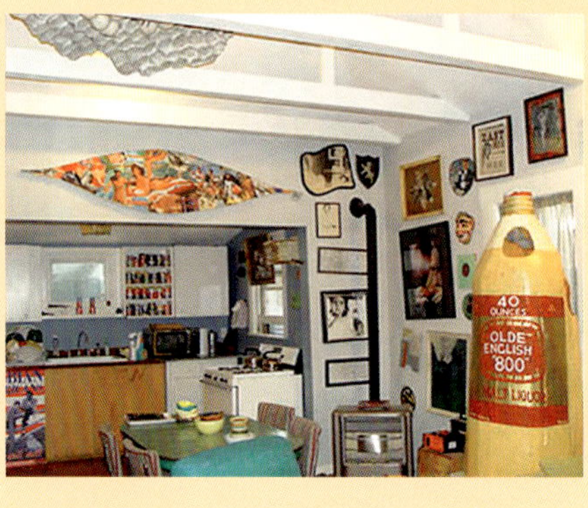

Interior displays at the Museum of the Weird, 2008

El Palomar Restaurant
Artists Lucas Johnson, Dick Wray, and Lynne Foster began programming exhibitions in El Palomar Restaurant, a modest Mexican café on White Oak Drive in Houston's Heights. For every exhibition, Foster produced a catalogue comprising photocopies of photographs taken at the exhibition opening.

Gallery One Three Seven
Sharon Engelstein opened Houston's smallest gallery, a 1.37-square-foot space modeled after the main space at the Texas Gallery. This portable space, whose floors were made of coffee stir sticks to simulate hardwood, hosted exhibitions of miniature work by a number of other artists.

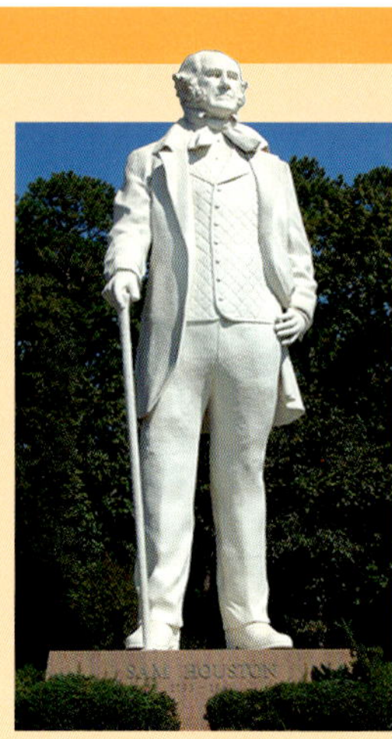

David Adickes' *A Tribute to Courage*, 1994

Sam Houston by David Adickes
A Tribute to Courage, a sixty-seven-foot tall statue of Sam Houston on a ten-foot granite base, created by David Addickes, was erected on Interstate 45 in Huntsville, Texas, Sam Houston's home.

Pigdom
Victoria Herberta moved to Houston and began to create a "Shrine to Swine" at her Crawford Street home. (*see photo p. 39*)

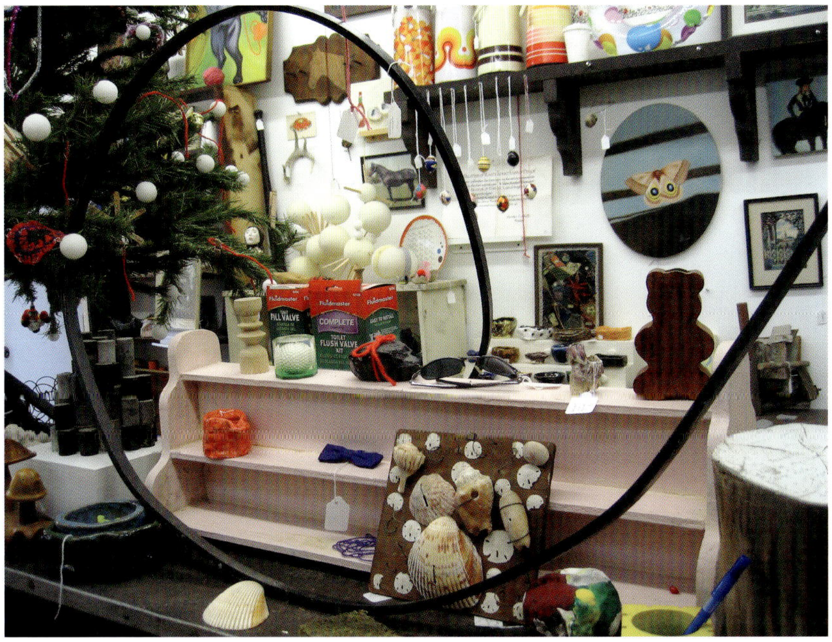

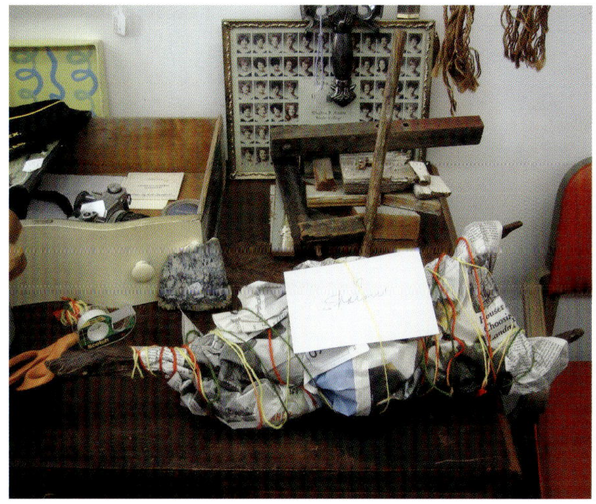

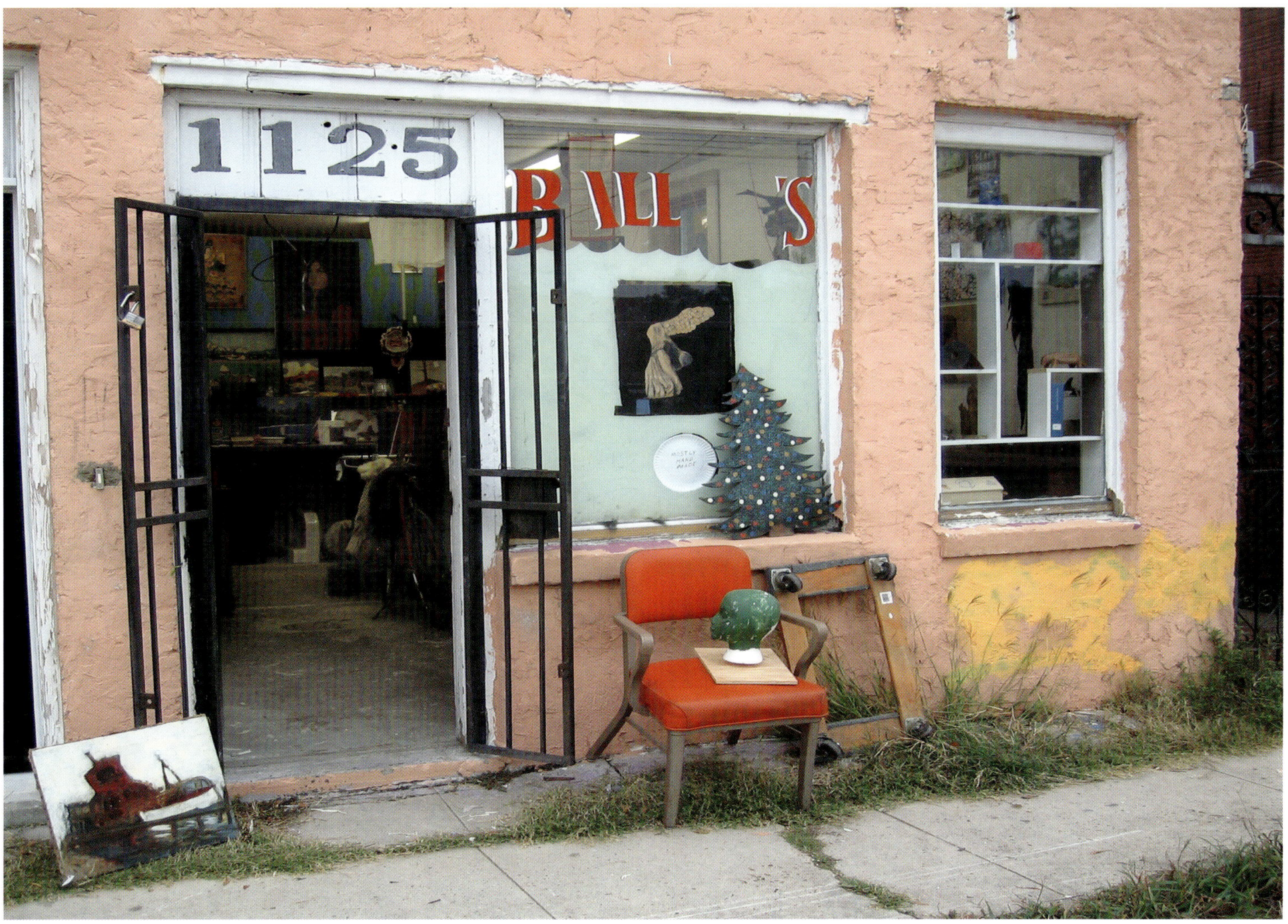
1125

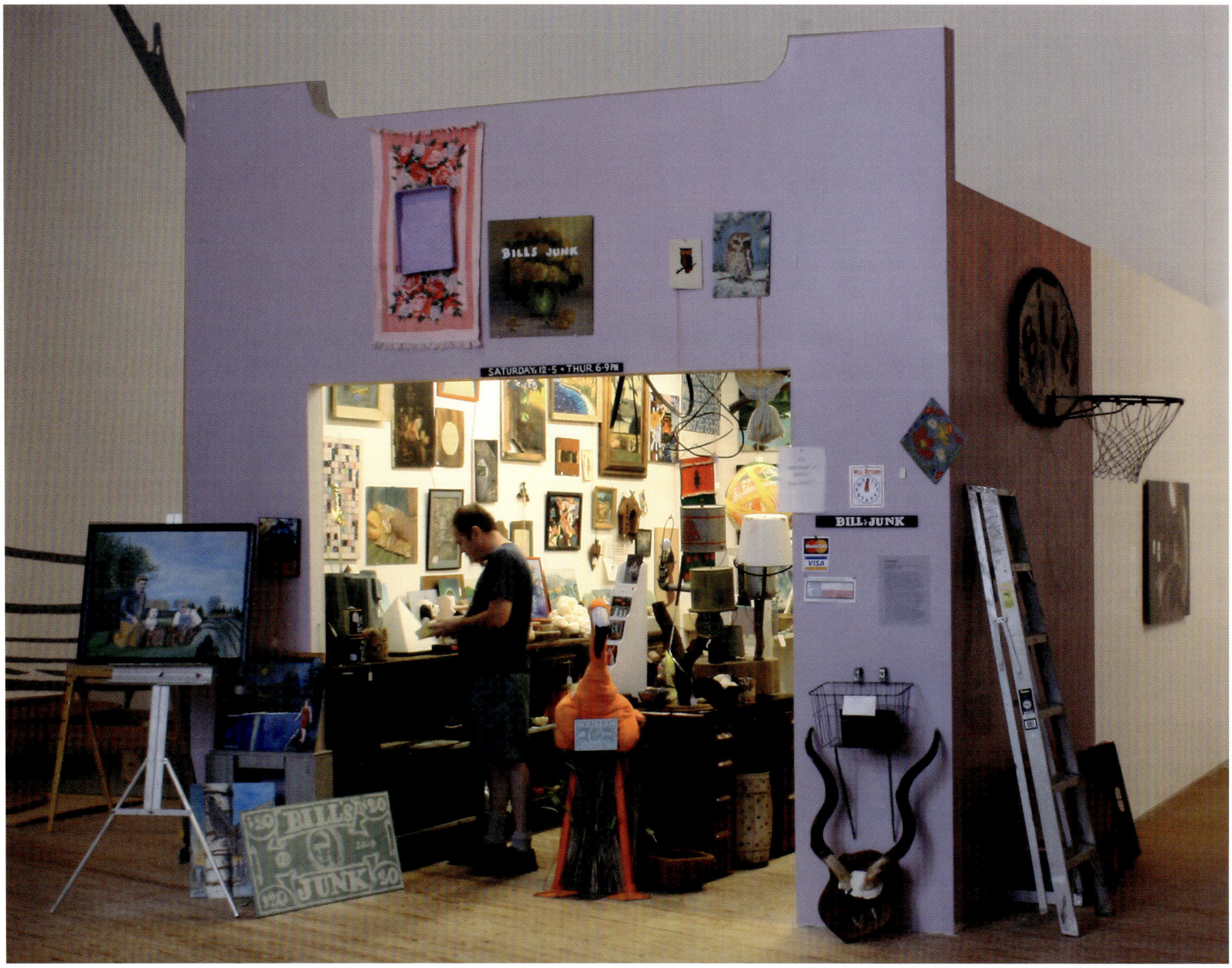

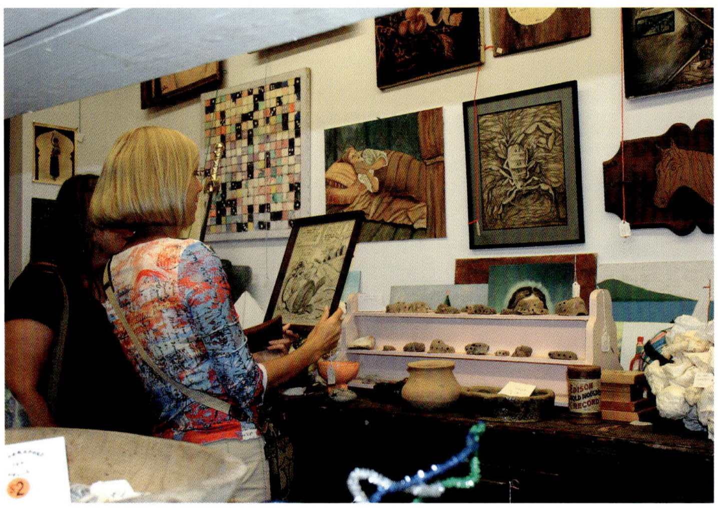

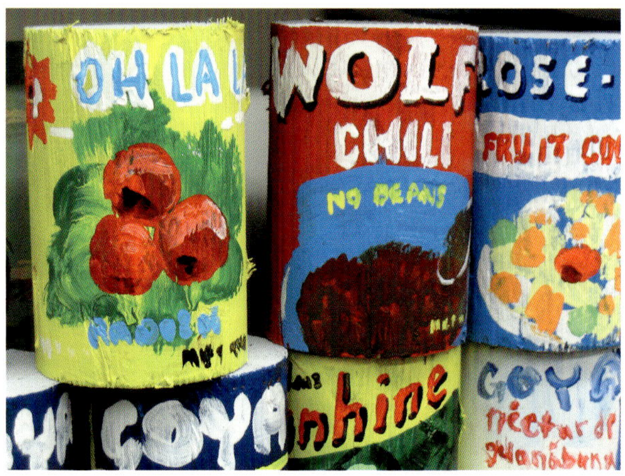

Bill Davenport
Bill's Junk, 2009
Wood, drywall, paint, fluorescent lights, electric fixtures, computer, handmade furniture, pottery, art, gifts, curios
12 x 12 x 20 feet
Installation view, Contemporary Arts Museum Houston
Interior details with the artist (*top*) and shoppers (*bottom left*)

Pop Art Cans, 2009
Wood, acrylic paint
Dimensions variable
All courtesy the artist and Inman Gallery, Houston

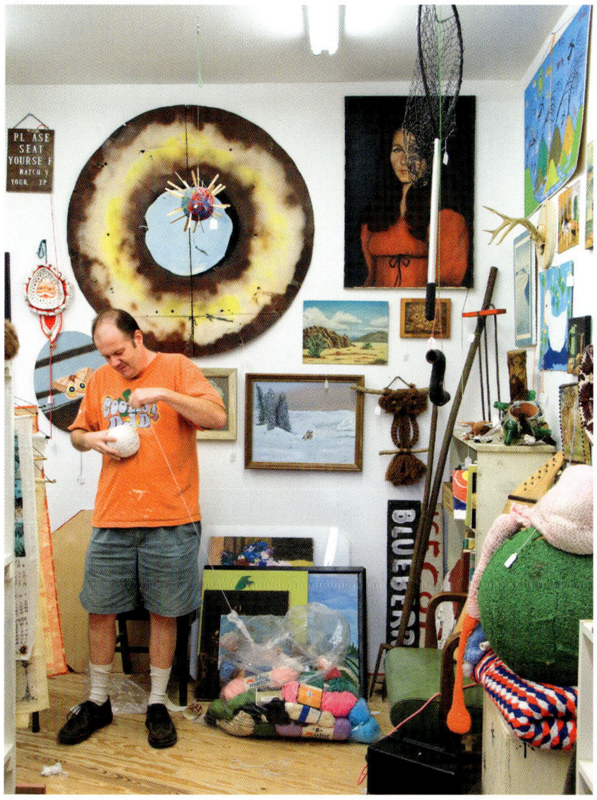

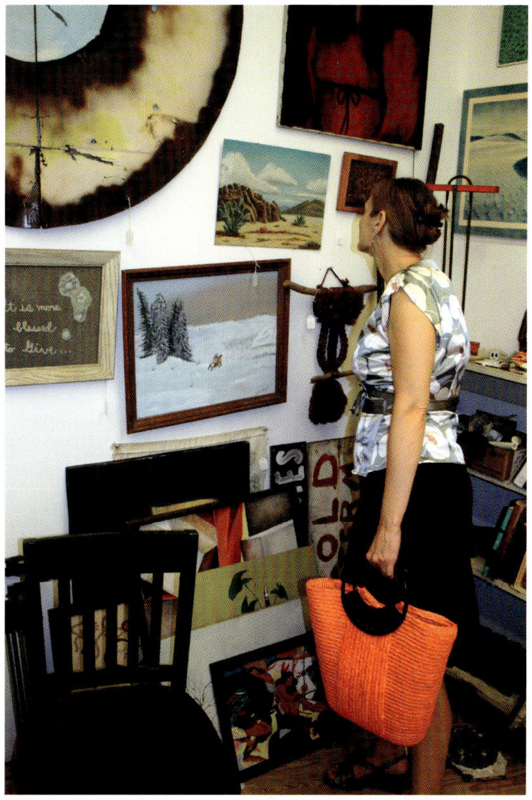

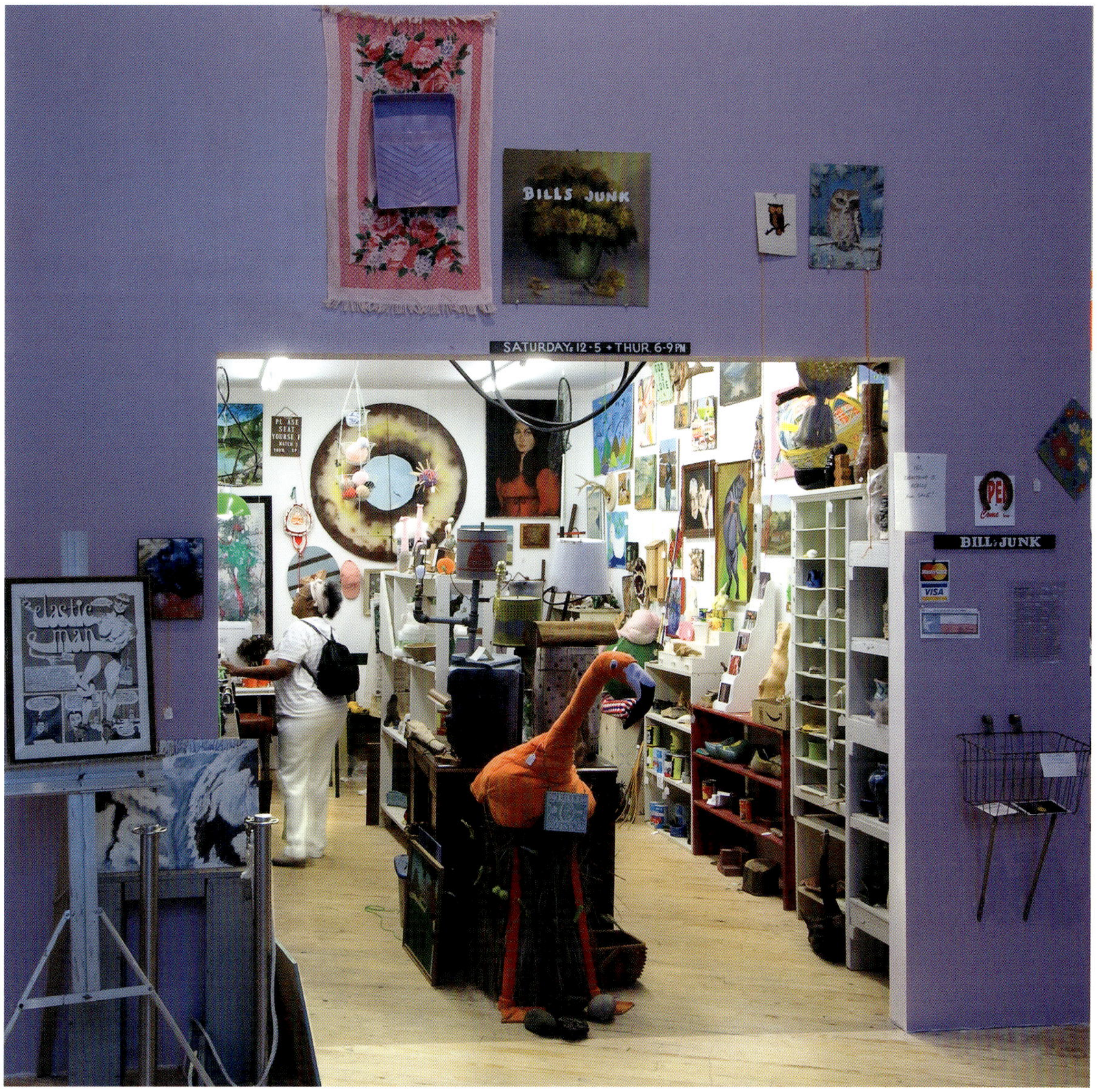

Bill's Junk, 2009
Three interior details with artist (*top left*) and shoppers (*top right, bottom*)
All courtesy the artist and Inman Gallery, Houston

Ben Tecumseh DeSoto

As a photojournalist for the *Houston Chronicle* from 1981 to 2006, Ben Tecumseh DeSoto documented almost every facet of the city, from Astros baseball games to public protests. When not on assignment, he captured life and events in the more offbeat margins of Houston, developing a large personal body of work that he terms "environmental portraits." In 2008 he presented *Understanding Poverty*, an exhibition of photographs documenting Houston's urban poor, at DiverseWorks. DeSoto's other portrait subjects, which include the homeless, children, and many of Houston's visual artists, are often pictured in the places where they live or work, revealing both the aesthetics of these individuals and the spaces they fashion for themselves.

Over the past twenty-five years, DeSoto has made almost two hundred photographs depicting artists in their studios, building one of the most in-depth archives of Houston's creative community. His images are portraits of Houston's most accomplished artists and a visual history of the myriad personalities shaping the city's artistic landscape. Among DeSoto's subjects are Dr. John Biggers, legendary Texas Southern University professor, painting in his studio; installation artist Toby Topek seated before an array of books and drawings; and James Bettison, smiling while at work on the floor among his colorful paintings. Other images document a life drawing class at The Artery, an exhibition and performance venue founded by Mark Larsen; sculptors Paul Kittelson, Jim Love, and Jesse Lott at work; and artist and home-studio space visionary Nestor Topchy, first in 1986 in a hammock in his Commerce Street Artists' Warehouse studio, cradling one of his early sphere sculptures, and then, twenty-three years later, holding one of his tempera and gold-leaf icon portraits of local artists in the domed annex he built in his backyard to house them.

Drawing from this archive for a project made especially for *No Zoning*, DeSoto presents thirty-two of these artist portraits, as well as photographs of such local folk-art landmarks as The Orange Show, the Beer Can House, and the Flower Man's house. Through this project, titled *The Significance of Making Art,* DeSoto seeks to understand what drives his fellow Houstonians to create and the ways they make places in which to do so.

Ben Tecumseh DeSoto
Bert Long, 1986
James Surls, Splendora, Texas, 1986
Color photographs
11 x 14 inches each
Courtesy the artist

1994

Rolywholyover–A Circus for Museum by John Cage
The exhibition *Rolywholyover–A Circus for Museum by John Cage,* presented by the Menil Collection, included the rotating display of objects from all the museums in Houston (including the National Museum of Funeral History, among others) and a multidisciplinary, multi-organizational series of events staged throughout the city by local artists and organizations.

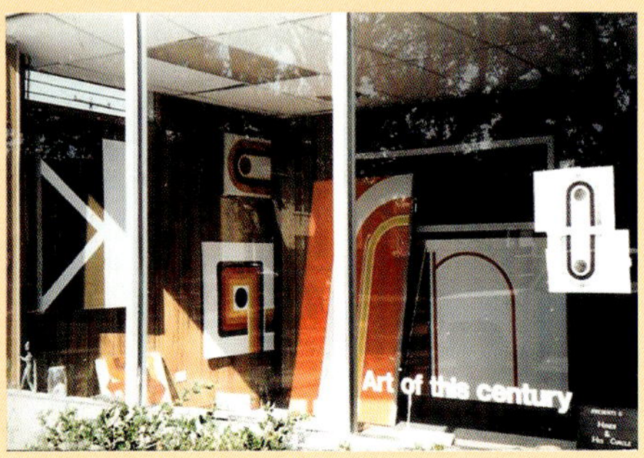

Tragic Fading Super-Graphic: Hines and His Circle exhibition installation view, Art of this century gallery, 1996

1995

Art of this century
Jeff Elrod and Mark Flood opened a gallery in Elrod's storefront studio on West Gray Street and named it Art of this century (after Peggy Guggenheim's 1940s New York gallery). It mounted four shows, but the space was not open to the public: Elrod explained, "I like having a gallery, but I hate having to be here to let people come in. Now they can just look in the window." Each show was accompanied by a handmade catalogue with an essay, and boasted lively openings attended by artists and art world insiders. The inaugural exhibition, *Objects Beside the Economy*, was curated by Robert Montgomery.

Bobbindoctrin Puppet Theatre
Founded by Joel Orr, this puppet theatre presented experimental adult puppet performances with low admission prices, giving actors, directors, playwrights, musicians, sculptors, dancers, and engineers a singular outlet for their creativity. Bobbindoctrin has since performed original work hundreds of times in both traditional and nontraditional places.

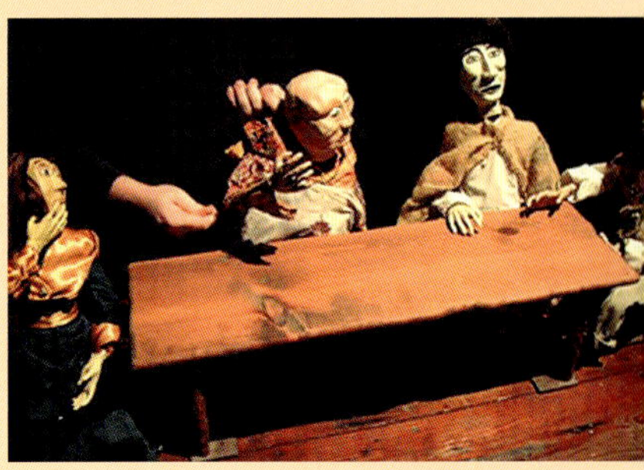

Bobbindoctrin Puppet Theatre's *Ivan the Fool*, 1999

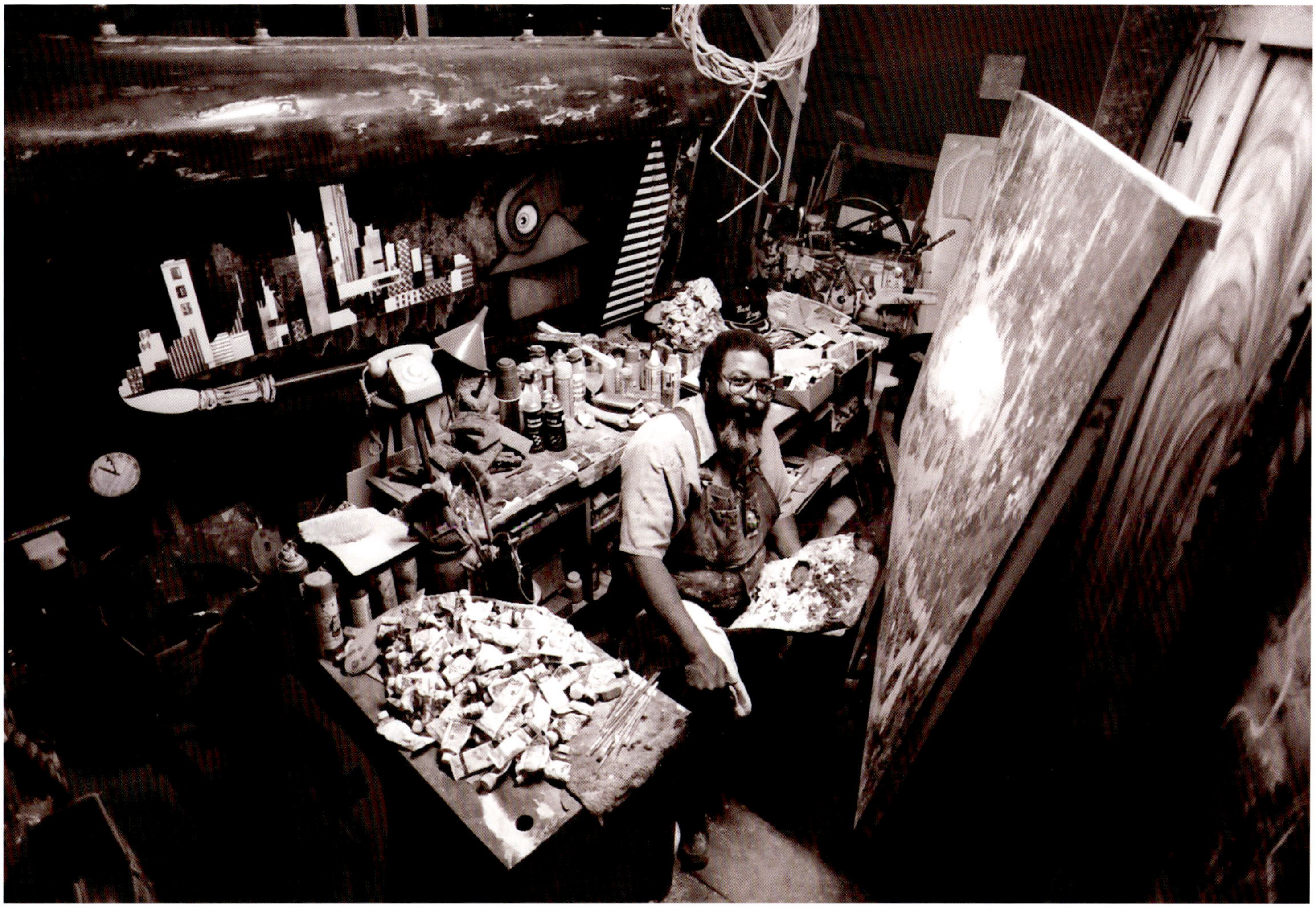

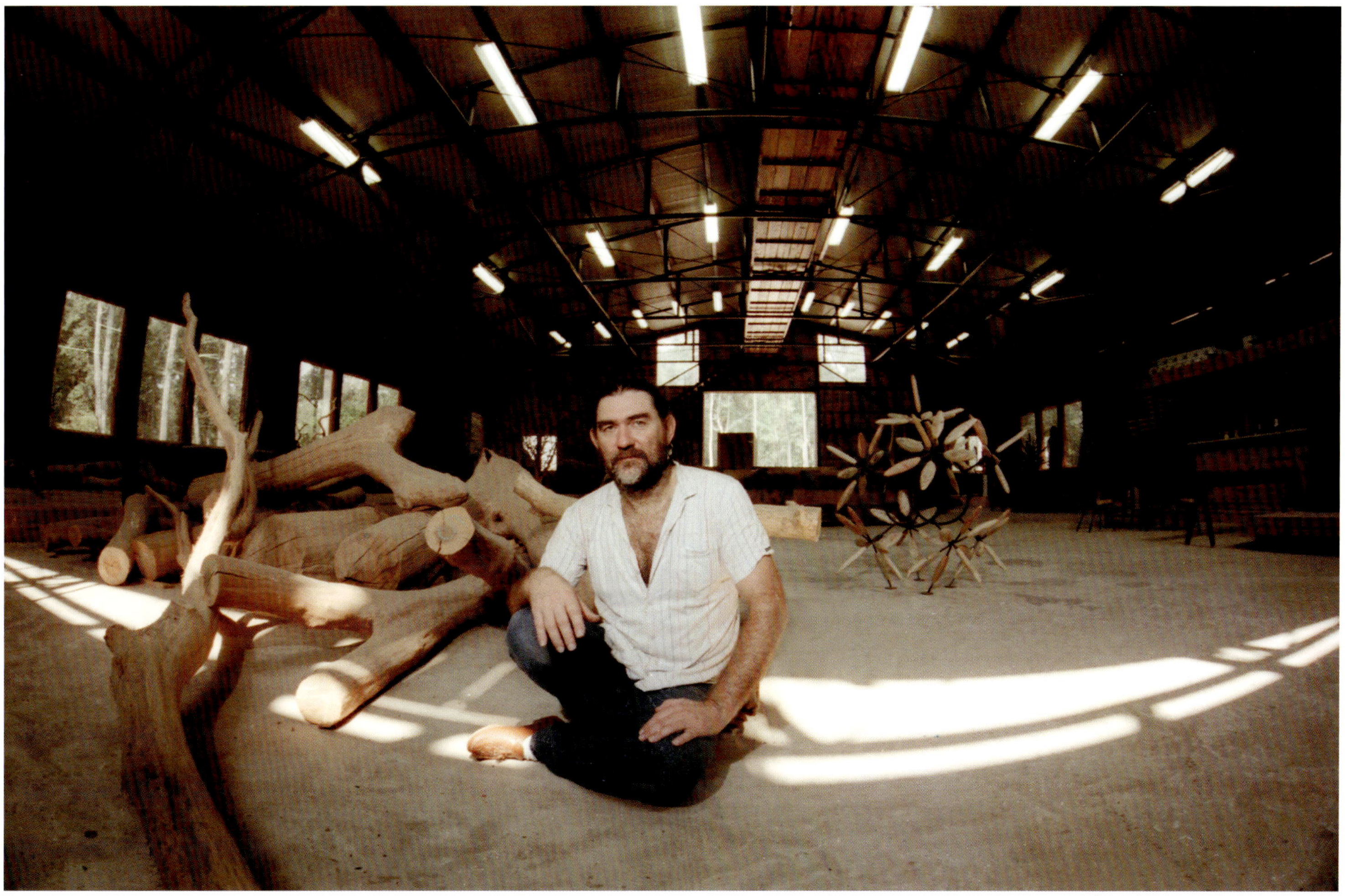

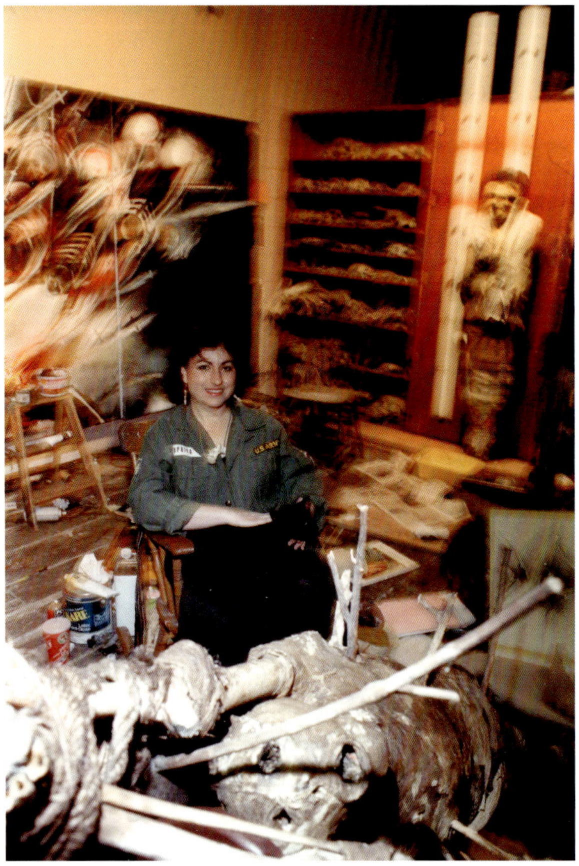

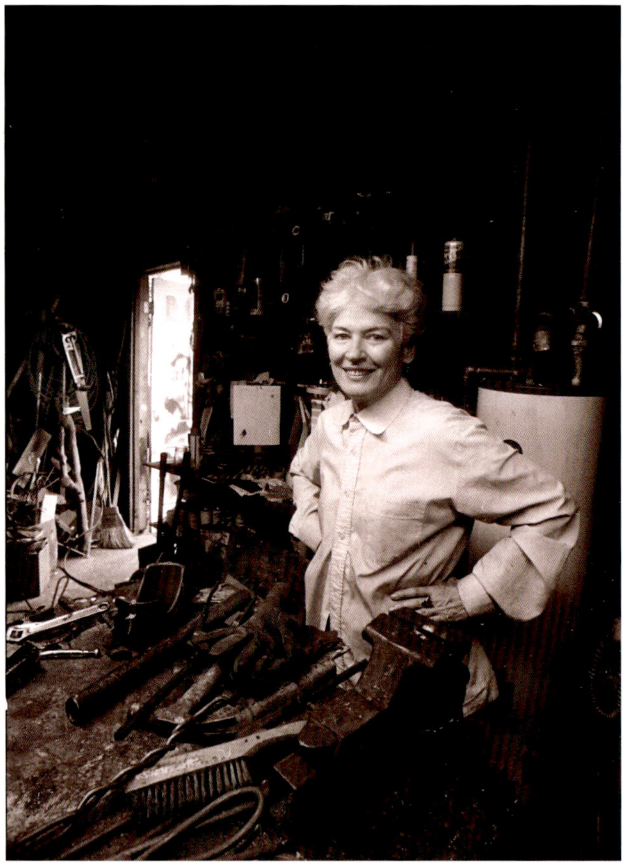

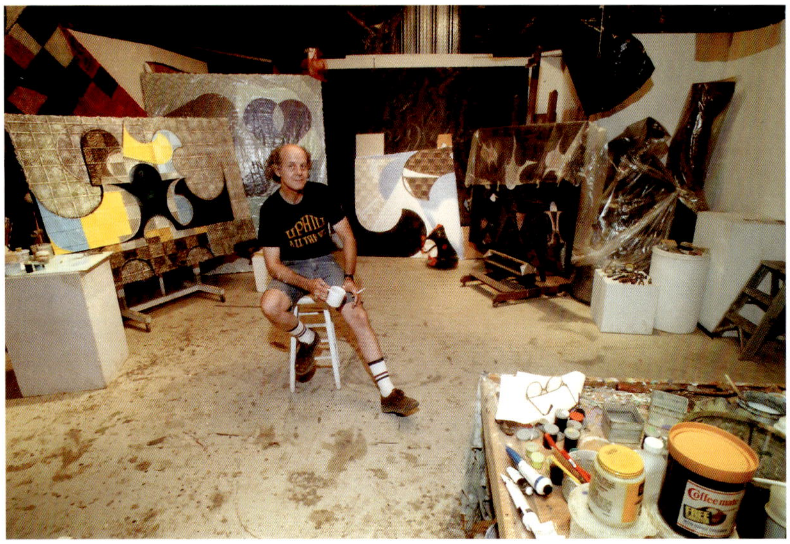

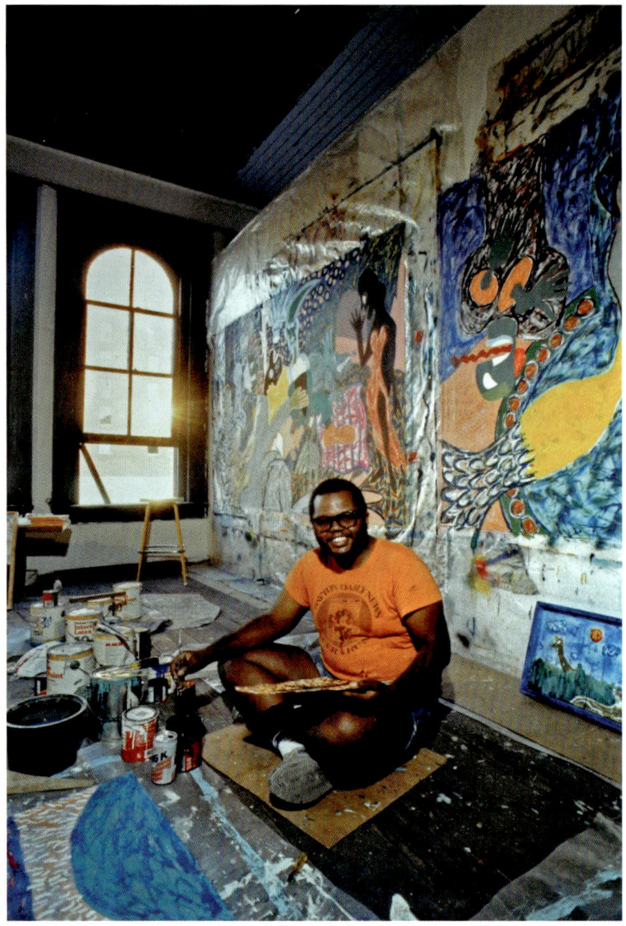

Ben Tecumseh DeSoto
clockwise from top left:
Sharon Kopriva, 1985
Gertrude Barnstone, 1986
James Bettison, DiverseWorks Artist Studio, 1986
Color photographs
14 x 11 inches, each

bottom left:
Harvey Bott, 1986
Color photograph
11 x 14 inches

opposite:
Paul Kittelson (with his *Stegosaurus*, under Highway 59 at Montrose Blvd.), 1987
Beth Secor, DiverseWorks Artist Studio, 1986
Color photographs
11 x 14 inches each
All courtesy the artist

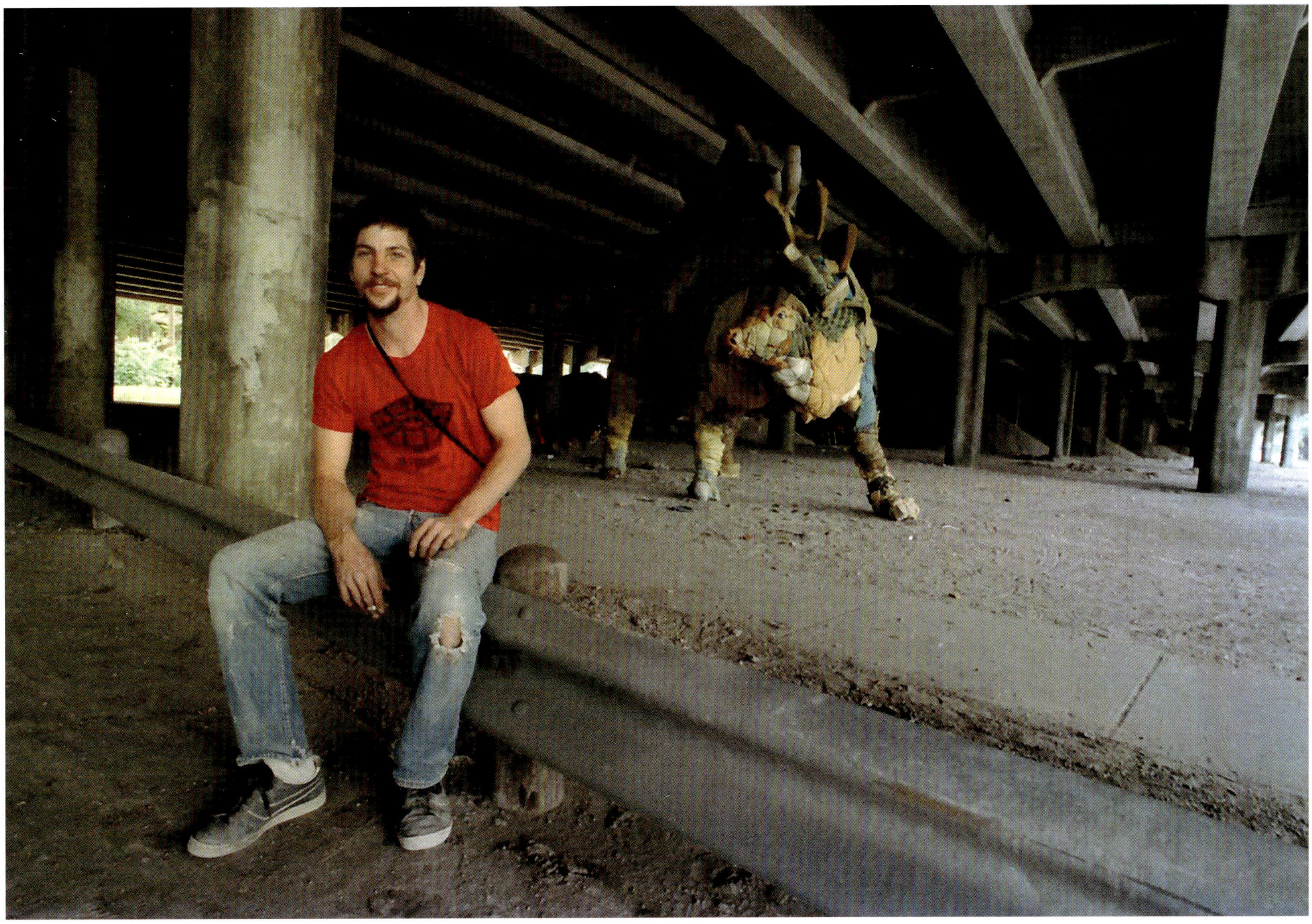

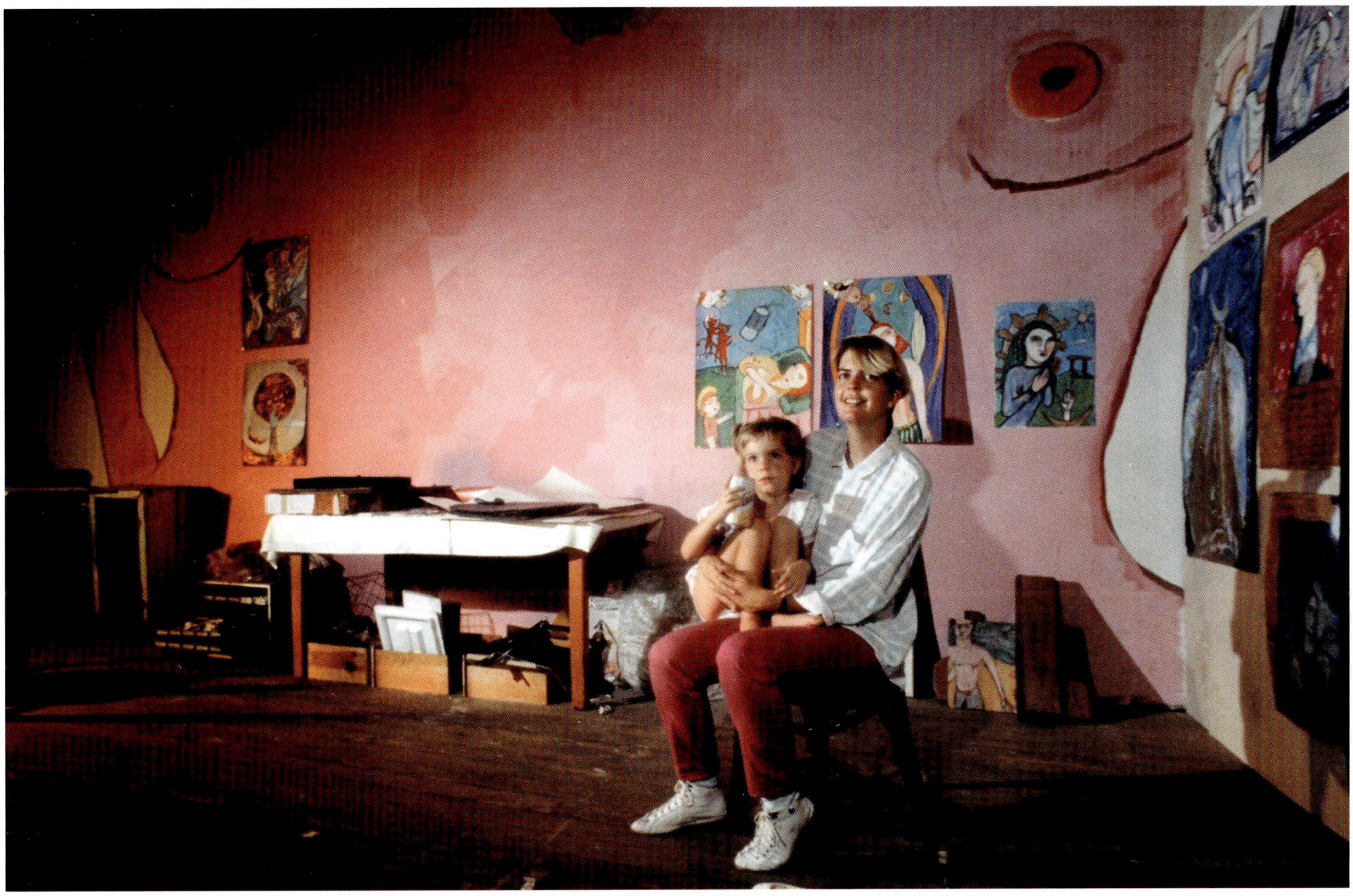

Sharon Engelstein

Sharon Engelstein, who came to Houston in 1990 as a Core Fellow in the artist-in-residence program at the Museum of Fine Arts, Houston, is known primarily for her ceramic sculptures—biomorphic abstractions that are mysterious, sensual, and playful—that she decorates with splatters and drips of acrylic paint, covers in sequins, or dresses in ready-made accessories. She also has worked with 3-D modeling software to turn her bulbous, alien shapes into larger installations made of colorful inflated nylon.

In 1994, however, Engelstein also became known as the proprietor of the smallest gallery in Houston, *Gallery One Three Seven*, named for its diminutive size—a mere 1.37 square feet. She originally built the structure as a mockup of Houston's Texas Gallery to help her plan an installation in that space. The tiny gallery has two white-painted walls, both 7½ inches high, and a 20¾ x 10¾-inch base made of coffee stir sticks to imitate hardwood flooring. The idea for the project came to Engelstein at one of the regular Friday night "soirees" she and her husband, artist Aaron Parazette, hosted for local artists. She recalls, "It was a down time in the economy, like now, and this was a successful grassroots operation. We were downsizing!"[1] In its inaugural year, *Gallery One Three Seven* hosted the exhibition *Killer Painting* in which Jeff Elrod presented miniature works inspired by the O. J. Simpson saga, including a painting tracing the notorious highway chase and, presented on a small pedestal, a miniscule sculpture based on Simpson's Heisman trophy.

In 1996 Engelstein created a second miniature gallery, this time modeled on one of the exhibition spaces at Project Row Houses, where she had been invited to participate in the *Round Five* exhibition. During its run, her replica shotgun house—a painstakingly detailed model, which came complete with a tiny tin roof and working windows—sat within the original, serving as the venue for a series of small-scale installations by local artists, which she organized as exhibitions within the exhibition.

Engelstein has revived *Gallery One Three Seven* for *No Zoning* and organized a series of seven exhibitions in the tiny space, presenting works by local artists David McGee, Amber Eagle, Jay Giroux, and Victoria Whitaker, as well as Hills Snyder, Alex Kvares, and Andrea Corson. Within the context of an exhibition that examines works of art that were never intended to be shown in a space like the CAMH, Engelstein's micro-gallery undermines the institutional power of the museum by slyly reminding viewers that Houston is a place where artists make things, like gallery shows, happen on their own terms.

1. Sharon Engelstein, conversation with the author, March 2009.

Sharon Engelstein
Gallery One Three Seven, 1994–ongoing
Exhibition of works by Mark Flood, 1994

Gallery One Three Seven, 1994–ongoing
Exhibition of works by Nicola Thompson, 1994

Wood, paint, works of art
7½ x 20¾ x 10¾ inches
All courtesy the artists

1995

O House
Sculptors Dan Havel, Dean Ruck, and Kate Petley collaborated on *O House*, a large-scale installation that transformed a small bungalow slated for demolition in Houston's West End neighborhood into a camera obscura. The work featured an interior circular room, earth floors, and pinhole projections of surrounding trees and the sky. The artists funded the project with proceeds from a tip jar at the front door.

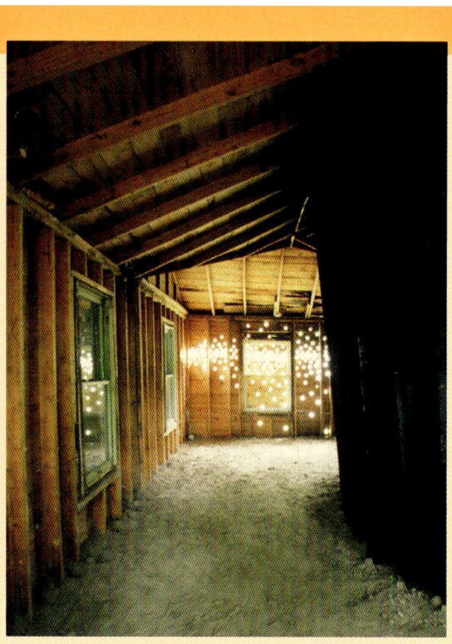

O House, 1995

Jim Pirtle Is Forrest Gump
Artist Jim Pirtle produced a video parody of the famous Hollywood movie by lip-synching the actual appropriated soundtrack with himself in the starring role. Shooting entirely on the grounds of the Zocalo artists' compound, he enlisted many artist friends (Nestor Topchy, Mark Flood, George Hixson, Michael Battey, Giles Lyon, The Art Guys, among others) to play various characters in the movie. The video was later screened at various underground and alternative venues such as Aurora Picture Show and Cue Foundation.

1996

Mural on William Steen's Studio
In association with the community service group Youth Advocates, William Steen made available a 16-foot high wall on the side of his studio building on Harrisburg Boulevard as a site for a constantly changing painting created by a core group of graffiti artists including Daniel Anguilu, Guillermo Morales, Carlos Martinez, Chris Rodriguez, Jason Nava, and Roland Saldana. Though sanctioned, the paintings provoked the Houston Police Department's attention and in July 2000 were overpainted in an anti-graffiti campaign.

ARTPIX
Fredericka Hunter and Ian Glennie formed ARTPIX, an experiment to explore new media and commission young artists to create new work on CD. Ongoing today, it has evolved to include archival projects that bring little-known work forward.

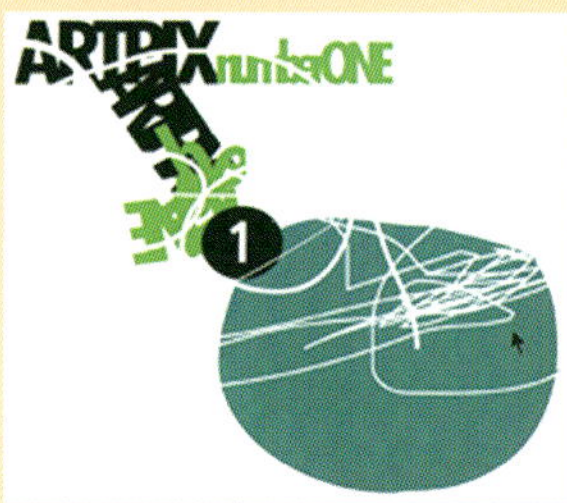

Cover of the first ARTPIX CD, published in 1999

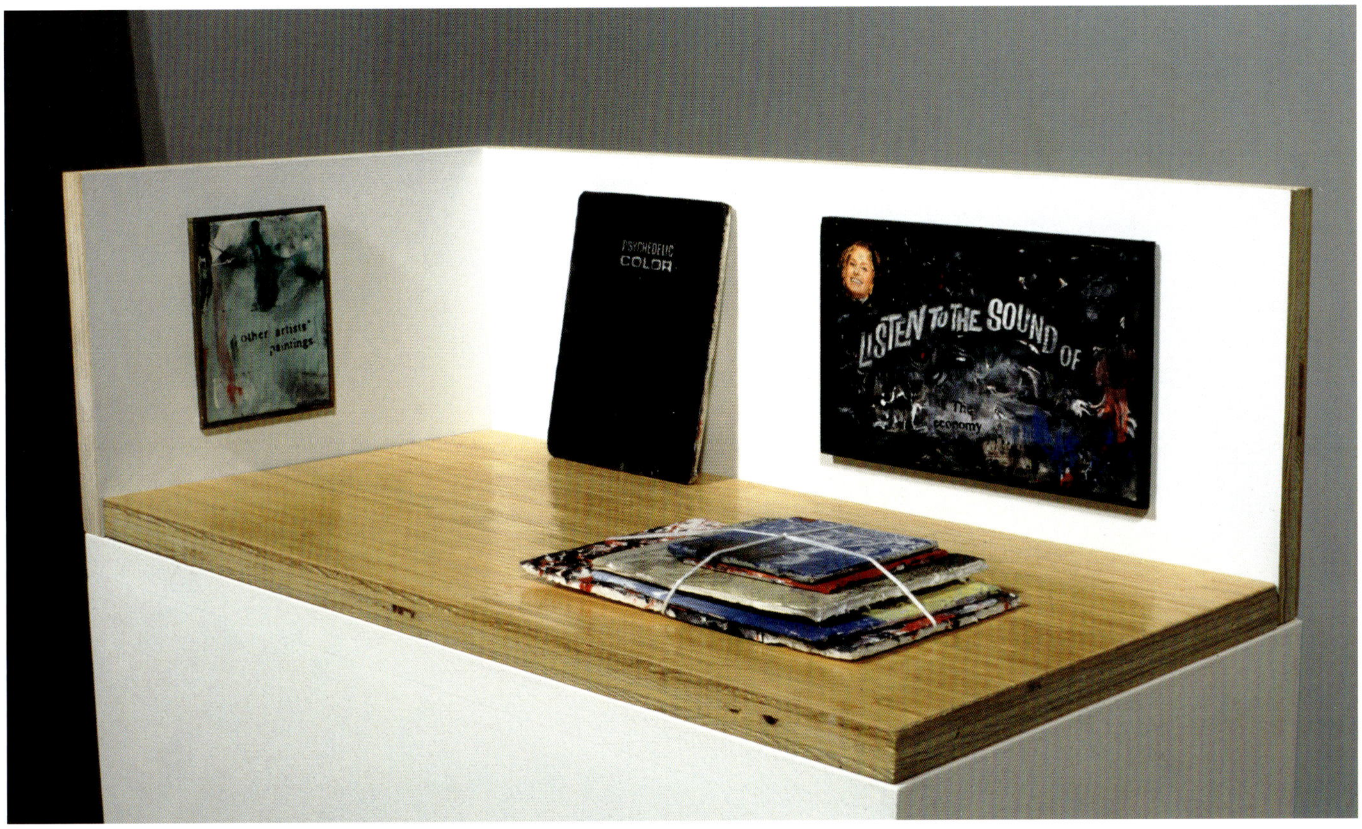
other artists' paintings
PSYCHEDELIC COLOR
LISTEN TO THE SOUND OF
The economy

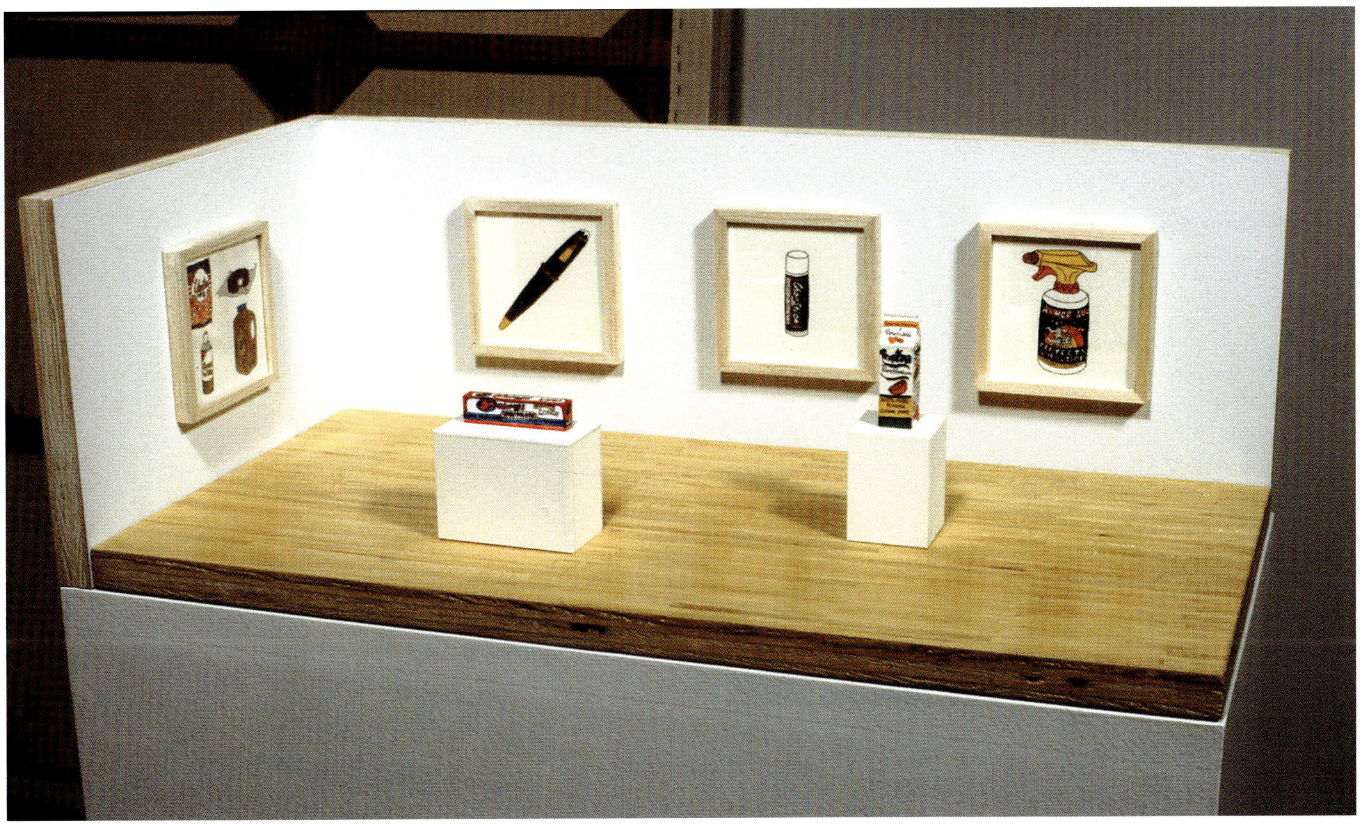

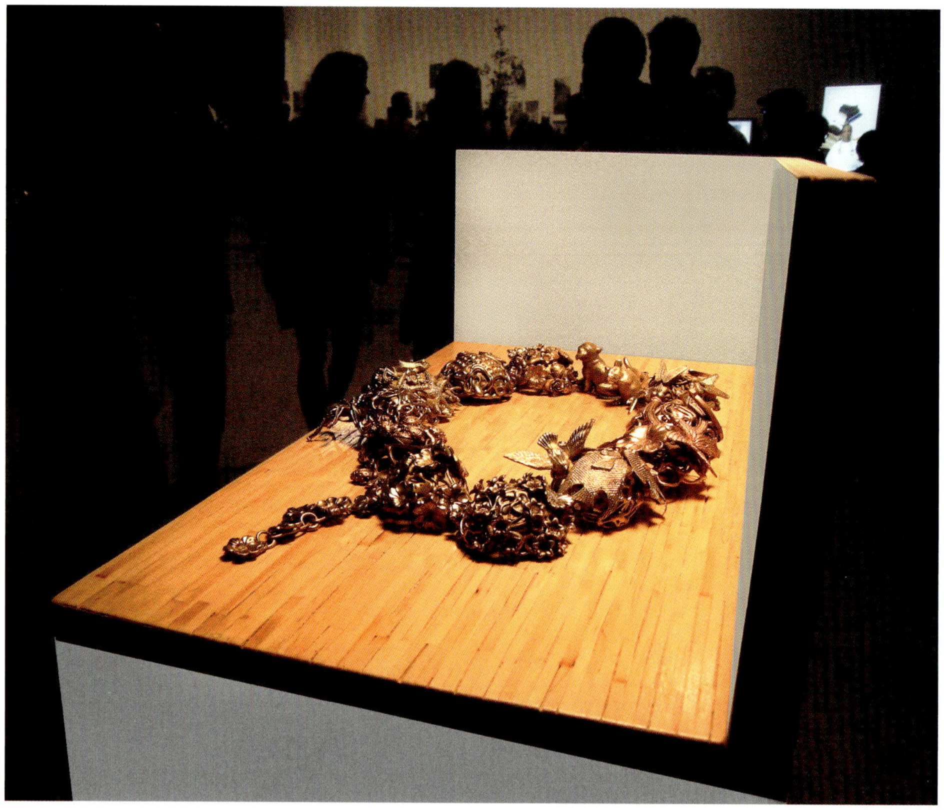

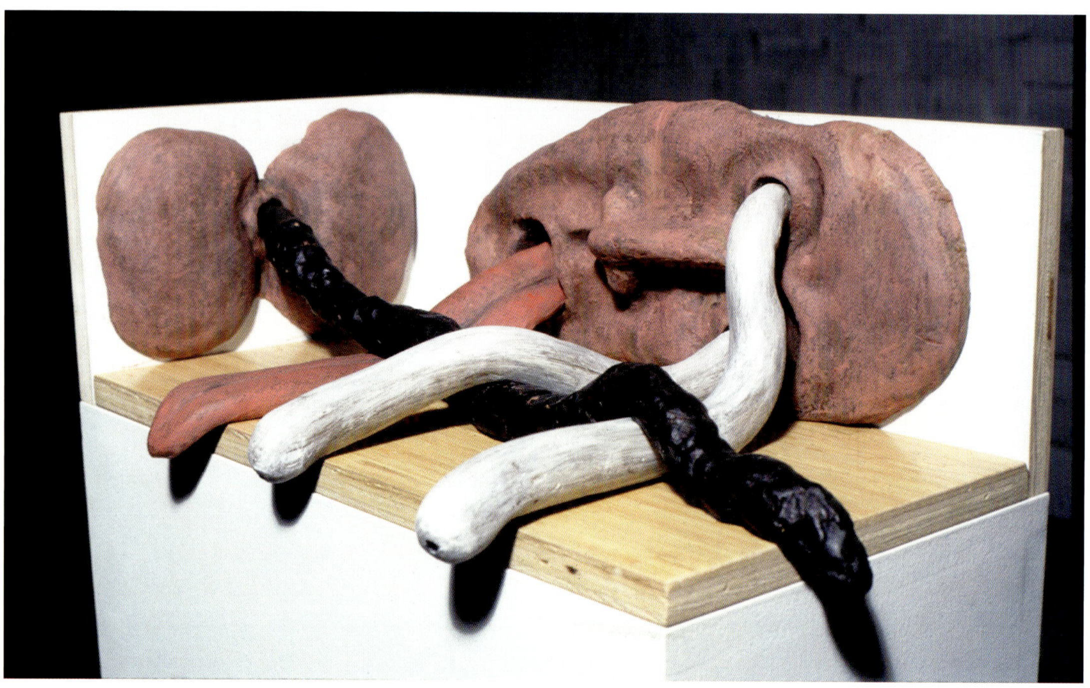

Sharon Engelstein
Gallery One Three Seven, 1994–ongoing
Exhibition of works by Andrea Corson, 2009

Gallery One Three Seven, 1994–ongoing
Exhibition of works by Mark Adams, 1994

Wood, paint, works of art
7½ x 20¾ x 10¾ inches
All courtesy the artists

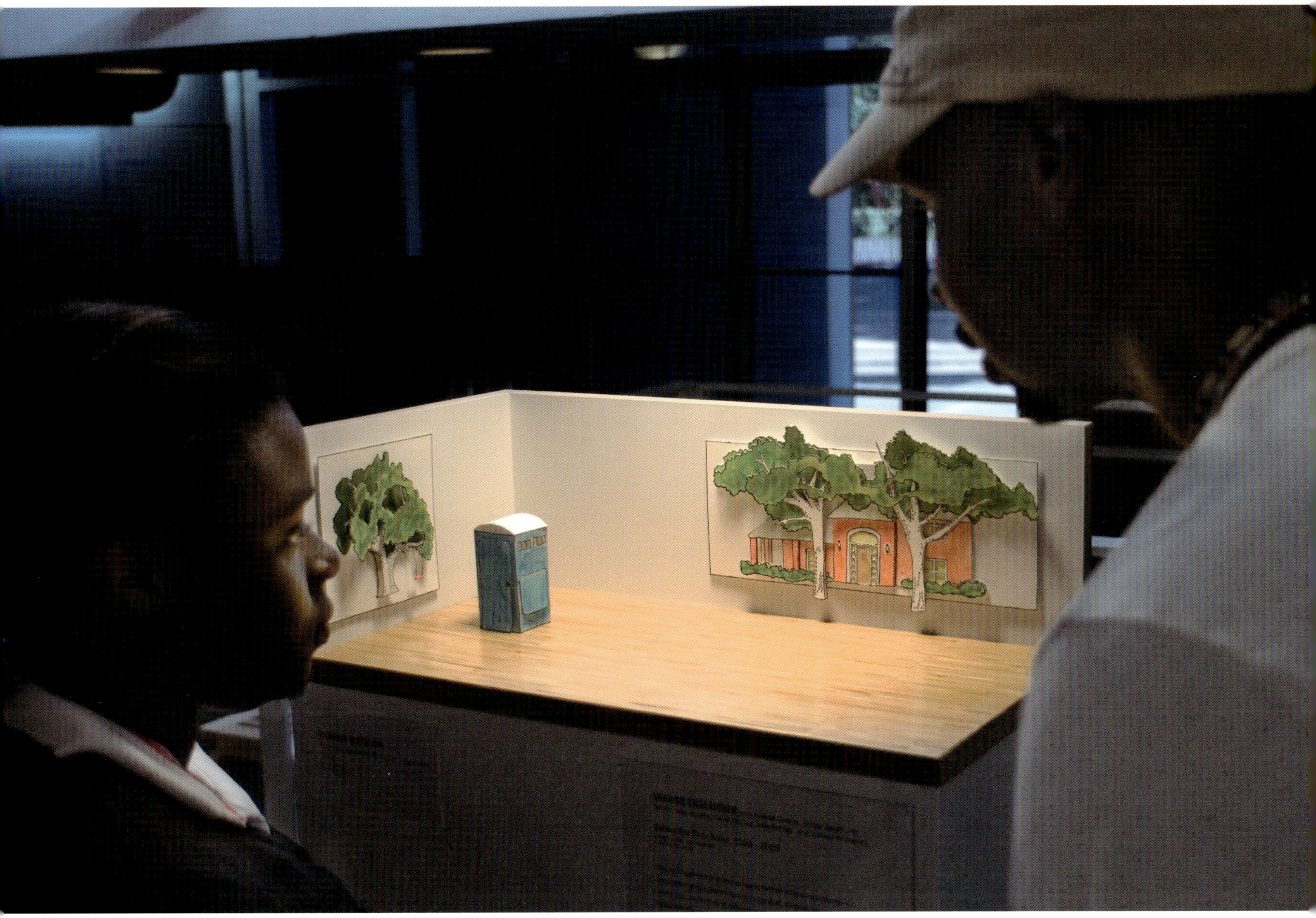

Sharon Engelstein
Gallery One Three Seven, 1994–ongoing
Exhibition of works by Victoria Whitaker, 2009
Wood, paint, works of art
7½ x 20¾ x 10¾ inches
Courtesy the artists

The Flower Man (Cleveland Turner)

Cleveland Turner is a visionary. Known throughout Houston and beyond as a legendary folk artist, The Flower Man, as he is called, has turned three successive yards into large-scale environmental artworks made from a dizzying symphony of junk and real and artificial flowers and plants. Like many artists in the *No Zoning* exhibition, Turner first stopped in Houston on his way somewhere else, in this case to California from his native Mississippi, and ended up staying. Unfortunately, after he arrived in 1961, a friend introduced him to Thunderbird wine, to which he became addicted. He eventually lost his job and spent the next seventeen years living on the street. One day in 1983, a woman found Turner unconscious, half-dead from alcohol poisoning, and took him to the hospital, where he spent several weeks recovering. Near the end of his convalescence, he had a vision of an ascending swirl of colorful junk, and he swore that he would stay sober and make something beautiful out of what others threw away.

To realize this vision, he began collecting neighborhood detritus, including old signs, discarded toys, bicycle rims, and plastic flowers, while riding around town on a flower-bedecked bicycle, nicknamed "the flower cycle." He then assembled his finds in outdoor installations at his rented homes—first on Sauer Street (1986), then at on Sampson Street (1988)—which he augmented by cultivating teeming flower and vegetable gardens, exploiting a knack for gardening that he inherited from an aunt in Mississippi. His quirky creation attracted so much admiration that when the Sampson Street house was destroyed by vandals and fire in 2003, community members pitched in to help him relocate to his current home on Francis Street, near Project Row Houses in Houston's Third Ward. They returned again in 2008 to help him reassemble his outdoor installation and repair his roof after Hurricane Ike blew through. Because of these vagaries of fate and The Flower Man's own ongoing quest for salvaged treasures, his creation is continually changing.

For *No Zoning*, Turner uses the lawn in front of the CAMH as the site for a similarly evolving work of art. Combining junk from Houston's streets with his own assemblage artworks, he has built an installation resembling the one in his own yard. This commission is not Turner's first. He has produced similar installations for Joan Wich's downtown gallery and Project Row Houses in 2002. By making trash useful again, and even beautiful, Turner not only redeems his own life, but also contributes a powerful form of beauty to Houston's cityscape.

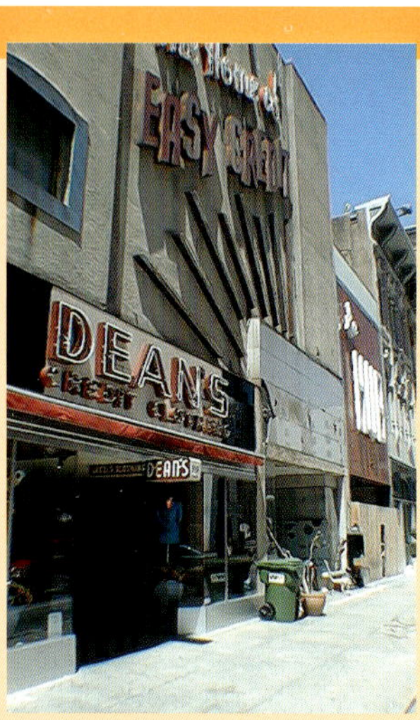

notsuoH exterior on Main Street, late 1990s

1997

notsuoH
Artist Jim Pirtle renovated a nineteenth-century storefront building on Main Street in downtown Houston into a coffee bar/chess club/gallery/performance space that he dubbed notsuoH–Houston spelled backwards and the name of an early twentieth-century civic celebration. notsuoH became one of the most notorious, complicated, experimental "social-sculpture" environments in Houston. On any given night, one could converse with physicists while playing chess with a homeless alcoholic against the background noise of a Japanese speed punk band.

Revolution Summer
Before he moved to California, Mark Allen opened an art space called Revolution Summer where he walled off and painted the interior of his rented house and mounted three conceptual art exhibitions.

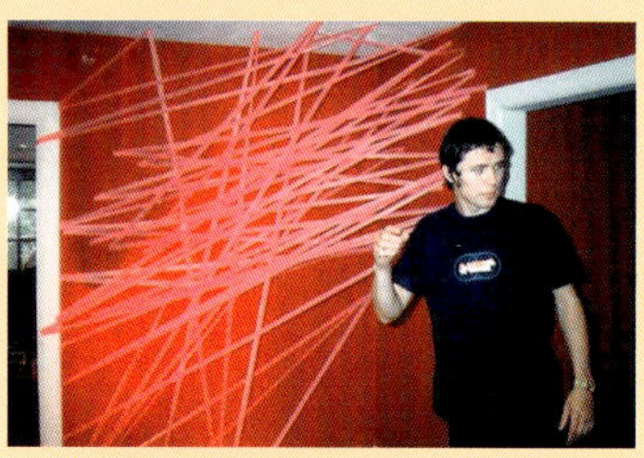

Robert Montgomery with *Constructivist Composition*, Revolution Summer gallery, 1997

1998

Aurora Picture Show
Artist Andrea Grover founded the Aurora Picture Show, a micro-cinema, in her home in a former church in the Sunset Heights. Programming was dedicated to noncommercial film, video, and media, often presented in other nontraditional venues. To date, they have screened over four thousand films and videos and hosted over four hundred artists.

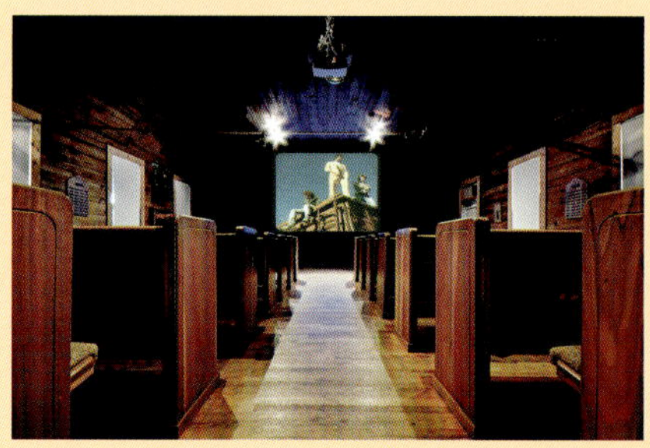

Interior, Aurora Picture Show, 2007

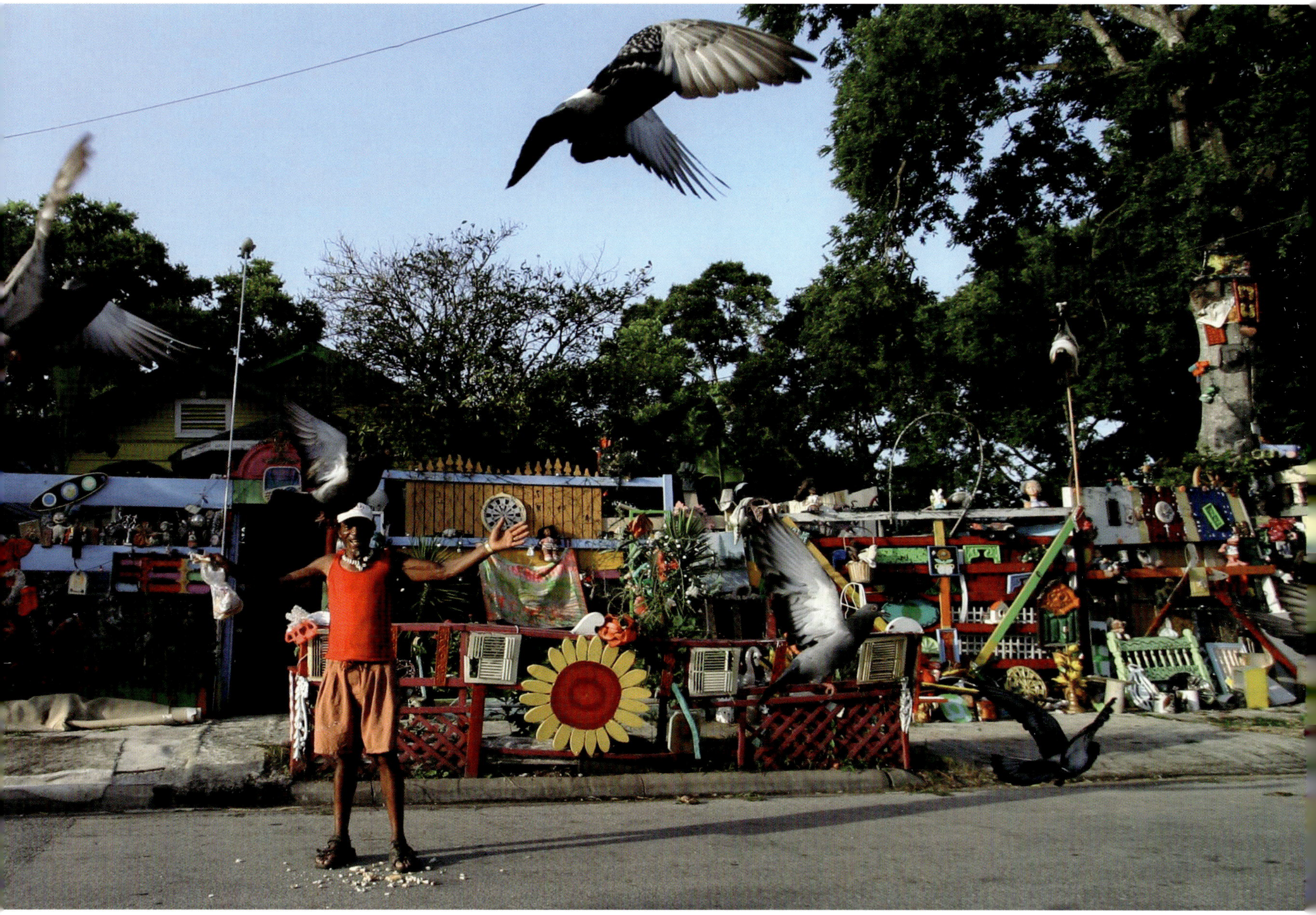

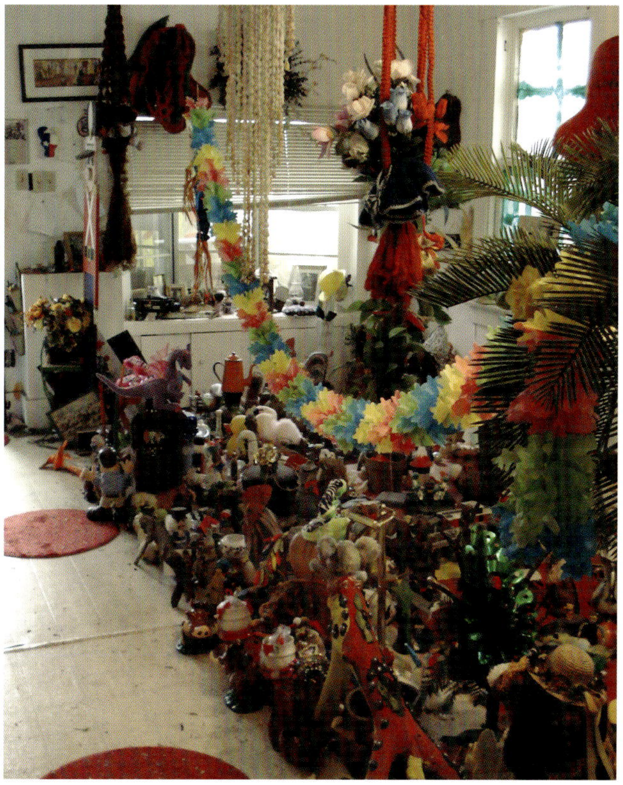

The Flower Man (Cleveland Turner)
The Flower Man House (exterior, with The Flower Man, and interior, Francis Street, Houston), 2003–ongoing
Paint, found objects, assemblages, plants, and flowers
Courtesy the artist and The Orange Show, Houston

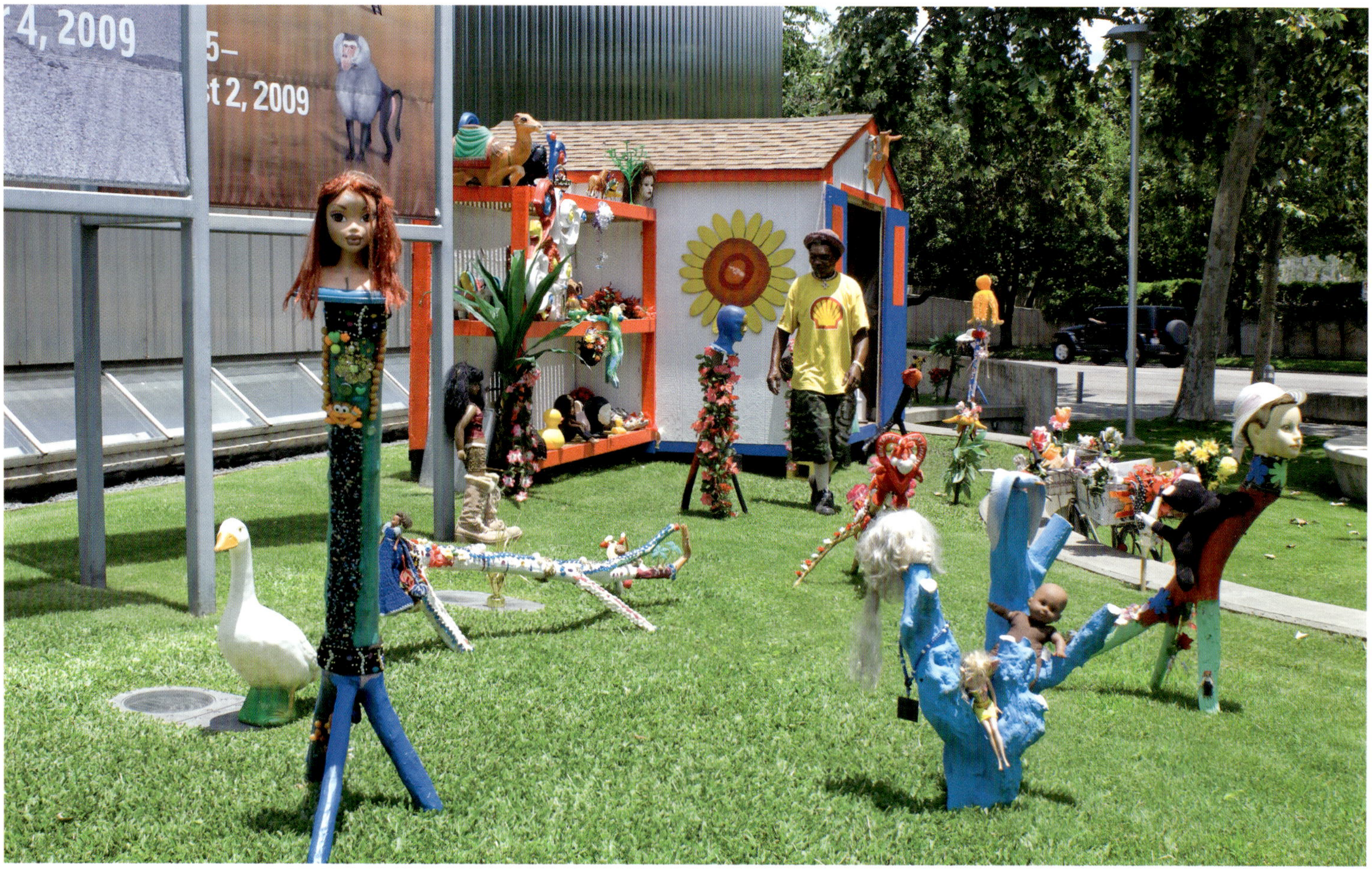
4, 2009
5–
t 2, 2009

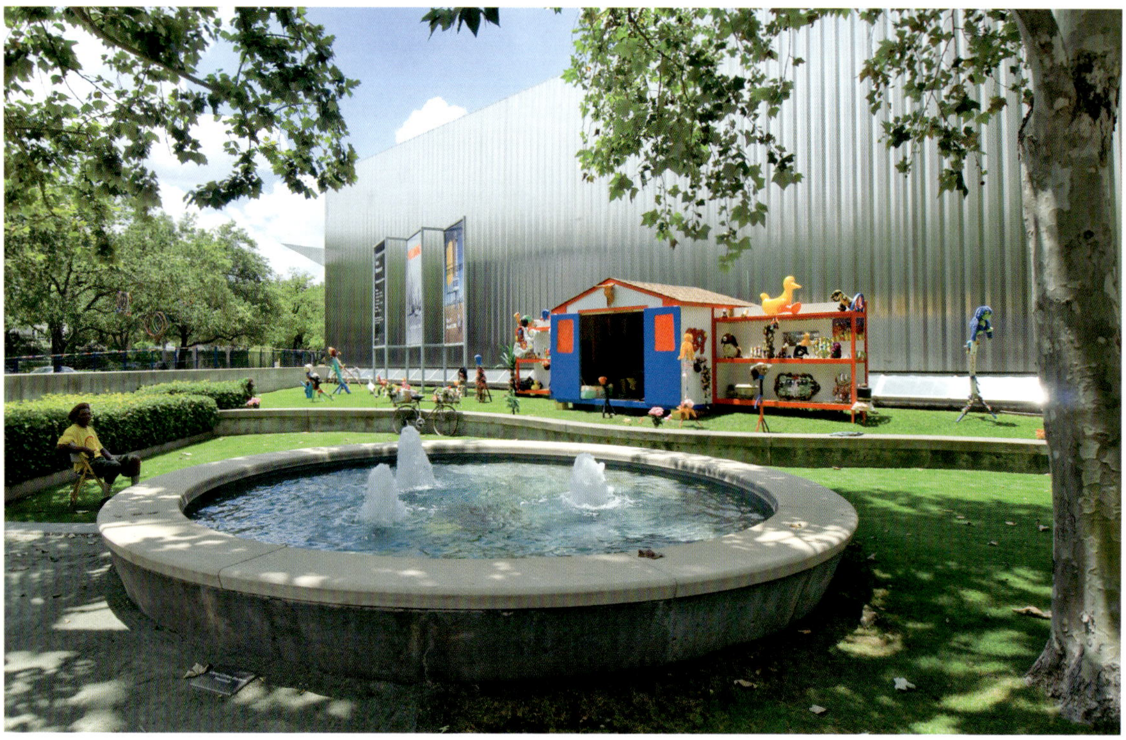

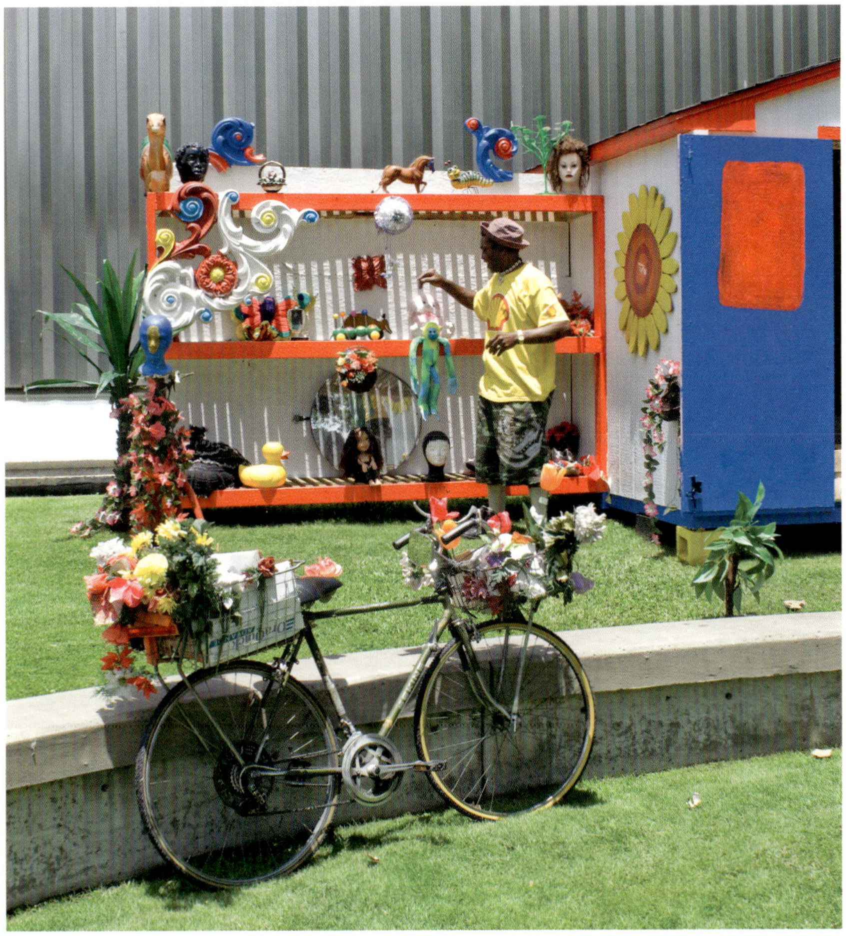

The Flower Man (Cleveland Turner)
The Flower Man Art, 2009
Wood, latex paint, found objects, artificial flowers, plants, CAMH front lawn
Structure: 10 x 10 x 17 feet
Installation views with the artist, Contemporary Arts Museum Houston
All courtesy the artist

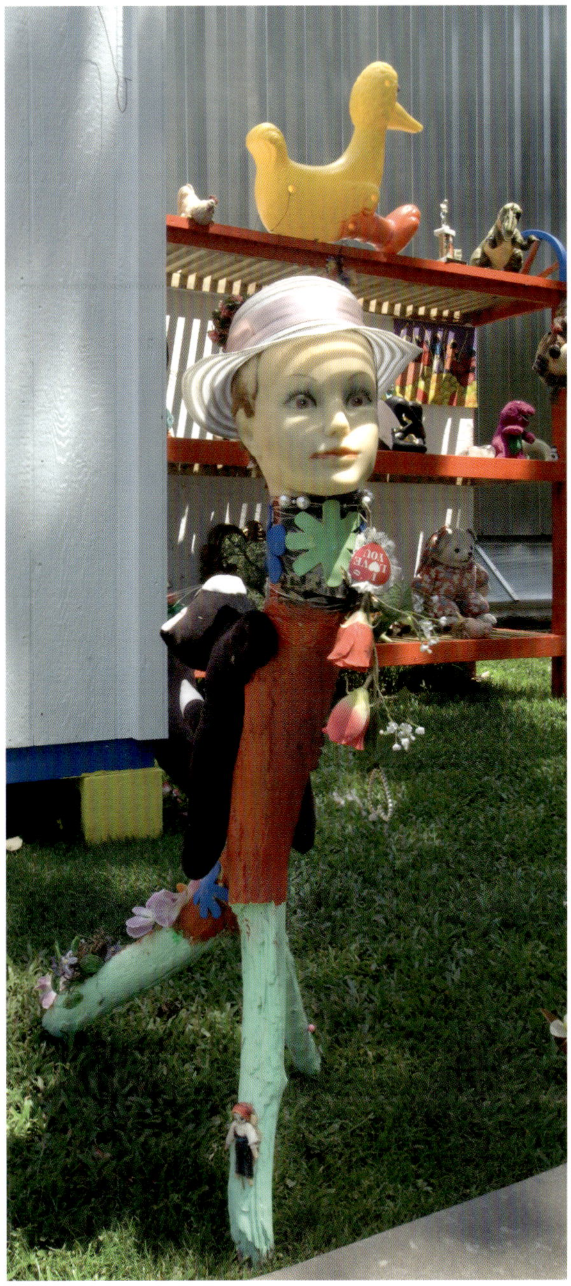

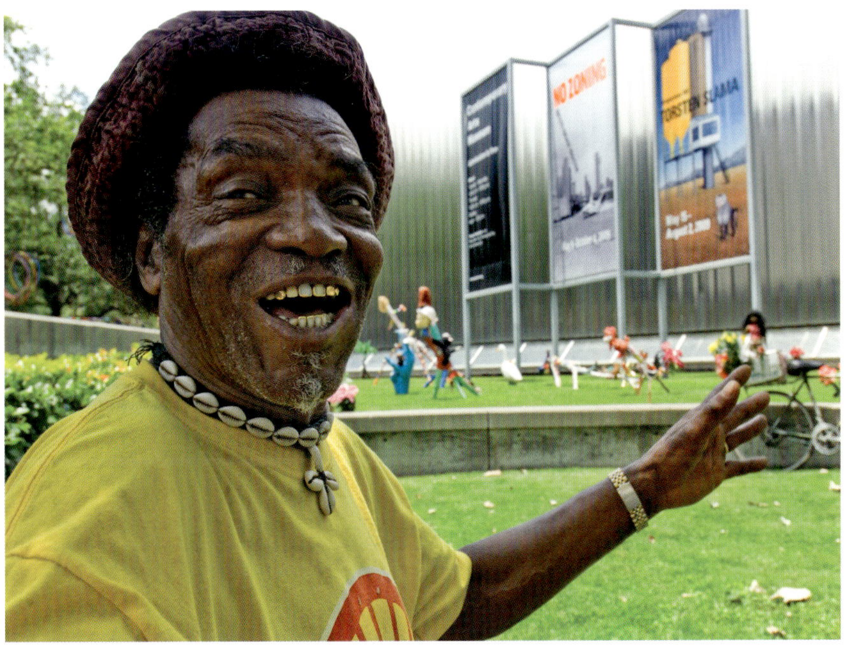

The Fundred Dollar Bill Project (Mel Chin et al.)

Mel Chin, often called the godfather of socially engaged public art in Houston, is renowned for pushing the boundaries of traditional art practice. He works across disciplines and against stylistic and thematic conventions, incorporating ecology, software engineering, economics, animation, and television production into his artwork.

In 1997 Chin developed the project *In the Name of the Place* in collaboration with other artists and students working under the name GALA Committee. Over the course of one season of the television series *Melrose Place*, the group responded to its plot twists by designing props and sets for the show with imbedded social and political messages.

In his groundbreaking 1991–93 work *Revival Field,* installed in Pig's Eye Landfill, St. Paul, Minnesota, and Palmerton, Pennsylvania, Chin worked with scientists to create sculpted gardens of hyperaccumulators—plants that can draw heavy metals from soil—at heavily polluted sites, where they served as both art installations and outdoor laboratories.

He has expanded his environmental focus with *Operation Paydirt* (2008–10), a multipart project designed to increase awareness of the dangers of lead contamination in New Orleans neighborhoods. Lead, a toxin that can enter the topsoil and household dust through flaking paint and automotive exhaust, has terrible impacts on children, including learning disabilities and behavioral problems. Working with scientists, health care professionals, designers, urban planners, engineers, political officials, and artists in New Orleans, Chin and his team identified a method of rendering the lead inert using calcium phosphate. This process, they calculate, if used at other sites, will cost the federal government $300 million per major city. To raise both money for remediation and awareness, Chin has developed *The Fundred Dollar Bill Project*, offering an "even exchange"[1] of $300 million for 3 million drawings on "fundred" dollar bill cutouts made by individuals across the country, which will be collected and delivered to Washington, D.C., in a modified armored car powered by vegetable oil.

In New Orleans, Chin and volunteers altered a house in a badly contaminated neighborhood, abandoned after Hurricane Katrina, to resemble a bank vault and turned its interior into a center for creating and displaying the customized dollar bills. Children and members of the public visiting the house could use a blank template of a "fundred" dollar bill—a name he says combines "fun, funds, and hundreds"[2]—to draw their own elements such as portraits, seals, and signatures. For people across the country interested in the project and the problem of lead pollution, Chin has established a website, www.fundred.org, where they can download templates for the bills and find nearby collection centers for the completed drawings.

During the run of *No Zoning*, visitors can make and display their own "fundreds" at the CAMH, which will also serve as the Houston collection site for bills created by local schoolchildren. Each of these drawings, Chin says, is "worth more than a hundred dollars. This is somebody's imagination, which is what is being laid waste by lead."[3] Chin intends *Operation Paydirt* to serve as a model for projects in other cities with severe lead problems, including Houston.

1. http://fundred.org/pages/Project/project_more_about.html (accessed March 24, 2009).
2. http://fundred.org/pages/Project/project_faq.html (accessed March 24, 2009).
3. Mel Chin, conversation with the author, March 2009.

1998

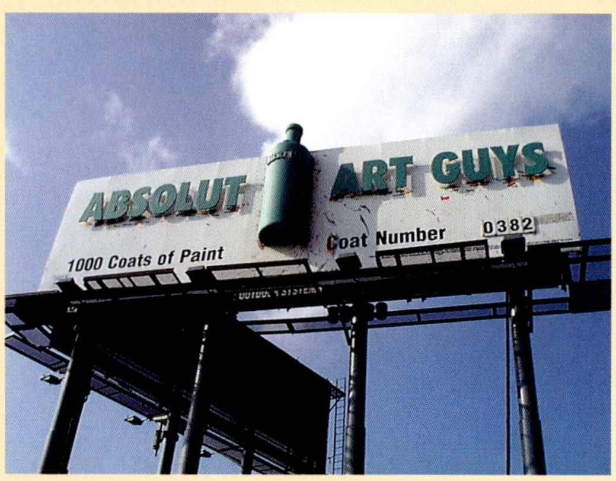

Coat Number 382 of the *Absolut Art Guys Billboard*, 1998

Absolut Art Guys Billboard
The Art Guys were commissioned by Absolut Vodka to create a billboard. Located on the West 610 Loop freeway near the Galleria, the billboard featured a giant Vodka bottle that was painted with a thousand separate coats of paint over a nine-month period.

SUITS: The Clothes Make the Man
The Art Guys unveiled their conceptual artwork *SUITS* with a two-man parade in downtown Houston. After leasing advertising space on two business suits designed by Todd Oldham, The Art Guys wore them for a year, promoting their "clients."

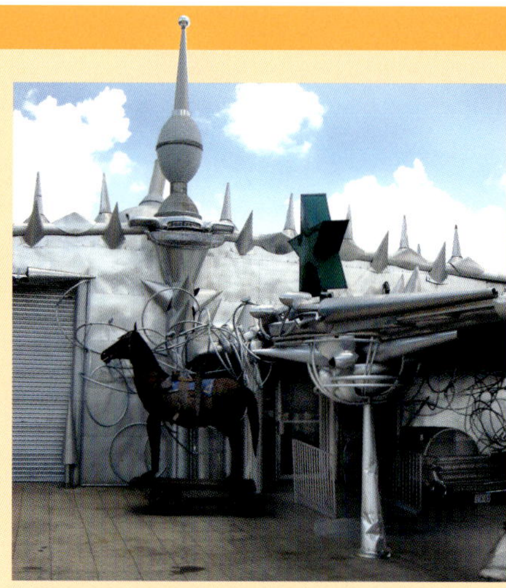

Art Car Museum, exterior, Heights Boulevard, 2009

Art Car Museum
Artist and patron Ann Harithas and former Contemporary Arts Museum Director James Harithas founded the Art Car Museum at the southern end of Heights Boulevard. Today it presents exhibitions and programs featuring art and art cars.

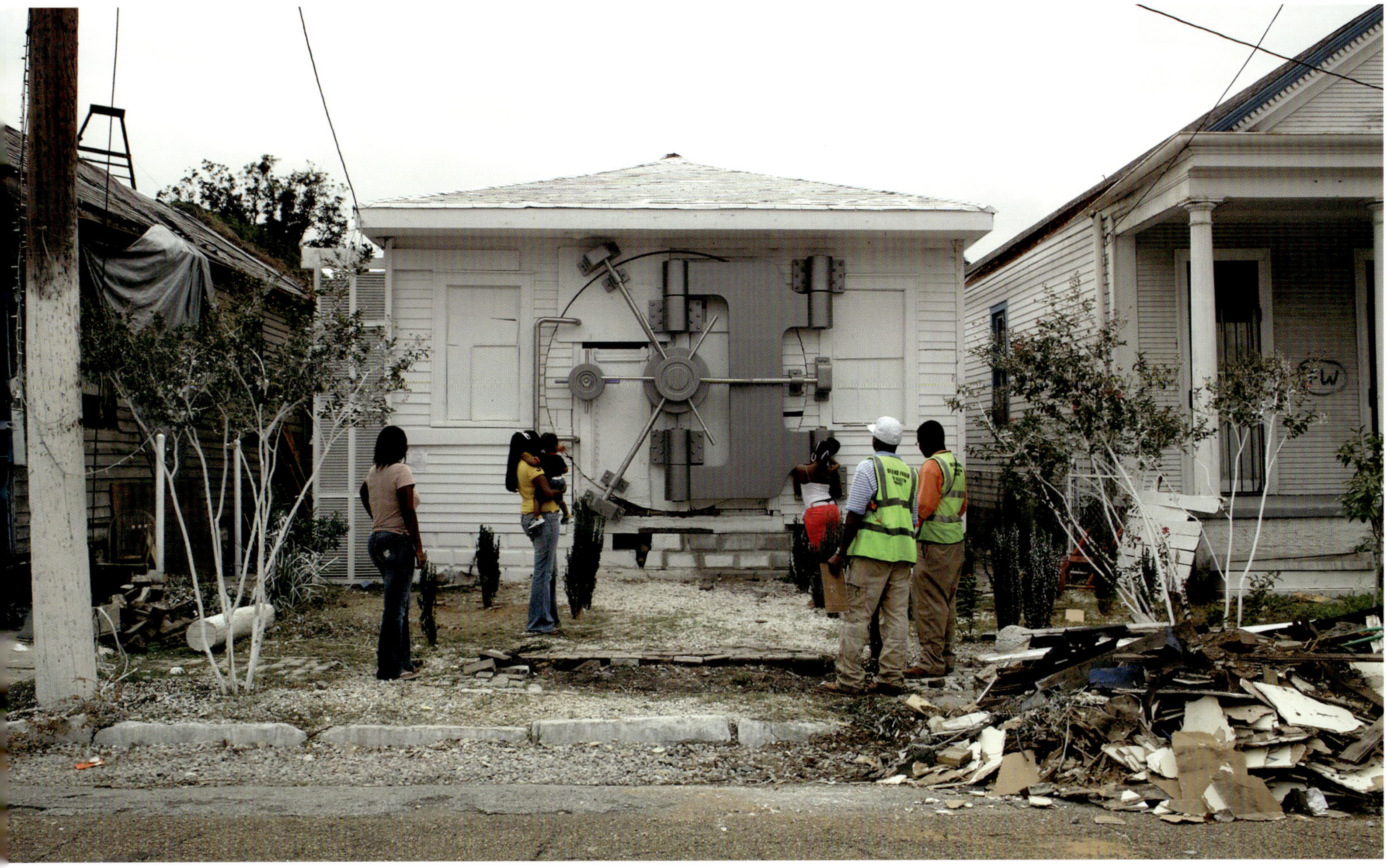

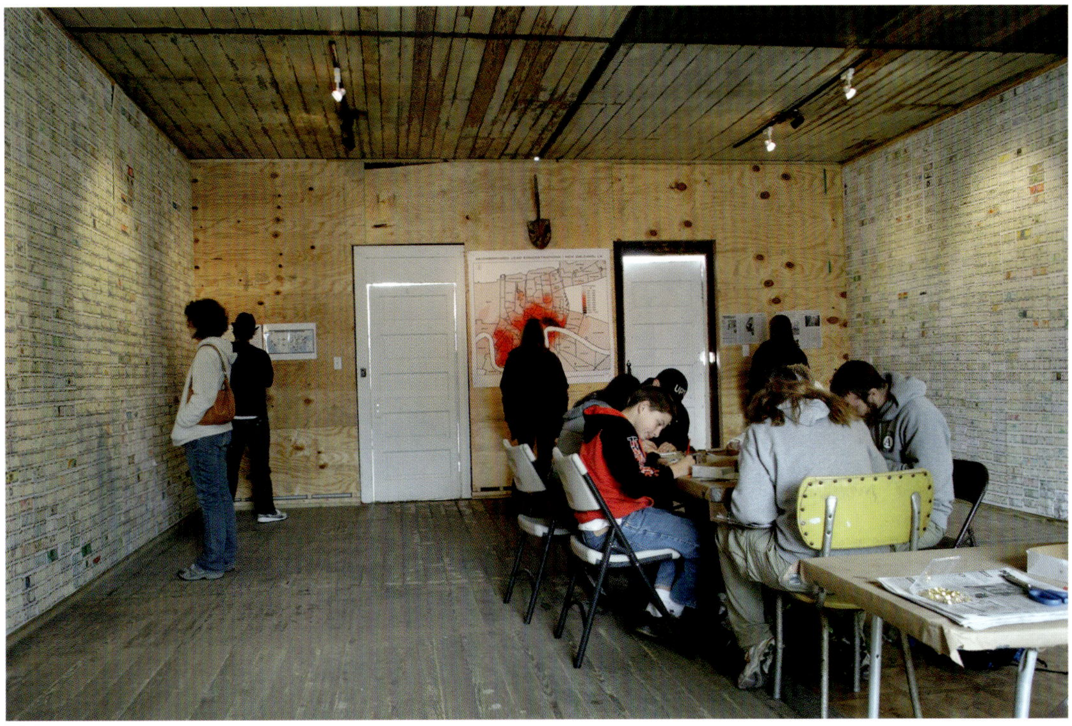

The Fundred Dollar Bill Project **(Mel Chin et al.)**
SAFEHOUSE (exterior and interior with *Fundreds*), 2008
2461 North Villere Street, St. Roch neighborhood, New Orleans
Courtesy the artist

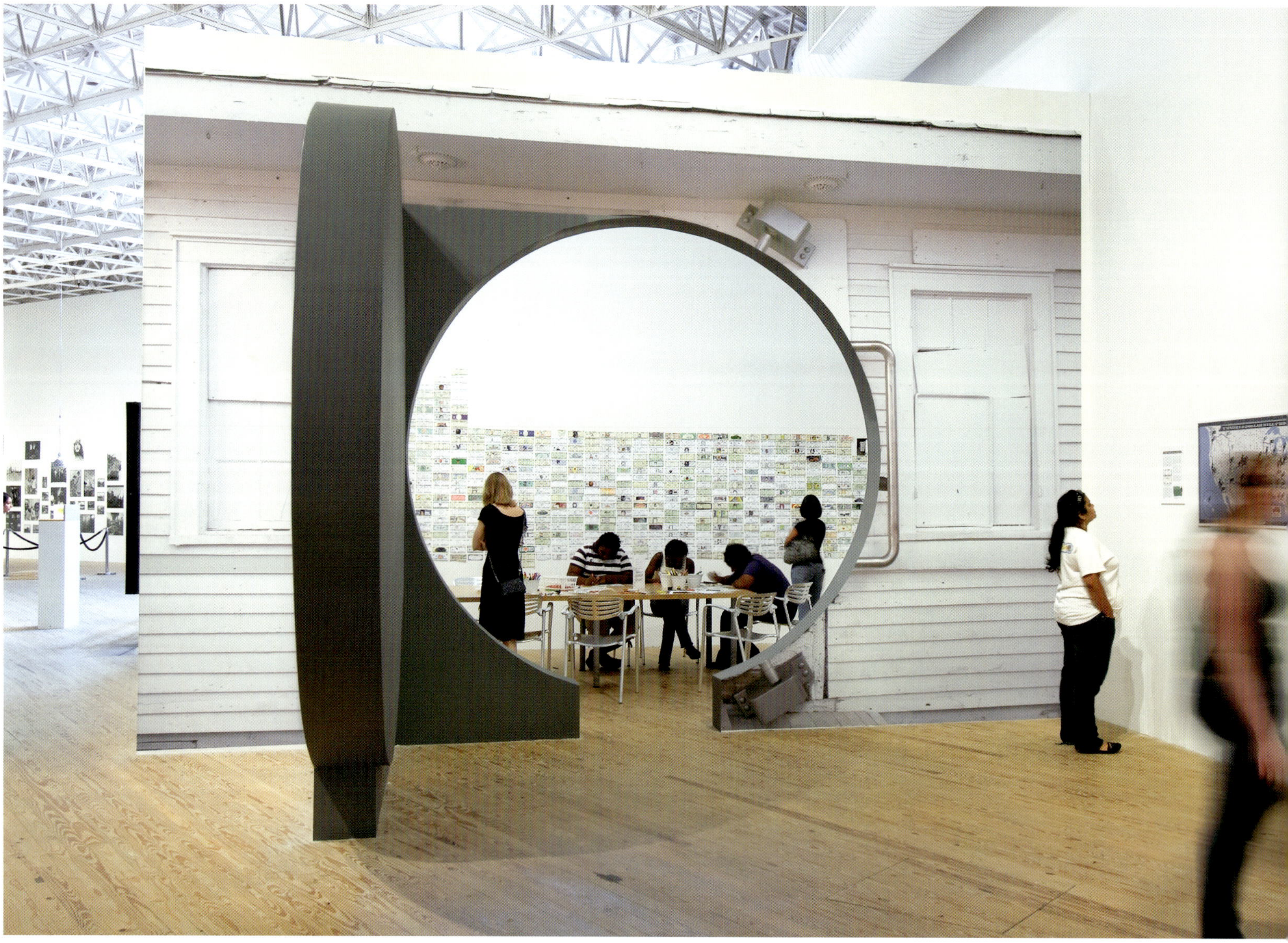

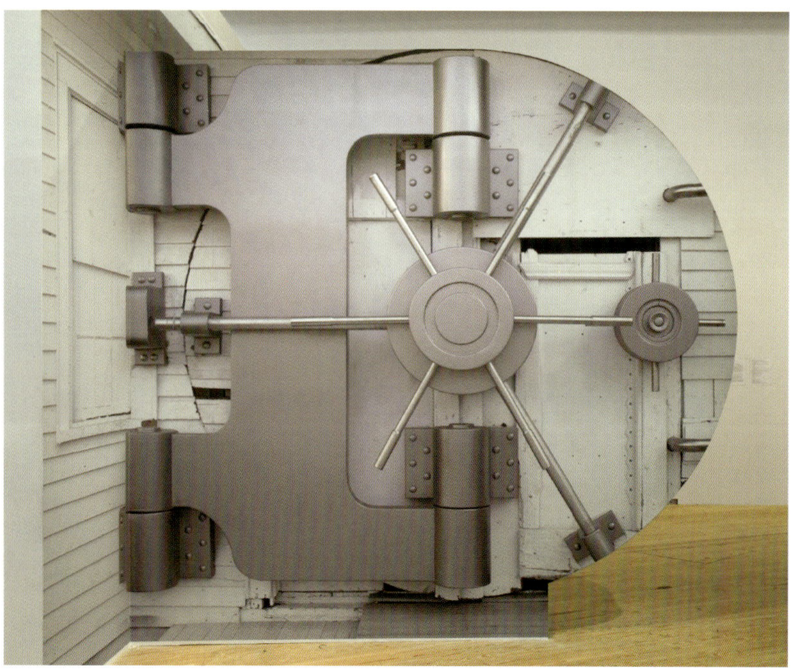

The Fundred Dollar Bill Project, 2008–10
(Houston portion of three million *Fundred* drawings by various contributing artists, all works signed)
Wood, drywall, paint, wallpaper photograph of *SAFEHOUSE*, paper templates, markers, pencils, gold tacks, chairs, table, participants
Installation: 14 x 19¾ x 27 feet
Drawings: 2⅝ x 6⅛ inches each
Installation views and detail of *Fundred* drawings, Contemporary Arts Museum Houston

All courtesy *The Fundred Dollar Bill Project* (Mel Chin et al.), Organizing Principal, and Sabrina Franzheim, donor of *Fundreds* templates for Houston

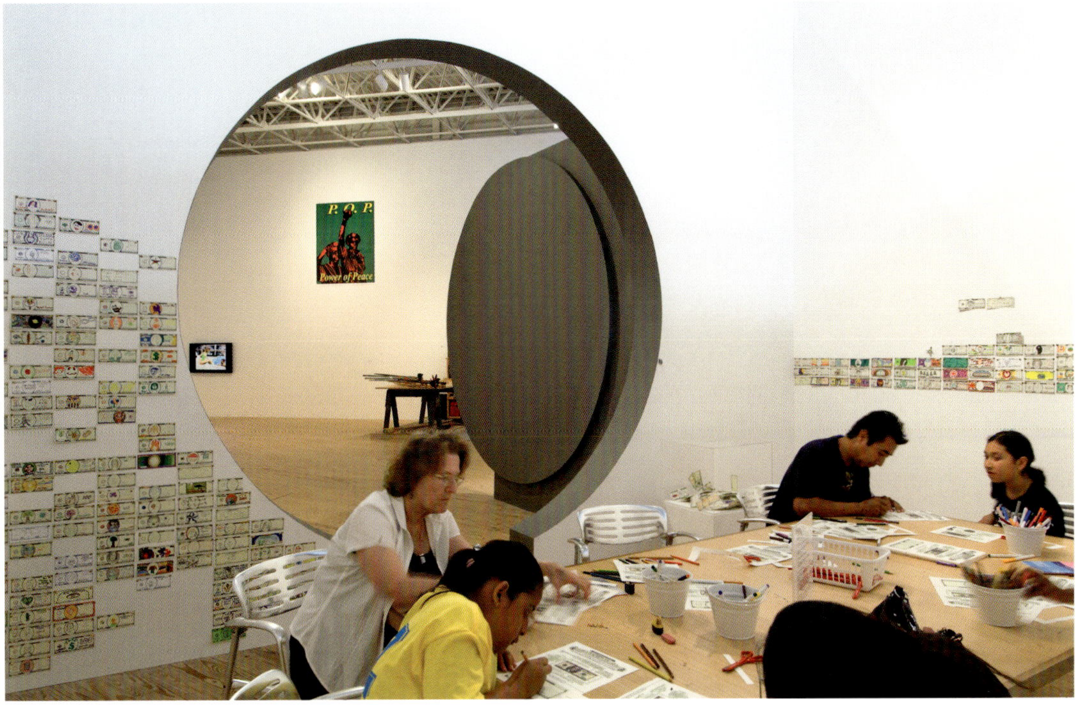
P.O.P.
Power of Peace

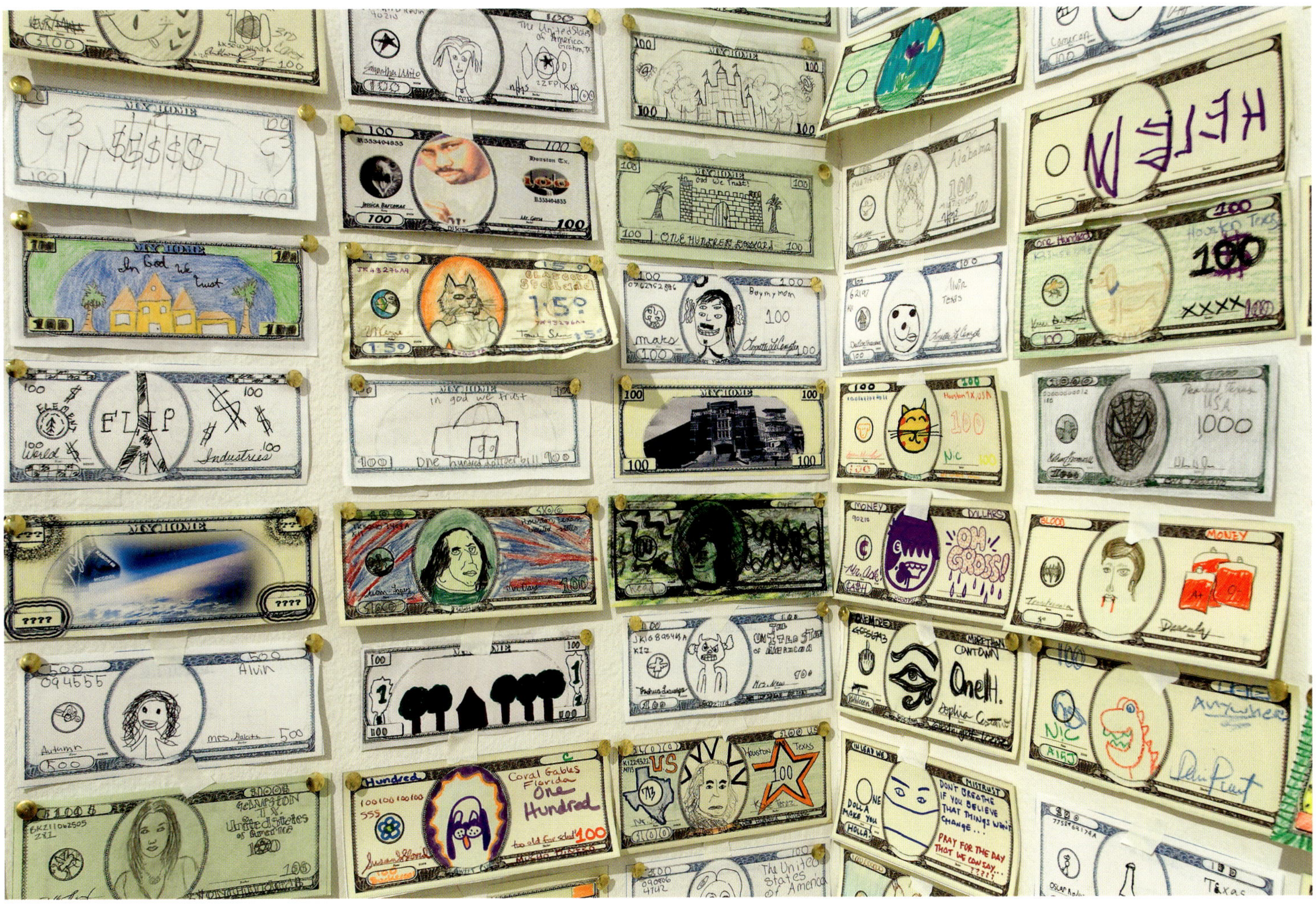
MY HOME
In God We trust
FLIP
Industries
OH GROSS!
Coral Gables Florida One Hundred

Andrea Grover

Andrea Grover began her career in Houston as an artist and film-maker in 1995, when she participated in the Core Program, an artists' residency program offered by the Museum of Fine Arts, Houston. She has lived in the city ever since. By 1998 she realized that she was more interested in presenting the work of other artists who were making films and videos, and so converted a small 1924 church in a Heights neighborhood into the Aurora Picture Show, a hundred-seat micro-cinema.

With Grover as its artistic director, the Aurora Picture Show flourished and expanded its reach by offering screenings at other locations around the city. It has hosted an outdoor film series on the Menil Collection campus and has broadcast videos from the back of a Toyota Scion for its *Mobile Cinema* project. In 2006 Aurora was part of the collaborative initiative *Floating Cinema*, a barge equipped with a screen that showed films by James Benning, Peter Hutton, and Andy Warhol while afloat on Buffalo Bayou.

Grover resigned her role as artistic director in 2008 to pursue writing and independent curating. She was the curator for the 2006 exhibition *Phantom Captain: Crowdsourcing and Art* at Apex Art in New York. In 2007 she served as co-curator for three exhibitions: *Never Been to Houston* at the Lawndale Art Center, in which world-wide contributors could upload photos of what they imagined Houston looks like to a website; *Never Been to Tehran,* a sequel project that traveled to international exhibition spaces; and the participatory camera-phone exhibition *Text Me L8r* at the Houston Center for Photography.

For *No Zoning*, Grover debuts three projects that draw on her personal film collection and her interest in cooperative creative production. *Astrodome Cinema* is an evening screening at the CAMH of Geoff Winningham's *The Pleasures of This Stately Dome* (1975), a 16mm film about the construction of this "Eighth Wonder of the World," along with *Lord of the Universe* (1974), Top Value Television's documentary about a sixteen-year-old guru Maharaji Ji's attempts to levitate this behemoth landmark. *Houston Lyceum* offers two evening presentations at the CAMH with participants recreating original lectures and debates that took place at the Houston Lyceum, a precursor to the Houston Public Library founded in 1854. Grover hopes that these voices from the past will shed light on the city's evolution, noting, "The mind-set of early citizens might (or might not) reveal a developing pattern or character."[1] Her third project, *Jacuzzi Movies*, features a collage of Jacuzzi and re-laxing water scenes culled from various movies to be screened for audiences soaking in a hot tub located on the CAMH's back lawn.

1. Andrea Grover, conversation with the author, March 2009.

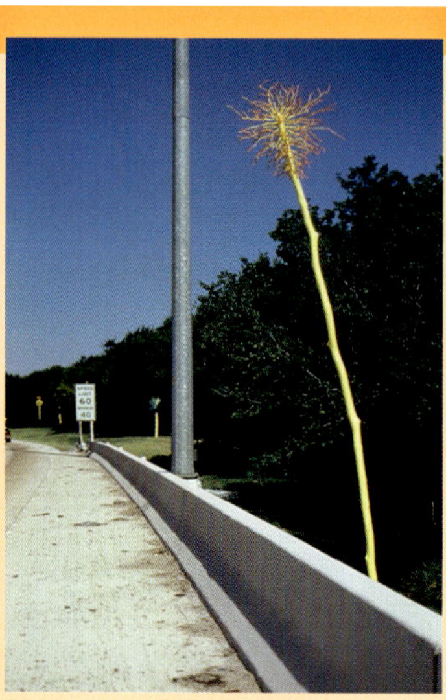

Lee Littlefield, *Pop-Up: Reach*, 2000

1998

Pop-Up Sculpture for the Millennium
Artist Lee Littlefield installed his first artist-initiated *Pop-Up* sculpture along Interstate 10 near downtown Houston. Typically painted in eye-catching yellow and made from willowy vines and branches, the sculptures now number in the hundreds and have become well known to travelers in and around the city.

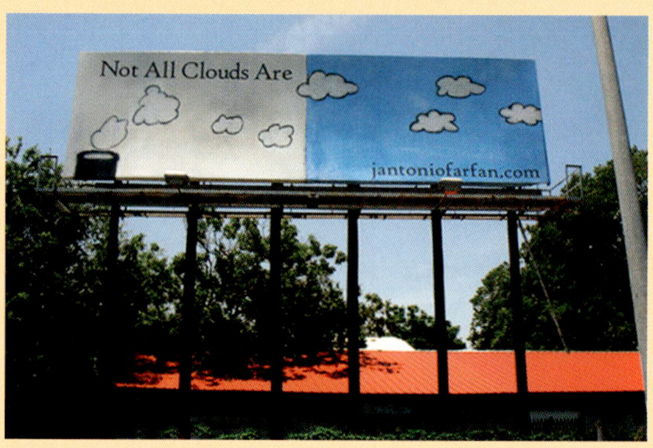

Watershed Collective billboard and studio, 2007

1999

Watershed Collective
A group of artists known as the Watershed Collective, occupying a group of buildings on property at TC Jester and Interstate 10, began a yearly program of allowing other artists to create an artwork on a billboard on their property that faces the interstate, directing its message to the passing traffic on the freeway.

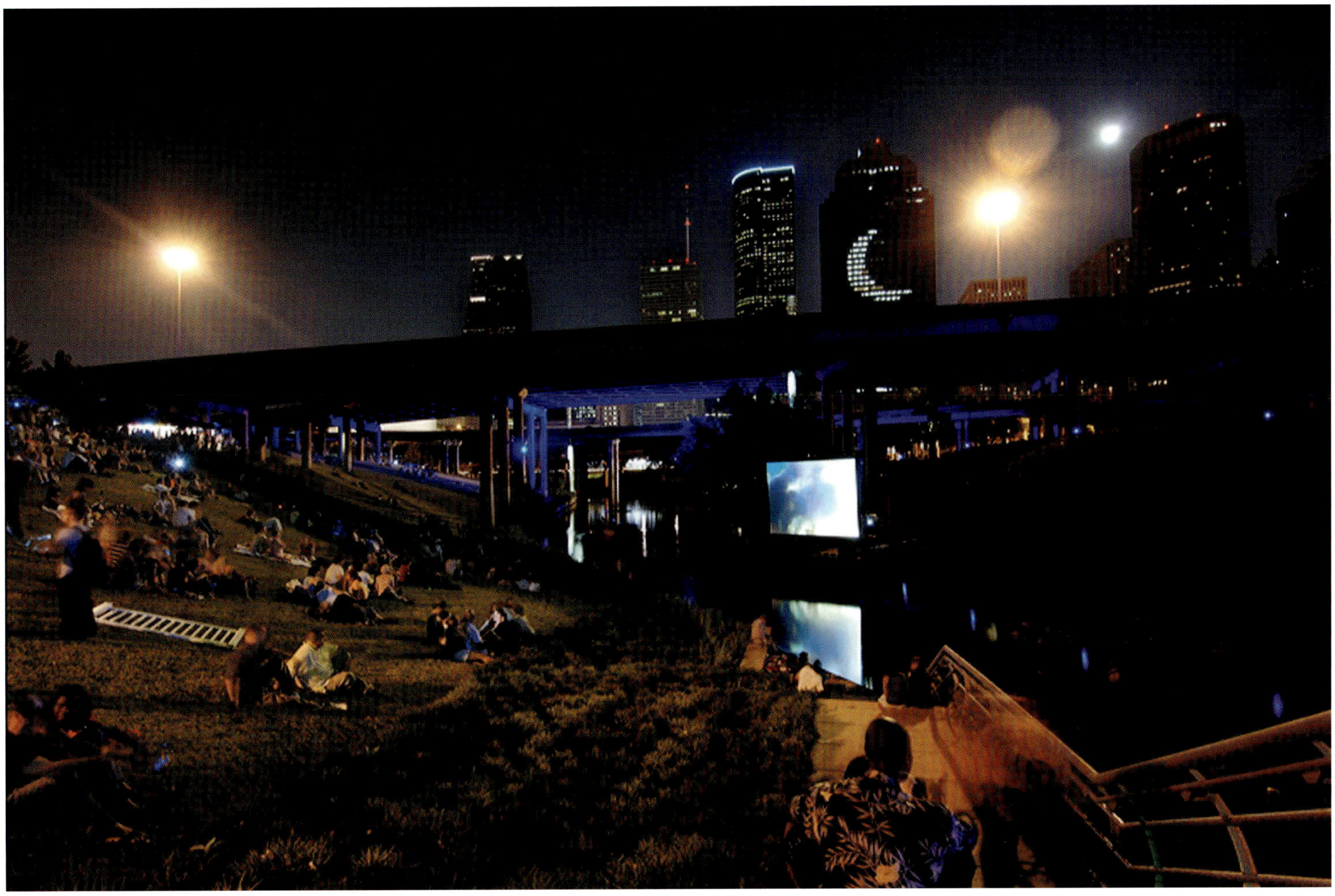

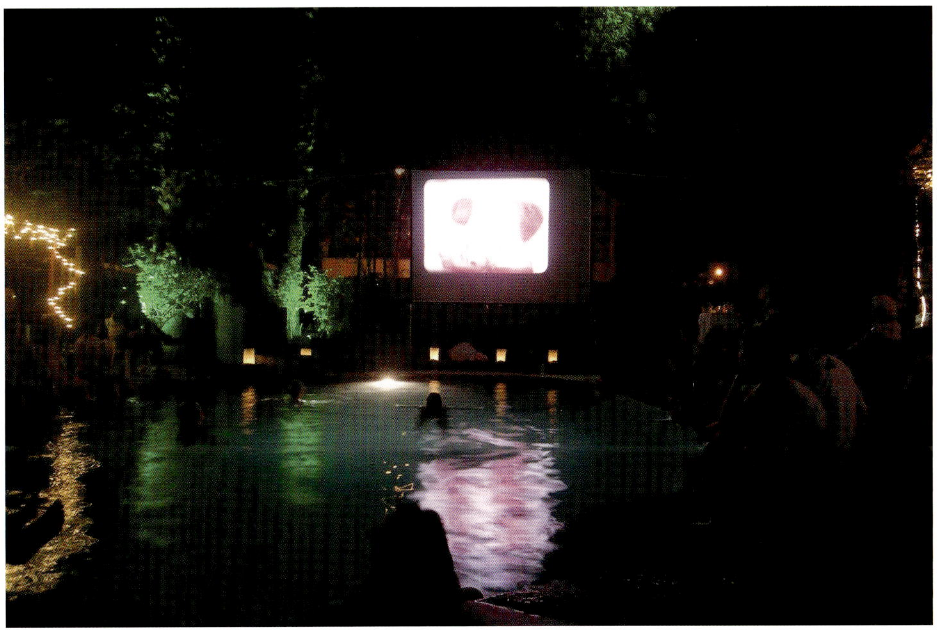

Andrea Grover
Floating Cinema (video screening event, Buffalo Bayou, Houston), 2006
Courtesy Aurora Picture Show, Minetta Brook, and Buffalo Bayou Partnership

Pool Rulez (video screening event, private pool, Houston), 2008
Courtesy Aurora Picture Show and A/V Geeks

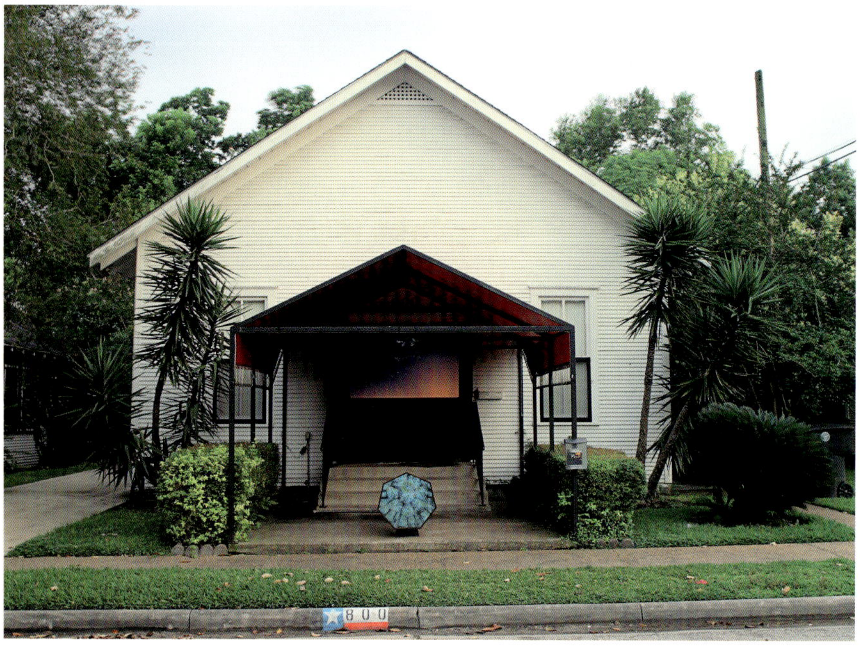

Andrea Grover
Aurora Picture Show, 1998–present
100-seat micro-theater in converted 1924 church, Houston, Texas

left:
Exterior view, 2007, with Andy Mann's *Sparkle Box* video sculpture

below:
Interior view, 2007
All courtesy Aurora Picture Show

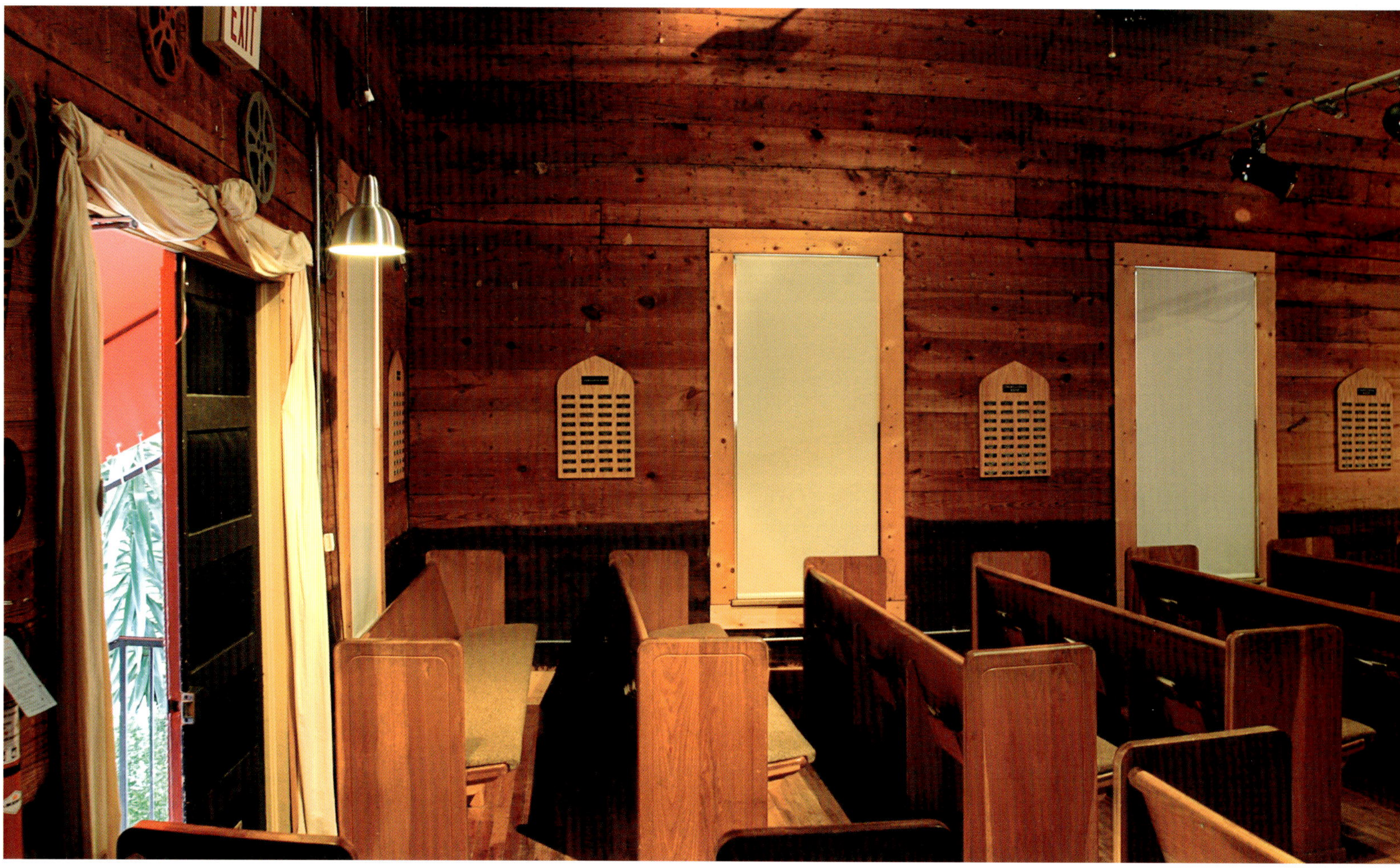

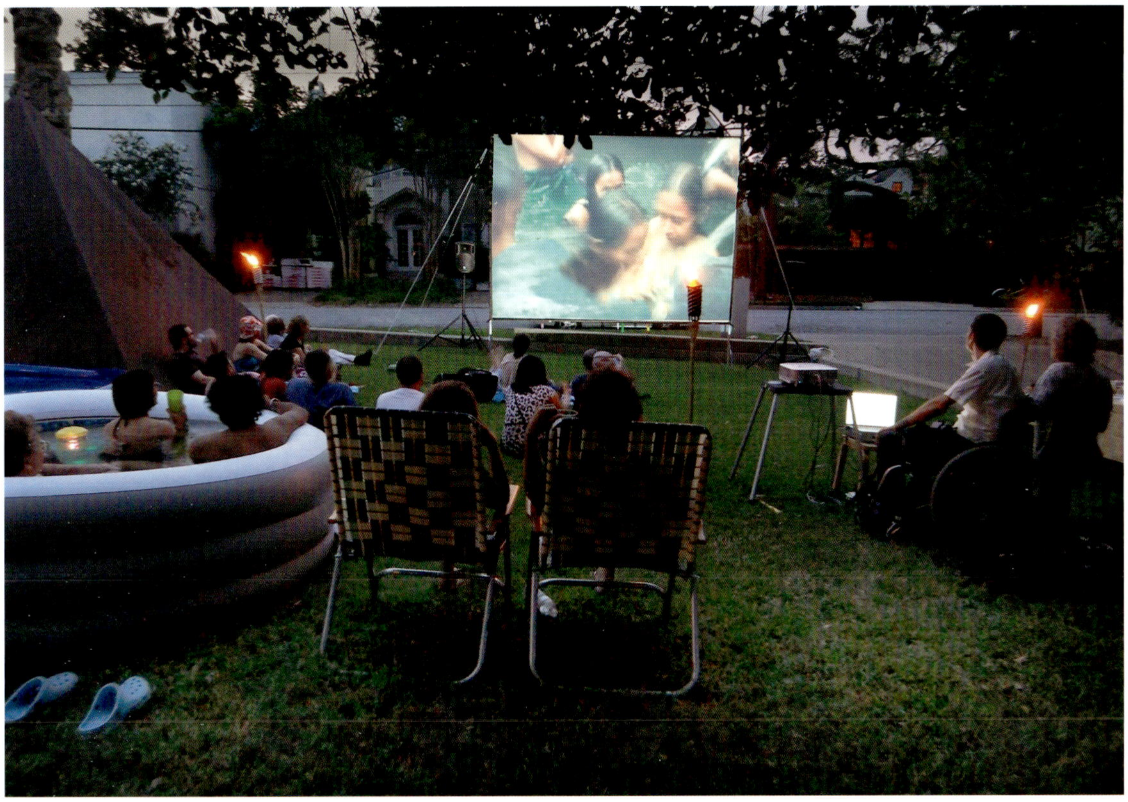

Andrea Grover
Jacuzzi Movies (video screening event, CAMH lawn), 2009
Courtesy the artist

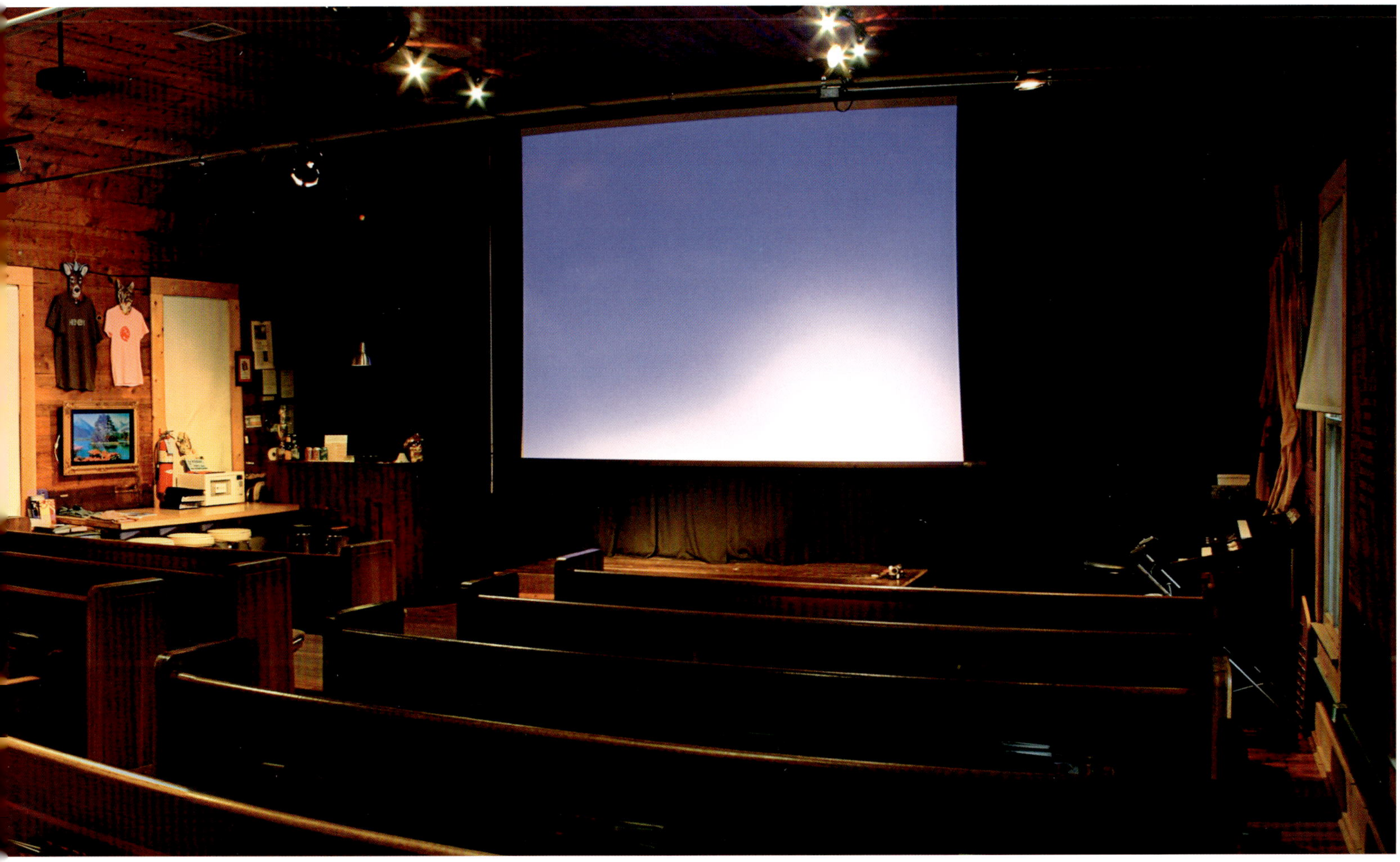

Dan Havel and Dean Ruck

Dan Havel and Dean Ruck make temporary sculptures out of Houston houses slated for demolition. In 1994 Havel completed his first architectural intervention, *Alchemy House*, a multimedia installation in a West End home in Houston. The work featured performances staged in rooms transformed by the materials for which they were named; for example, the Earth Room had walls caked with mud, and the Salt/Lead Room featured water from a lead funnel dripping onto a mound of salt.

In 1995 Havel collaborated with Ruck and Kate Petley to produce *O House*, which transformed another condemned West End bungalow. Drilling hundreds of holes along the house's exterior produced spots of golden light that circled an inner chamber with a dirt floor and a small pool of water at its center. By cutting a small hole in the roof, they turned this chamber into a camera obscura, which projected the shadowy forms of clouds and the surrounding trees onto the interior walls.

Ten years later Havel and Ruck established their formal partnership, Havel Ruck Projects, and created a large-scale work entitled *Inversion*, which transformed two condemned bungalows on Montrose Boulevard belonging to the Art League of Houston into a vortexlike tunnel. Havel and Ruck stripped the outer wood siding to construct a thirty-five-foot passage that began with a two-foot diameter hole at the rear exterior of one house and continued into the next house. This ever-widening tunnel eventually broke through the street-side wall of the second house, in a twelve-foot diameter opening fringed by a starburst of jagged boards of various length, making it look like the source of a massive explosion or implosion. The project was an instant sensation. Drivers rubber-necked and made U-turns to get closer looks; children and adults crawled through the tunnel again and again; bridal parties posed for pictures inside it; and "Inversion" even became the name for the coffeehouse that the Art League built on the site.

Havel and Ruck have developed a new architectural intervention for *No Zoning,* entitled *Give and Take*, which the public may experience at two locations: in the CAMH and in an abandoned bungalow on Cottage Street in Houston's Heights neighborhood. The artists have essentially "cored" this house, cutting away a 30 x 15 x 15-foot, egg-shaped section that includes parts of the walls, doors, floor, ceiling, and roof. They have reinstalled the excised portion—the "give" of the work's title—as a sculptural installation in the CAMH. In the hollowed-out house—the "take" of the work's title—viewers can walk the perimeter of the oval void to observe the remains, from the dismantled roof above to the dirt below. The peeling paint, termite-nibbled studs, and worn floors of both portions of the work attest to Houston's relentless cycles of demolition and construction, and the passage of time and lives within the city's houses and neighborhoods.

2000

2000s

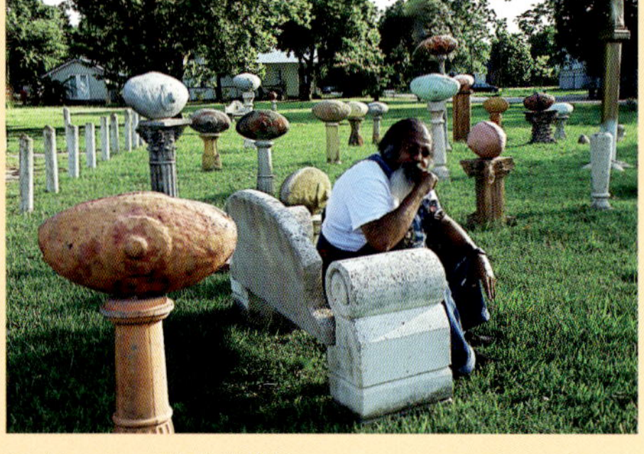

Bert J. Long, Jr., and his *Field of Vision*, 2000

Field of Vision
Bert L. Long, Jr., created *Field of Vision*, a series of eyes resting on pedestals fashioned out of concrete and installed in a parklike setting in the Fifth Ward; each was dyed a different color to reflect the diversity of the neighborhood. After it was vandalized, it was relocated in 2008 to a site on the Project Row Houses campus next to the El Dorado Ballroom.

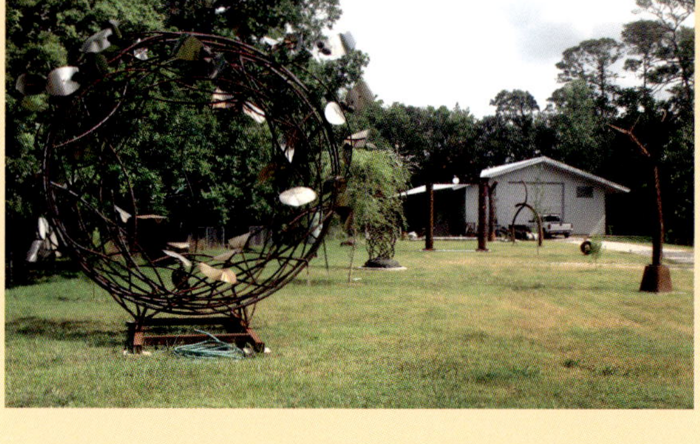

Sculpture at *Itchy Acres*, 2000

Itchy Acres
Area artists including Paul Kittelson, Carter Ernst, Ed Wilson, Lee Littlefield, and Tim Glover, among others, relocated their studios and residences in a neighborhood in North Houston between Yale and North Shepherd Streets on various plots of wooded acreage. Today they use the shared compound for exhibitions and musical performances.

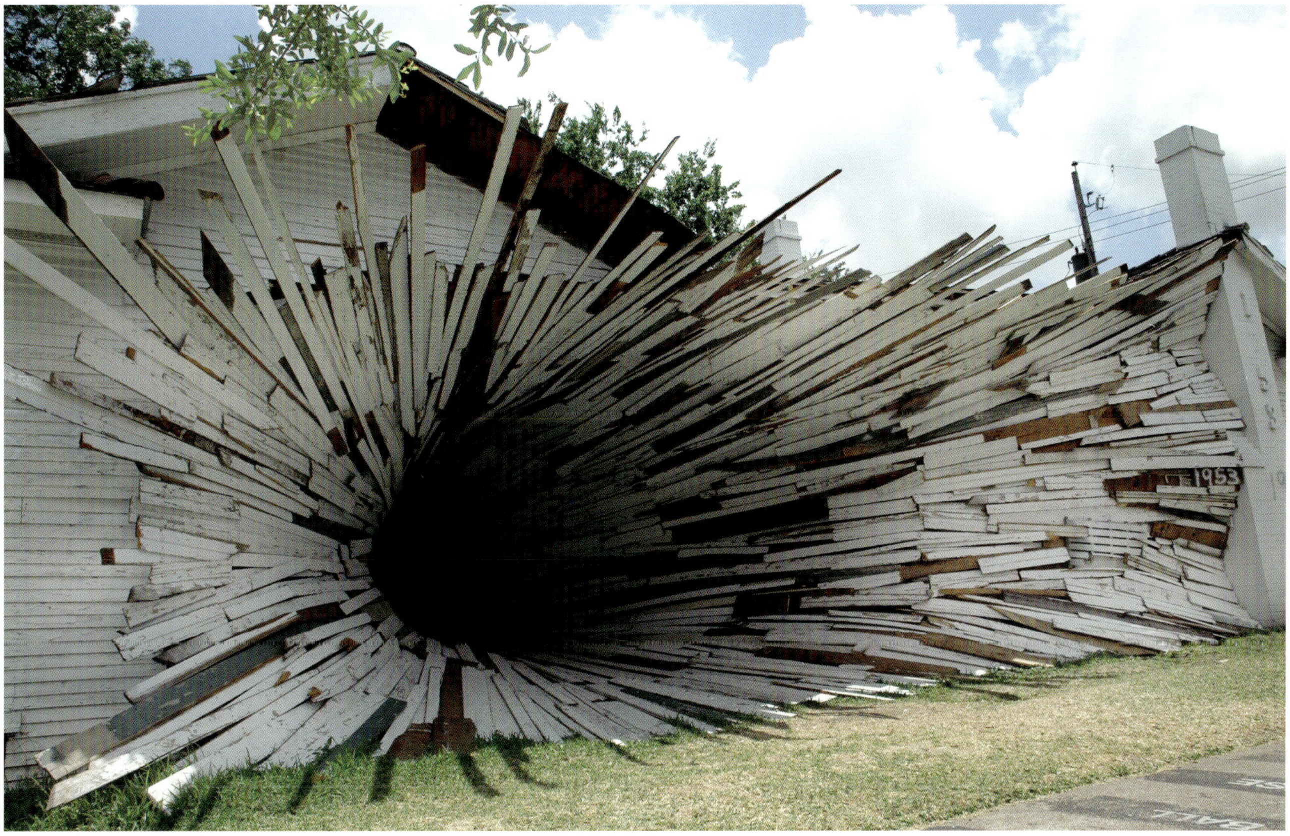

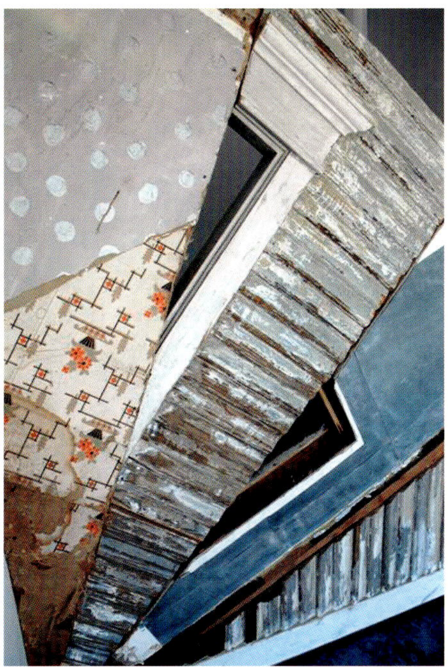

Trespass 5319, 2007
Wood from condemned bungalow, Houston
96 x 36 x 12 inches each section
All courtesy the artists

Dan Havel and Dean Ruck

top:
Inversion, 2005
Two condemned bungalows formerly housing the Art League of Houston, Montrose Boulevard, Houston

bottom right:
Apt. Suite, 2005
Condemned apartment complex at 1711 Winbern Street, Houston

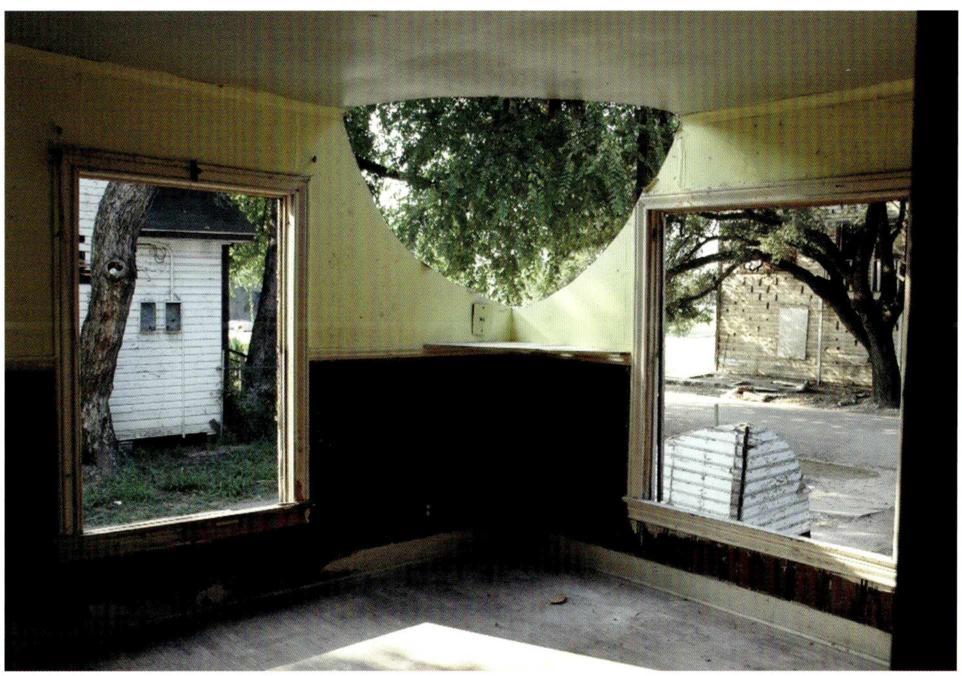

Dan Havel and Dean Ruck
top left:
"Take" site of ***Give and Take***, condemned bungalow at 931 Cottage Street, Houston

Dan Havel
top right:
Give and Take Drawing 6, 2009
Graphite, chalk, on paper
32 x 24 inches
All courtesy the artists

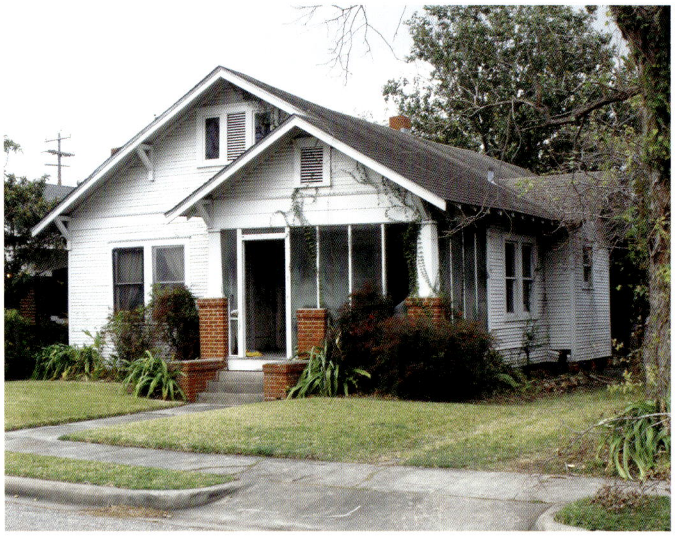

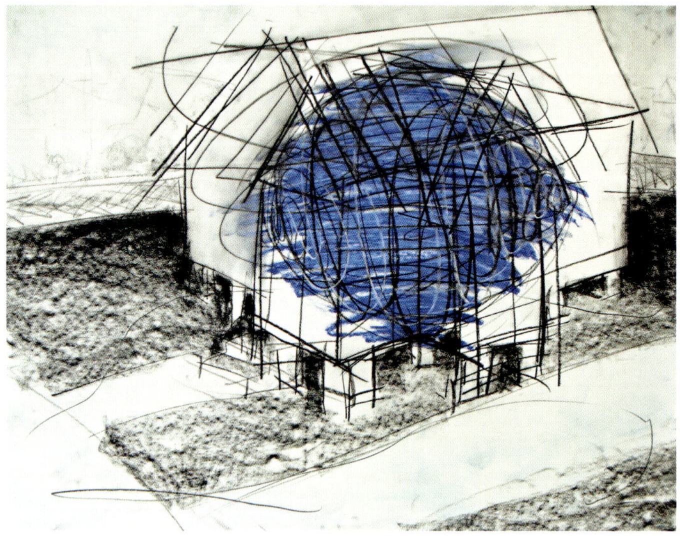

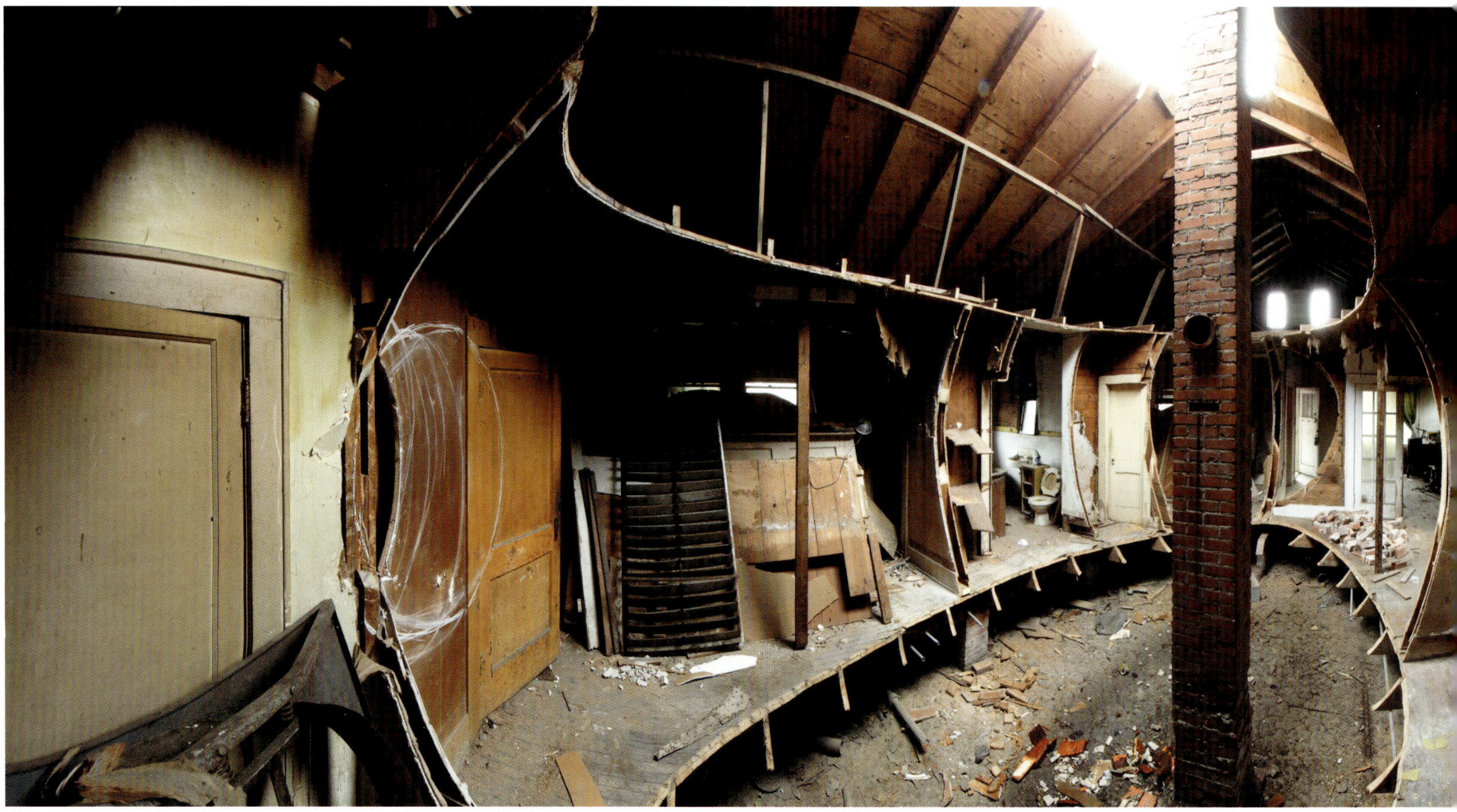

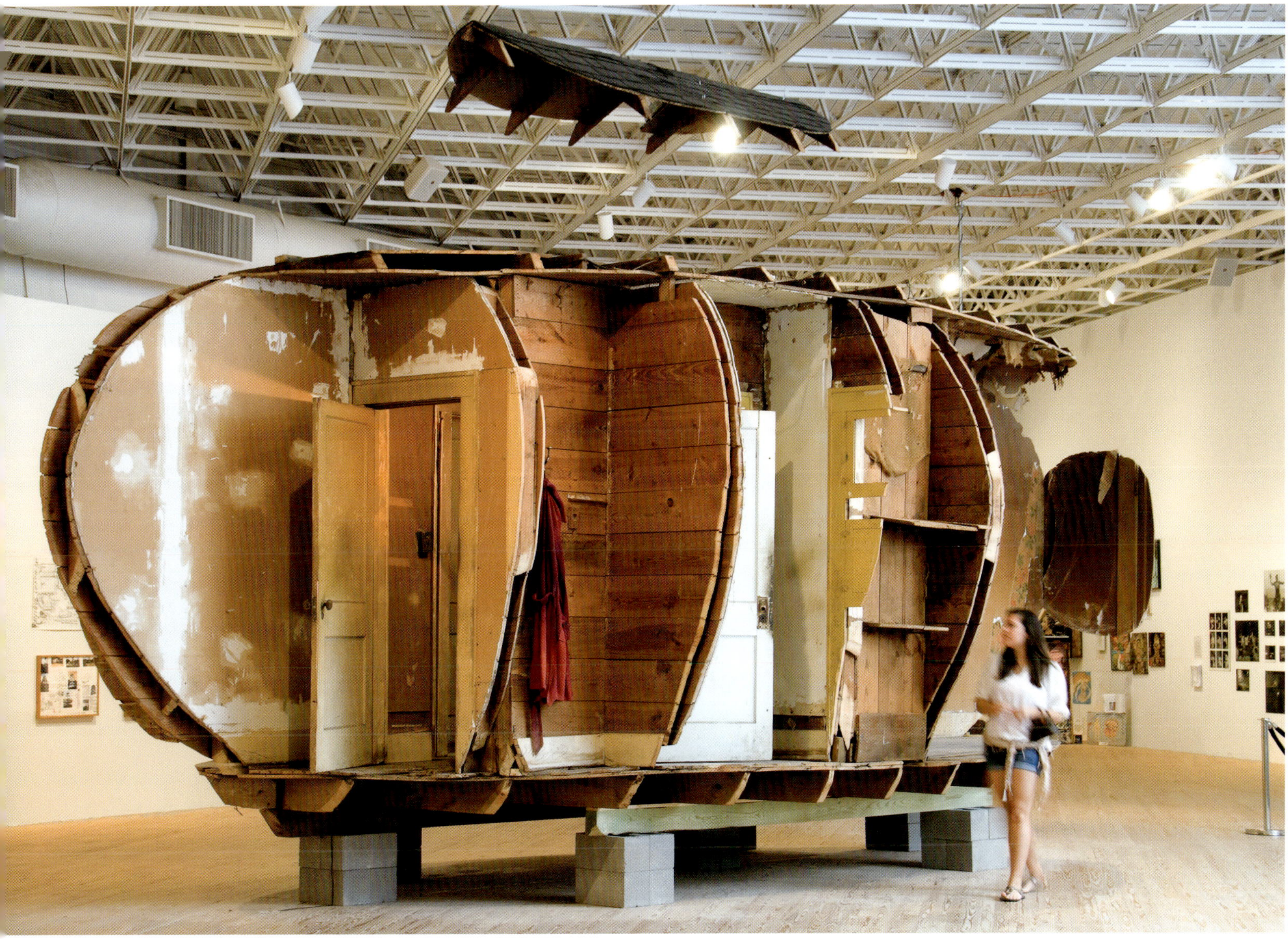

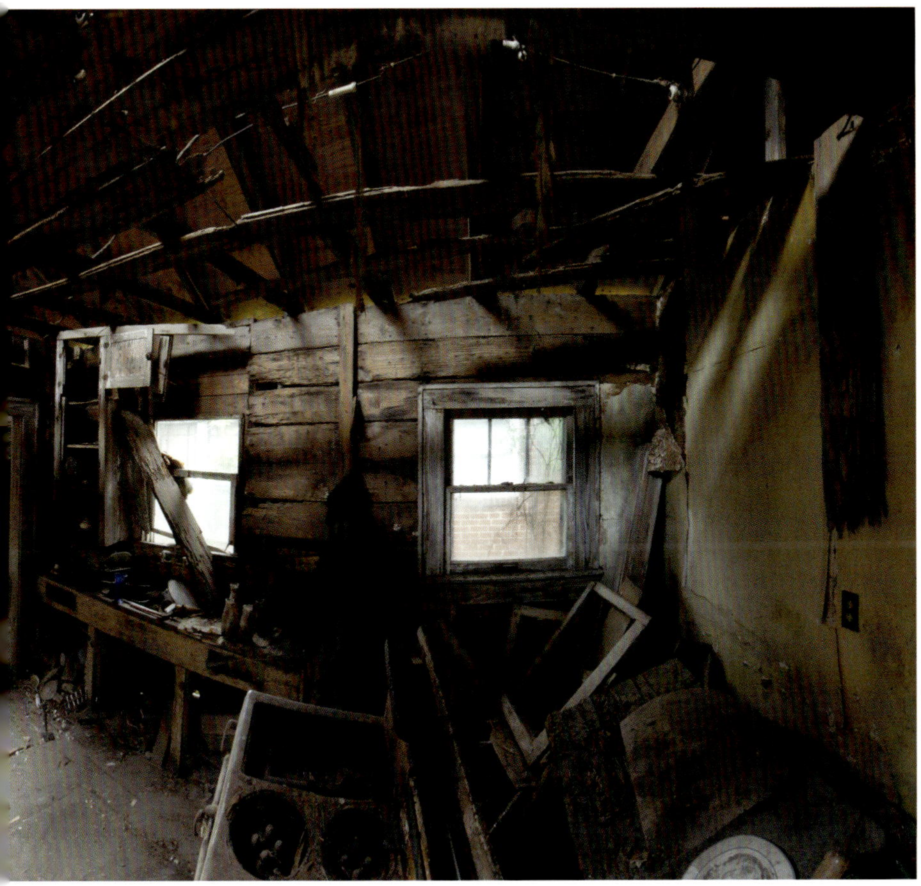

Dan Havel and Dean Ruck
top:
Give and Take, 2009
Reclaimed material from condemned bungalow at
931 Cottage Street, Houston
Approximately 20 x 30 x 15 feet
Installation view, Contemporary Arts Museum Houston

left:
Give and Take, 2009
Interior of condemned bungalow, 931 Cottage Street, Houston
All courtesy the artists and Devin Borden Hiram Butler Gallery, Houston

George Hixson

George Hixson has been the unofficial photographer of the Houston alternative art scene for over thirty years. After growing up in Buffalo and attending college in Connecticut, Hixson hitchhiked west, headed for California. He stopped to visit a friend in Houston in 1981, was offered a job as a photographer at the University of Houston, and has been here since.

Although he holds a degree in photography and film, Hixson says he got his "real art education"[1] among the artists at Commerce Street Artists' Warehouse (CSAW), an artist-run studio and exhibition space where he maintained a studio from 1986 to 1990. While there, he expanded his practice to include painting, assemblage, and even pyrotechnics. In 1989 he burned down the set for a staging of local artist Joel Orr's play *Free Advice* at Little Egypt Gallery, and he blew up the CSAW toilet in his solo performance *Paint Bomb* in 1990.

Every underground scene needs its own documentarian, and Hixson placed himself and his camera in the middle of an astounding number of art events and performances, some staged and some spontaneous, between 1981 and today. Among his sixty-two black-and-white images in *No Zoning* are photographs of Scott Prescott of the Urban Animals in roller skates catching air off a slope on the McKee Street Bridge in 1987; The Art Guys in one of their first performances of *Fifty Things at Once* in 1988; and the mirrored "Shark Car," created by art car pioneer Tom Kennedy, who passed away in early 2009, peeling out from CSAW in 1993 with Houston's gleaming skyline in the distance (shown on this catalogue's cover).

Hixson's photographs appeared in columns he contributed to two of Houston's weekly newspapers. His column "Eye Spy" ran in *Public News* from 1985 to 1998, and his column "9X" ran in *Houston's Other* from 1998 to 2001. As the number of performances and art exhibitions at alternative spaces exploded in the 1980s, these papers were vital to artists and audiences who wanted to learn what was happening. The landscape of artist-built venues changed constantly (many were in houses and vacant structures with no signage), making the newspapers' listings indispensable. Each week the single image of "Eye Spy" reflected what had debuted the previous week, showing what Hixson had seen, where readers had been, or what they had missed.

Houston's cultural landmarks and topography change constantly, and so does its underground scene. In a city that saves so little history, Hixson's archive is a black-and-white treasure trove of the people, places, events, and everyday life in Houston during an especially energetic period.

1. George Hixson, conversation with the author, January 2009.

George Hixson
Mike Scranton, 1998
Gelatin silver print
24 x 17 inches

Scott Prescott and the Urban Animals, McKee Street Bridge, 1987
Gelatin silver print
24 x 20 inches

All courtesy the artist

2001

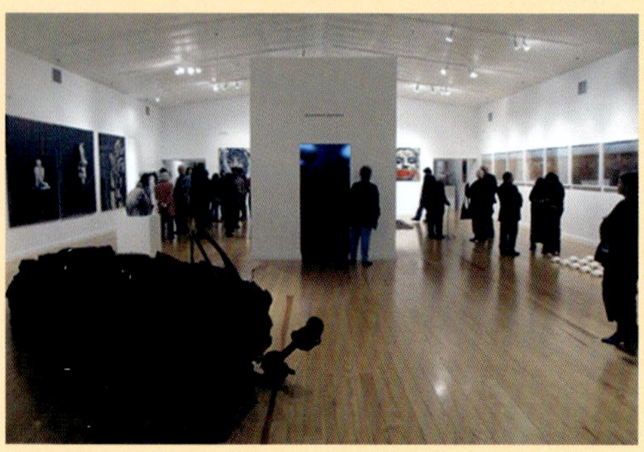

Iraqi Artists in Exile opening at The Station Museum, 2008

The Station Museum
Ann and James Harithas established the Station Museum of Contemporary Art to present topical exhibitions of works by artists from around the world and to serve as a platform for artists to express progressive alternative political and artistic points of view.

Live Oak Friends Meeting House
Live Oak Friends Meeting House was built in a collaboration initiated and organized by Hiram Butler that involved light artist James Turrell, architect Leslie Elkins, and the Live Oak Friends Meeting. Notable for Turrell's open-roof *Skyspace*, this Quaker place of worship, funded largely through the generosity of the arts community, today is open for public viewing every Friday evening.

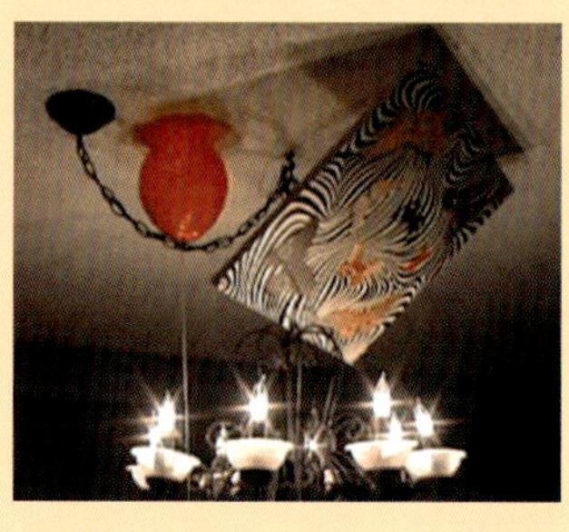

Installation by Bill Davenport hung on the ceiling at *The Million Dollar Hotel* exhibition, 2001

2002

The Million Dollar Hotel
Artist Paul Horn, in collaboration with Dolan Smith, took over the entire top floor of the Holiday Inn Select at Highway 59 and Kirby for the exhibition *The Million Dollar Hotel*. The show brought together more than twenty artists, each exhibiting in a separate room or suite, for a long night of exhibition, performance, and general mayhem.

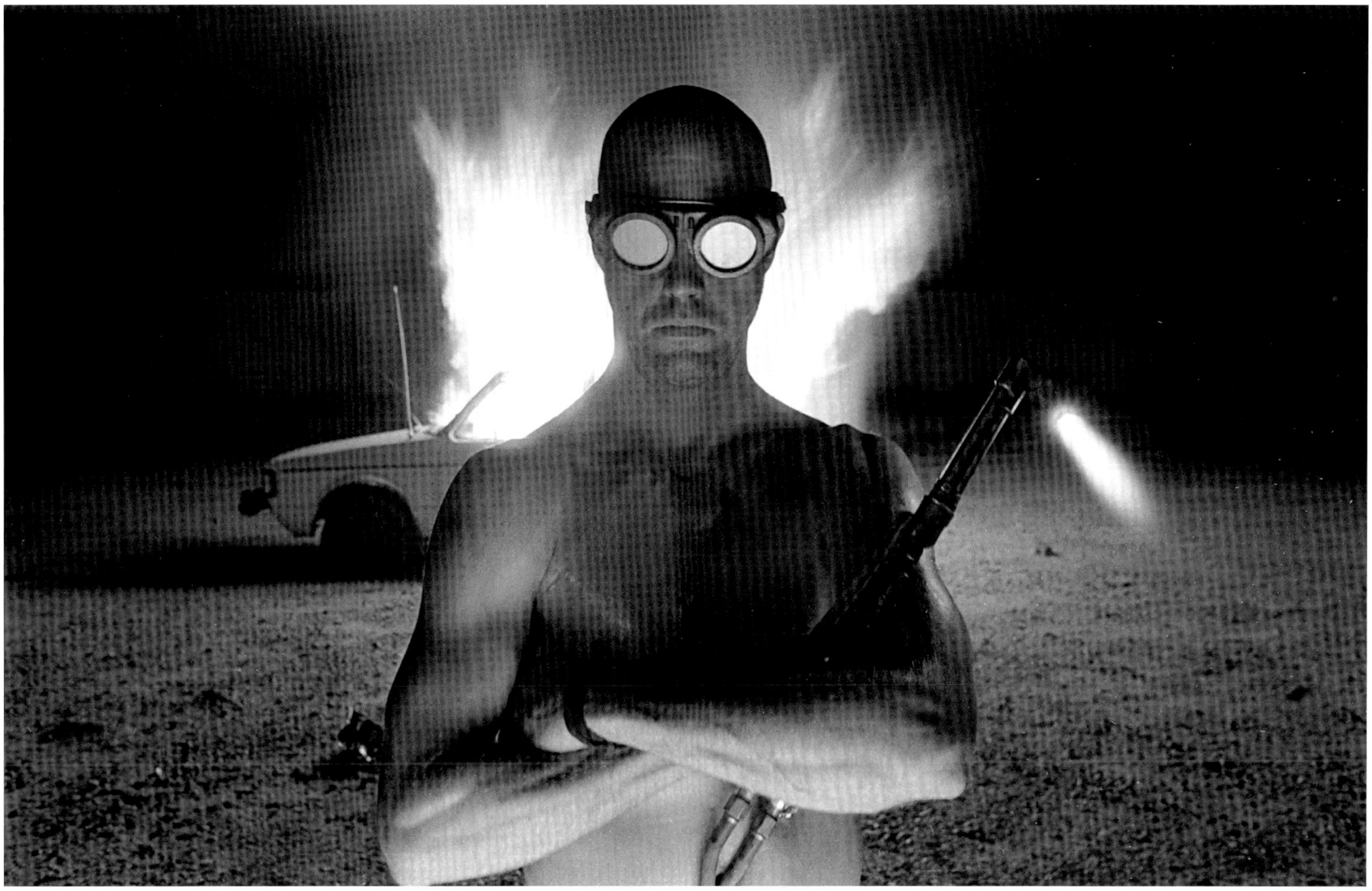

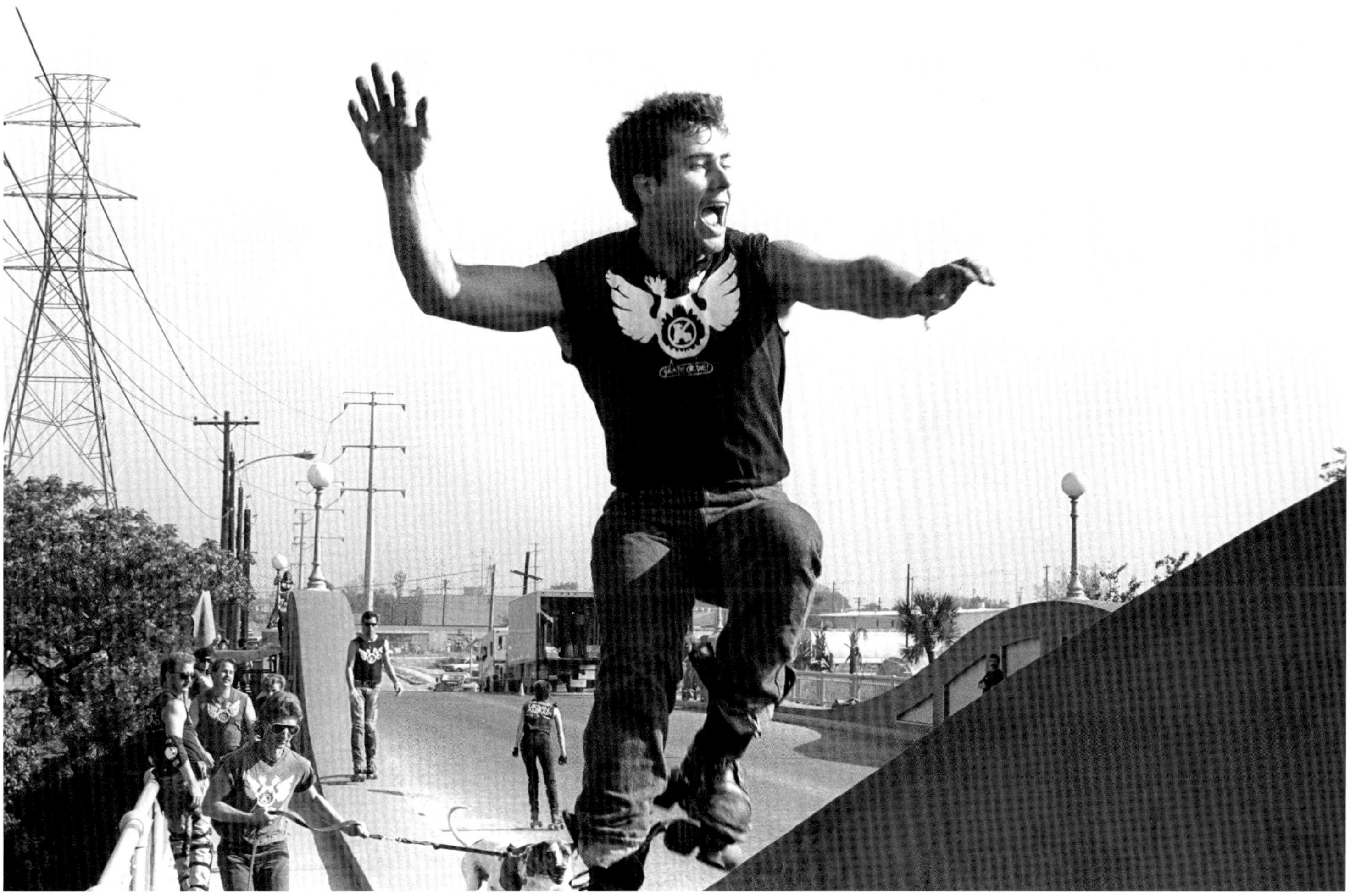

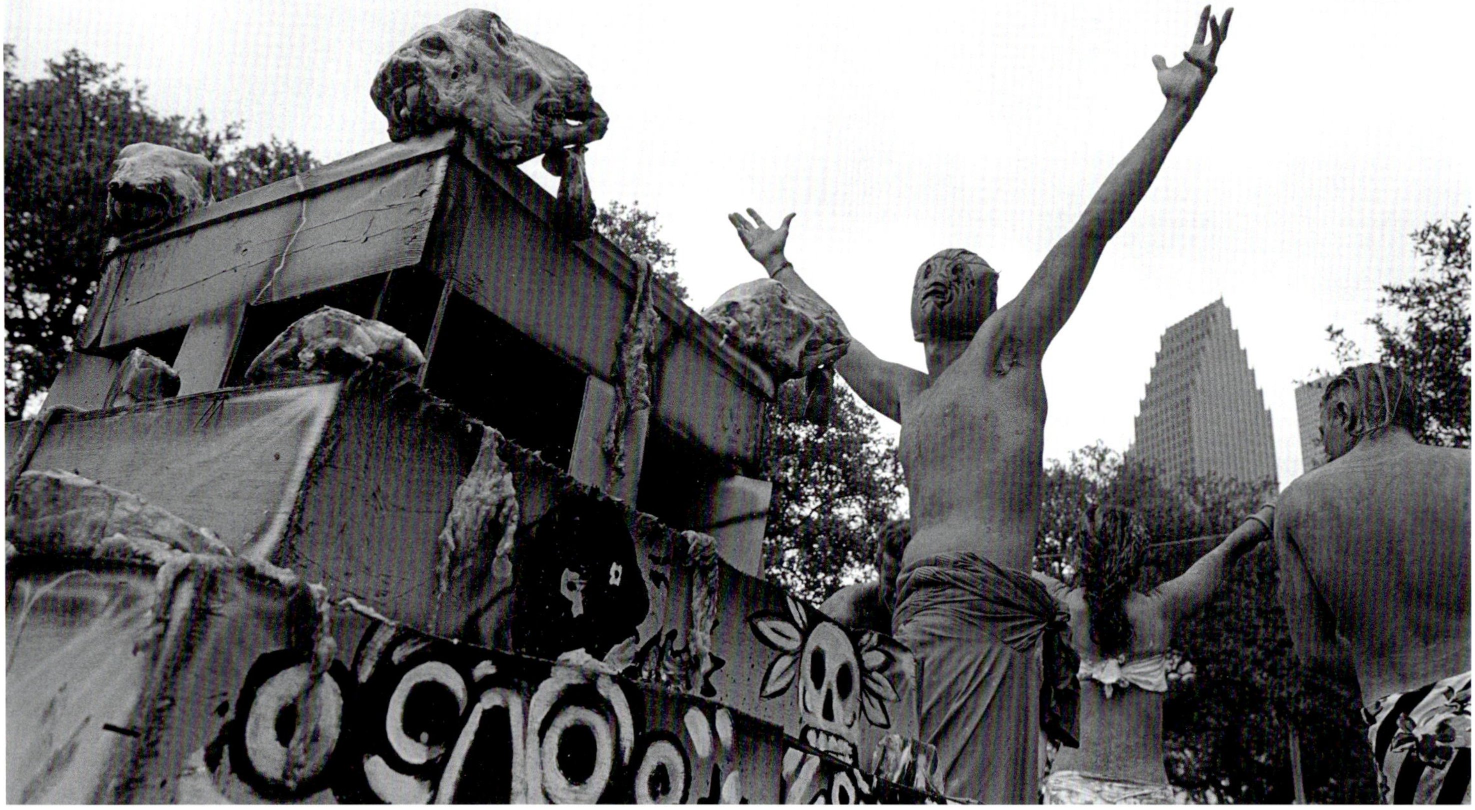

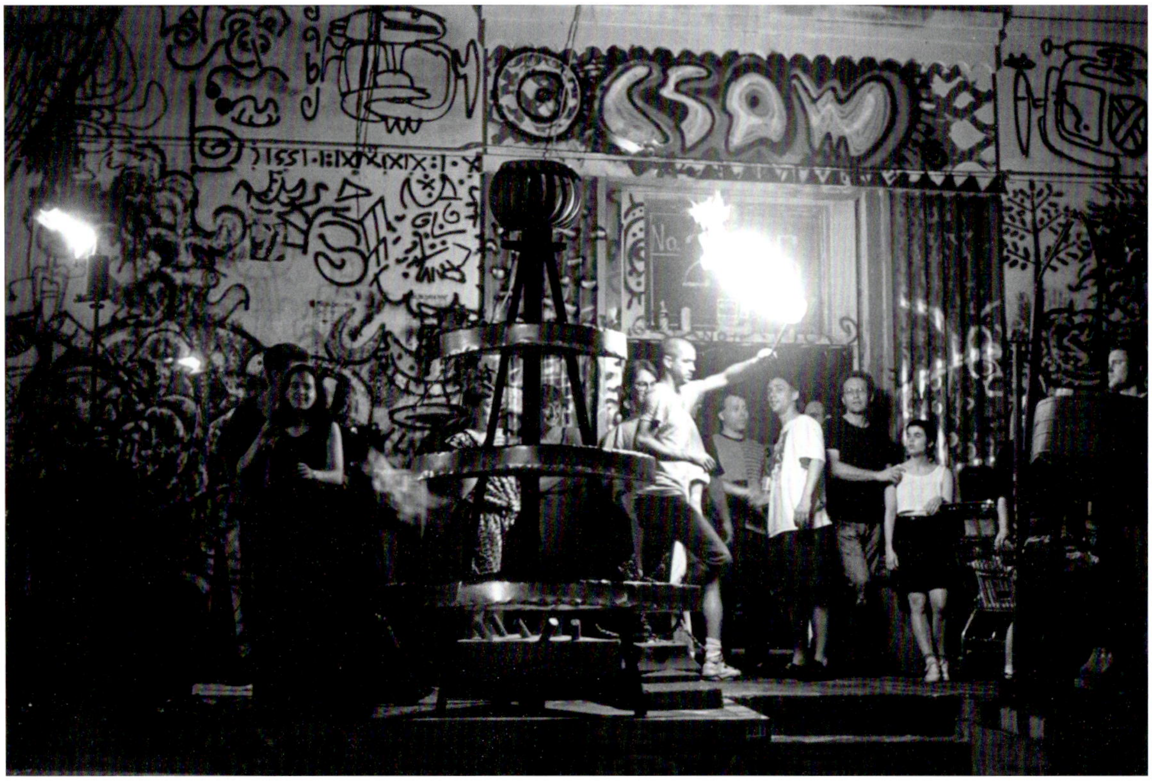

George Hixson
Piazza della Morte (Nestor Topchy's art car, Art Car Parade), 1993

Commerce Street Artists' Warehouse, 1992
Gelatin silver prints
24 x 20 inches
Courtesy the artist

George Hixson
top left and top right:
***Lamar Hotel Demolition*, 1985**
Gelatin silver print
8 x 10 inches (not in exhibition)

***James Bettison*, 1991**
Gelatin silver print
20 x 24 inches

bottom:
62 gelatin silver prints, 1981–2006
Installation view, Contemporary Art Museum Houston, 2009
Dimensions variable

All courtesy the artist

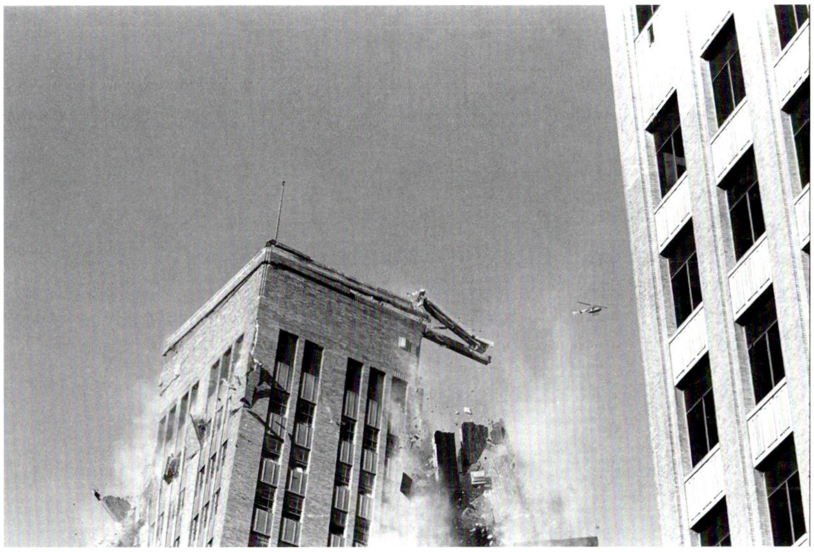

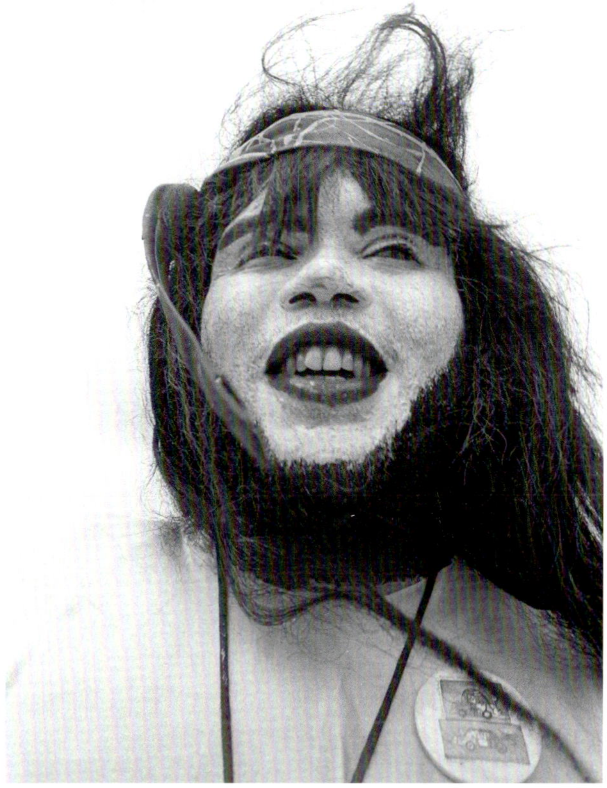

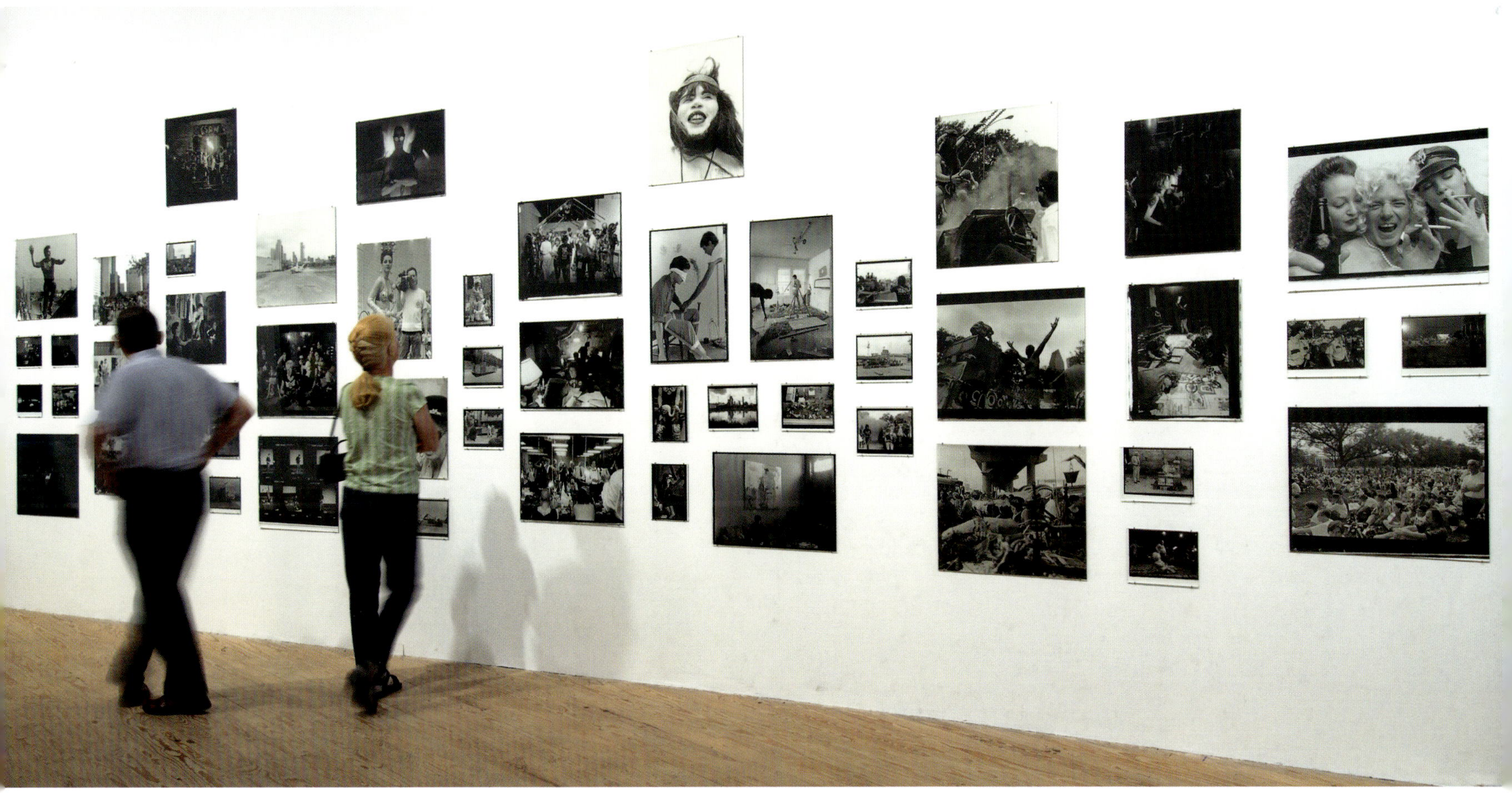

Lauren Kelley

With humor and heart, Lauren Kelley employs a variety of media, including sculpture, drawing, photography, and video, to explore perceptions and expressions of female and black identity. Her photography and video works offer satirical portrayals of characters in their efforts to navigate a hypersexualized, materialistic world.

The stories Kelley tells in her art are often based on events in the lives of her friends and family, and the environments she creates are sometimes drawn from her own experiences growing up in Houston. Using elaborate small-scale sets and brown-skinned Barbie-like dolls in stop-motion animation, she creates short video narratives in which female leads confront such social themes as dating, relationships among co-workers, body image, unplanned parenthood, weddings, and family dynamics. Kelley sometimes augments the dolls' features and attire. For example, in *Big Gurl* (2006), she used clay to enhance a doll's lips, causing them to expand until they filled the entire frame, suggesting how the character's self-image slowly aligns with others' stereotypical perceptions of her.

For this exhibition, Kelley debuts an episode from a series of animated videos entitled *Limited Edition Logic*, which she is currently producing with the intention of airing them biweekly on a Houston public-access cable television channel. The episode, *Prototypical Obsession/Oppression* (2009), chronicles a day in the life of several female flight attendants who just cannot work well together, clashing over differences rooted in their varying ages and ethnic backgrounds.

This and other episodes that Kelley is making for broadcast are undeniably comic despite the gravity of their subjects. "I think I'm funniest when I'm trying to be serious," Kelley says. Yet she hopes to deliver at the end of each episode what she calls "a thought-provoking punch line."[1] By using television to broadcast her art, she will be able to engage Houstonians at large in their living rooms, conveying her messages beyond traditional gallery spaces to a wider audience. Using smart art and humor to invade a mindless medium, Kelley's works subvert the stereotypes and materialistic lifestyles that other sitcoms perpetuate.

1. Lauren Kelley, e-mail correspondence with author, January 2009.

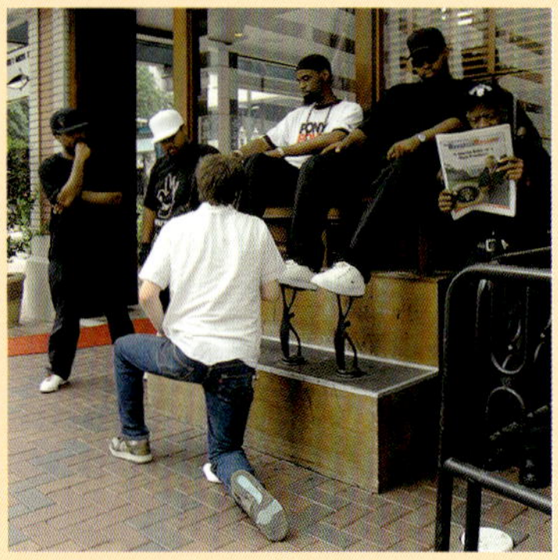

Otabenga Jones & Associates, *Self Portrait as N.W.A.*, 2006

2002

Otabenga Jones & Associates
Otabenga Jones & Associates, the Houston-based artist collective of Dawolu Jabari Anderson, Jamal Cyrus, Kenya Evans, and Robert Pruitt, began staging artworks and installations dealing with African American social and historical issues. The group's work was featured in the 2006 Whitney Biennial.

2003

Workshop Houston
Workshop Houston was founded by artists Zach Moser, Katy Goodman, Seth Capron, and Benjamin Mason. Today it has five workshops in Houston's Third Ward that provide resources and support for young people: a do-it-yourself bike repair shop, a welding and metal fabrication shop, the Beat Shop for music production, a fashion design shop, and the Scholar Shop for tutoring and academic enrichment.

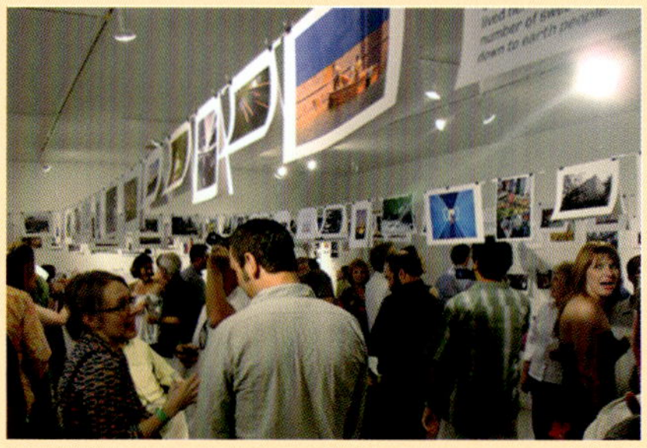

Party celebrating the *HIWI: The Book* release, with enlarged pages from the book, 2007

2004

HIWI (Houston. It's Worth It.)
Dave Thompson and Randy Twaddle created HIWI (Houston. It's Worth It.), launching a website where Houstonians could express in their own words why Houston is worth it. Later HIWI partnered with the Houston Center for Photography to present the open call exhibition *Houston. It's Worth It.—Show Us Why*. The exhibitors received and displayed over six hundred images. Created from the exhibition and website, the landmark book *Houston. It's Worth It. (HIWI: The Book)* was published in 2007.

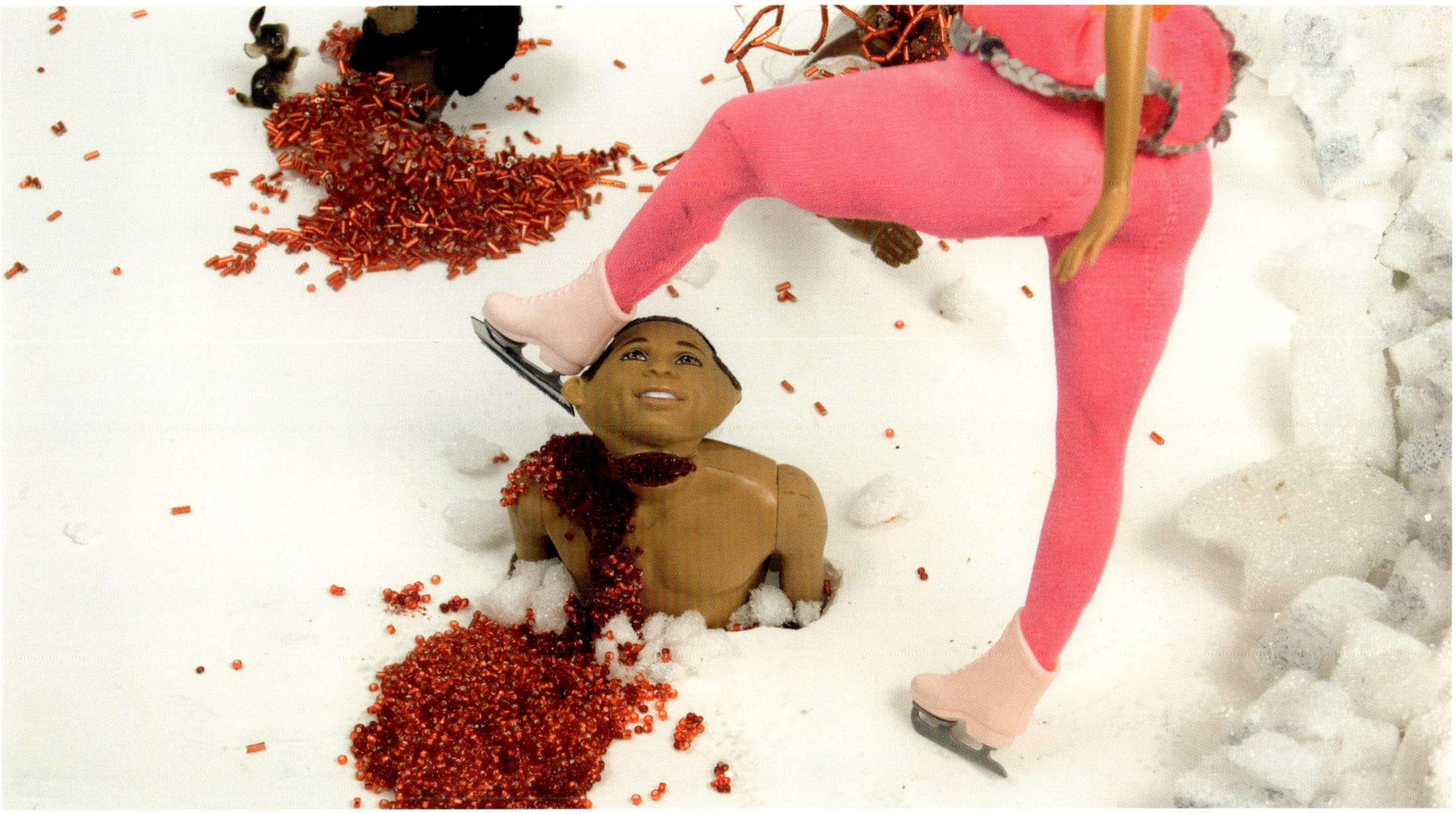

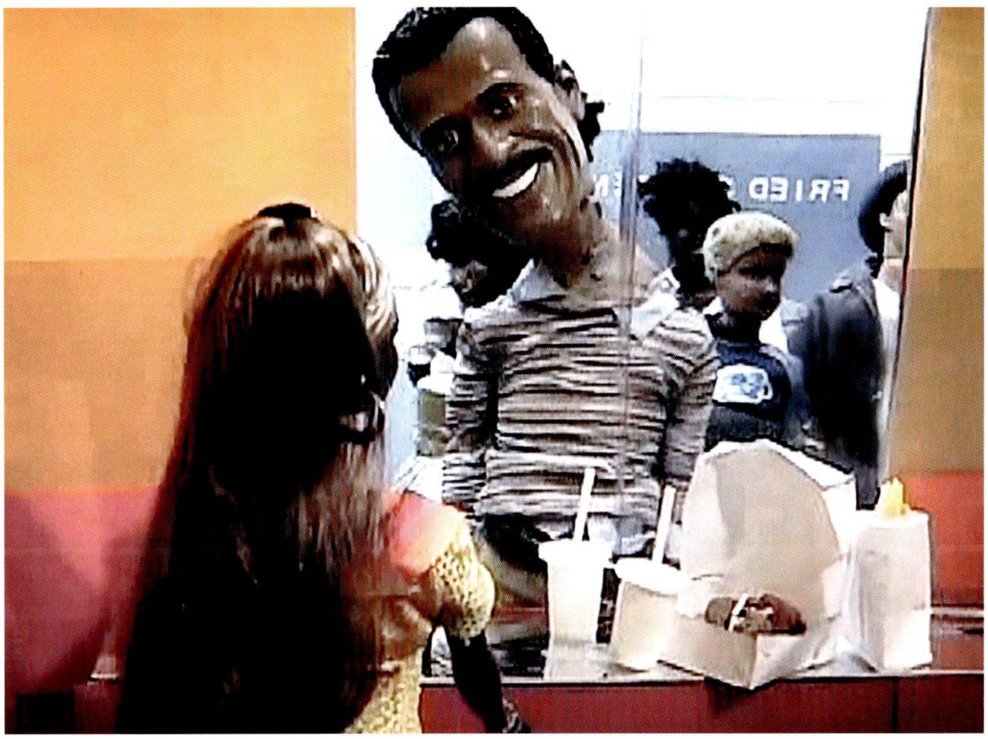

Lauren Kelley
Twice, 2007
Lightjet print
16 x 20 inches

Big Gurl (still), 2006
DVD video, running time: 8:12 minutes, color, sound
All courtesy the artist

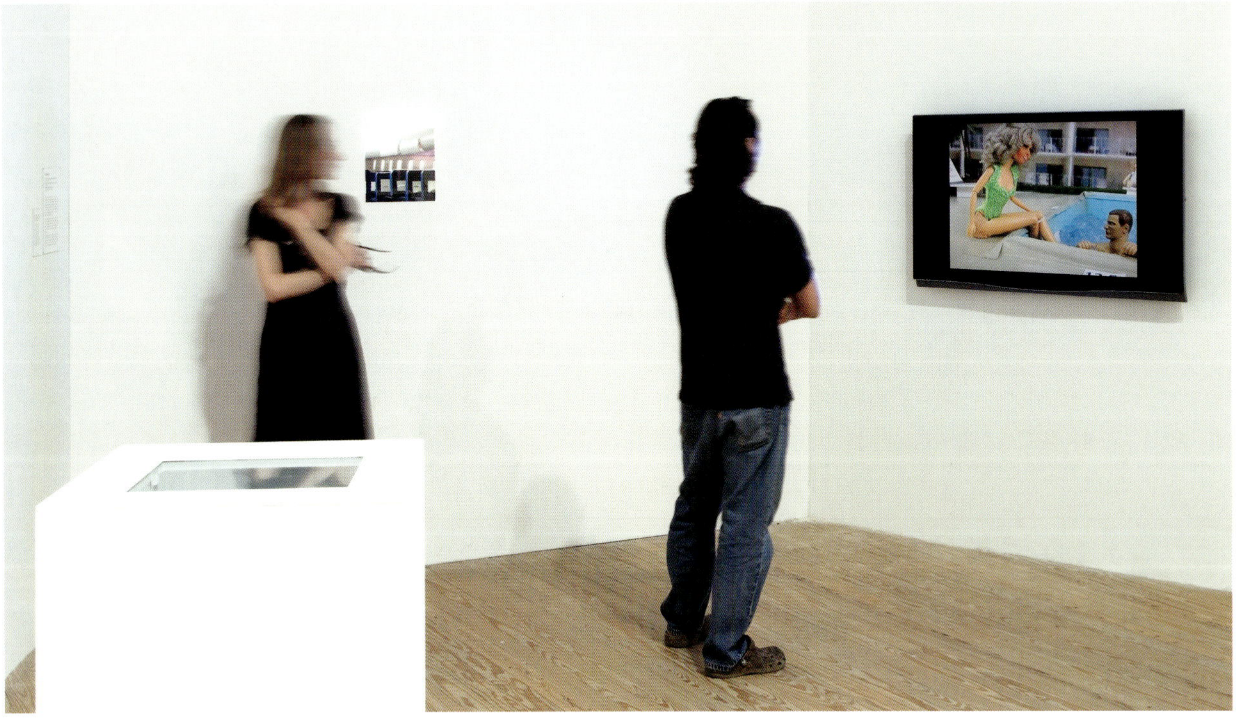

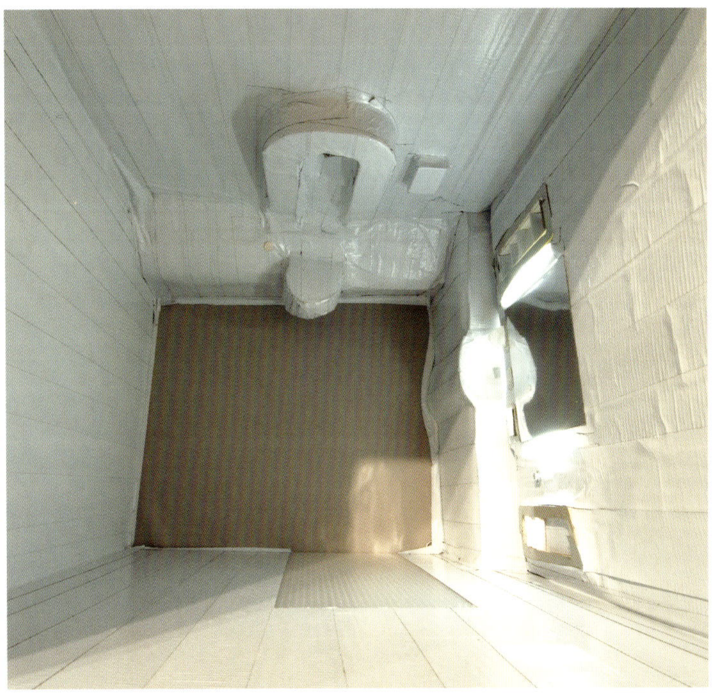

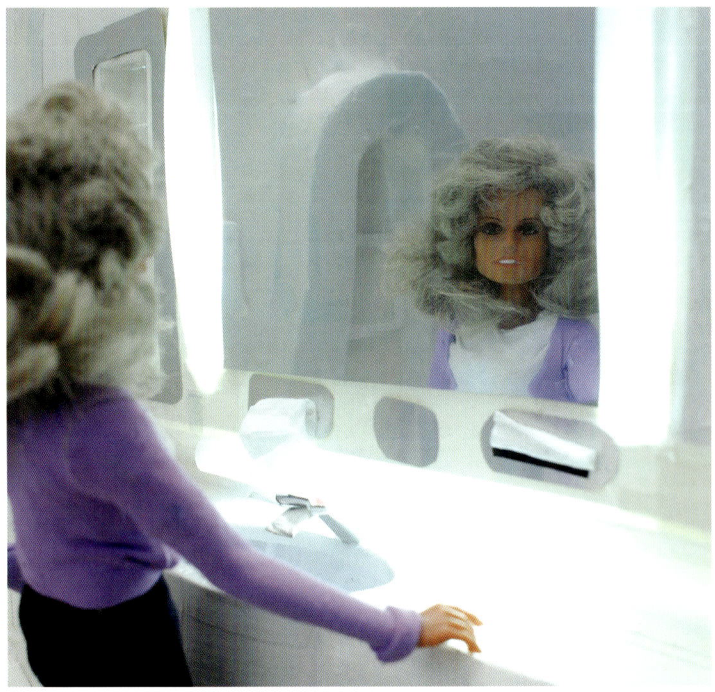

Lauren Kelley

top:
Prototypical Obsession/Oppression, 2009
DVD video, running time: 4:32 minutes, color, sound
Installation view, Contemporary Arts Museum Houston

bottom left:
Prototypical Obsession/Oppression (bathroom set), 2007
Mixed media and lights in pedestal
36 x 30 x 30 inches
Installation detail, Contemporary Arts Museum Houston

bottom right:
Prototypical Obsession/Oppression (still), 2009
DVD video, running time: 4:32 minutes, color, sound
All courtesy the artist

opposite:
Prototypical Obsession/Oppression (airplane set), 2008
Mixed media and lights in drywall
36 x 36 x 60 inches
Installation detail, Contemporary Arts Museum Houston
All courtesy the artist

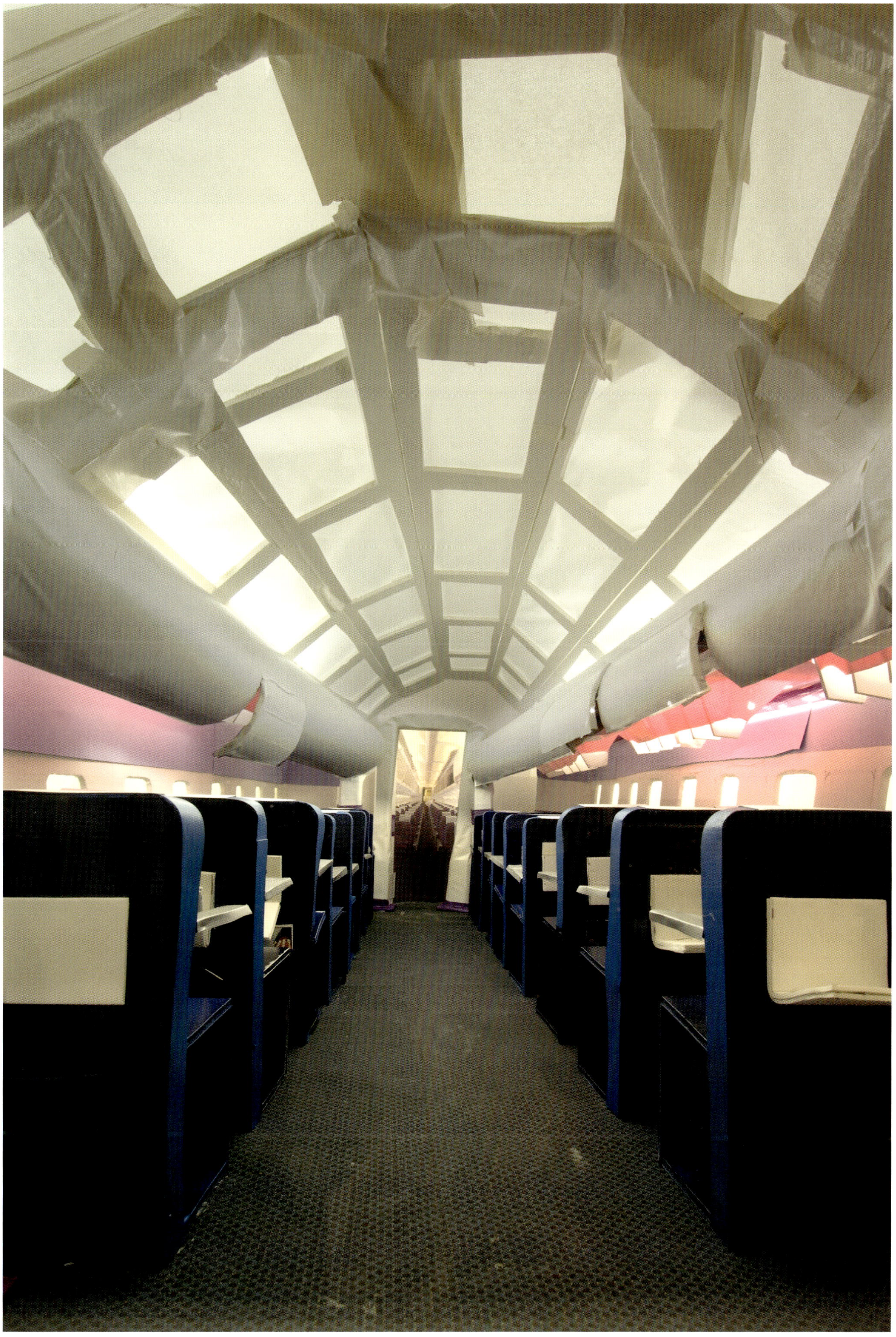

KnittaPlease (Magda Sayeg et al.)

The craft art collective KnittaPlease began in 2005 when Magda Sayeg wrapped the door handle of her clothing boutique Raye in Houston's Montrose district with some of her unfinished knitting. The act of transforming something cold, gray, and metal into something warm, colorful, and soft opened her eyes to other possibilities. "I looked across the street," she says, "and thought, I want to cover that stop sign."[1] Along with a friend, she "yarn-bombed" the stop sign post, delighting passersby and giving the utilitarian street fixture personality, making it irresistible to touch. With this act, the KnittaPlease crew was born.

The group quickly attracted other members, who assumed noms-de-knit such as PolyCotN, GrannySQ, and MascuKnitity. They worked under cover of night to adorn Houston's tree trunks, bridge supports, and other easily overlooked aspects of the urban landscape. Sayeg, who relishes the ways these interventions make anonymous forms come alive and bring joy to those who see them, reminisces fondly, "I remember the first time I put a hat on a fire hydrant."

Sayeg cultivates the outlaw aspect of the group by giving it a faux "gangsta" name and finds inspiration in the work of artists Barry McGee and Banksy, who utilize spray-paint graffiti and tagging as part of their art. Yet many people find KnittaPlease's creations more delightful than defacing, which means that, unlike other graffiti, the works often remain undisturbed until the fibers deteriorate. The group has even been invited by cities such as Paris, Mexico City, Seattle, and Tilberg in the Netherlands to "tag" them without consequence.

With Sayeg serving as the constant in the group while other members come and go, KnittaPlease has widened its circle of activity to cover everything from rocks on the Great Wall of China, to the interior door handles of taxi cabs in New York City, to standpipes, street sign posts, and many other objects in Los Angeles, San Francisco, Montreal, Milan, and Stockholm. In 2008 the group expanded the scale of its projects when it knitted together thrift-store afghan blankets to cover an entire bus in Mexico City.

Continuing their unique brand of smiling subversion, KnittaPlease has "yarn-bombed" the railing on the CAMH's exterior terrace for the *No Zoning* exhibition, as well as the front desk inside the Museum, using both handmade and ready-made knitted materials. Despite the increasing legitimacy and expanding scale of these projects, KnittaPlease continues its clandestine efforts to add color and texture to Houston, contributing quite literally to the city's funky urban fabric.

1. This and subsequent quotes by Magda Sayeg are from a conversation with the author, February 2008.

KnittaPlease
opposite top:
Mexico City Bus, 2008
Knitted and crocheted yarn, glue, city bus
Courtesy the artists and Absolut Vodka

2004

Billboard Series
While its gallery was undergoing renovation, Lawndale Art Center moved its programming to the streets with the Billboard series. A billboard at Highway 59 and Montrose Boulevard provided a venue from June through November for the works of five artists: Ryan Molloy's *The Jones' Got Platinum Doorknobs*; Katrina Moorhead's *Sampled Sky*; Fannie Taper's *Trust*; Mark Wade's *Manifest Destiny*; C. Andrew Byrd's *Hero 1K*; and Danny Yahev-Brown's untitled project.

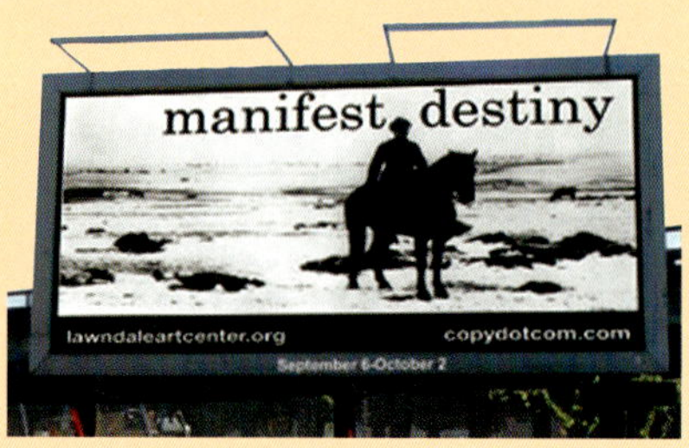

Mark Wade's *Manifest Destiny*, Lawndale Art Center Billboard series, 2004

2005

Sketch Klubb
Sketch Klubb was organized to meet bimonthly and produce drawings and a 'zine. The group now counts fourteen members, including artists Patrick Phipps, J. Michael Stovall, Rene Cruz, Michael Harwell, Lane Herachtus, and Nick Meriwether, and bookseller Russell Etchen. They have produced over forty 'zines and have compiled an anthology through lulu.com.

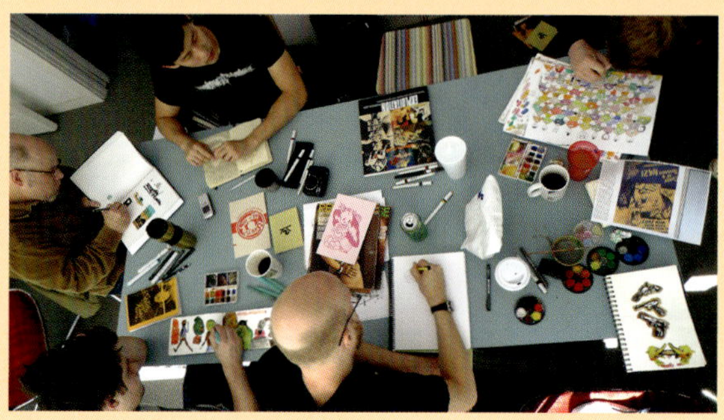

Sketch Klubb members at a bimonthly meet-up, 2006.

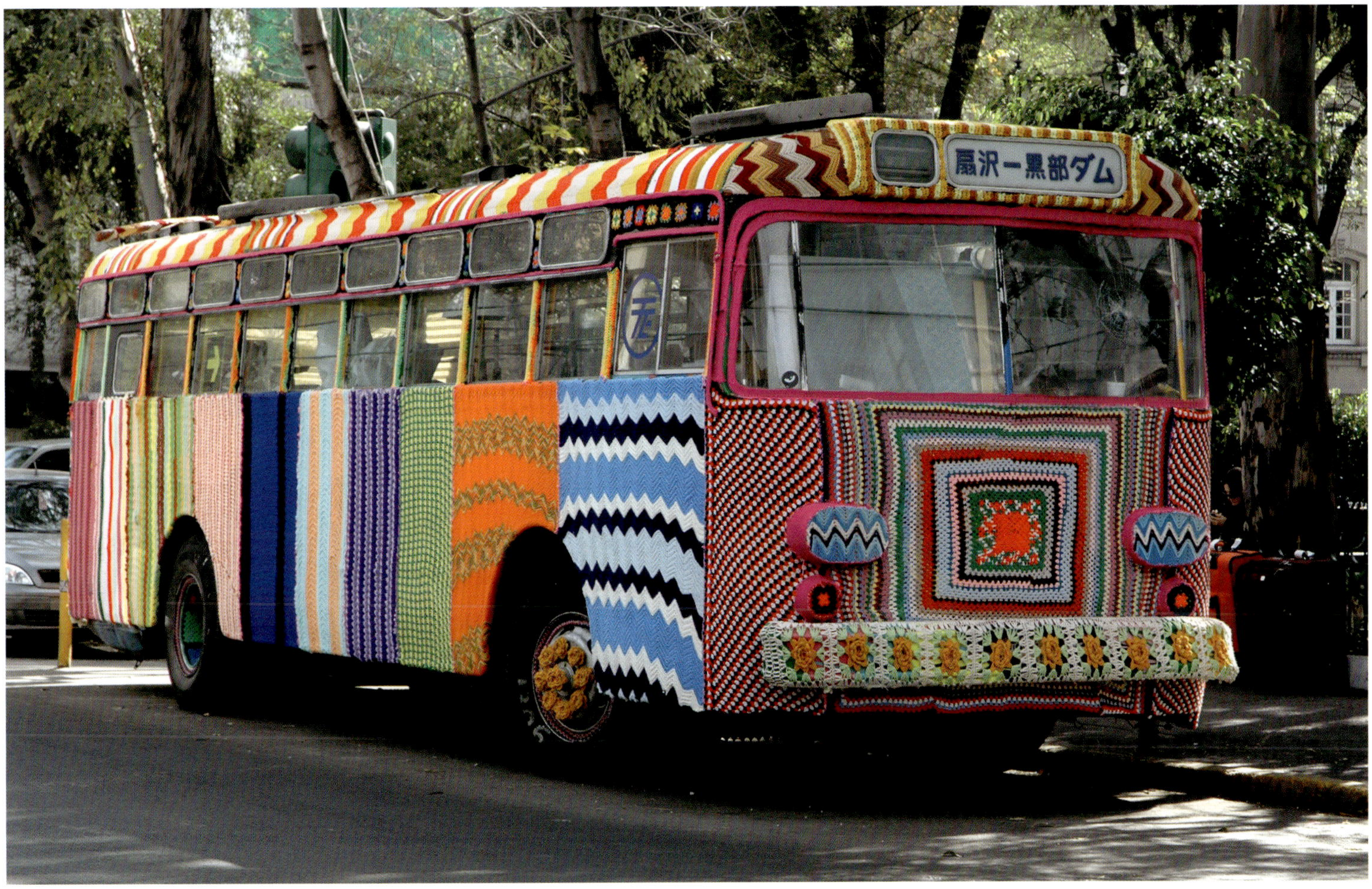

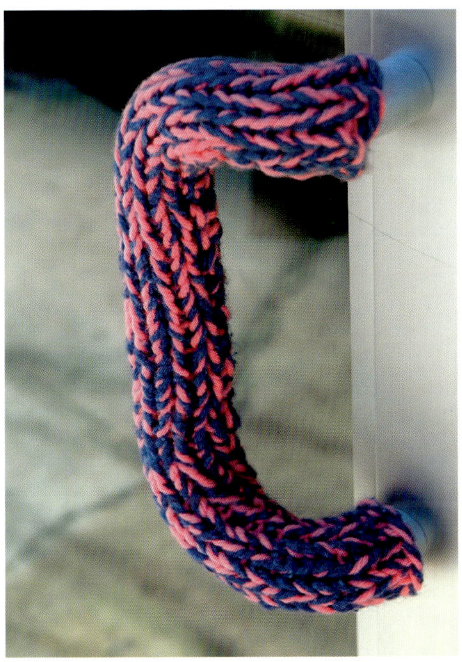

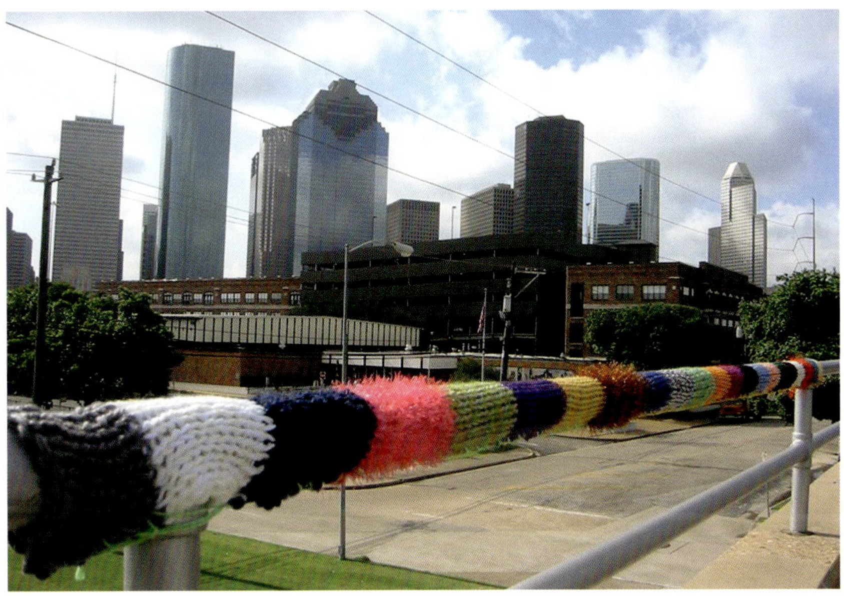

KnittaPlease
Tagged Door Handle (Knitta Alpha), Houston, 2005
Knitted yarn

Tagged Bridge Over Memorial Drive, Houston, 2007
Knitted yarn, ink on paper label
All courtesy the artists

KnittaPlease (Magda Sayeg et al.)

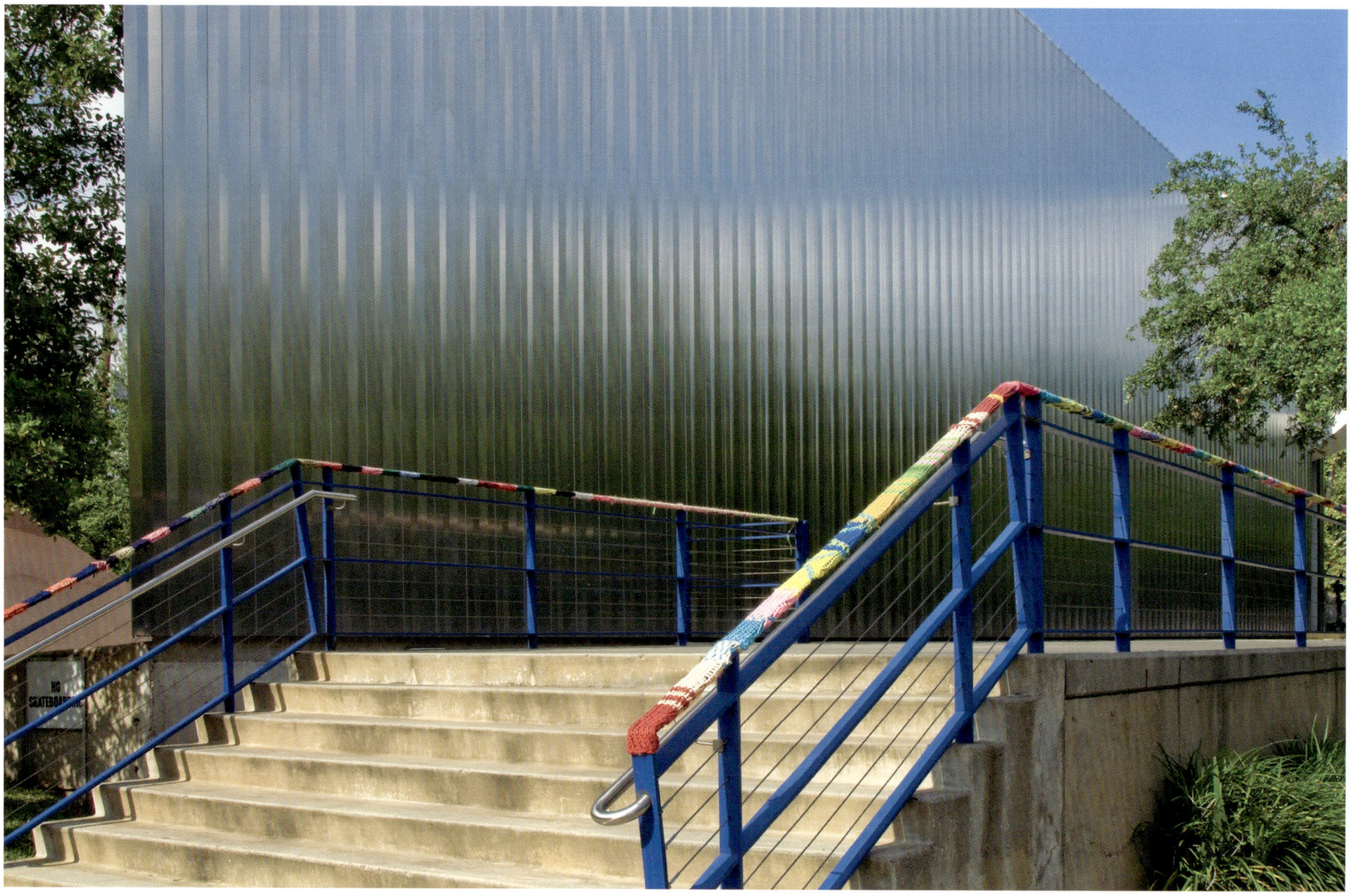

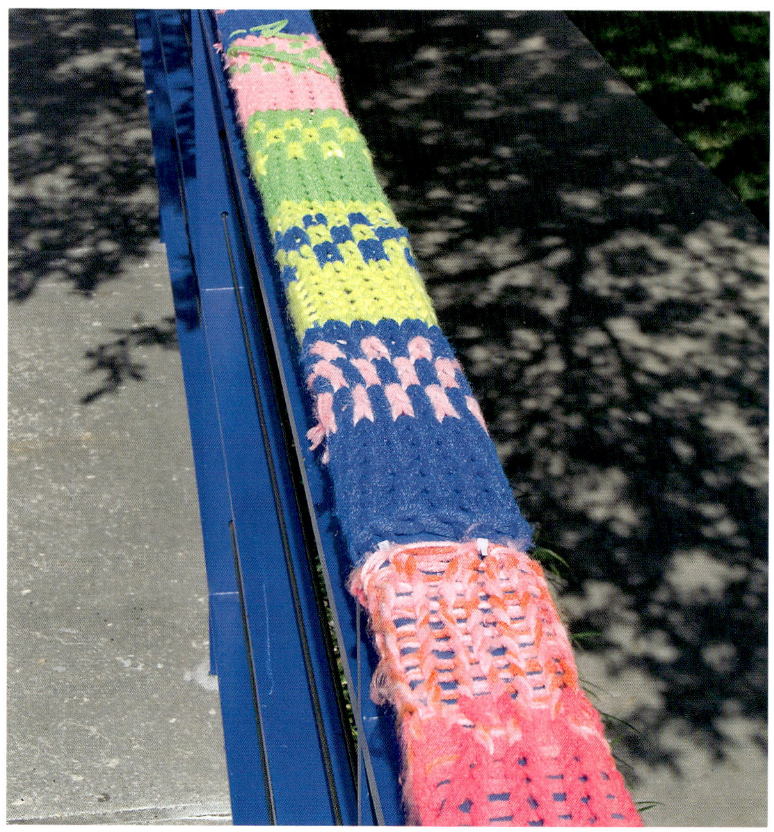

KnittaPlease (Magda Sayeg with Peggy Fergus and Michael Sayeg)
Untitled, 2009
Knitted and crocheted yarn, zip ties, CAMH terrace railing
194 feet x 4 inches
Installation views, Contemporary Arts Museum Houston
Courtesy the artists

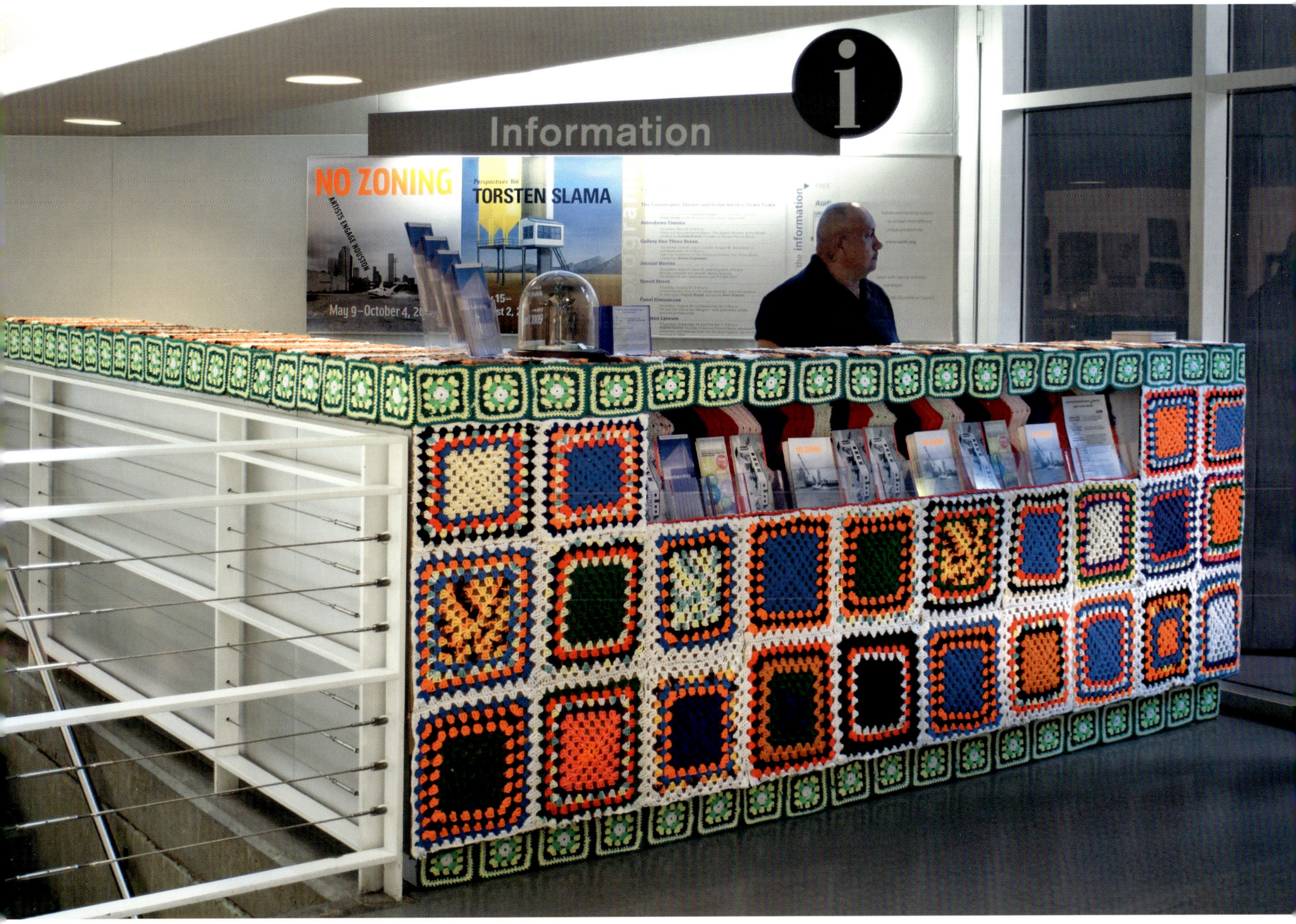

Untitled, 2009
Knitted and crocheted yarn, cardboard, glue,
on CAMH information desk
$4^{1/2}$ x $125^{1/2}$ x 142 inches
Courtesy the artists

Eric Leshinsky

Eric Leshinsky is an architect who employs temporary structures, graphic design, and urban studies scholarship to investigate public spaces. Before moving to Houston in 2002 to enter the graduate program at the Rice School of Architecture, he lived in Baltimore and New York City. There the complex push-and-pull between the wish to preserve historic buildings and the demand to serve new public needs sparked his interest in studying architecture as an expanded field that includes not only individual structures but also the entirety of city life. During a pivotal research trip to the former Yugoslavia, he began developing theoretical architecture projects that explored peoples' collective memories and cultures. Social relations became the inspiration for his innovative architectural practice.

During his four years in Houston, Leshinsky lived in the Museum District (he is now based in Baltimore). He was struck by the fact that the neighborhood, whose name connotes conservation and history, was changing rapidly due to redevelopment. His initiation of the interactive project and website *Museum for Missing Places* (2005–06) was in part a response to the dynamics of his immediate neighborhood and in part a way to go beyond his formal academic training and engage with other Houstonians directly through the subject of land use.

The *Museum for Missing Places* is designed to provoke dialogue through online exhibitions that, he says, "propose alternative ways of mapping the present condition of a city in the context of rapid and unregulated urban change and the uncertainty of enduring architectural landmarks."[1] The "missing" of the museum's title refers both to the lack of spaces dedicated to public activity in Houston and to the architectural features we often ignore or for which we have no names. For example, Leshinsky asks his online visitors probing questions: "What does it take to turn a Houston esplanade into a functioning public space?" "With virtually no laws for the preservation of historic landmarks...what happens if we tweak our understanding of architectural monuments to include places that already exist in Houston as personal landmarks?" "Vacant lots are created in Houston...at an astounding rate.... Can these lots be seen as something more than absence?"

Leshinsky has updated his website, www.missing-places.org, for *No Zoning*. Viewers can visit and respond to the site from the computer in the gallery or from their own computers at home. The eight *Museum for Missing Places* exhibitions include *Re-Districting*, which debates where the Museum District begins and ends; *Event: Passing Thru*, which proposes a drive-thru recycling center in Houston as a potential public meeting place; and *Valuing Vacancy*, a campaign to interrogate the vacant lots of Midtown by erecting signs that ask passersby, "What was here? What should be here? What do you know?" By archiving, analyzing, and otherwise making permanent the constant state of change in Houston, Leshinsky's *Museum of Missing Places* performs a crucial public service—one perhaps equal to the acts of art and history preservation performed by the real-world institutions in Houston's Museum District.

1. This and all subsequent quotes by Eric Leshinsky are from http://www.missing-places.org (accessed March 26, 2009).

2005

Cynthia Woods Mitchell Center for the Arts
The Cynthia Woods Mitchell Center for the Arts, a center for artistic collaboration at the University of Houston, presented its inaugural performance, *DUGOUT III: WARBOY (and the backboard blues)*, a musical theatre piece written and directed by multidisciplinary artist Terry Allen. Featuring original music by Terry Allen, Richard Bowden, and Lloyd Maines, it starred veteran actress Jo Harvey Allen.

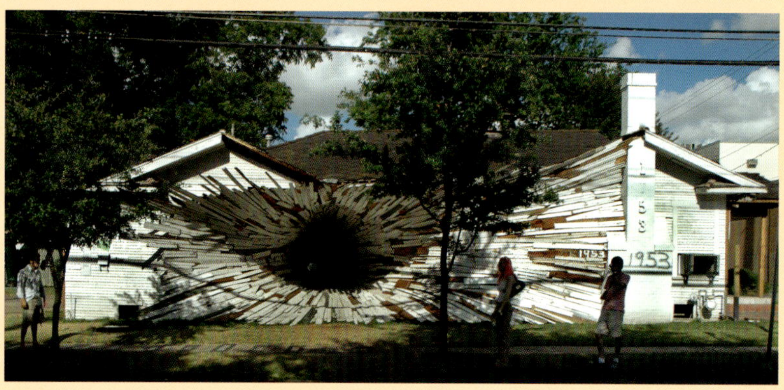

Dan Havel and Dean Ruck's *Inversion*, 2005

Inversion
Sculptors Dan Havel and Dean Ruck altered two buildings owned by the Art League of Houston on the corner of Montrose Boulevard and Willard Street. The exterior skins of the houses were peeled off and used to create a large vortex that funneled into the small central hallway connecting the two buildings and eventually exited through a small hole into an adjacent courtyard. *Inversion* has become one of Houston's most well-known, albeit vanished, sculptures. The structure was later demolished to make way for a new Art League building.

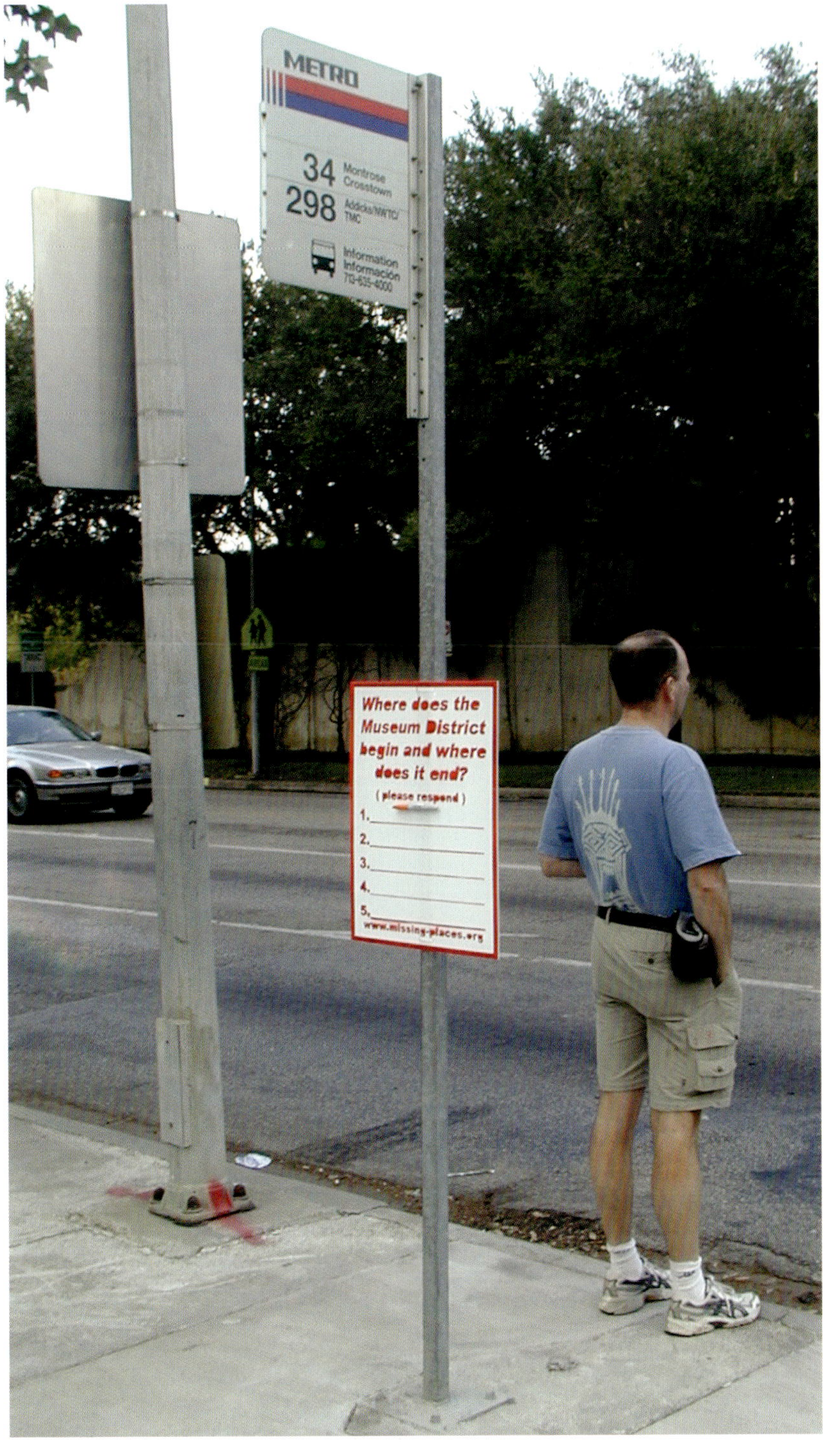

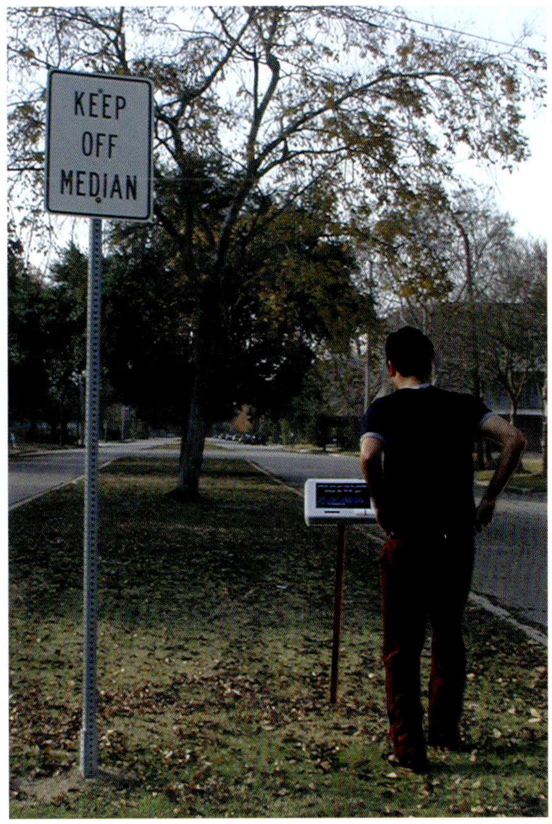

Eric Leshinsky
Museum for Missing Places (photograph of poster mounted on bus stop, Montrose Boulevard at Bissonnet Street, Houston, from ***Exhibit 2: Re-districting***), 2005–06
Interactive website: www.missing-places.org

Museum for Missing Places (photograph of signs erected on Houston esplanades from ***Exhibit 7: This is between you and me***), 2005–06
Interactive website: www.missing-places.org
All courtesy the artist

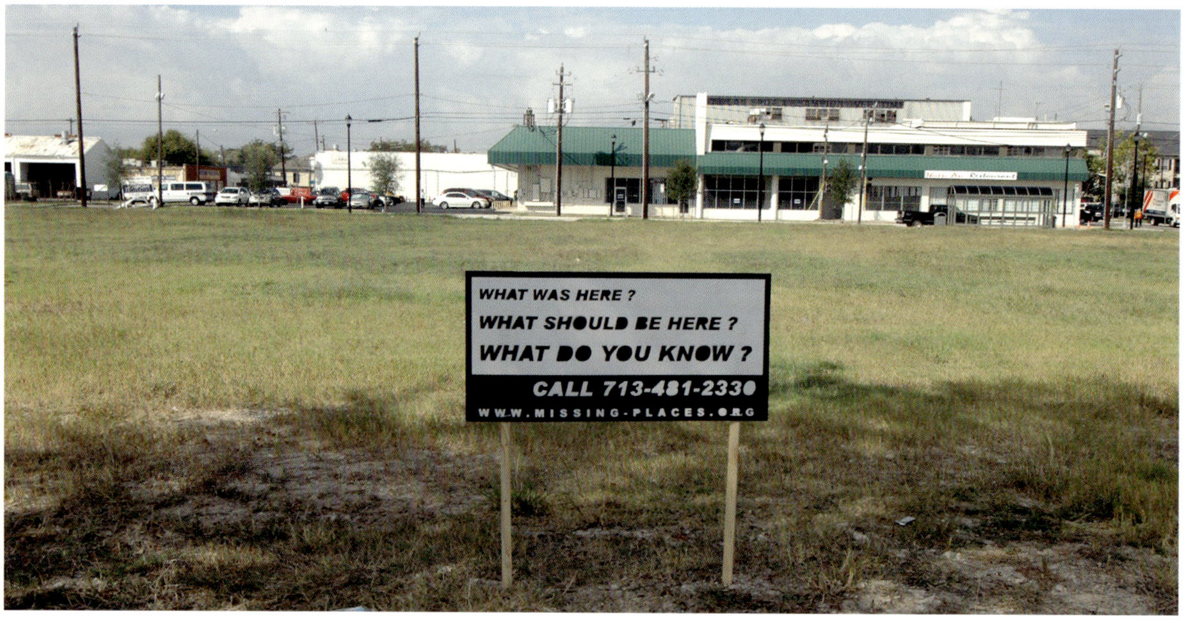

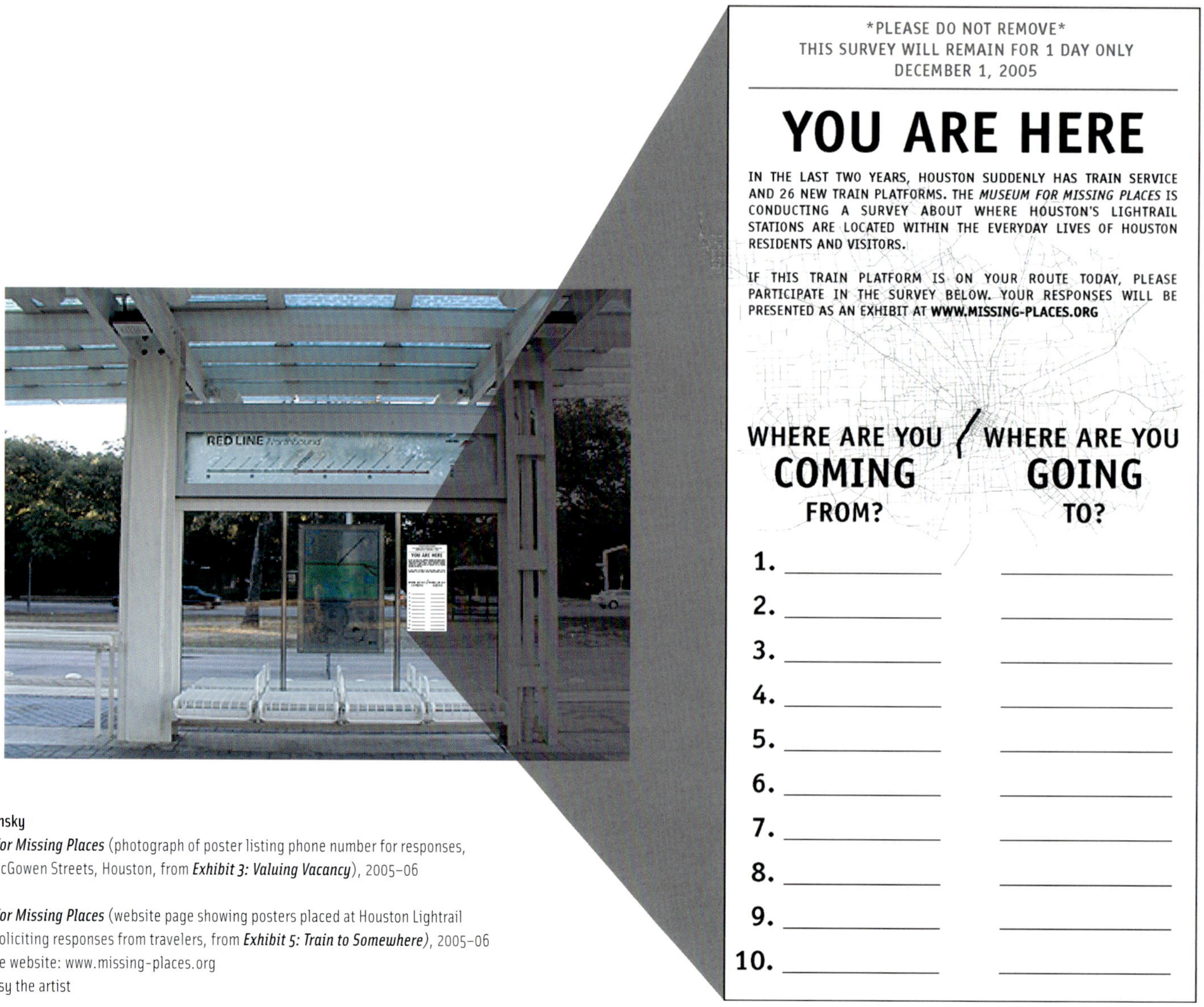

Eric Leshinsky
Museum for Missing Places (photograph of poster listing phone number for responses, Main at McGowen Streets, Houston, from ***Exhibit 3: Valuing Vacancy***), 2005–06

Museum for Missing Places (website page showing posters placed at Houston Lightrail stations soliciting responses from travelers, from ***Exhibit 5: Train to Somewhere***), 2005–06
Interactive website: www.missing-places.org
All courtesy the artist

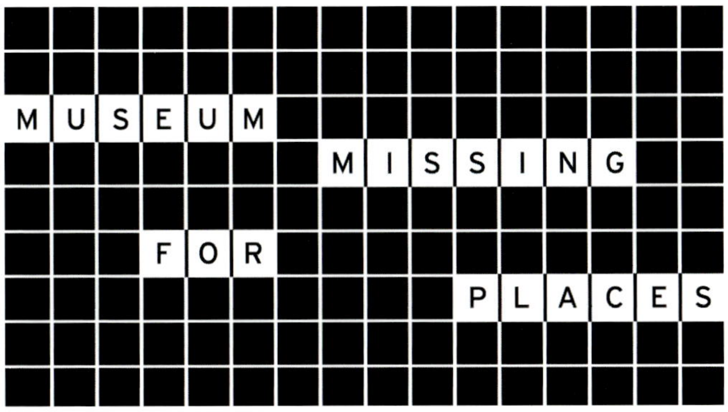

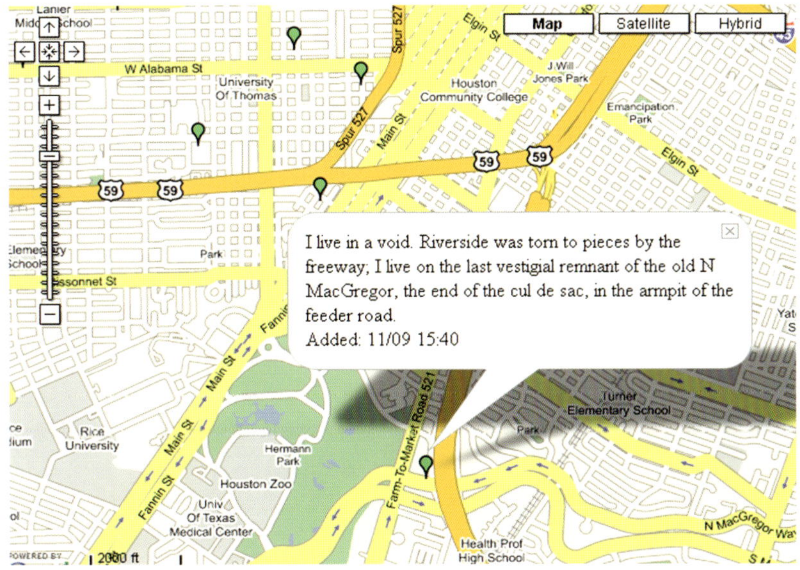

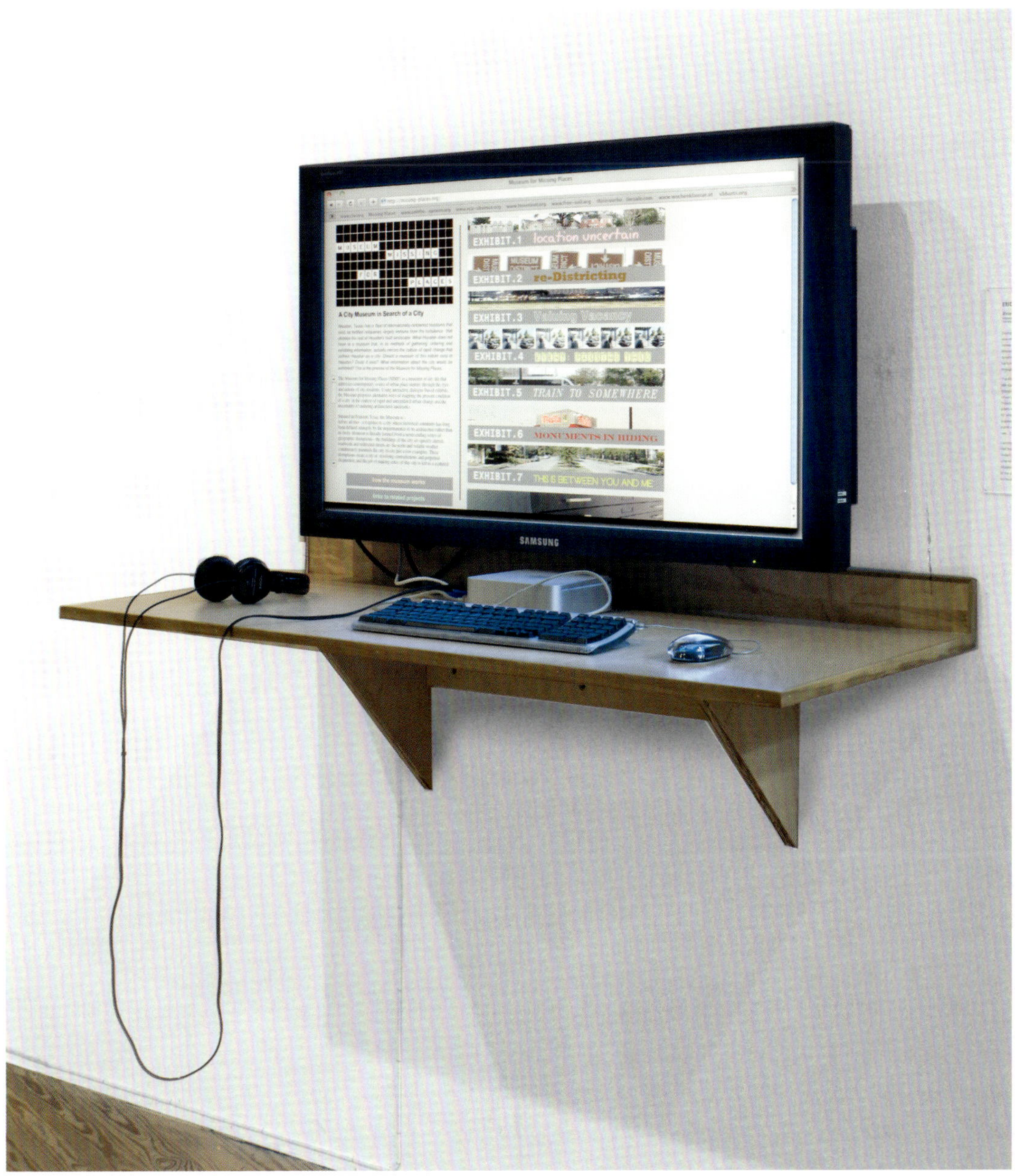

Eric Leshinsky

top left:

Museum for Missing Places (Exhibit 1: Location Uncertain), 2005–06

Website page with Google Maps feature soliciting and collecting responses

top right:

Museum for Missing Places (logo), 2005–06

Digital artwork

Dimensions variable

bottom:

Museum for Missing Places, 2005–06

Interactive website: www.missing-places.org

Installation view, Contemporary Arts Museum Houston

All courtesy the artist

Lee Littlefield

Since 1998 sculptor Lee Littlefield has installed colorful wooden sculptures alongside Houston freeways. Called "Pop-Ups," after a friend's observation that they spring suddenly into a driver's field of view, these works, some of which are more than twenty feet tall, resemble otherworldly plants and flowers. They are made from brightly painted and inventively reshaped vines and wood harvested from Houston's bayous. At first, Littlefield would simply park his pickup truck on the highway shoulder and bury the bases of his Pop-Ups by underpasses and on embankments along Houston Interstates 10 and 45. However, the works, which are painted in a trademark scheme of ascending and blending yellows, reds, and greens, and have swamp-inspired titles like *Greens Bayou Crawfish, Swamp Critter,* and *Atchafalaya Spiders*, were quickly plucked from the ground by the agencies responsible for the land adjacent to the roads as soon as they were discovered. Gradually, however, Littlefield developed relationships with the Texas Department of Transportation and Harris County Flood Control, which now allow him to use their land provided he follows a set of safety rules.

For *No Zoning*, Littlefield has installed a small grove of three twenty-foot tall reedlike works made from bamboo alongside the Museum's "backyard" on Bayard Lane, just west of Montrose Boulevard. He also bedecked the branches of the live oak trees along the CAMH's Bissonnet façade with "rings," painted hoops made from easily shaped mustang grapevines. Littlefield, who began his career as a narrative painter describing his life and the lives of his friends in symbolic images, now devotes himself and the large yard of his house just north of the 610 Loop freeway to the production of sculpture. Clearly, though, he has not lost his interest in art as a form of storytelling. His Pop-Ups conjure up tales of mysterious growth and life in overlooked corners of the city.

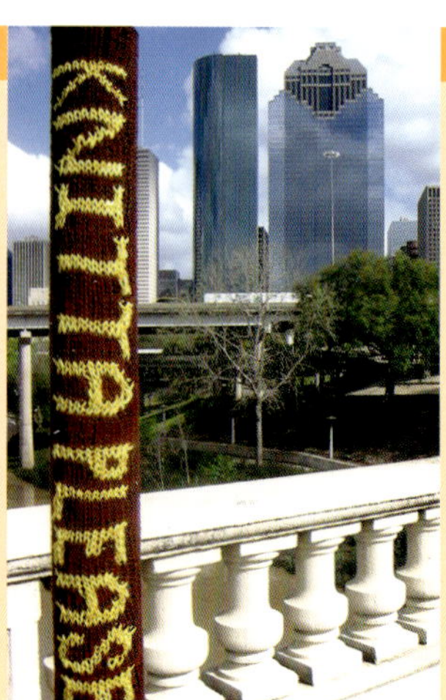

KnittaPlease, tagged pole near downtown Houston, 2005

2005

KnittaPlease
A group of anonymous knitters began to tag public signage, doorknobs, railings, trees, fences, and public sculptures on the streets of Houston with custom-knitted sculptures wrapped around the objects.

Westheimer Block Party
The traditional Houston street art festival began on Westheimer Street in the 1970s. A group of young artists, led by independent curator/writer Sean Carroll, revived the festival to include drive-by painting exhibitions, a bike-ride exhibition through the neighborhood, graffiti, busking, site-specific installation, performance art, and social interactions. Participants included Elia Arce, Robert Pruitt, Will Boone, JoAnn Park, Cheyenne Ramos, Matthew Dupont, YAR!, BLOWJACK, B~Kay, and Skeez-181, among others.

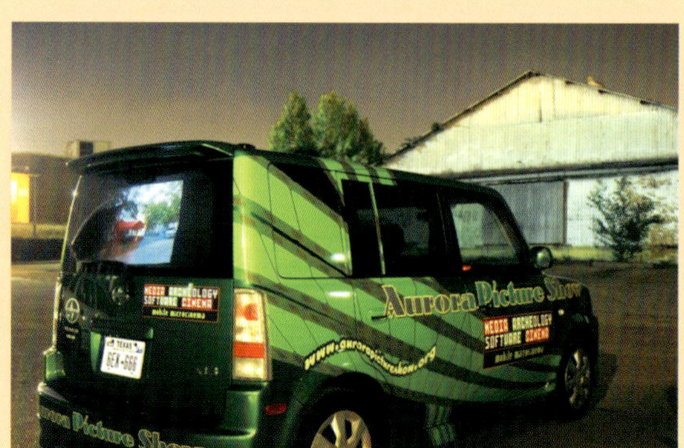

One of the Aurora Picture Show's mobile micro-cinema vehicles, 2006

2006

Mobile Cinemas
In April the Aurora Picture Show converted two Toyota Scions into mobile micro-cinemas using portable projectors with the rear windows as projection surfaces. In June the Aurora Picture Show, the nonprofit arts organization Minetta Brook, and the Buffalo Bayou Partnership presented a floating cinema barge for viewing by an audience sitting on the banks of the bayou.

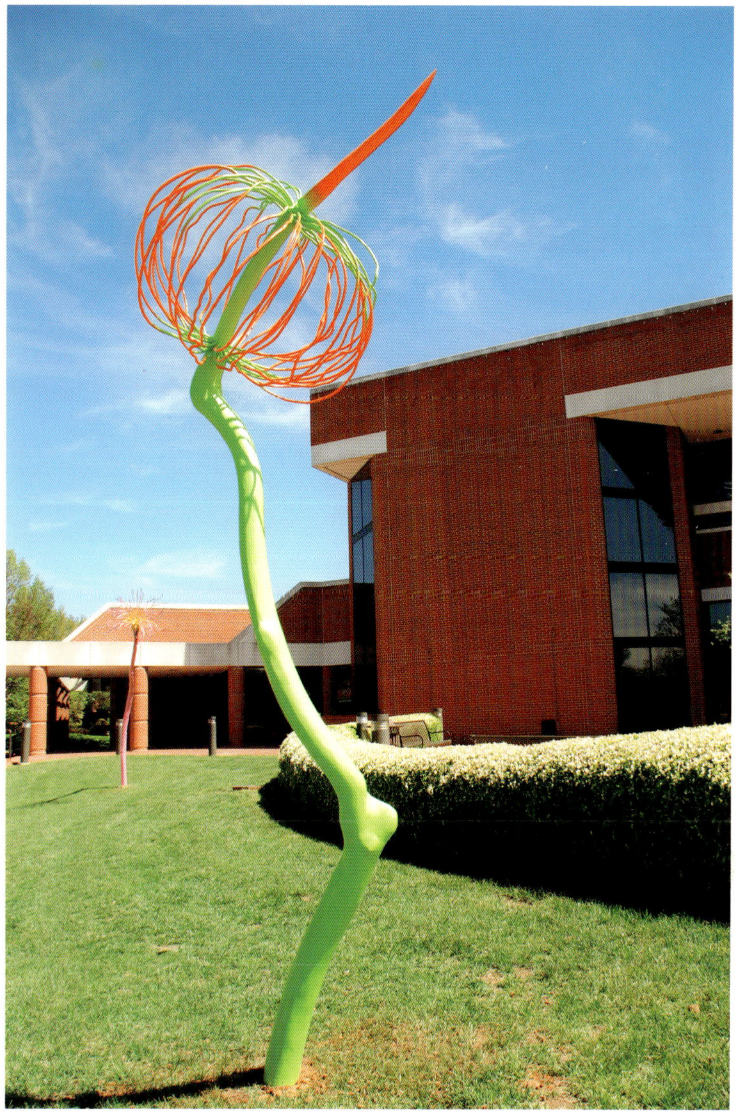

Lee Littlefield
below:
I-540 Flowers, 2007
Bamboo, vines, enamel paint,
Installation view, Interstate 40,
Lowell Exit, Arkansas

right:
Ball, 2007
Bamboo, vines, enamel paint,
Installation view

All courtesy the artist and Poissant Gallery, Houston

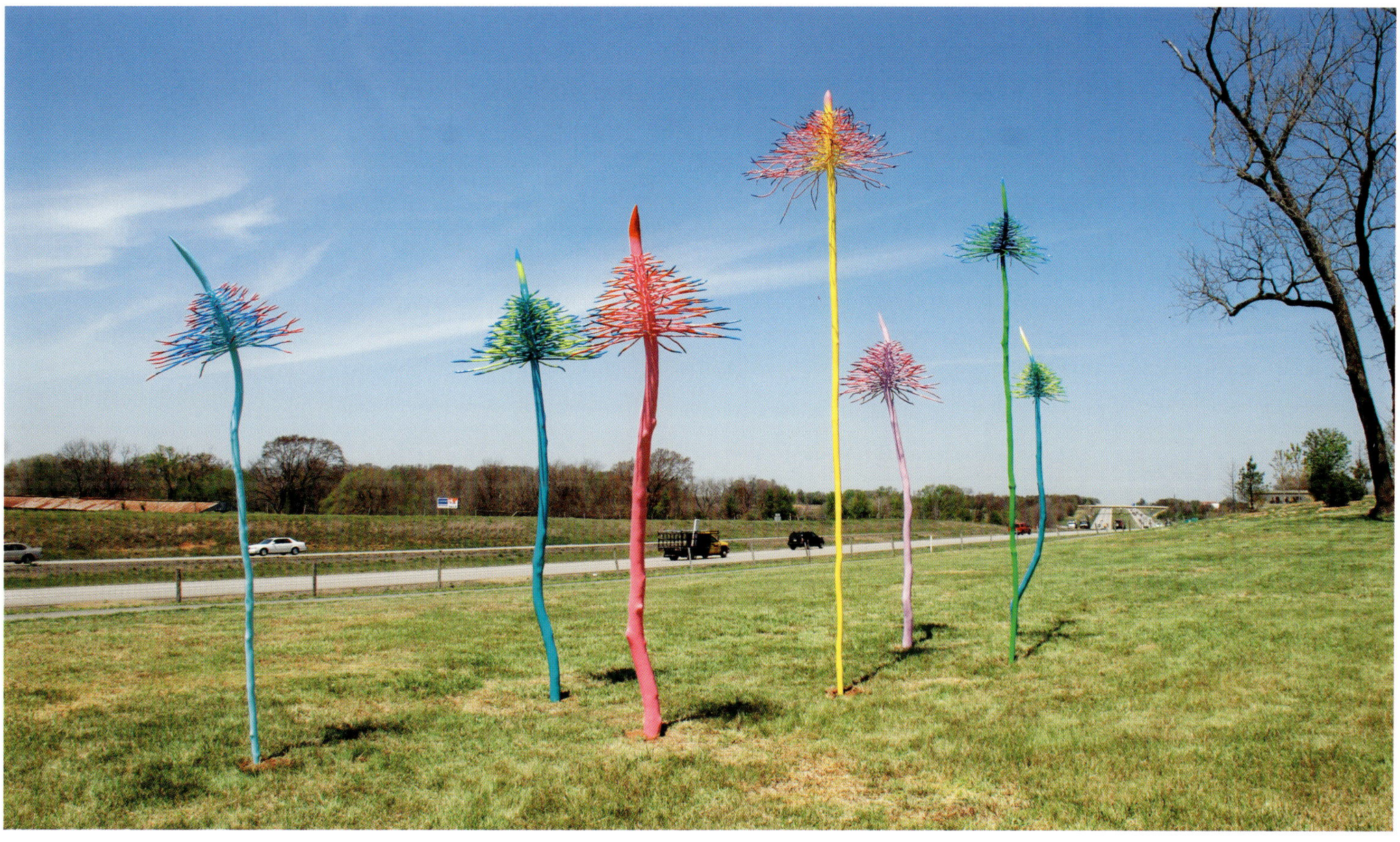

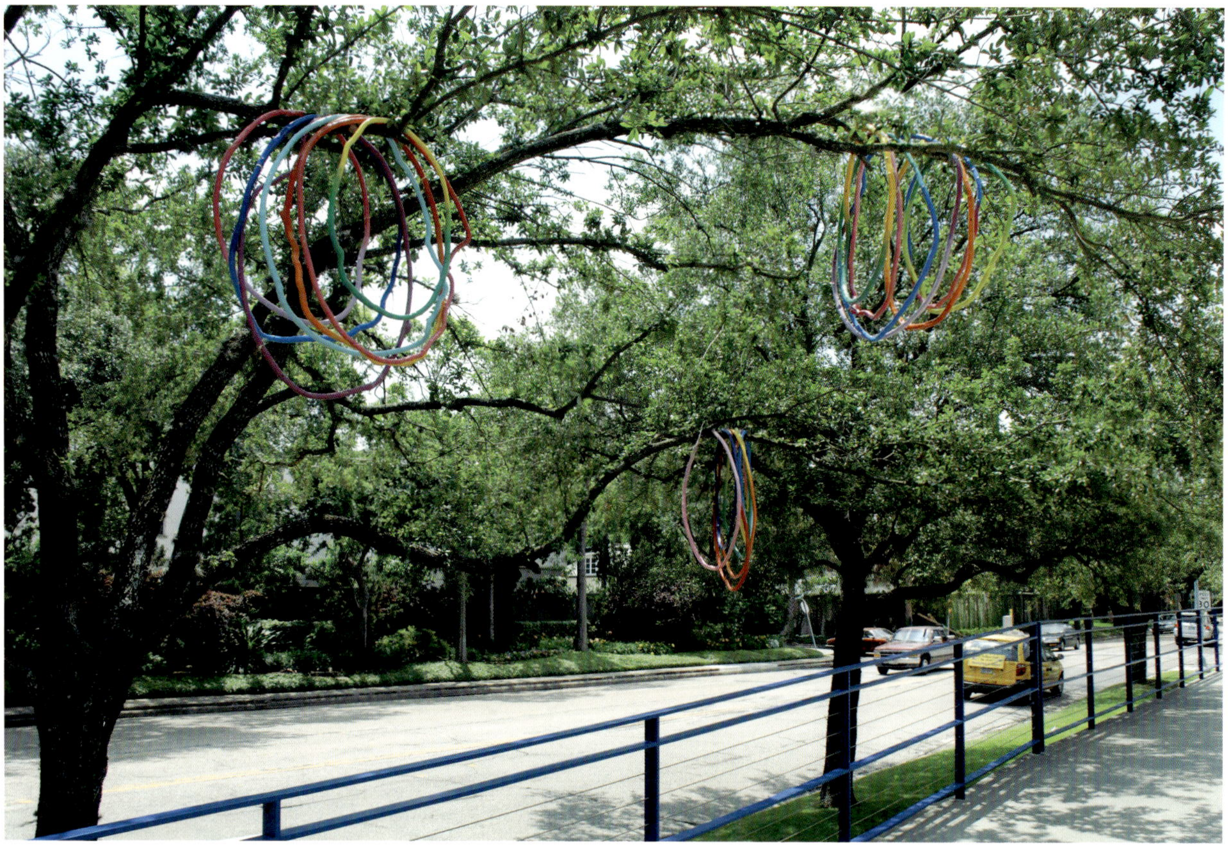

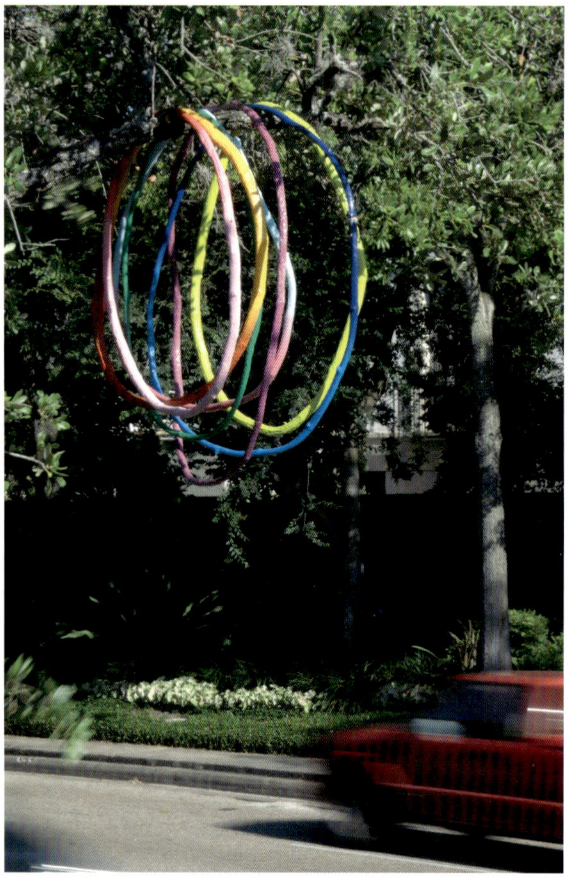

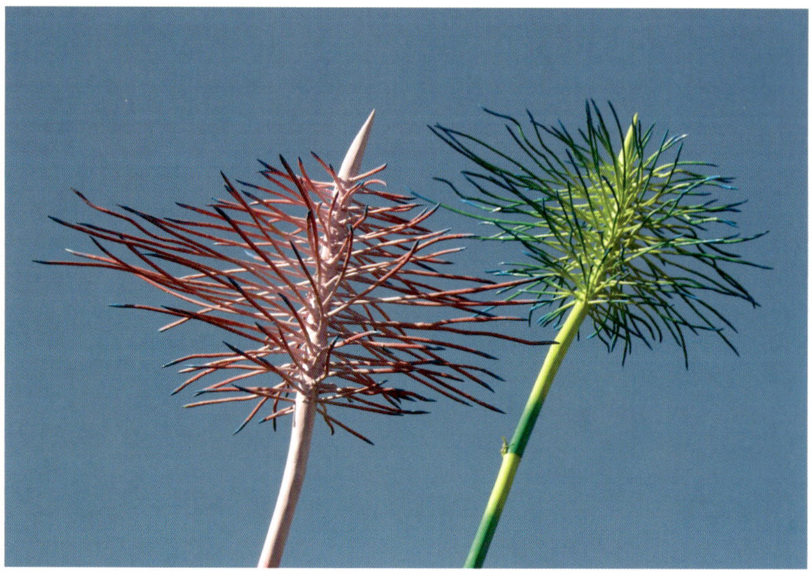

Lee Littlefield

top and bottom left:
Rings on Bissonnet, 2009
Vines, oil paint
Dimensions variable
Installation views, Contemporary Arts Museum Houston

bottom right and opposite:
New World Bamboo Flowers, 2008
Bamboo, vines, enamel paint
Approximately 26 x 3 x 3 feet each
Installation views, Contemporary Arts Museum Houston
(in background: Mel Chin, *Manila Palm*, 1979)
All courtesy the artist and Poissant Gallery, Houston

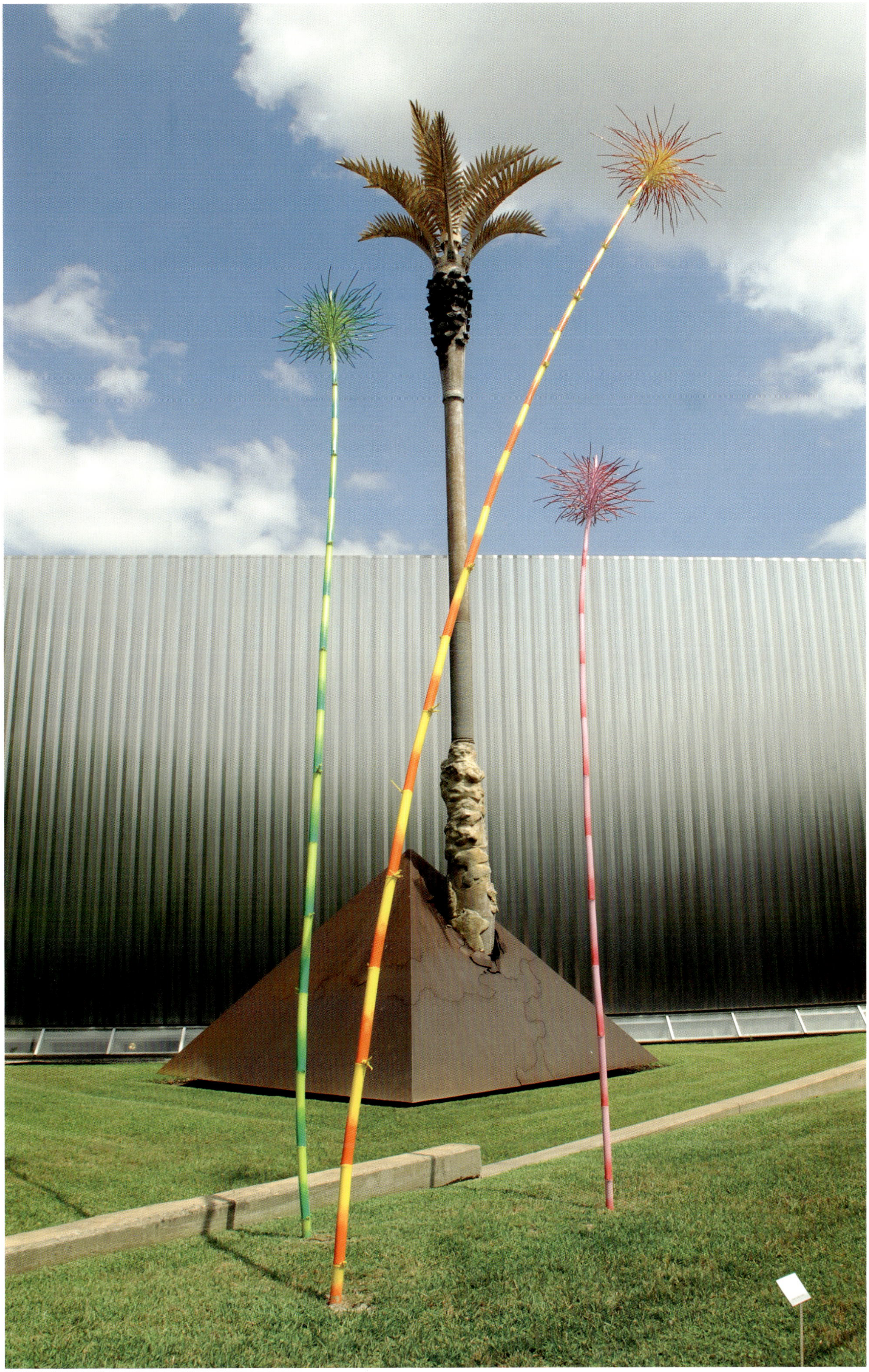

Rick Lowe

Born in Alabama, Rick Lowe studied art and played basketball at Columbus State University in Georgia. Inspired by a professor's strong faith in "the great power of art,"[1] he trained as a painter, but the school's art department was focused on landscape painting, and Lowe found he could not express the socially conscious themes he wanted to explore in that genre. So in 1985 he drove with a friend to the nearest big city with a vibrant arts scene—Houston.

In Houston Lowe became an active member of the art community, helping found Commerce Street Artists' Warehouse (CSAW), an artist-run studio and exhibition space, shortly after his arrival. At CSAW, he met Nestor Topchy and Jim Pirtle, with whom he collaborated to start the art community Zocalo in 1989. Lowe's work in the 1980s mainly consisted of paintings on 8 x 4-foot plywood sheets that addressed issues such as human rights and poverty and functioned like modular, freestanding billboards.

Lowe is best known for his work as the founder of Project Row Houses, an arts organization located in Houston's culturally rich and historically African American Third Ward. Established in 1993, Project Row Houses encompasses a two-block campus of twenty-two shotgun houses that serve as artist studios, housing for young single mothers, and exhibition spaces, as well as venues for social events, cultural festivals, and children's arts programs. Lowe was influenced by the idea of social sculpture developed by shamanistic German artist Josef Beuys (1921–86). Beuys believed certain human interactions could be works of art, and Lowe based Project Row Houses on his belief that living with art and its makers can revitalize depressed inner-city communities.

Lowe's project for *No Zoning* combines elements of his early billboard-style works with aspects of his later social sculpture. Using a digital camera and computer photo-editing software, he has made images of Third Ward residents that promote and celebrate the ways their talents and activities contribute to the community. *Brother-N-Law's, Every Neighborhood Needs One* features Brother-N-Law, a friend of a staff member at Project Row Houses who, Lowe says, "just showed up one day" and hung around until there was a job to do. Eventually Brother-N-Law's barbecuing talent was discovered, and since then he has become an occasional in-house caterer for Project Row Houses and other neighborhood events. "He had been incarcerated and came back to this community with nothing," Lowe says. "He made a niche for himself by doing something valuable." Another image, *Power of Peace,* features Kenya Shabazz, proprietor of the Pyramid Store, known for dressing in a military-style uniform and voluntarily patrolling the neighborhood to safeguard children as they return home from school.

By placing images of these individuals in the kind of light boxes and printed-vinyl banners used for commercial signage, Lowe seeks to advertise the unconventional yet meaningful services they provide. "I want to re-brand these people," he says. He wants to make them icons of the Third Ward, just like the shotgun house architecture that, through Project Row Houses, has become a positive symbol for the city. Lowe hopes that the individual "social sculptors" depicted in his images will, in this way, gain wide recognition for their contributions to Houston.

1. This and all subsequent quotes by Rick Lowe are from conversations with the author, November 2008–February 2009.

2007

This Old House by Aerosol Warfare
Aerosol Warfare was invited to paint the exterior of a house acquired by DiverseWorks at Alabama Street and Almeda Road in a project called *This Old House*.

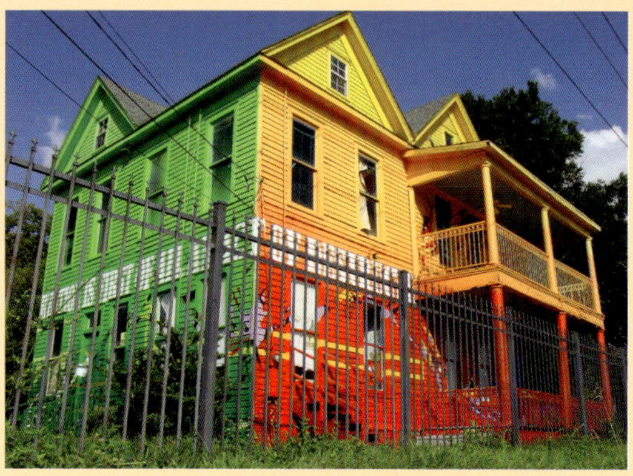

Aerosol Warfare's *This Old House*, 2007

Performance Art Lab (PAL)
Performance Art Lab (PAL) was founded by Elia Arce, then a graduate art student at the University of Houston. She taught performance art and worked with her students to create the collective. When the class ended in 2008, PAL was launched as an independent performance collective. Guerilla performances staged in 2008 included *Sexy Attack*, inspired by an eighties-style aerobic workout video. PAL members choreographed their own version and took it to the streets. Showing up unannounced in public places like a Kroger's grocery store, performers played a boombox and did their workout. Rehearsals and participation are open to all today.

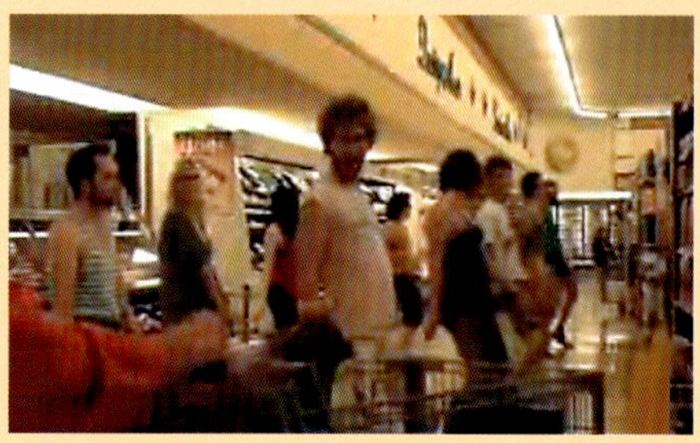

PAL performance *Sexy Attack*, Kroger's grocery store, Montrose Boulevard, 2008

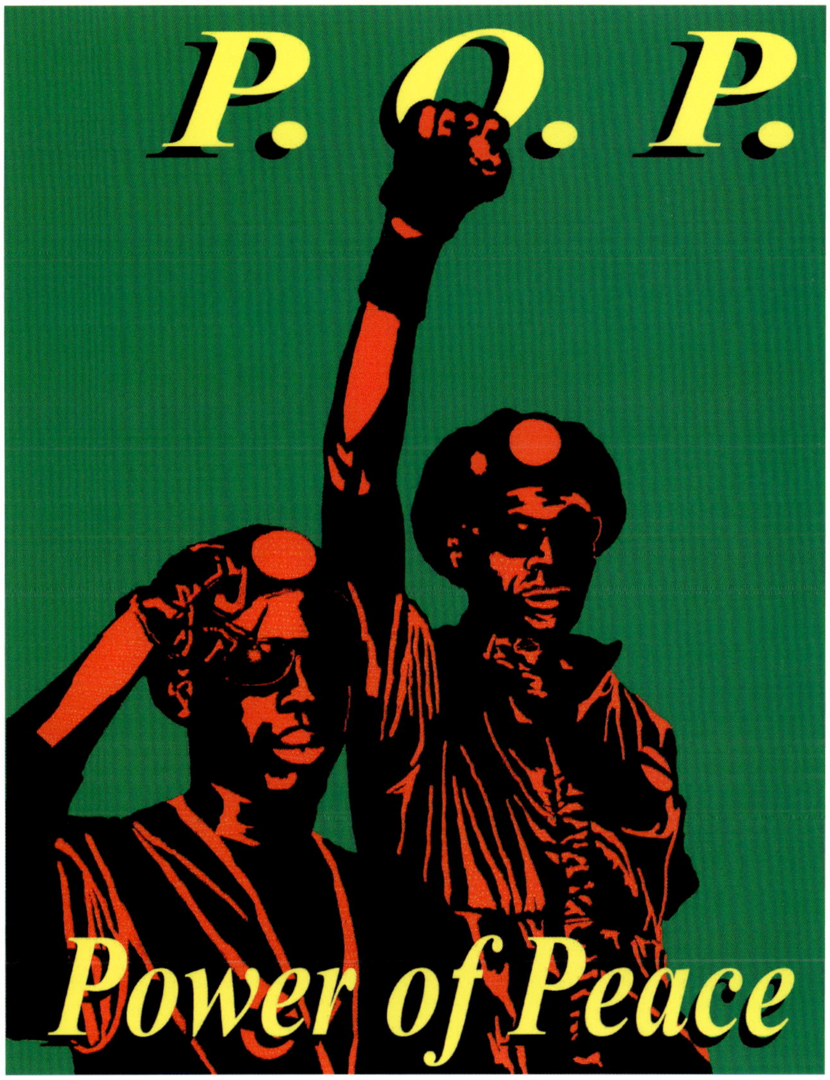

Rick Lowe
Power of Peace, 2009
Digital print on vinyl banner
77 x 60 inches

The Burning Sounds of Progress and Loss, 2009
Photograph on aluminum
36 x 70 x 1½ inches
All courtesy the artist

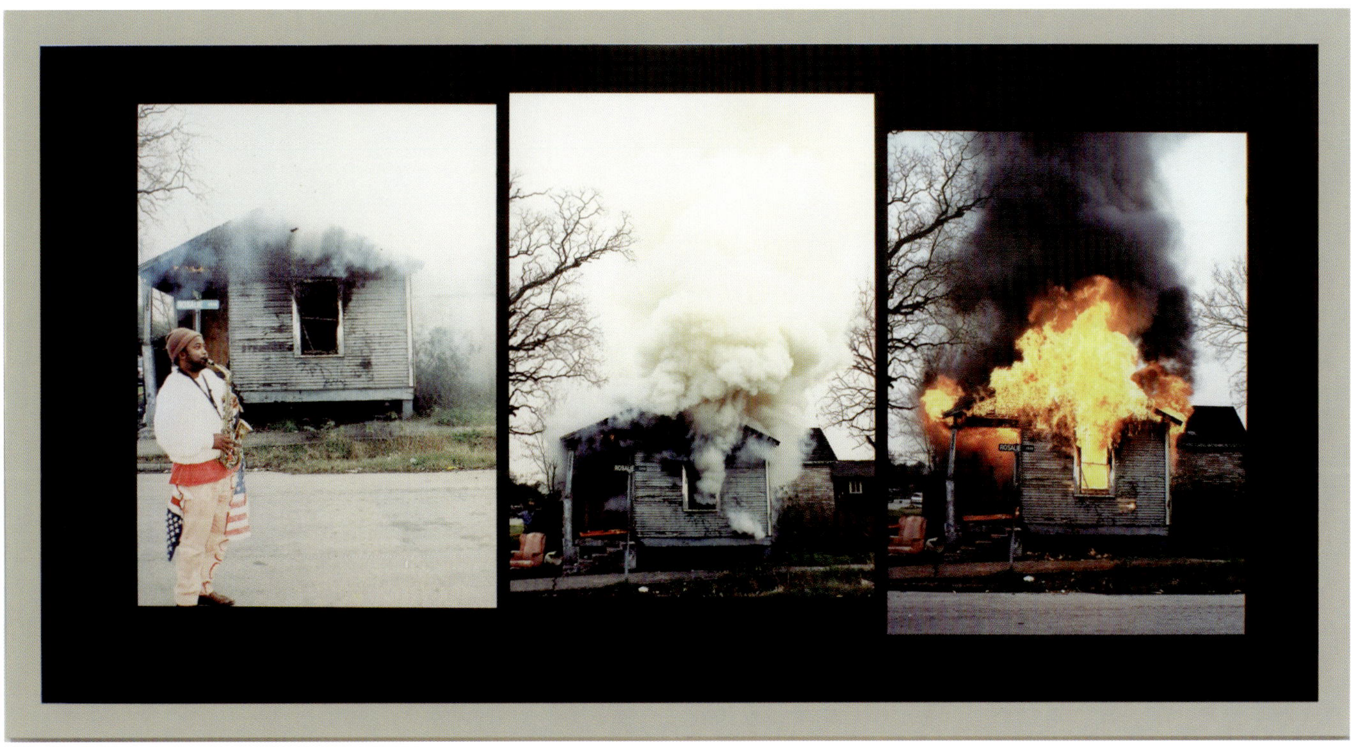

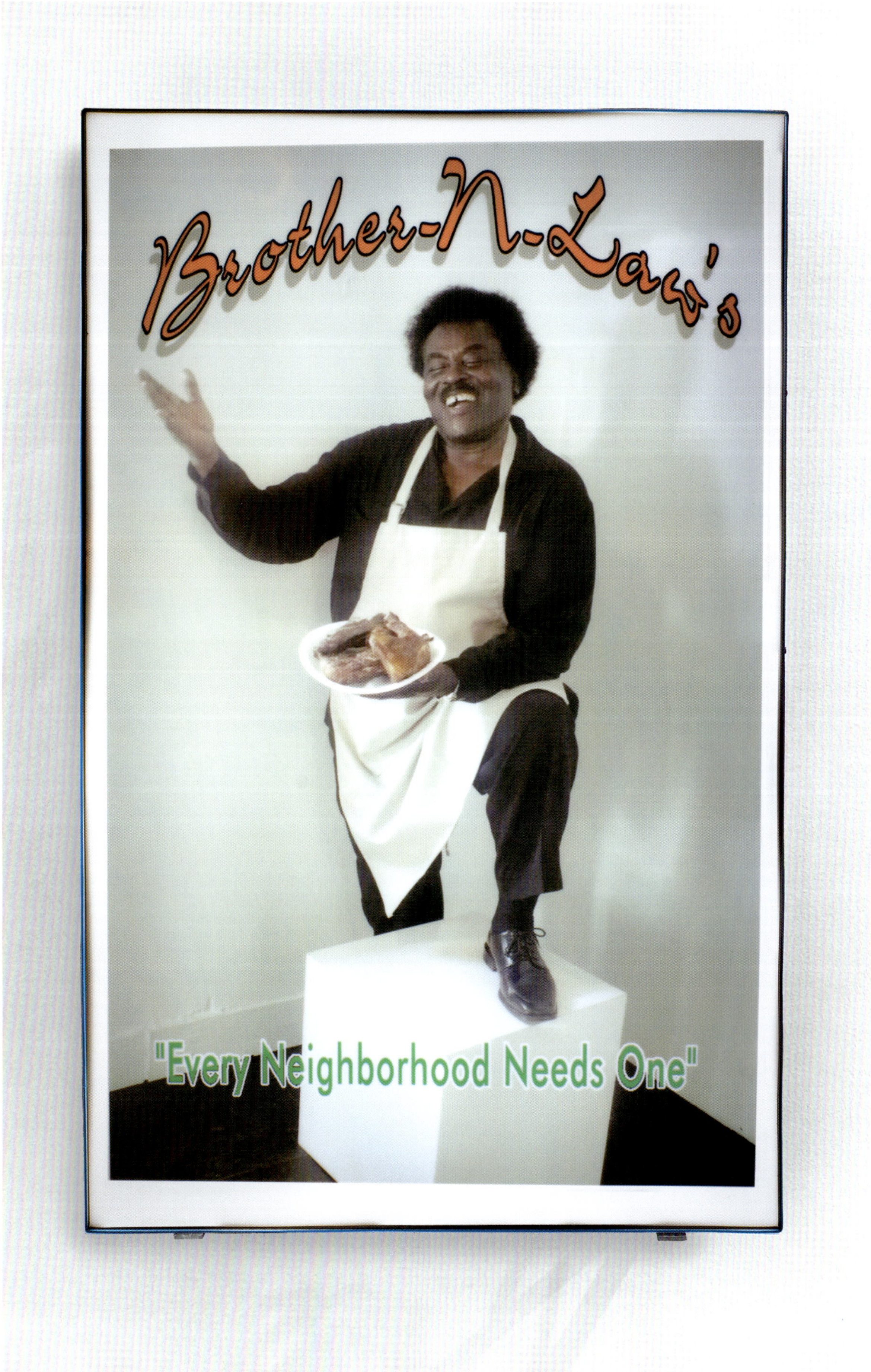

Rick Lowe
Brother-N-Law's, Every Neighborhood Needs One, 2009
Photograph and light box
48 x 30 x 5½ inches
Courtesy the artist

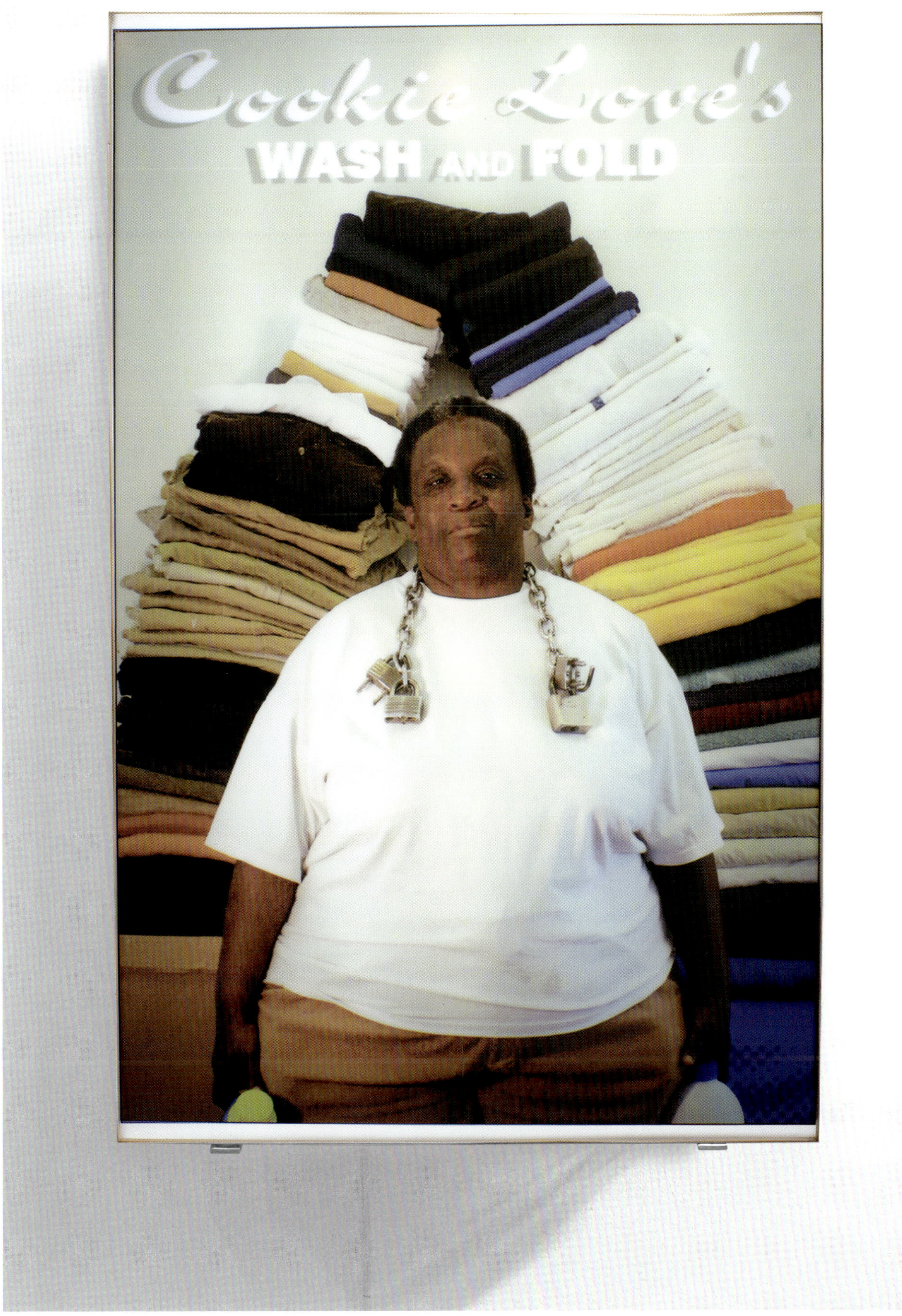

Rick Lowe
Cookie Love's Wash and Fold, 2009
Photograph and light box
48 x 30 x 5½ inches
Courtesy the artist

Benjy Mason and Zach Moser

Zach Moser and Benjy Mason have been using art to foster collaboration and community since their student days at Oberlin College in Ohio. They first joined forces in 2001, when they worked together to establish Oberlin's Big Parade, an annual citywide parade of bikes and other human-powered vehicles that have been converted into mobile works of art. After graduating in 2002, they moved to Moser's hometown of Houston and became two of the co-founders of Workshop Houston, a community bike building and repair shop that opened in 2003 to serve youths in the city's Third Ward neighborhood. Over the years, the Workshop has expanded, now offering kids training in metal fabrication, fashion design, and music production, as well as a place to receive academic assistance.

Moser and Mason's commitment to community manifests itself in public art projects whose final outcome is determined by group, rather than individual, dynamics. Mason has often collaborated with others to make works that involve hands-on exploration and play. In 2006 he partnered with artist Danny Kerschen to present *B.Y.O.B.B.* ("Bring Your Own Boom Box") at Houston's DiverseWorks. They outfitted toy vehicles with speakers, each transmitting parts of a sound composition on separate frequencies. As children pedaled the vehicles in the art space, they produced a mobile radio network.

Like Mason, Moser has also invited participation in his works. In 2008 during a summer residency in Skowhegan, Maine, he began the project *Voyages to the Unknown* by constructing a sailboat. He then asked several fellow artists to join him on a series of voyages in the vessel in search of such ephemeral destinations as Utopia, Meaning, Freedom, Happiness, and the Sublime. They later collaborated to produce maps of their journeys.

In their work together, Moser and Mason have often sought to build a sense of community empowerment. For *Yacht Shop*, their contribution to *No Zoning*, they have purchased the plans for a nineteen-foot sailing skiff and will invite the public to help construct it inside the CAMH over the course of the exhibition. After the exhibition, they plan to burn the boat, Viking funeral-style, at a location to be determined. Mason says, "We are very interested in all this community effort coming together, working so hard on this project, and then destroying it in the end."[1] Much as Tibetan Buddhists brush away elaborate sand mandalas after days of painstaking labor, Mason and Moser's destruction of the boat will be an act that emphasizes the artists' belief that the importance of any project lies in the process, not the end result.

1. Benjy Mason, conversation with author, January 2009.

2007

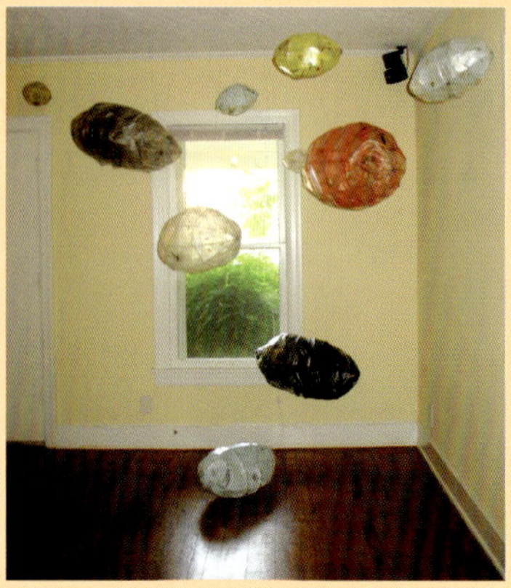

Francis Giampietro's *Zeppelins*, in the exhibition *No Skeleton Armies, Please*, the joanna, 2007

the joanna
In March artists Cody Ledvina and Brian Rod created "the joanna," an artists' collective and space for presenting art, performances, and collaborative endeavors in what was Rod's and is currently Ledvina's home on Graustark Street. Using the bedroom, living room, kitchen, garage, and backyard for staging programs, it is open today for special events and by appointment.

Never Been to Houston
Co-curated by the Aurora Picture Show's Andrea Grover and artist Jon Rubin for Lawndale Art Center, *Never Been to Houston* invited artists from around the world to photographically document (without leaving home) what they imagined Houston looked like. They uploaded their photos on a daily basis to an on-line photo-sharing site; the images were projected as an evolving slide show at Lawndale Art Center. A sequel exhibition, *Never Been to Tehran*, was presented by Parkingallery, Tehran.

Hello Lucky
A group of artists led by Teresa O'Connor founded Hello Lucky, an artists' boutique on Studewood Street in Houston's Heights. Artists consign their works for sale, and part of the proceeds go to nonprofit arts organizations across Houston.

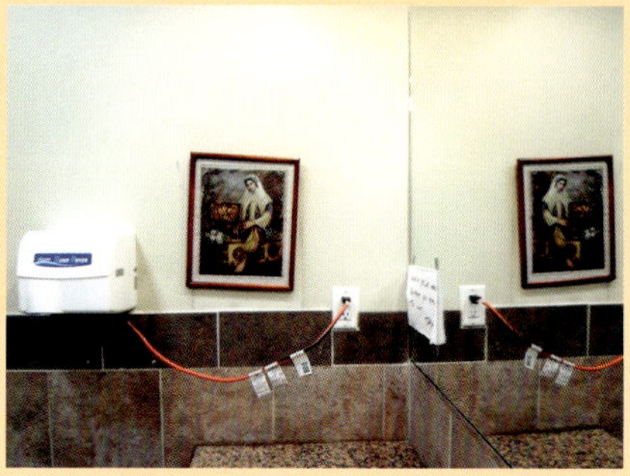

Crowd-sourced image from *Never Been to Tehran*, co-curated by Andrea Grover and Jon Rubin, 2007

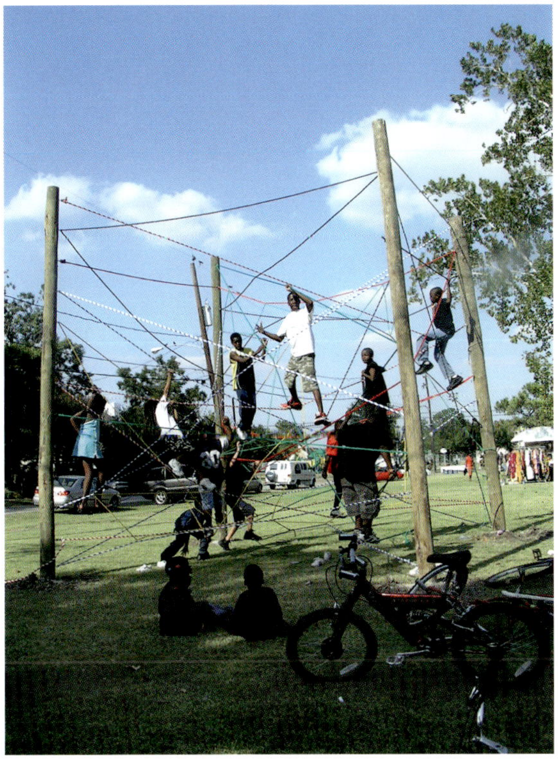

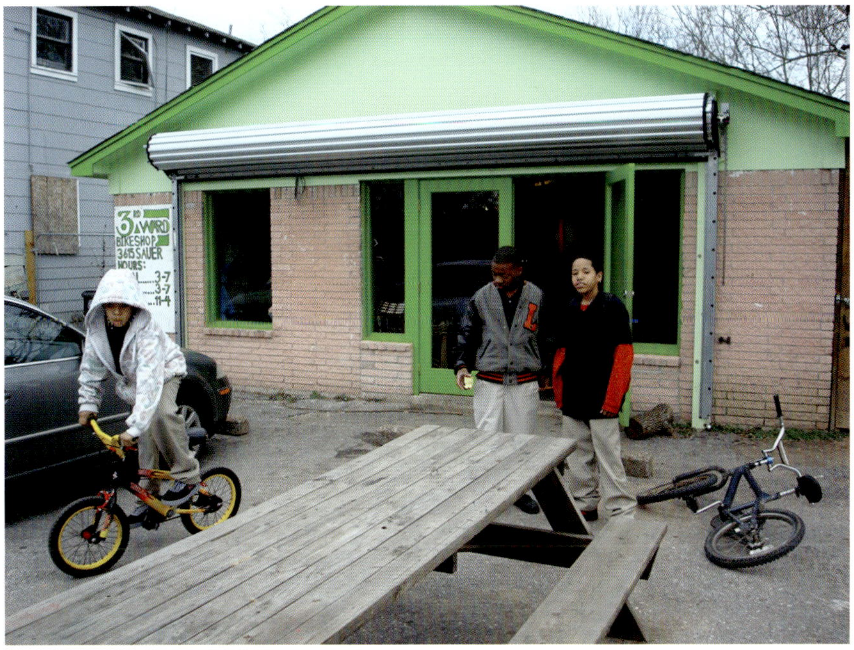

top left:
Zach Moser
New Space, 2005
Telephone poles, rope
10 x 10 x 10 feet

top right:
Workshop Houston
Bike Shop exterior, participants
3615 Sauer Street, Houston

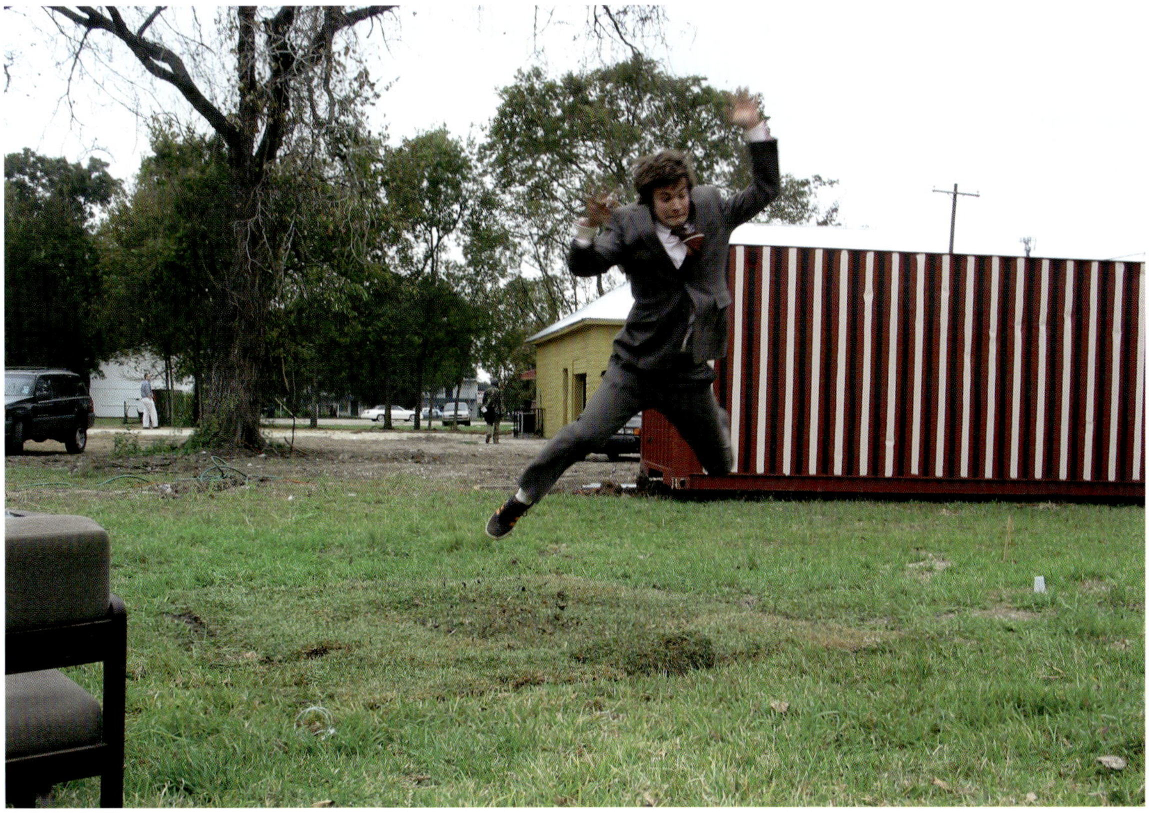

Benjy Mason and Zach Moser
Mario World, 2004
Buried trampoline with sod grass mat
96 x 96 inches
Courtesy the artists

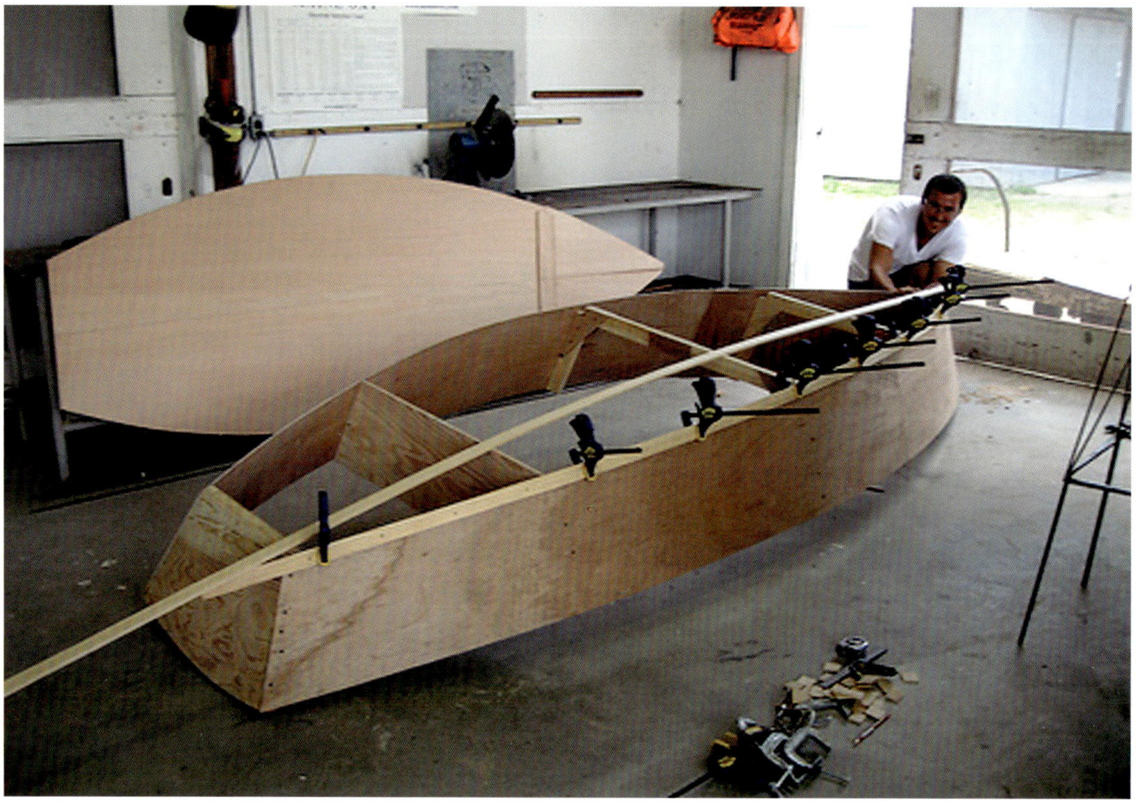

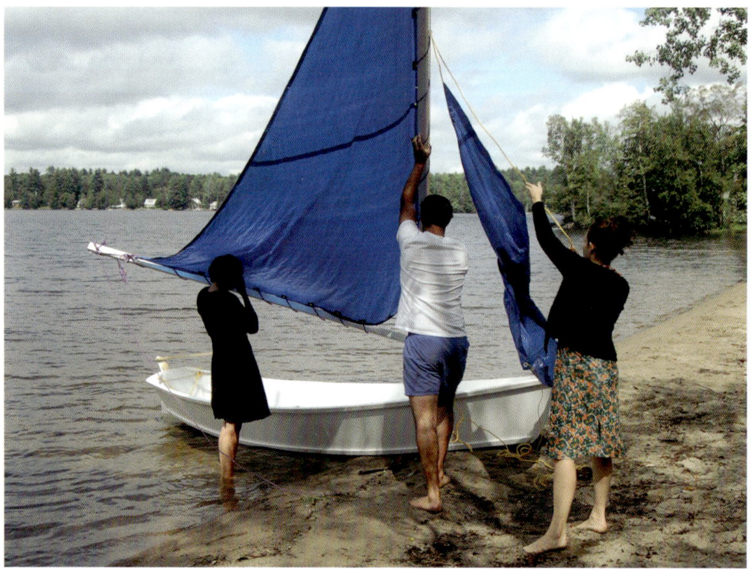

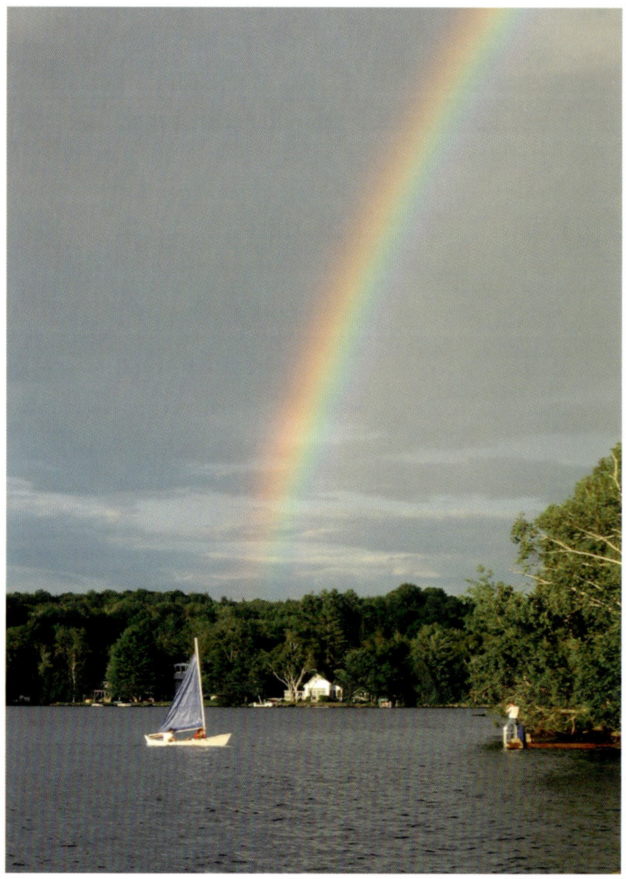

Zach Moser
top:
Voyages to the Unknown (construction view), 2008
Luan plywood, drywall screws, wood glue, tarp

bottom left and right:
Voyages to the Unknown (Search for Meaning, with Kristin Wanek and Liz Lazer), 2008
Luan plywood, drywall screws, wood glue, tarp, participating artists
Courtesy Zach Moser

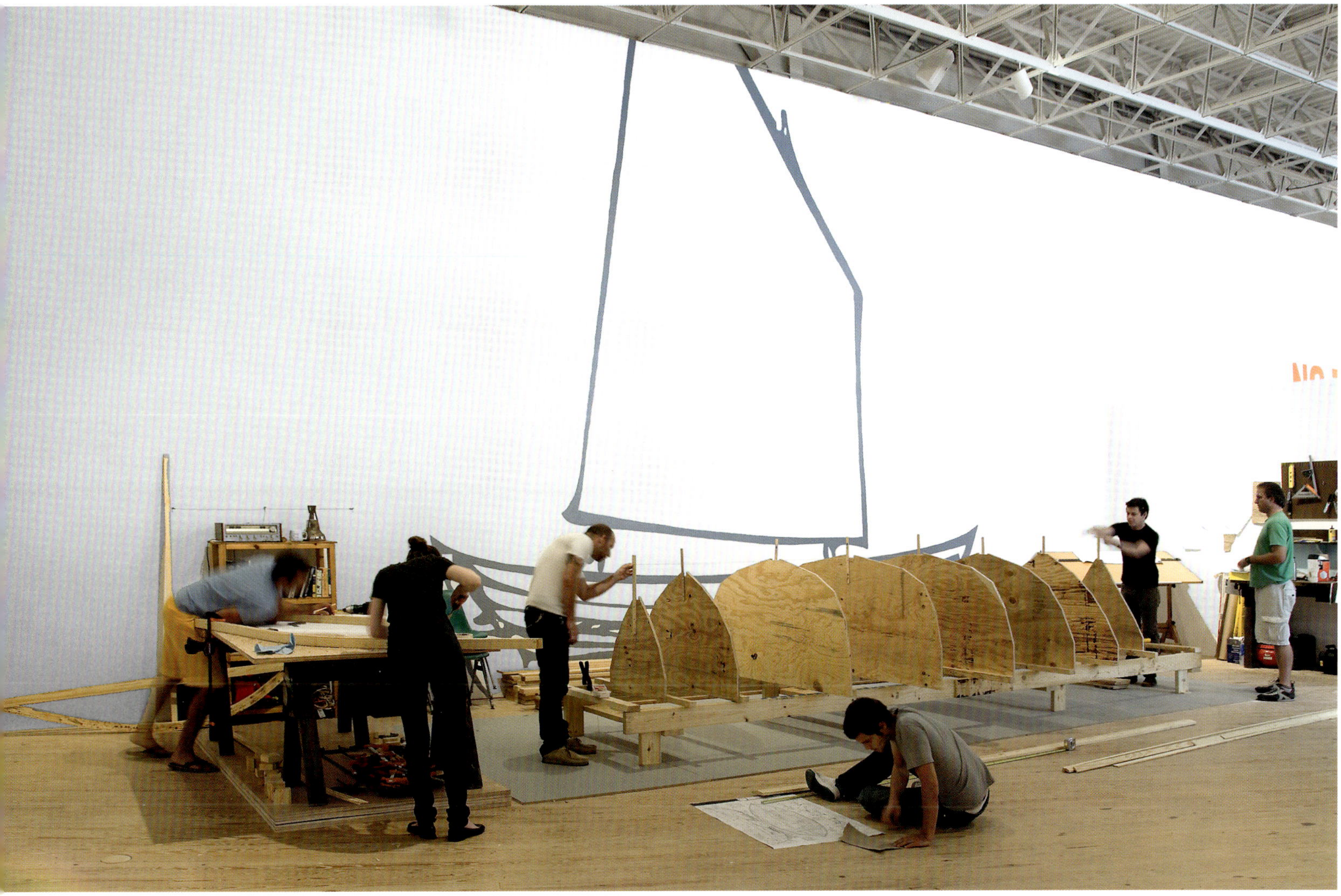

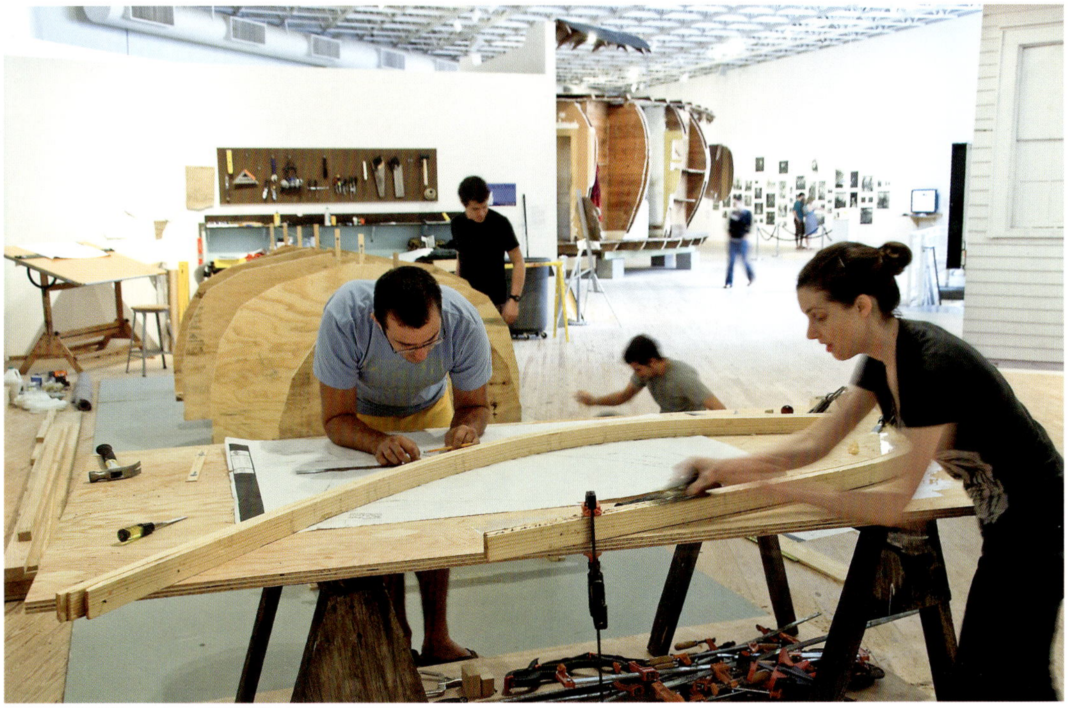

Benjy Mason and Zach Moser
Yacht Shop, 2009
Building plans for a nineteen-foot skiff, paint, wood, tools, participants
20 x 35 x 20 feet
Installation views, Contemporary Arts Museum Houston
Courtesy the artists

Jim Pirtle

Painter, performance artist, and club proprietor Jim Pirtle, a Houston native, has had many artistic incarnations. Before he became an artist, he was a member of the NoZE Brotherhood at Baylor University, an underground society of satirists, and an orderly at the Austin State Hospital, where he worked with the mentally ill. In the mid 1980s, he began painting, taking a studio at the Commerce Street Artists' Warehouse (CSAW) and making portraits of his friends and fellow artists using fabric from polyester garments for his canvases. At CSAW he met artists Nestor Topchy and Rick Lowe, and in 1989 he helped establish Topchy's communal artist space and performance venue Zocalo. There Pirtle also started working as a performance artist, often portraying "Stu Mulligan," a lounge singer who covered his face in mayonnaise, chugged hot sauce until he vomited, and ate bouquets while singing "You Don't Bring Me Flowers."

Pirtle embraced Zocalo's concepts that life and art can and should be intertwined, that anything can be an artistic gesture, and that the execution of that gesture is an invitation to others to add their own. He made this notion of communal creativity central to notsuoH ("Houston" spelled backwards), a bar, social hall, and eclectic performance venue that he founded in 1995 in an historic building in downtown Houston. Erected in 1836, the building had housed various retail enterprises over the years; when Pirtle purchased the property, it was still filled with thousands of unopened boxes of women's shoes, sales slips detailing years of purchases, and everyday antiques. All of these objects became part of notsuoH's décor.

Recent events in Pirtle's life have inspired him to look back at the various artworks and acts for which he is known. For the *No Zoning* exhibition, he has fabricated a new sculpture entitled *Ghost Bar*, made from iconic objects from his life. It functions both as a bar, serving adult refreshments during Thursday evening programs, and as a time capsule of Pirtle's career. *Ghost Bar* consists of display cases housing examples of materials he has used in performances, sculptures, and paintings—polyester fabric, vinyl records, jars of mayonnaise and hot sauce—and examples of the vintage objects he has collected for decades. "What is a bar?" Pirtle asks rhetorically. "A table and some liquor, that's a bar."[1] Throughout his career, Pirtle has used the objects close at hand to explore various forms of spontaneous creation. In the improvised, mini-retrospective *Ghost Bar*, he creates a satellite of notsuoH at the CAMH and a platform for creative conversations and acts.

1. Jim Pirtle, conversation with the author, February 2009.

2008

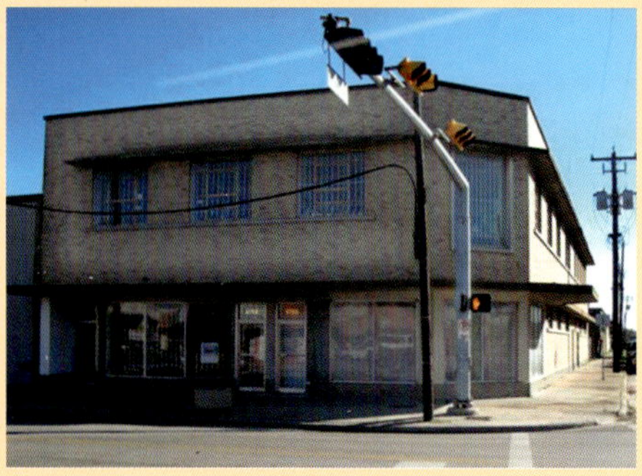

BOX 13 Artspace
Located in Houston's East End at Harrisburg Boulevard and Cesar Chavez Street, the nonprofit artist-run exhibition and studio space BOX 13 was founded by Elaine Bradford, Woody Golden, Michael Henderson, Young-Min Kang, Kathy Kelley, Teresa O'Connor, Whitney Riley, and Mat Wolff. The space today offers affordable studios for emerging and established artists, with two roomy exhibition galleries, a window gallery for installations, and an outdoor performance and exhibition space.

BOX 13 Artspace exterior, 2009

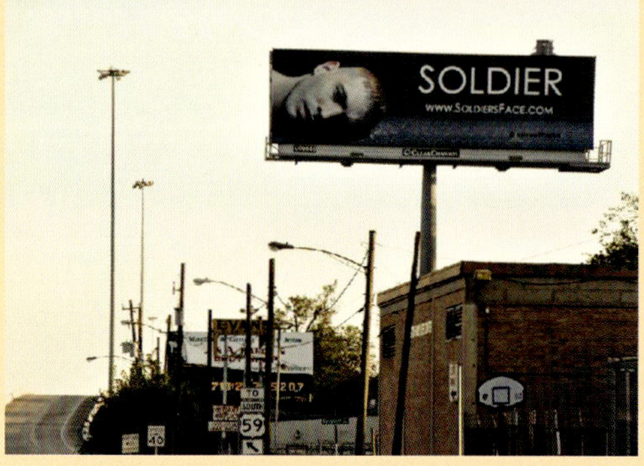

The Soldier Billboards
DiverseWorks organized *The Soldier Billboards* by Suzanne Opton. Appearing on billboards throughout Houston were photographs of soldiers who had been deployed more than once to Afghanistan and Iraq, and a website address where one could go to get more information about the individuals represented.

One of Suzanne Opton's *Soldier Billboards*, 2008

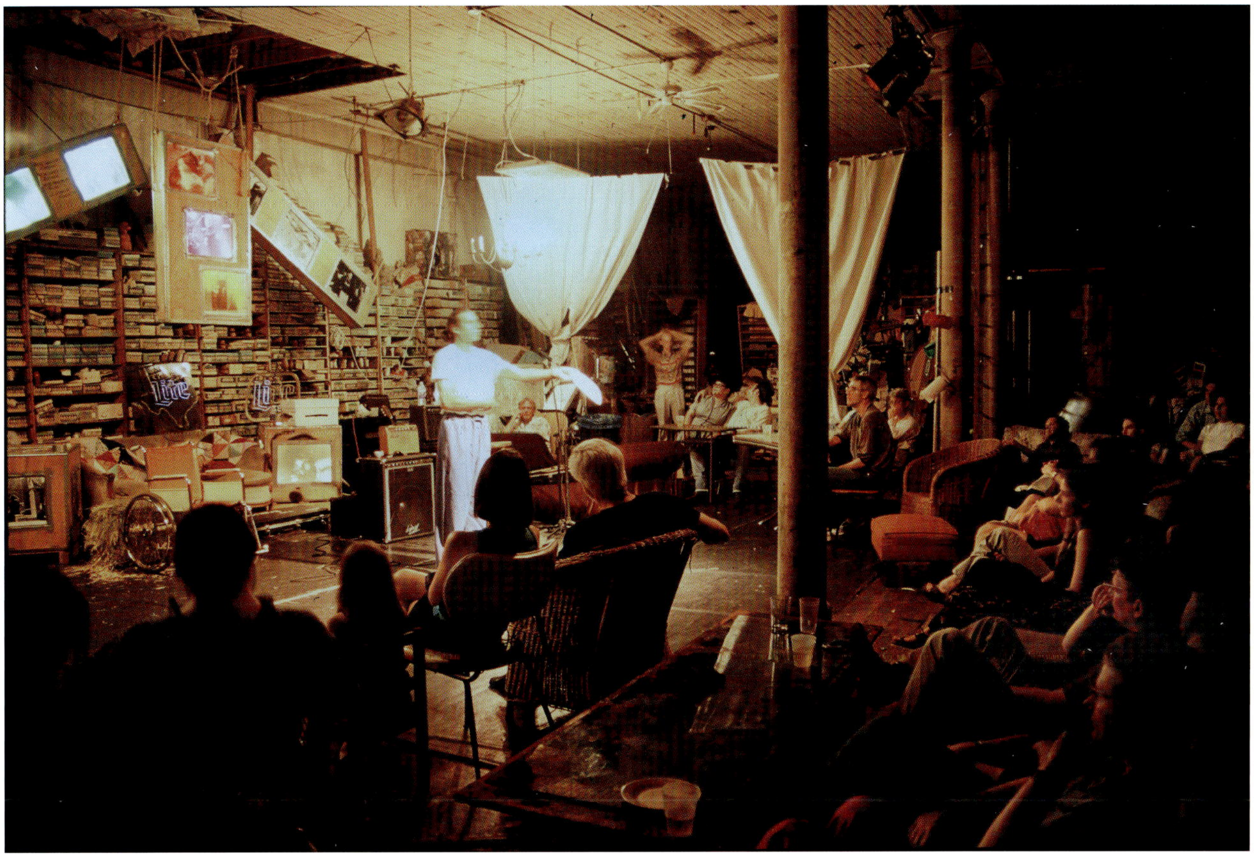

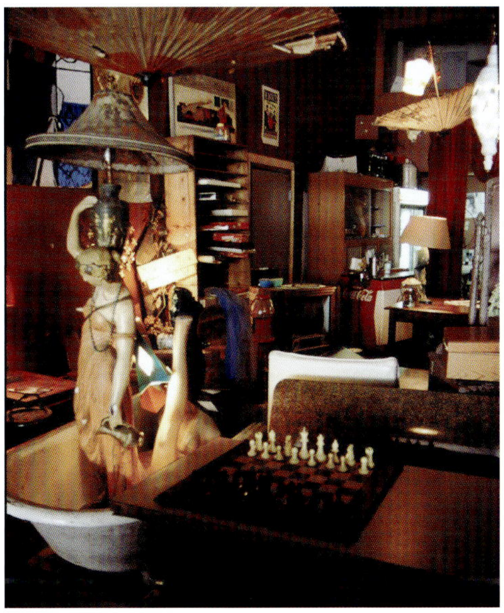

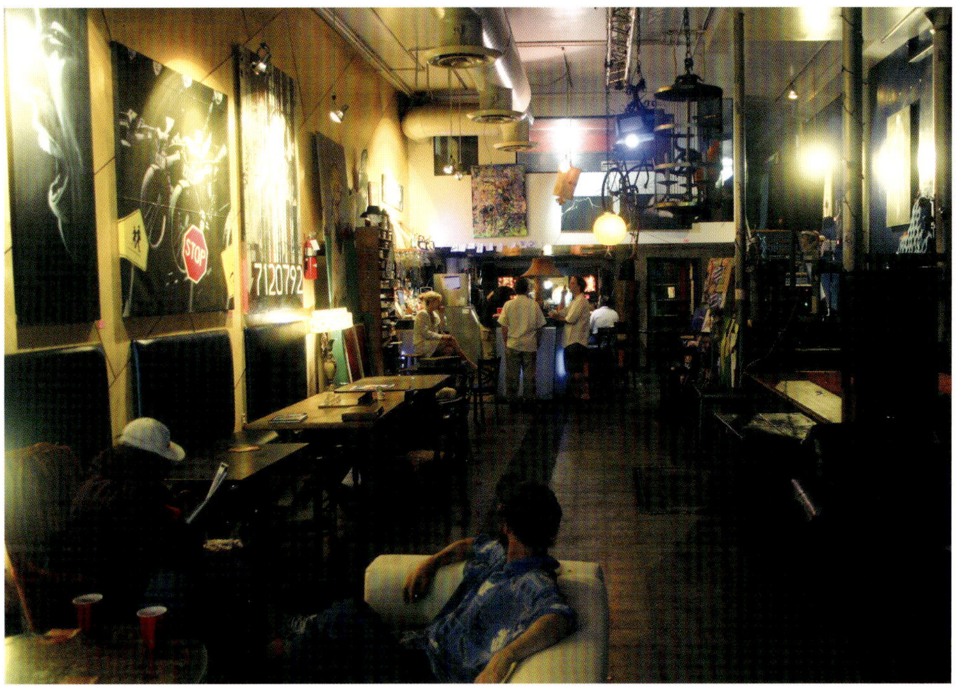

Jim Pirtle
notsuoH (*top:* upstairs performance; *bottom:* downstairs interior views), 1995–ongoing
314 Main Street, Houston
All courtesy the artist

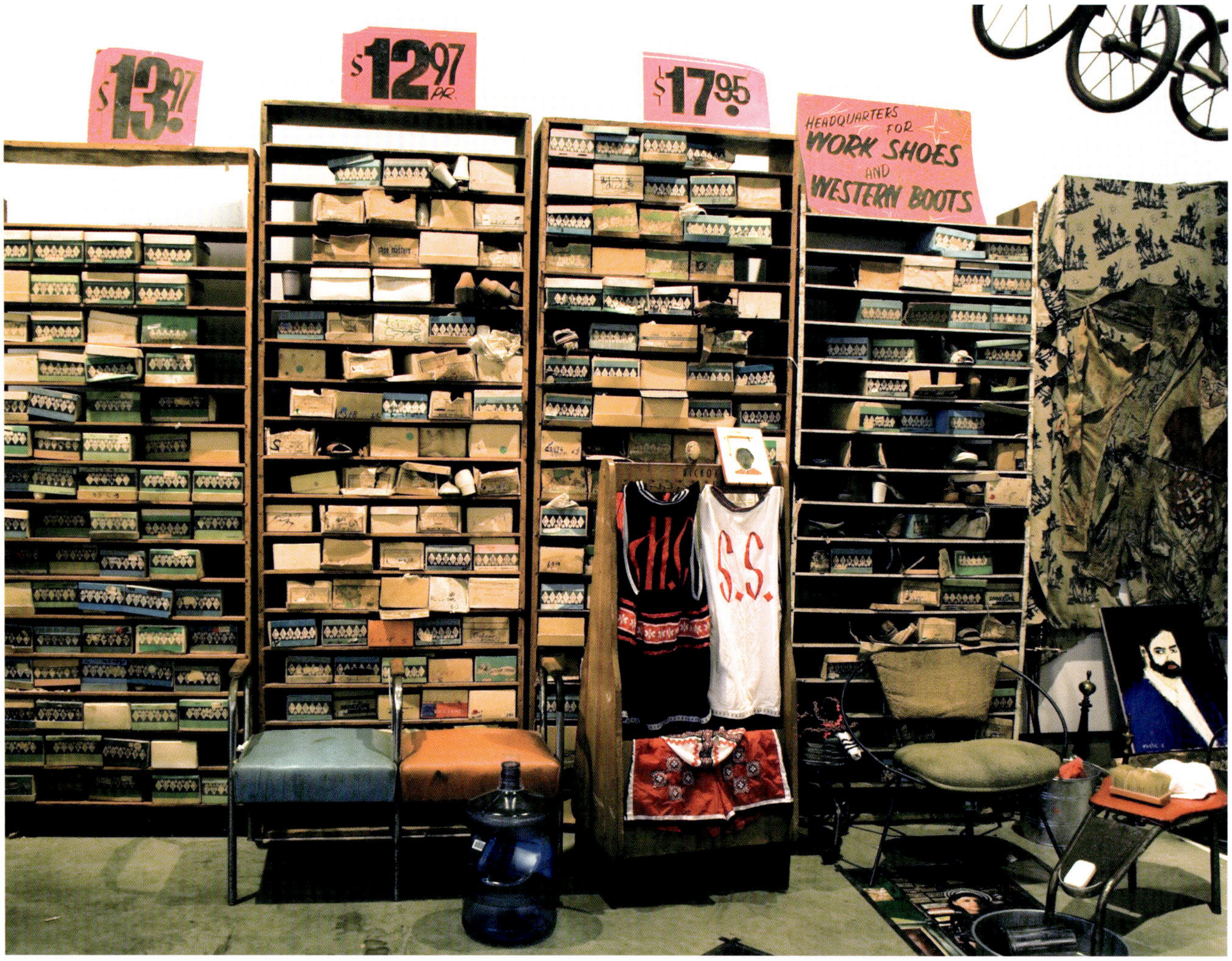

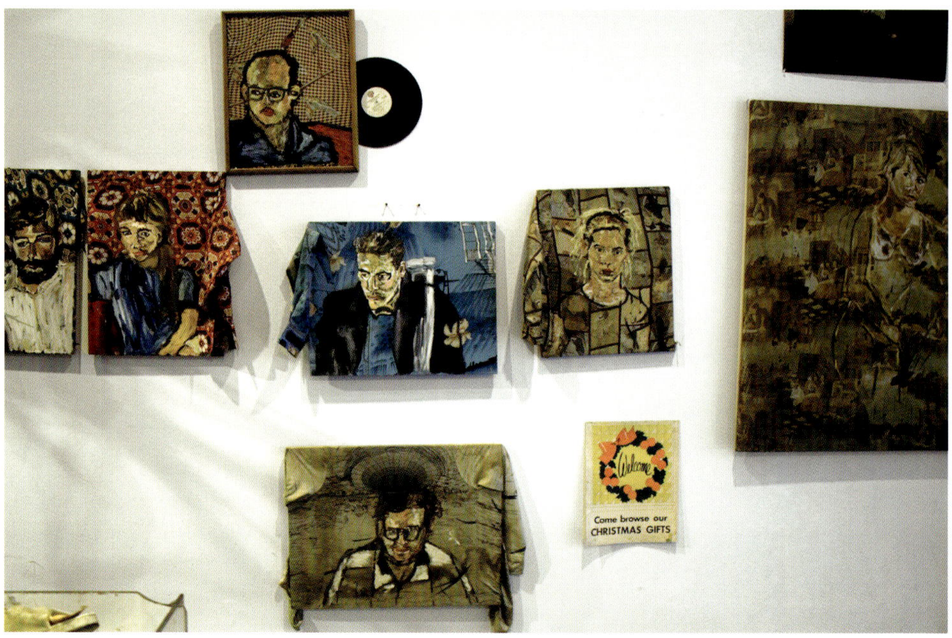

Jim Pirtle
notsuoH, 2008
Installation views, Cue Art Foundation, New York
Courtesy the artist and Cue Art Foundation, New York

opposite:
Ghost Bar, 2009
Plexiglas display cases, mixed media, found materials, artworks, alcohol
14 x 20 x 16 feet
Installation views, Contemporary Arts Museum Houston
Courtesy the artist

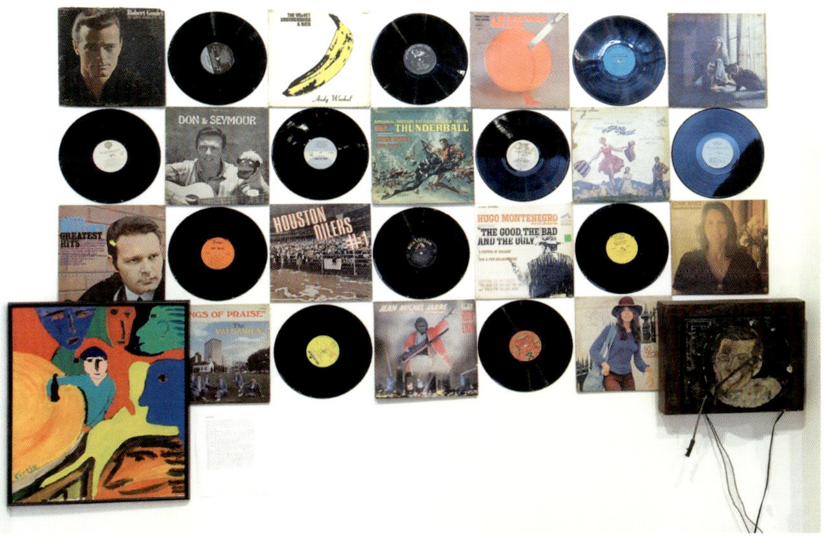
DON & SEYMOUR
THUNDERBALL
HOUSTON OILERS
HUGO MONTENEGRO
"THE GOOD, THE BAD AND THE UGLY"
JEAN MICHEL JARRE

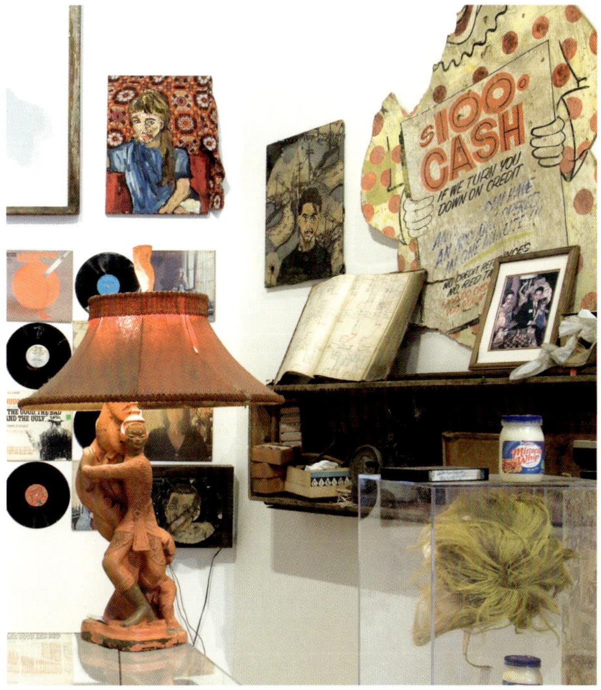
$100 CASH
IF WE TURN YOU DOWN ON CREDIT

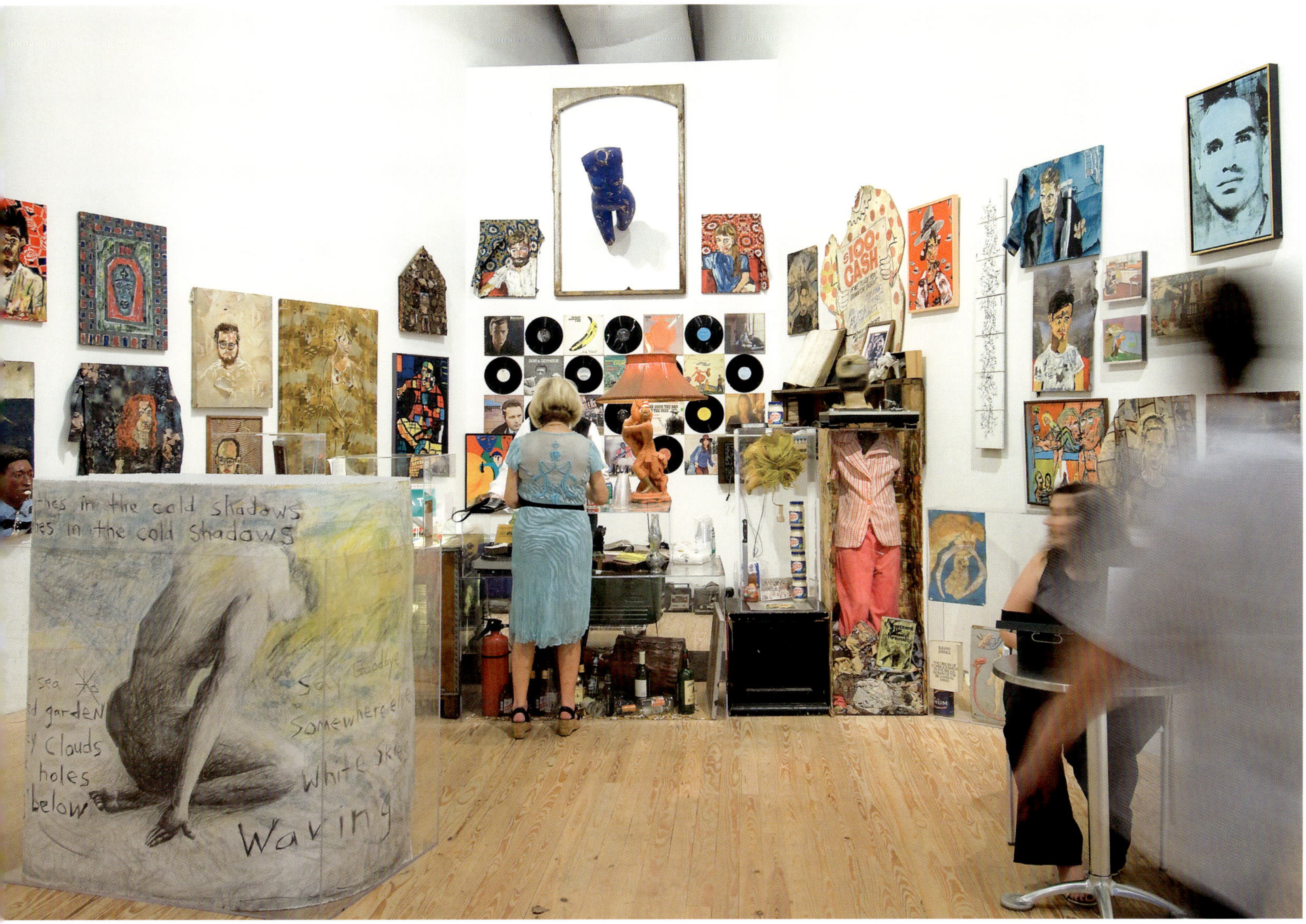
$100 CASH
Say Goodbye
Somewhere else
Waving

Nestor Topchy

Nestor Topchy is a true believer in, and dedicated facilitator of, communal living and art-making environments. In 1989 he rented two acres of semi-industrial property in Houston, where he and *No Zoning* artists Jim Pirtle and Rick Lowe founded Zocalo, an artist-run exhibition, performance, and residency space in the Heights neighborhood of Houston. He and his cohorts converted a truck-washing station on the property into a theater that served as the home of the Zocalo Theater and Performance Art Company when the group was not touring in the "Zocalo Mobile Village," a modified 1971 Department of Corrections transport bus.

In 1996 Topchy reestablished the organization as a nonprofit, renaming it Templ0 after a five-story, metal, pagoda-like structure he had erected on the property. Building on Zocalo's existing features, the nonprofit eventually came to include a drive-in cinema with a two-story screen, a community kitchen with a café and bar, a sculptural pond with a fountain made from hundreds of beer bottles, and corrugated-tin studios and offices. The communal work environment was a venue for avant-garde poetry readings, dance and theatrical performances, and visual art exhibitions until Topchy lost the lease in 2001.

Through five documentary photo and text collages, along with hand-drawn blueprints of the site's various incarnations, visitors to *No Zoning* can trace "the rise and fall of Templ0."[1] Also on display are drawings and models for Organ, Topchy's latest grand plan for a communal living and working site in Houston. Topchy's team, including architect Si Dang, engineer Hisham El-Chaar, and builder John Walker, envisions Organ as a self-sustaining environment contained within an immense square ringed by 288 shipping containers. This perimeter will house the "Bazaar," with the shipping containers modified to hold such elements as "artisan shops, farmers market, service micro-enterprises, spay and neuter clinic, health clinic, child care, restaurants, cafes, galleries, architecture studios, and a recycling center, just to name a few."[2] At the center of the compound will be the "Hive," 148 shipping containers stacked in the domelike form of its namesake to a height of seventy-two feet. Here will be undertaken "any positive intellectual or spiritual activity which can be done quietly, including visual and performing artists/writers studios." Topchy believes the contemplative creative work done in the Hive will be symbiotically supported by "the micro-economy of the surrounding Bazaar," while the gardens, orchards, and water elements planned around the Hive "will provide much of the produce for the farmers market and restaurants in the Bazaar."

Working with limited resources and groups of friends, Topchy took advantage of Houston's openness to construct oases of creativity in the city through Zocalo and Templ0. With Organ, he seeks to institutionalize and monumentalize this impulse. He is borrowing a page from the playbooks of Houston's many successful developers to lay the groundwork for a master-planned artist-centric utopia in the city's largely commercial and residential landscape.

1. Nestor Topchy, conversation with the author, February 2009.
2. This and all subsequent quotes by Nestor Topchy are from the artist's unpublished document describing Organ, reviewed January 2009.

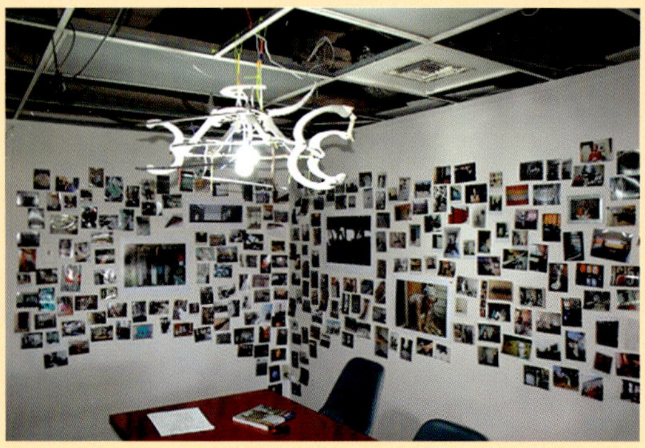

Sarah Wagner and Jon Brummit, *Open House*, installation view, Skydive, 2008

2008

Skydive
Artists Sasha Dela and Ariane Roesch founded Skydive, an exhibition space in their studio on the ninth floor of the office building on Montrose Boulevard that houses the Skybar. Skydive was established to create opportunities for artists and to broaden the spectrum of arts dialogue in the city by bringing artists from around the country to Houston. Many of the artists presented are exploring relational aesthetics, a form of art that relies on a direct interaction between the art and the viewer.

Quitta
A number of knitters broke with KnittaPlease to form their own subversive yarn-tagging group.

2009

Sunday Soup
Sunday Soup, a community meal that functions as a grant funding process, was launched at the exhibition space Skydive. Proceeds from the $5 meal go to support an artist initiative or community project.

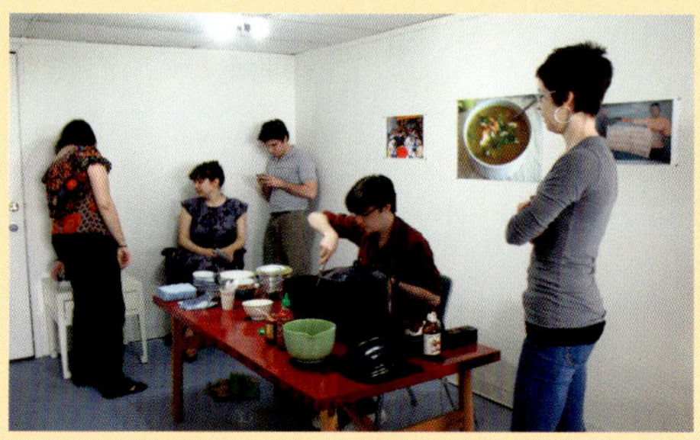

inCUBATE's Sunday Soup event at Skydive, 2009

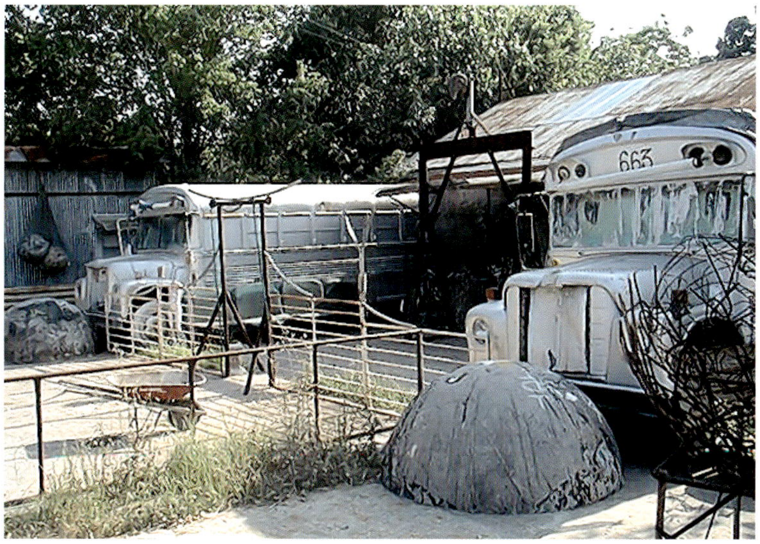

Nestor Topchy
Templo, late 1990s

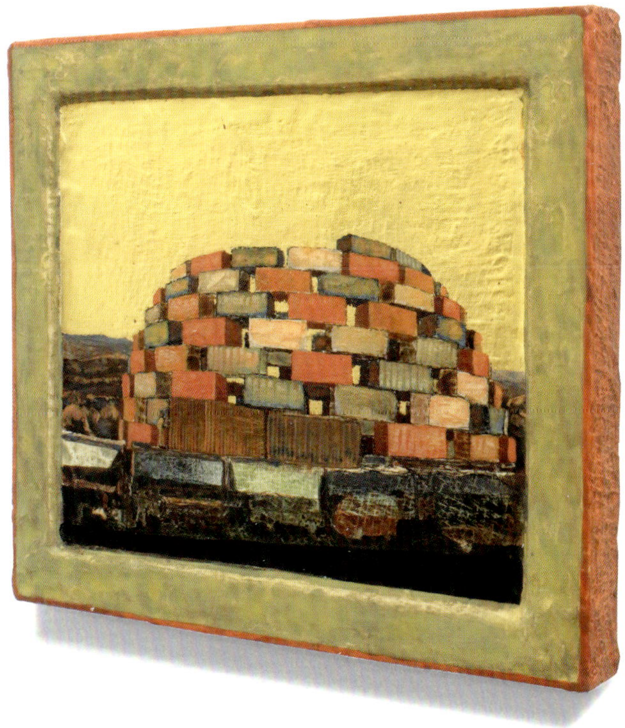

Nestor Topchy
right:
Organ Demekon, 2009
Egg tempera, gold leaf, on wood
13 1/4 x 11 3/4 inches

bottom:
Organ Maquette, 2008
Painted wood on board, string
48 x 41 1/2 x 13 1/2 inches
All courtesy the artist

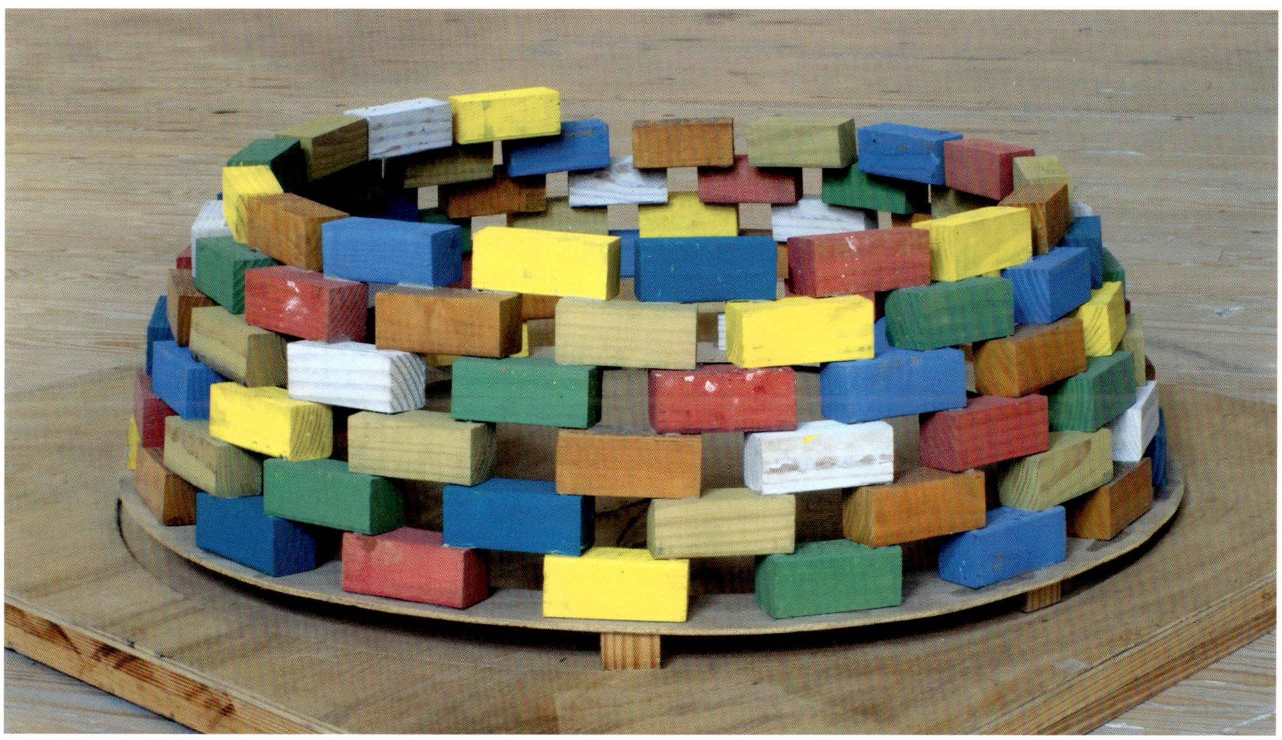

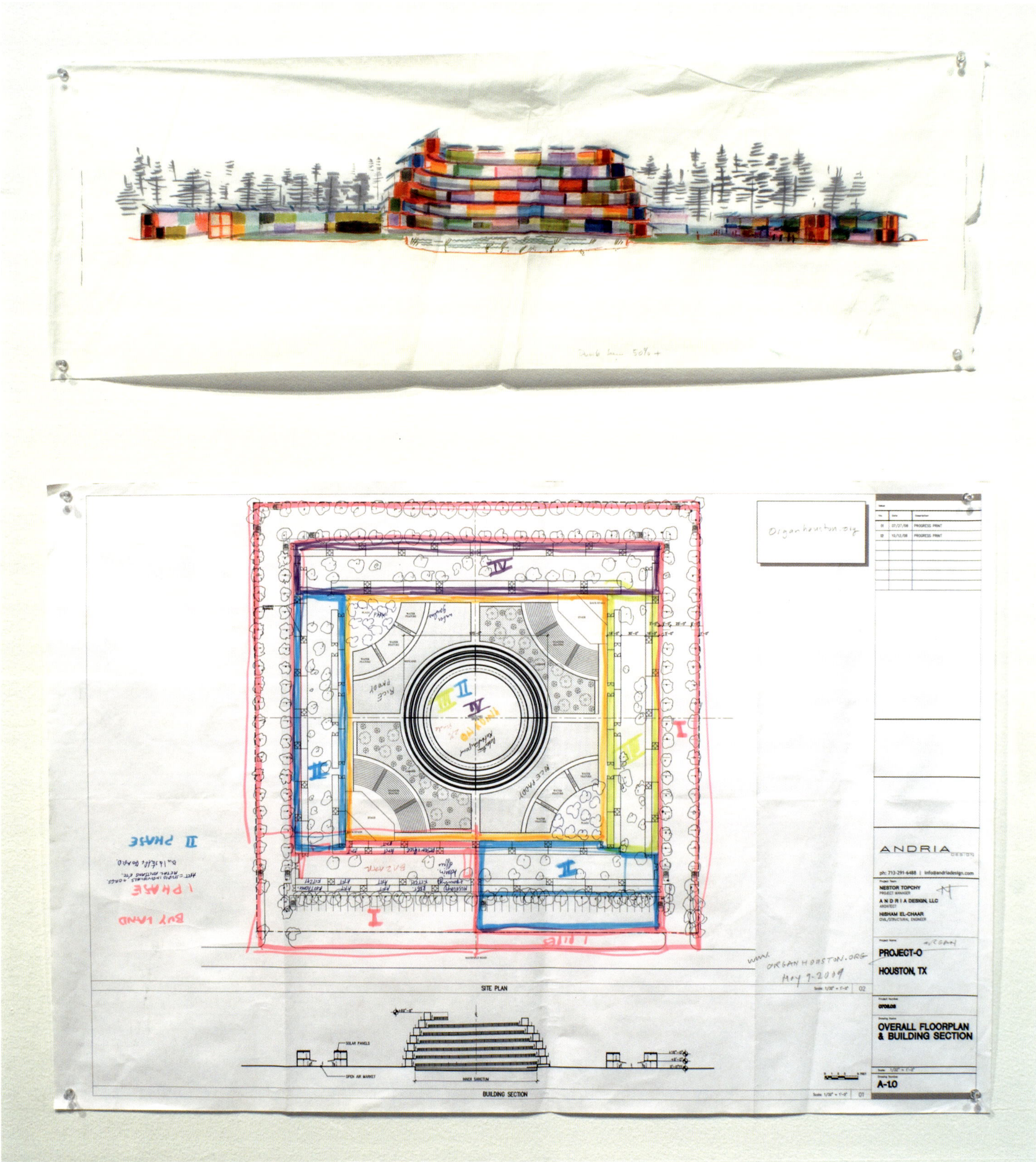

Nestor Topchy

top:
Organ Elevation Drawing, 2008
Ink on paper
12 x 35 1/2 inches
Courtesy the artist

bottom:
Organ Floorplan, 2008
Computer printout on paper
24 x 36 inches
Courtesy the artist

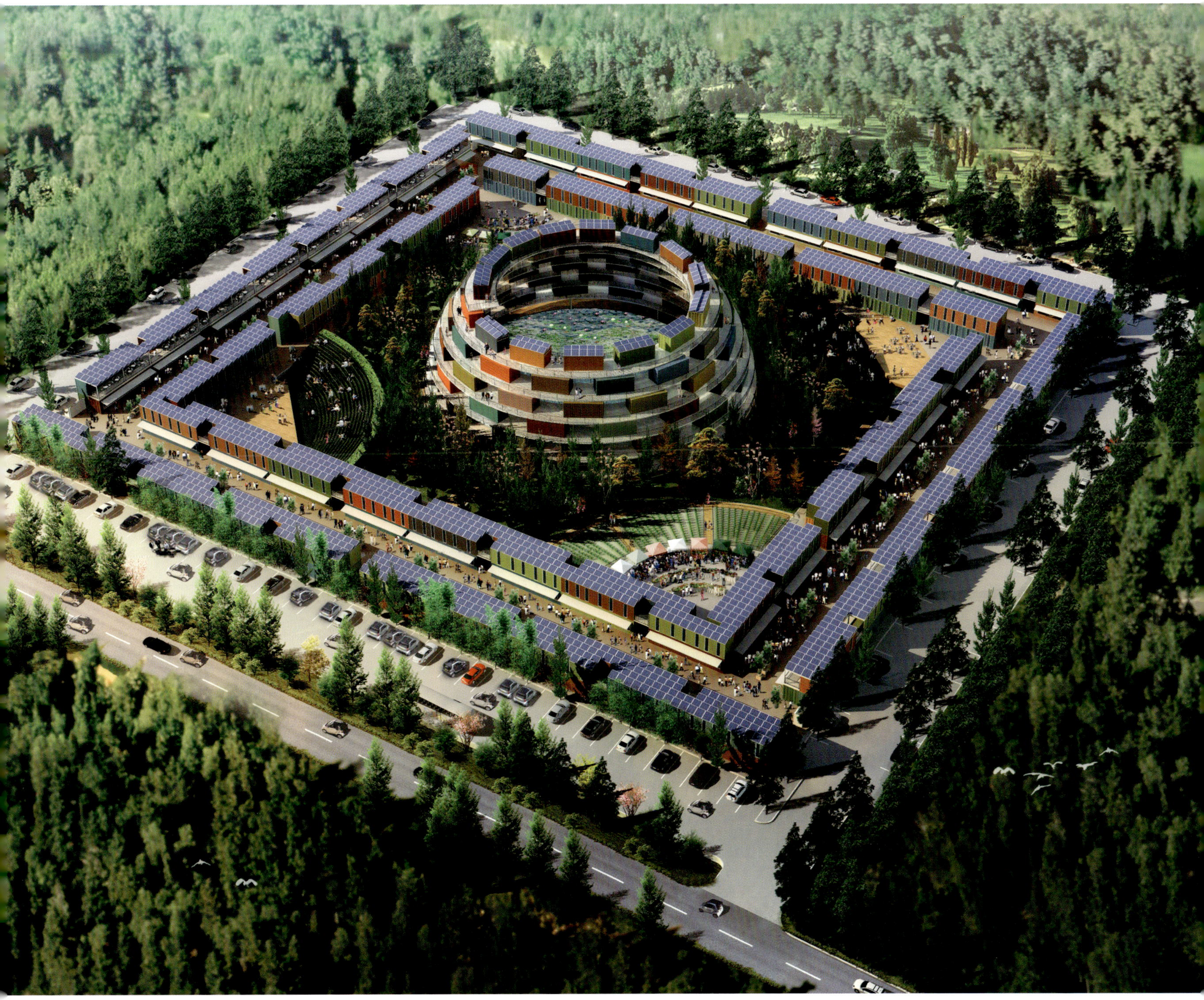

Nestor Topchy (with Si Dang)
Organ Computer Rendering, 2009
Computer rendering on photo paper
50 x 74 inches
Courtesy the artists and Que Imaging

Catalogue of the Exhibition

Dimensions are listed as height, preceding width, preceding depth

THE ART GUYS
The Art Guys Marry a Plant, 2009
Live oak tree, dirt, clay pot, gold ring
Tree: 104 x 18½ x 18½ inches
Courtesy the The Art Guys and McClain Gallery, Houston

MARY ELLEN CARROLL
prototype 180: table, 2009
Wood, laminate flooring, pipe, stools
32⅝ inches, height x 192 inches, diameter
Courtesy the artist and Galerie Hubert Winter, Vienna

BILL DAVENPORT
Bill's Junk, 2008
Wood, drywall, paint, fluorescent lights, electric fixtures, computer, handmade furniture, pottery, art, gifts, curios
12 x 12 x 20 feet
Courtesy the artist and Inman Gallery, Houston

BEN TECUMSEH DeSOTO
The Significance of Making Art, 2009
32 color photographs
11 x 14 inches each
Courtesy the artist

SHARON ENGELSTEIN (with Andrea Corson, Victoria Whitaker, David McGee, Jay Giroux, Alex Kvares, Amber Eagle, and Hills Snyder)
Gallery One Three Seven, 1994–2009
Wood, paint, works of art
7 ½ x 20 ¾ x 10 ¾ inches each
Courtesy the artists

THE FLOWER MAN (CLEVELAND TURNER)
The Flower Man Art, 2009
Wood, latex paint, found objects, artificial flowers, plants, CAMH front lawn
Structure: 10 x 10 x 17 feet
Courtesy the artist

MEL CHIN et al.
The Fundred Dollar Bill Project (Houston portion of three million *Fundred* drawings by various contributing artists, all works signed), 2008–10
Wood, drywall, paint, wallpaper photograph of *SAFEHOUSE*, paper templates, markers, pencils, gold tacks, chairs, table, participants
Installation: 14 x 19¾ x 27 feet
Drawings: 2⅝ x 6⅛ inches each
Courtesy Mel Chin, Organizing Principal, and Sabrina Franzheim, donor of *Fundreds* templates for Houston

OPERATION PAYDIRT/FUNDRED and *SAFEHOUSE* are made possible in part with support from Transforma Projects / National Performance Network (NPN), with major contributions from The Andy Warhol Foundation for the Visual Arts, The American Center Foundation, Creative Capital, Nathan Cummings Foundation, CrossCurrents Foundation and Project Row Houses.

SAFEHOUSE is installed in the St. Roch neighborhood of New Orleans at KKProjects, Art is Life Foundation.

ANDREA GROVER
Astrodome Cinema, May 28, 2009, 6:30 pm
Video screening: *The Pleasures of This Stately Dome* (1975), Geoff Winningham, running time: 54 minutes, 16mm on video, color, sound, and *The Lord of the Universe* (1974), TVTV (Top Value Television), running time: 58 minutes, black and white video, sound
Courtesy the artist, Geoff Winningham, and TVTV

Houston Lyceum, September 10, 2009, 6:30 pm and October 1, 2009, 6:30 pm
Public lecture series: "Eloquence," presented by Dr. Mike Fain, Director of Forensics, University of Houston Forensic Society, and "The Cause and Laws of Storms," presented by Lew Fincher, President of the Houston Chapter of the American Meteorological Society
Courtesy the artist

Jacuzzi Movies, June 11, June 25, and August 6, 2009, 6:30 pm
Video screenings, inflatable jacuzzi, participants
Courtesy the artist

DAN HAVEL and DEAN RUCK
Give and Take, 2009
Reclaimed material from condemned bungalow at
931 Cottage Street, Houston, and C-print
Approximately 20 x 30 x 15 feet
Courtesy the artists and Devin Borden Hiram Butler
Gallery, Houston

GEORGE HIXSON
Untitled, 1981–2006
62 gelatin silver prints
Dimensions variable
Courtesy the artist

LAUREN KELLEY
Prototypical Obsession/Oppression (bathroom set),
2007
Mixed media and lights in pedestal
36 x 30 x 30 inches

Prototypical Obsession/Oppression (airplane set),
2008
Mixed media and lights in drywall
36 x 36 x 60 inches

Prototypical Obsession/Oppression, 2009
DVD video, running time: 4:32 minutes, color, sound

All courtesy the artist

KNITTAPLEASE
(Magda Sayeg with Peggy Fergus and Michael Sayeg)
Untitled, 2009
Knitted and crocheted yarn, zip ties, front railing at
the CAMH
194 feet x 4 inches

Untitled, 2009
Knitted and crocheted yarn, cardboard, glue, on information desk at the CAMH
$48\frac{1}{2}$ x $125\frac{1}{2}$ x 142 inches

Both courtesy the artists

ERIC LESHINSKY
Museum for Missing Places, 2005–06
Interactive website: www.missing-places. org
Courtesy the artist

LEE LITTLEFIELD
New World Bamboo Flowers, 2008
Bamboo, vines, enamel paint
Approximately 3 x 26 x 3 feet each

Rings on Bissonnet, 2009
Vines, oil paint
Dimensions variable

Both courtesy the artist and Poissant Gallery, Houston

RICK LOWE
Brother-N-Law's, Every Neighborhood Needs One,
2009
Photograph and light box
48 x 30 x $5\frac{1}{2}$ inches

The Burning Sounds of Progress and Loss, 2009
Photograph on aluminum
36 x 70 x $1\frac{1}{2}$ inches

Cookie Love's Wash and Fold, 2009
Photograph and light box
48 x 30 x $5\frac{1}{2}$ inches

Power of Peace, 2009
Digital print on vinyl banner
77 x 60 inches

All courtesy the artist

BENJY MASON and ZACH MOSER
Yacht Shop, 2009
Building plans for a nineteen-foot skiff, paint, wood,
tools, participants
20 x 35 x 20 feet
Courtesy the artists

JIM PIRTLE
Ghost Bar, 2009
Plexiglas display cases, mixed media, found materials,
artworks, alcohol
14 x 20 x 16 feet
Courtesy the artist

NESTOR TOPCHY
Organ Demekon, 2009
Egg tempera, gold leaf, on wood
$13\frac{1}{4}$ x $11\frac{3}{4}$ inches

Organ Elevation Drawing, 2008
Ink on paper
12 x $35\frac{1}{2}$ inches

Organ Floorplan, 2008
Computer printout on paper
24 x 36 inches

Organ Maquette, 2008
Painted wood on board, string
48 x $41\frac{1}{2}$ x $13\frac{1}{2}$ inches

Zocalo and TemplO memorabilia/ephemera,
1989–2001
Five framed photo and text collages, blueprints,
photocopies on paper, drawings
Dimensions variable

(with Si Dang)
Organ Computer Rendering, 2009
Computer rendering on photo paper
50 x 74 inches
Courtesy the artists and Que Imaging

(with Si Dang and Andria Design)
Organ Elevation Model, 2009
Plastic print
4 x 18 x 20 inches

All courtesy the artist

The Art Guys

Michael Galbreth
Born 1956, Philadelphia
1984, MFA, University of Houston
1980, BFA, Memphis State University
1975–1977, Middle Tennessee State University
Lives and works in Houston

Jack Massing
Born 1959, Buffalo, New York
1984, BFA, University of Houston
1981, Glassell School of Art, Houston
1977–1979, Niagara Community College, New York
Lives and works in Houston

Selected Solo Exhibitions

2007
The Art Guys: Seeing Double, Tampa Museum of Art, Florida

2001
SUITS: The Clothes Make the Man, Museum of Fine Arts, Houston

1999
The Art Guys Again and Again, Tacoma Art Museum, Washington

Kit and Caboodle, Scottsdale Museum of Contemporary Art, Arizona

1996
Visualize The Art Guys, Kemper Museum of Contemporary Art and Design, Kansas City

1995
The Art Guys: Think Twice, Contemporary Arts Museum, Houston; traveled

Selected Group Exhibitions

2008
Agency: Art and Advertising, McDonough Museum of Art, Youngstown, Ohio

MashUp, University of South Florida Contemporary Art Museum, Tampa

2007
Duiying-Yingdui –Corresponding & Responding, Zhongguo Gongyi Meishuguan, Beijing

2005
Pattern Language: Clothing as Communicator, Tufts University Art Gallery, Medford, Massachusetts; traveled

2003
2003 Biennial Exhibition of Public Art, Neuberger Museum of Art, Purchase College, New York

Selected Performances

2008
Nothing To It (An Evening Of Itty Bitty Witty Ditties), Cynthia Woods Mitchell Center for the Arts, University of Houston

The Art Guys Lie in State, City Hall, Houston

2005
Nothing To It, University of Dayton, Ohio

2000
The Art Guys Are This Evening's Entertainment, San Jose Museum of Art, California

1999
101 of the World's Greatest Events All In A Row Tonight Right Before Your Very Eyes And We're Not Kidding And This Time We Really Mean It For Sure And How, Museum of Contemporary Art San Diego

Selected Bibliography

The Art Guys. *SUITS: The Clothes Make the Man*. New York: Harry N. Abrams, Inc., 2001.

French, Christopher. "Working in the World: A Conversation with The Art Guys." *Sculpture* 24, no. 1 (January/February 2005).

Gray, Lisa. "The Art Guys attempt to sell themselves." *Houston Chronicle*, January 27, 2008, Zest section.

Herbert, Lynn. *The Art Guys: Cloud Cuckoo Land*. Exh. cat. Galveston, Texas: Galveston Arts Center, 2007.

Herbert, Lynn, et al. *The Art Guys: Think Twice*. Exh. cat. Houston: Contemporary Arts Museum, 1995.

Klaasmeyer, Kelly. "The Art Guys: To the outer loop and beyond." *Art Lies*, no. 44 (Fall 2004).

Klein, Sheri. *Art and Laughter*. London: I.B. Tauris & Co., 2007.

Mary Ellen Carroll

Born 1962, New York
1989, MFA, School of the Art Institute of Chicago
1986, BS, University of Colorado at Boulder
Lives and works in Houston and New York

Selected One-Person Exhibitions

2008
Angles Gallery, Santa Monica, California

Galerie Hubert Winter, Vienna

2007
The Power House Memphis

2006
The Precipice Alliance, New York

2005
Storefront for Art and Architecture, New York

Selected Public Projects

1999–2009
prototype 180, 6513 Sharpview Street, Houston

Selected Group Exhibitions

2006
Soft Sites, Institute of Contemporary Art, Philadelphia

2005
We Keep Working, To No Longer Work, Staatliches Museum für Völkerkunde, Munich

2004
A Perfect Union...More or Less, The Renaissance Society at the University of Chicago

2003
100 Artists See God, Independent Curators International; traveled

2002
Itinerant Gastronomy, Apex Art, New York

2001
Out of Order: Mapping Social Space, University Memorial Center Art Gallery, University of Colorado at Boulder; traveled

Selected Bibliography

Barliant, Claire. "Mary Ellen Carroll: Cinema Village/Storefront for Art and Architecture." *Artforum* 44, no. 3 (2005): 256.

Boyle, Frank. *A Modest Proposal /A Modist Prepozel*. New York: Presse Endémique, 1994.

Carroll, Mary Ellen. *All of the Men Who Think That They Can Be Me*. Paris: OneStar Press, 2004.

Elias, Norbert, and Harald Welzer. *100 German Men*. New York: Presse Endémique, 1998.

Flatley, Jonathan, and Hamza Walker. *Mary Ellen Carroll* (monograph). London: Steidl Mack, forthcoming.

Henderson, Stephen. "Think Again." *Gourmet Magazine* (February 2008): 64.

Johnson, Ken. "Art Guide." *New York Times*, November 23, 2001, Arts section.

Mel Chin (of *The Fundred Dollar Bill Project*)

Born 1951, Houston
1975, BA, Peabody College, Nashville
Lives and works in Burnsville, North Carolina

Selected One-Person Exhibitions

1997–1999
Inescapable Histories, Exhibits USA; traveled

1995
Anxious Objects, Colorado State University, Fort Collins

1992
Soil and Sky, The Fabric Workshop and Swarthmore College, Philadelphia

1991
Degrees of Paradise, Storefront for Art and Architecture, New York

1990–1992
Mel Chin, Walker Art Center, Minneapolis; traveled

Selected Public Projects

2008–2010
The Fundred Dollar Bill Project and *Operation Paydirt*, national art/science project in conjunction with *SAFEHOUSE*, New Orleans

2007
9/11-9/11, animated film, with Chip Schneider, Houston, and Planovisual Estudio de Animación, Santiago, Chile

1992
Revival Field/Netherlands: Simultaneous Replicated Field Test, Floriadepark, Zoetermeer, The Netherlands

1991–1993
Revival Field/Minnesota, Pennsylvania, hazardous waste state Superfund sites, Pig's Eye Landfill, St. Paul, Minnesota, and Palmerton, Pennsylvania

Selected Group Exhibitions

2008
Ornithology: Looking at Birds, University of Connecticut, Storrs

2005
Down the Garden Path: The Artist's Garden After Modernism, Queens Museum of Art, New York

2003
Signatures of the Invisible, P.S.1 Contemporary Art Center, New York

2002
The Culture of Violence, Mead Art Museum, Amherst College, Massachusetts; traveled

A New World Trade Center: Design Proposals, Max Protetch Gallery, New York

One Planet Under A Groove, Bronx Museum of the Arts, New York; traveled

Selected Bibliography

Art:21 Art in the Twenty-First Century [PBS television series]. New York: Art21, Inc., 2001.

Boswell, Peter. *Viewpoints: Mel Chin*. Exh. cat. Minneapolis: Walker Art Center, 1990.

Decter, Joshua. "Prime Time: 'In the Name of the Place' of Art and Television." In *In the Name of the Place*. Exh. cat. Kansas City, Missouri: Grand Arts, 1998.

Finkelpearl, Tom. *Dialogues in Public Art*. Cambridge, Massachusetts: MIT Press, 2000.

Kastner, Jeffrey, ed. *Land and Environmental Art*. London: Phaidon, 1998.

Knight, Christopher. "The Socio-Art Genre." *Los Angeles Times*, March 18, 1997.

Lippard, Lucy. *The Lure of the Local: Senses of Place in a Multi-Centered Society*. New York: New Press, 1997.

———. *Mixed Blessings: New Art in Multicultural America*. New York: Pantheon, 1990.

McEvilley, Thomas. "Explicating Exfoliation in the Work of Mel Chin." In *Soil & Sky*. Exh. cat. Philadelphia: The Fabric Workshop, 1993.

Rifkin, Ned. *Directions: Mel Chin*. Exh. cat. Washington, D.C.: Hirshhorn Museum and Sculpture Garden, 1989.

Bill Davenport

Born 1962, Greenfield, Massachusetts
1990, MFA, University of Massachusetts, Amherst
1986, BFA, Rhode Island School of Design, Providence
Lives and works in Houston

Selected One-Person Exhibitions

2006
Forever Rafter, Inman Gallery, Houston

2004
Poetry of the Thirties, Inman Gallery, Houston

2003
Slow Birds, Angstrom Gallery, Dallas

2001
The Modern Blacksmith, Inman Gallery, Houston

Spectaculess, Homeroom, Munich

1999
Nothing Special, Angstrom Gallery, Dallas

Selected Public Projects

2009
Giant Mushroom Forest, City of Austin Art in Public Places Program, 2009 Texas Biennial

2007
Theory of Macramé Owls, Visual Arts League, Lewisville, Texas

2006
The Stream of Conscious-ness (my secret journal from 1974–1977 posted in real time), http://billdavenport.blogspot.com

Timberland Art Corral, Westheimer Street Festival, Houston

Selected Group Exhibitions

2008
Material Culture, Fort Worth Contemporary Arts

2007
Arthouse Texas Prize Exhibition, Arthouse, Austin, Texas

2006
COMPLICIT!, Bayley Art Museum, University of Virginia, Charlottesville

2002
Blip, University of South Florida Contemporary Art Museum, Tampa

2000
Natural Deceits, Modern Art Museum of Fort Worth

1998
Blunt Object, David and Alfred Smart Museum of Art, Chicago

Selected Bibliography

Bourbon, Matthew. "Bill Davenport: Slow Birds." *Art Lies* 38 (Spring 2003): 71.

Colpitt, Frances. "Bill Davenport at Inman." *Art in America* (March 1996): 105.

________. "Southern Sensibilities." *Art in America* (November 2001): 58.

Dewan, Shaila. "The Antihero." *Houston Press*, October 28–November 3, 1999.

Mitchell, Charles Dee. "Bill Davenport at Angstrom Gallery." *Art Lies* 23 (Summer 1999): 42.

Moody, Tom. "Bill Davenport at Cristinerose." *Artforum* (April 1997): 95.

Ben Tecumseh DeSoto

Born 1958, Jacinto City, Texas
1978–1981, University of Houston
1978, AA, San Jacinto College, Houston
Lives and works in Houston

Selected One-Person Exhibitions

2008
Understanding Poverty, DiverseWorks, Houston

2007
Understanding Poverty Project Presentation #1, Bohemeo's, Houston

1992
Urban Poverty, FotoFest, DiverseWorks, Houston

1990
Fellowship Exhibition, Houston Center for Photography

1989
Urban Poverty, United Way Coalition of Churches Homeless Campaign, Houston

Selected Group Exhibitions

1998
Local Heroes, FotoFest, Menil Collection, Houston

1989
Can Religion Make a Difference?, Margolis Gallery, Congregation Beth Israel, Houston

Messages from the South, Sewell Gallery, Rice University, Houston

1988
Houston Area Exhibition, Blaffer Gallery, University of Houston

Selected Bibliography

Afra, Omar. "Understanding Poverty." *Houston Free Press* (September 2008): 22–23.

"Alternative Space Preview." *Art in America 2008 Guide: Galleries, Museums, & Artists* (August 2008): 35.

Britt, Douglas. "A photographer's view of the homeless." *Houston Chronicle*, October 23, 2008.

Hennington, Jason. "Creating Medicine from Poison." *Living Buddhism* (November–December 2008): 30–31.

Huber, Caroline. "Introduction." In *Urban Poverty: Photographs by Ben DeSoto*. Exh. cat. Houston: DiverseWorks, 1992.

Schultze, Troy. "Rich 'Poverty.'" *Houston Press*, October 2–8, 2008.

Sharon Engelstein

Born 1965, Montreal
1990, MFA, Claremont Graduate School, California
1987, BFA, University of South Florida, Tampa
Lives and works in Houston

Selected One-Person Exhibitions

2009
Light as Air, Discovery Green, Houston

Site Flavor, Shaw Center for the Arts, Louisiana State University, Baton Rouge

2008
Blowdup, Sunday L.E.S., New York

2004
Tethertwin, Sioux City Art Center, Iowa

2002
Air GA, Artpace, San Antonio

2000
Boolean Unions, Contemporary Arts Museum Houston

Selected Group Exhibitions

2008
Sculpture at Evergreen Biennial, Evergreen Museum, Johns Hopkins University, Baltimore

2007
Big, Cameron Art Museum, Wilmington, North Carolina

2005
Partners, Kirkland Arts Center, Washington

2004
Feed, Bakalar and Paine Galleries, Massachusetts College of Art and Design, Boston

From the States, National Museum of Women in the Arts, Washington, D.C.

Selected Bibliography

Colpitt, Frances. "Space City Takes Off." *Art in America* (October 2000): 67–75.

Dumbadze, Alexander. Review. *New Art Examiner* (April 2000): 57.

Friis Hansen, Dana. *Boolean Unions*. Exh. cat. Houston: Contemporary Arts Museum, 2000.

Linden, Christina. "Sharon Engelstein: Sunday." *Art Lies* (Fall 2008): 114.

McQuaid, Cate. "Sculptures Are Both Playful and Powerful." *Boston Globe*, January 31, 2003.

Olsen, Valerie Loupe. *Inflated*. Exh. cat. Houston: Museum of Fine Arts, Houston, 2001.

O'Sullivan, Michael. "Nature Pushes Back." *Washington Post*, August 15, 2008.

Rushing, Jackson. Review. *Sculpture* (June 2000): 79.

The Flower Man (Cleveland Turner)

Born 1935, Mississippi
Lives and works in Houston

One-Person Exhibition

2002
Joan Wich & Co., Houston

Public Projects

2004–ongoing
The Flower Man's House, 2305 Francis Street, Houston

2002
Project Row Houses, Houston

1988–2003
The Flower Man's House, 3311 Sampson Street, Houston

1986–88
The Flower Man's House, Sauer Street, Houston

Selected Bibliography

Beardsley, John. "Salvage/Salvation: Recent African American Yard Shows." In *American Sanctuary: Understanding Sacred Spaces*. Edited by Louis P. Nelson. Bloomington: Indiana University Press, 2006.

Maizels, John. *Raw Creation: Outsider Art & Beyond*. New York: Phaidon Press, 1996.

Manley, Roger, and Mark Sloan. *Self-Made Worlds: Visionary Folk Art Environments.* New York: Aperture, 2005.

Mason, Randy, Don Mayberger, and Mike Murphy. *Rare Visions & Roadside Revelations*. Kansas City: Kansas City Star Books, 2002.

Nokes, Jill, with Pat Jasper. *Yard Art and Handmade Places: Extraordinary Expressions of Home*. Austin: University of Texas Press, 2007.

Rowden, Deb, ed. *Detour Art: Outsider, Folk Art, and Visionary Environments Coast to Coast–Art and Photographs from the Collection of Kelly Ludwig.* Kansas City: Kansas City Star Books, 2007.

Sellen, Betty-Carol, with Cynthia J. Johanson. *Self Taught, Outsider, and Folk Art: A Guide to American Artists, Locations and Resources.* Jefferson, N.C.: McFarland & Company, 1999.

Wardlaw, Alvia. "The Flower Man's Corner." In *Souls Grown Deep: African American Vernacular Art of the South*. Vol. 2. Edited by William Arnett and Paul Arnett. Atlanta: Tinwood Books, 2001.

Wertkin, Gerard, ed. *Encyclopedia of American Folk Art*. New York: Routledge, 2004.

Andrea Grover

Born 1970, Long Island, New York
1995, MFA, School of the Art Institute of Chicago
1992, BFA, Syracuse University, New York
1991, Central/St. Martin's College of Art and Design, London
Lives and works in Houston

Selected Curated Film and Video Exhibitions

2008
At Your Service: Escaping the Progress Trap, DVD for *Art Lies*, no. 57

2007
Never Been to Houston, co-curated with Jon Rubin, Lawndale Art Center, Houston

Never Been to Tehran, co-curated with Jon Rubin, Parkingallery, Tehran

Txt Me L8r, Houston Center for Photography, Houston

2006
Phantom Captain: Art and Crowdsourcing, Apex Art, New York

Selected Professional Projects

2007–ongoing
Confluence Points of View on Buffalo Bayou, co-curator, Buffalo Bayou Partnership, Houston

1998–2008
Founder and director, Aurora Picture Show, Houston

Selected Bibliography

2007

Cotter, Holland. "Phantom Captain: Art and Crowdsourcing." *New York Times*, November 24, 2006, Arts section.

DeVun, Leah. "Your Assignment: Art." *Assignment Zero,* in collaboration with *Wired News.* http://www.wired.com/techbiz/media/news/2007/07/crowd_captain (accessed March 20, 2009).

Gray, Lisa. "Houston, imagined by people who've never been here." *Houston Chronicle*, March 11, 2007, Zest section.

________. "The Moving Picture Show." *Houston Chronicle,* December 5, 2007, Star section.

Handwerker, Margo. "Never Been to Houston." *Art Lies*, no. 54 (Summer 2007).

Meltzer, Eve. "Phantom Captain." *Frieze* , no. 104 (February 2007).

Taylor, Tess. "See Modern Art in Houston." *New York Magazine* (May 2007).

Woodward, Richard B. "Keeping it Reel." *Departures* (November/December 2005).

Dan Havel and Dean Ruck

Havel Ruck Projects
Founded 1995

Dan Havel
Born 1959, St. Peter, Minnesota
1983, MFA, Minnesota State University, Mankato
1981, BFA, Southwest State University, Marshall, Minnesota
Lives and works in Houston

Dean Ruck
Born 1962, Hamden, Connecticut
1987, MFA, Cranbrook Academy of Art, Bloomfield Hills, Michigan
1984, BFA, University of Colorado, Boulder
Lives and works in Houston

Solo Exhibition

2009
Architectural Euthanasia, Architecture Center Houston

Selected Public Projects

2005
Apt. Suite, 1711 Winbern, Houston

Inversion, Art League of Houston

Scatterboats, Estudio Abierto, Buenos Aires

1995
O House, Houston (collaboration with Kate Petley)

Selected Group Exhibitions

2008
False Space and Time in the Apartment, CentralTrak, Dallas

2007
Artadia 2006 Exhibition, DiverseWorks, Houston

Selected Bibliography

Feireiss, Lukas, and R. Klanten, eds. *Spacecraft: Fleeting Architecture and Hideouts*. London: Die Gestalten Verlag, 2007.

Gray, Lisa. "After the Whirlwind." *Houston Chronicle*, February 8, 2009, Star section.

Greene, Alison de Lima. "To Continue." *Gulf Coast* 18, no. 1 (Winter/Spring 2006): 171.

Johnson, Patricia. "The Art Shack." *Houston Chronicle*, April 28, 1995, Star section.

________. "Art Turned Inside Out: Bringing Down the House." *Houston Chronicle*, May 20, 2005, Star section.

Klaasmeyer, Kelly. "Tunnel of Love." *Houston Press*, June 23, 2005.

Peters, Patrick. "Casa Lucida/Casa Obscura." *Cite* 34 (Spring 1996).

________. "Curb a Peel Along Montrose." *Texas Architect* (July/August 2005).

________. "*Inversion*." *Cite,* no. 65 (Winter 2005).

Pruitt, Nicole. "Inversion." *artsHouston* (June 2005).

Ward, Liz. "O: A House Installation." *Gulf Coast* 18, no. 1 (Winter/Spring 2006): 157.

Worthmann, Arthur. "The Implosion." *Mark*, no. 2 (Spring 2006): 180–81.

George Hixson

Born 1956, Buffalo, New York
1986–1990, Commerce Street Artists' Warehouse, Houston
1975–1979, University of Bridgeport, Connecticut
Lives and works in Houston

Selected One-Person Exhibitions

2006
Dean's Clothing, Houston

Fotofest, Poissant Gallery, Houston

2004
Axiom, Houston

2002
Dog, City Gallery at Wells Fargo, Houston

Selected Group Exhibitions

2008
Green Texas, Art Car Museum, Houston

2005
Poissant Gallery, Houston

2004
Cross Current, Gallery 101, Houston

2000
Shudder Speed, Art Car Museum, Houston

1998
Local Heroes, The Menil Collection, Houston

1994
Project Landscape, Commerce Street Artists' Warehouse, Houston

1995
Changing Perspectives, Contemporary Arts Museum Houston

Performances and Media

1998–2001
"9X," weekly photography column, *Houston's Other*

1990
Paint Bomb, Bathroom, Commerce Street Artists' Warehouse, Houston

1985–1998
"Eye Spy," weekly photography column, *Public News* (Houston)

Lauren Kelley

Born 1975, Baltimore
1999, MFA, School of the Art Institute of Chicago
1997, BFA, Maryland Institute College of Art, Baltimore
Lives and works in Houston

One-Person Exhibition

2006
Collect Them All! Soft Brown Narratives, Lawndale Art Center, Houston

Selected Group Exhibitions

2009
Core 2009, Glassell School of Art, Houston

2008
Altoids Award, New Museum of Contemporary Art, New York

Cinema Remixed and Reloaded: Black Women Artists and the Moving Image Since 1970, Contemporary Arts Museum Houston

Core 2008, Glassell School of Art, Houston

2007
Nexus Texas, Contemporary Arts Museum Houston

Homage to Domestic Familiarity, Anya Tish Gallery, Houston

Reality Testing, LACE, Los Angeles

Round 27: Race and Class, Project Row Houses, Houston

2003
Telling Our Story: The Art of YBW, Prairie State College, Chicago Heights, Illinois

2002
Burnt, Fried, Pulled, Curled, Hyde Park Art Center, Chicago

2001
Wig Works, DiverseWorks, Houston

YBW, Young Black Women, Frick Center, Founder's Lounge Gallery, Elmhurst College, Illinois

Selected Bibliography

Davenport, Bill. "Barbie she's not..." *Houston Chronicle*, October 1, 2006, Zest section.

Goldsmith, Meredith. "Lauren Kelley: Collect Them All! Soft Brown Narratives, Houston." *Art Lies* 52 (Fall 2006).

Gray, Lisa. "Heartbreak in the dollhouse." *Houston Chronicle*, April 30, 2008, Star section.

Klaasmeyer, Kelly. "Home Improvements." *Houston Press*, May 4, 2000.

Vogel, Carol. "Altoids Award." *New York Times*, March 21, 2008, Arts section.

Wolmack, Ytasha. "Odditorium: Poet Brings Freak to Light." *Chicago Defender*, November 28, 2001.

KnittaPlease (Magda Sayeg et al.)

KnittaPlease (Magda Sayeg, et al.)
Founded 2005, Houston

Selected Public Projects
2008
Absolut Vodka, Mexico City (wrapped city bus in yarn)

J. Crew, New York (tagged flagship store and knit 100 belt loops on jeans)

ZXZW Music Festival, Tilberg, The Netherlands (tagged town square)

2007
AIGA Design Ranch, Austin, Texas (tagged compound and workshops)

Bergère de France, Paris (tagged various objects for ten days)

Neiman Marcus International, Chicago, Los Angeles, and Washington, D.C. (tagged interior of four C.U.S.P. stores)

Standard Hotel, Los Angeles (tagged vitrine in lobby)

2006
Bumbershoot Festival, Seattle (tagged monorail columns, trees, and center court columns)

Selected Group Exhibitions
2009
La Triennale di Milano, Triennale Design Museum, Milan

2008
400 ML Project, Le M.U.R., Paris

2007
PLAY, Urbis, Manchester, UK

Texas Uprising, Blue Star Contemporary Art Center, San Antonio

Thread, Wood Street Galleries, Pittsburgh

2006
After School Art, S.U.N. Arts, Brooklyn, New York

Fuzzy Logic, Dundee Contemporary Arts, Scotland

Nana Is the New Black, Centre of Contemporary Arts, Cairns, Australia

Softly Threatening, One Reel for Bumbershoot Festival, Seattle

Selected Bibliography

Gastman, Roger, Caleb Neelon, and Anthony Smyrski. *Street World: Urban Culture and Art from Five Continents*. New York: Harry N. Abrams, 2007.

Gavin, Francesca. *Street Renegades: New Underground Art*. London: Laurence King, 2007.

Gschwandtner, Sabrina. *KnitKnit: Profiles + Projects from Knitting's New Wave*. New York: Stewart, Tabori and Chang, 2007.

Hanaor, Ziggy, and Victoria Woodcock, eds. *Making Stuff: An Alternative Craft Book*. London: Black Dog Publishing, 2007.

Levine, Faythe, and Cortney Heimerl. *Handmade Nation: The Rise of DIY, Art, Craft, and Design*. New York: Princeton Architectural Press, 2008.

McCormick, Carlo, ed. *Trespass: A History of Uncommissioned Public Art*. Cologne: Taschen, forthcoming.

Moore, Mandy, and Leanne Prain. *Yarn Bombing: The Art of Crochet and Knit Graffiti*. Vancouver: Arsenal Pulp Press, 2009.

Spencer, Amy. *The Crafter Culture Handbook*. London: Marion Boyars, 2007.

Eric Leshinsky

Born 1976, Annapolis, Maryland
2006, MArch, Rice University, Houston
1998, BA, Columbia University, New York
Lives and works in Baltimore

Selected Public Projects
2008–ongoing
Baltimore Design Conversations, monthly curated forum, Baltimore (collaboration with Fred Scharmen, Ryan Patterson, Ben Stone, and Gary Kachadourian)

2008
The Plant, conceptual design for urban infill energy farm, Baltimore (collaboration with Fred Scharmen, Prescott Gaylord, Elizabeth Evitts Dickinson, and Thibault Manekin)

2007
Deck, architectural installation, 1428 Hollins Street, Baltimore

2006
Bambino, Airstream trailer architectural prototype, Houston (collaboration with Garrett Finney/FARO Studio)

2003–2005
Museum for Missing Places, art, architecture, and curatorial project, Houston. www.missing-places.org

Selected Group Exhibitions
2009
Baltimore Infill Survey, Baltimore Office of Promotion & Arts

2008
Colors, 2219 gallery, Baltimore

Stuttering: In a New Light, Carroll House Museum, Baltimore

Welcome to: One Park, Current Gallery, with Baltimore Festival of Maps (collaboration with Fred Scharmen)

2007
Home, 2219 gallery, Baltimore

Plastic: Landscape, Cityscape, Lifescape, Creative Alliance, Baltimore

2005
Indecent Proposals, Buffalo Bayou ArtPark, Houston

Selected Bibliography

"Design Conversation: Cultural Containers." *Urban Palimpsest*, October 23, 2008. http://urbanpalimpsest.blogspot.com/2008/10/design-conversation-cultural-containers.html (accessed April 6, 2009).

Dickinson, Elizabeth Evitts. "The Great Infill Challenge." *Metropolis Magazine POV,* March 2, 2009. http://www.metropolismag.com/pov/20090302/the-great-infill-challenge (accessed April 6, 2009).

Leshinsky, Eric. "Welcome to Houston, Texas." *MONU: Magazine on Urbanism*, no. 4 (January 2006).

"The New Power Plant." *Urban Palimpsest*, December 10, 2008. http://urbanpalimpsest.blogspot.com/2008/12/new-power-plant.html (accessed April 6, 2009).

Lee Littlefield

Born 1936, Cape Cod, Massachusetts
1968, MA, University of New Mexico, Albuquerque
1962, BA, Florida State University, Tallahassee
Lives and works in Houston

Selected One-Person Exhibitions

2007
Walton Arts Center, Fayetteville, Arkansas

2005
Dallas Center for Contemporary Art

Paul and Lulu Hilliard University Art Museum, University of Louisiana, Lafayette

2004
Daum Museum of Contemporary Art, Sedalia, Missouri

2001
Ann Norton Sculpture Gardens, West Palm Beach, Florida

Springfield Art Museum, Missouri

Selected Public Project

1998–ongoing
Pop-Up Sculpture for the Millennium, along Interstates 10 and 45, Houston

Selected Group Exhibitions

2008
The Great Texas Sculpture Roundup, Art Car Museum, Houston

2007
Sculpture Vision XV, North Harris College, Houston

2006
Houston Now, Williams Tower Gallery, Houston

2004
Texas Uprising, Blue Star Contemporary Art Center, San Antonio

2002
South Texas Sculpture Invitational, San Antonio

Selected Publications:

Armstrong, Cameron. "Site/Works, A Public Forum." *Sculpture* (October 2000).

Karkabi, Barbara. "Look Again, and Look Again, whimsical sculpture 'popping up' all over," *Houston Chronicle*, July 26, 2000, Star section.

Ponnekanti, Rosemary. "Hidden In Full View." *artsHouston* (2003): 14–19.

Rothman, Sabine. "Stopping Traffic." *House and Garden* (November 2001): 108–09.

Tennant, Donna. "Born in the Bayou." *artsHouston* (April 2005): 16–17.

Rick Lowe

Born 1961, Eufaula, Alabama
1982, BA, Columbus College, Georgia
Lives and works in Houston

Selected Public Projects

2008–ongoing
Time Bank, Amherst College, Massachusetts (collaboration with Wendy Ewald and students)

Vessel, Eatonville, Florida (collaboration with the community)

2006–ongoing
Transforma New Orleans Resource Team (collaboration with Jessica Cusick, Sam Durant, Robert Ruello, and MK Wegmann)

2003–2004
Delray Beach Cultural Loop, Delray Beach, Florida

2003
Borough Project, Spoleto Festival 2003, Charleston, South Carolina (collaboration with Suzanne Lacy and Mary Jane Jacobs)

2002
Freehouse, Rotterdam, The Netherlands

1993–ongoing
Project Row Houses, Houston

Selected Group Exhibitions

2009
Needle in a Haystack, Center for the Arts, Eagle Rock, Los Angeles

2008
In Katrina's Wake, Blanton Museum of Art, Austin, Texas (with Transforma New Orleans Resource Team)

Into the Open: Positioning Practice, Architecture Venice Biennale; traveled

2005
Towards Social Sculpture, Glassell School of Art, Houston

2001
New•Land•Marks, Pennsylvania Academy of the Fine Arts, Philadelphia

2000
OutBound, Contemporary Arts Museum, Houston

Selected Bibliography

Becker, Carol. "The Art of Crossing the Street." *Art Journal* 58, no. 1 (Spring 1999): 11–15.

Goldberg, Vicki. "Art: In Houston, Building by Creating." *New York Times*, July 16, 1995, Art section.

Johnson, Patricia. "Rick Lowe's World." *Houston Chronicle*, January 23, 2005, Zest section.

Kimmelman, Michael. "In Houston, Art Is Where the Home Is." *New York Times*, December 17, 2006, Art & Design section.

Lopate, Phillip. "Deep in the Heart of Houston." *New York Times Magazine*, (February 27, 2000): 21.

Ulbricht, J. "Learning About Community Art Behaviors." *Art Education* 55, no. 5 (September 2002): 33-38.

Benjy Mason and Zach Moser

Benjy Mason
Born 1980,Charlotte, Vermont
2002, BA, Oberlin College, Ohio
Lives and works in Houston

Selected Public Projects

2005
Land of Happy Feet, El Dorado Ballroom, Houston

2004
I dream of frogs (for Jeff), The Orange Show, Houston

Mario World, Project Row Houses Cultural Arts Festival, Houston (collaboration with Zach Moser)

2003–ongoing
Co-director, Workshop Houston

2003 and 2004
Community float building workshops, The Big Parade, Oberlin, Ohio

Selected Group Exhibitions

2009
Houston Bicentennial, the joanna, Houston

2006
B.Y.O.B.B, DiverseWorks, Houston (collaboration with Danny Kerschen)

Zach Moser
Born 1979, Houston
2008, Leadership Institute for Non-Profit Executives, Rice University, Houston
2008, Skowhegan School of Painting & Sculpture, Maine
2002, BA, Oberlin College, Ohio
Lives and works in Houston

Selected Public Projects

2005–ongoing
Shrimp Boat Project, Houston

2003–ongoing
Co-director, Workshop Houston

2001–2003
Organizer, The Big Parade, Oberlin, Ohio

Selected Group Exhibitions

2007
Reprised: The Artadia Awardees, DiverseWorks, Houston

2006
Take One, Glassell School of Art, Houston

2005
Thought Crimes: The Art of Subversion, DiverseWorks, Houston

2004
Mario World, Project Row Houses Cultural Arts Festival, Houston (collaboration with Benjy Mason)

2003
Delray Beach Cultural Loop, Delray Beach, Florida

Selected Bibliography

Ammirati, Domenick. "Belief Systems: Deep in the Art of Texas." *Modern Painters* (October 2006).

Brancaccio, David. "Ideas That Work: Earn-a-Bike." *Now* [PBS television series], May 18, 2007.

Fowler, Brendan. "Workshop Houston." *ANP Quarterly* 1, no. 8 (Summer 2007).

Gabe, Catherine. "Oberlin's town-gown parade brings college, city a step closer Big Parade two," *The Plain Dealer (Cleveland),* May 5, 2002.

Gray, Lisa. "Rebuilding Bikes, Rebuilding Lives, in Third Ward." *Houston Chronicle,* December 29, 2008, Star section.

Panis, Regina. "Workshop Houston: Life Is Like Riding a Bicycle." *002* (November 2008): 32.

Ritter, Travis. "You Fix It, You Keep It." *Houston Press*, November 6, 2003.

Sievert, Steve. "Community Bike Center Makes Impact in Third Ward." *Houston Chronicle*, October 30, 2003, Sports section.

Jim Pirtle

Born 1960, Houston
1983, BA, Baylor University, Waco, Texas
Lives and works in Houston

Selected One-Person Exhibitions

2008
notsuoH, CUE Art Foundation, New York

2004
I'm painting again, Helios, Houston

1990
Polyester, DiverseWorks, Houston

1989
Polyester World View, Axiom, Houston

1986
Connected Community, Treebeard's, Houston

Selected Group Exhibitions

2000
Site/Work/S, Sculpture2000 International Conference, Houston

1990
Avenues of Departure, Contemporary Arts Center, New Orleans

1988
The Commerce Street Artists, Commerce Street Artists' Warehouse, Houston

Selected Performances

2003
Drinking Pennzoil, Art Car Parade, Houston

1995
Narcissism, DiverseWorks, Houston

1994
Media Lounge, Dallas Museum of Art

1993
Stu Mulligan Self-destructive Consumption with Lounge Singing, International Performance Festival, Ex Teresa, Mexico City

Selected Bibliography

Cunningham, Kevin. "Gut Reaction." *Houston Press*, February 22, 1990.

Fludenheimer, Mark. "Notsuoh…Jim Pirtle spells Insanity Forwards." *Field and Stream* (July 2001).

Waddington, Chris. "Highs and Lows from Houston." *New Orleans Picayune*, January 1, 1993.

Nestor Topchy

Born Sommerville, New Jersey, 1963
1987, MFA, University of Houston
1985, BFA, Maryland Institute College of Art, Baltimore
Lives and works in Houston

Selected One-Person Exhibition

2008
Pysanky, Art League of Houston; traveled to Galveston Arts Center, Texas

Selected Public Projects and Performances

2008
notsuoH, CUE Art Foundation, New York

2006
I love You, Me, notsuoH, Houston

2004–2005
Seed / 0 co-op Project, Project Row Houses, Houston

1989–2001
Zocalo/Templ0, an outdoor stage, gallery, and artist studios, Houston

Selected Group Exhibitions

2007
Amistad: Texas Art in Peru, Museo de la Nación, Lima, Peru; traveled to Museo de Arte Moderno, Trujillo, Peru

Building a Legacy: Evergreen Scholars at MICA, Evergreen Museum, Johns Hopkins University, Baltimore

2005
Drawings, Devin Borden Hiram Butler Gallery, Houston

2003
The Passionate Pursuit of the Real: Collage, Assemblage, and Object in 20th Century Art, Museum of Fine Arts, Houston

2001
The Inward Eye: Transcendence in Contemporary Art, Contemporary Arts Museum, Houston.

Selected Bibliography

Colpitt, Frances. "Space City Takes Off." *Art in America* (October 2001).

Gambrell, James. "In the Third Coast Art Capital." *Art in America* (April 1987).

Harithas, James. *Art Cars: Revolutionary Movement.* Houston: Ineri Foundation, 1997.

Herbert, Lynn M., Klaus Ottman, and Peter Schjeldahl. *The Inward Eye: Transcendence in Contemporary Art*. Exh. cat. Houston: Contemporary Arts Museum, 2002.

Tyer, Brad. "Bringing Down the House: Nestor Topchy Deconstructs his Templo." *Houston Press*, March 22, 2001.

Contemporary Arts Museum Houston

Staff

Bill Arning, *Director*
Andriano Balajadia, *IT Manager / Webmaster*
Tim Barkley, Registrar
Cheryl Blissitte, *Administrative Assistant, Director's Office*
Robert Bowden, *Finance Officer*
Amanda Bredbenner, *Development Assistant*
Mario Cuellar, *Assistant Gallery Supervisor*
Kenya F. Evans, *Gallery Supervisor*
Natividad Flores, *Housekeeping*
Meredith Goldsmith, *Curatorial Associate (2008–2009)*
Toby Kamps, *Senior Curator*
Carlos Lama, *Education Associate*
Connie McAllister, *Communications and Marketing Manager*
Paula Newton, *Director of Education and Public Programs*
Valerie Cassel Oliver, *Curator*
Sue Pruden, *Museum Shop Manager*
Michael Reed, *Assistant Director*
Linda Shearer, *Interim Director (2007–2009)*
Jeff Shore, *Head Preparator*
Kristina Spritzer, *Grants and Gifts Manager*
Lana Sullivan, *Receptionist/Staff Secretary*
Vanessa Voss, *Museum Shop Assistant*
Justine Waitkus, *Curatorial Manager*
Amber Winsor, *Director of Development*

Photography Credits

Page numbers are listed. The designation "chrono" refers to photos appearing in the chronology band at the bottom of pages.

Mark Allen: p. 70 (chrono, center)

©Terry Allen: p. 22 (chrono, left)

Courtesy of Ant Farm: p. 17 (chrono, left)

Cameron Armstrong: pp. 16, 25, 30 (left and right), 32, 34 (left and right), 35 (center), 37 (center), 35 (chrono), 40 (chrono, left), 54 (chrono, left), 70 (chrono, left), 115 (top and bottom left), 119 (top)

The Art Guys: pp. 41 (chrono, right), 51 (top and center), 52 (left), 74 (chrono, left), 82 (chrono, right)

Courtesy of ARTCRAWL: p. 50 (chrono, right)

Courtesy of ARTPIX: p. 66 (chrono, right)

Chris Ballou: p. 54 (chrono, right)

Chuy Benitez: pp. 84–85 (bottom)

Courtesy of Bobbindoctrin Puppet Theatre: p. 62 (chrono, right)

Courtesy of H. J. Bott: p. 26 (chrono, center and right)

Courtesy of BOX 13 Artspace: p. 114 (chrono, left)

Courtesy of Bernard Brunon: p. 38 (chrono, left)

Jim Caldwell: p. 79 (top)

Mary Ellen Carroll: pp. 20 (bottom), 55 (all), 56 (bottom)

Mel Chin: pp. 20 (chrono, right: top and bottom), 75 (top)

Courtesy of Robbie Conal: p. 37 (chrono, left)

Contemporary Arts Museum Houston Archives: p. 18 (chrono, left)

Jim Culbertson: p. 15 (chrono, right)

Bill Davenport: pp. 21 (top right), 59 (all), 60 (bottom left and right), 61 (top right)

Courtesy of Frank Davis: p. 18 (chrono, right)

Ben Tecumseh DeSoto: pp. 14, 19, 28 (bottom), 40 (top), 63–65 (all)

Courtesy of DiverseWorks: pp. 29 (chrono, right), 43 (chrono, right), 45 (chrono, left and right), 106 (chrono, left), 114 (chrono, right)

Courtesy of Joe Dugan and Mary Louise Lopez: p. 25 (chrono, left)

Jeff Elrod: p. 62 (chrono, left)

Sharon Engelstein: pp. 26 (top left), 67 (all), 68 (bottom)

Kirk Farris: p. 27 (chrono, right)

John Filiss, courtesy of www.seriouswheels.com: p. 31 (chrono, right)

Michael Galbreth: p. 36 (chrono, left)

Courtesy of Scott Gilbert: p. 42 (chrono, left)

Courtesy Wayne Gilbert: p. 40 (chrono, right)

Courtesy of glasstire.com: p. 86 (chrono, right)

Courtesy of GONZO247: p. 41 (chrono, left)

Andrea Grover: pp. 79 (bottom), 81 (top)

Andrea Grover, courtesy of Andrea Grover and Jon Rubin: p. 110 (chrono, right)

Kenny Haner: pp. 80 (top), 80–81 (bottom)

Larry Harris (www.narrowlarry.com): pp. 26 (chrono, left), 28 (chrono, left), 38, 39 (chrono, left), 42 (top and bottom), 44, 71 (bottom)

Dan Havel: pp. 44 (chrono, left), 84 (top right)

Dan Havel and Dean Ruck: pp. 66 (chrono, left), 83 (all), 84 (top left), 98 (chrono)

Paul Hester: pp. 20 (top), 22 (bottom), 26 (top right), 34 (chrono, left), 53 (bottom right), 60 (top), 61 (top left and bottom), 69, 72–73 (all), 76–77 (all), 85 (top), 89 (bottom), 92 (top and bottom left), 93, 96–97 (all), 101 (bottom), 104–105 (all), 107 (bottom), 108–109 (all), 113 (all), 117 (all), 119 (center and bottom), 120

Leslie Hewitt: p. 90 (chrono, left)

George Hixson: cover; pp. 8, 22 (chrono, right), 28 (top), 30 (chrono, right), 37 (chrono, right), 42 (chrono, right), 50 (chrono, left), 87–88 (all), 89 (top left and right)

Courtesy of Houston Center for Photography: p. 27 (chrono, left)

Courtesy of Brian Huberman: p. 30 (chrono, left)

Courtesy of I Love You Baby: p. 43 (chrono, left)

Courtesy of the joanna: p. 110 (chrono, left)

Courtesy of Jim Kanan; photo by Ben DeSoto: p. 33 (chrono, right)

Patricia John Keightly: p. 14 (chrono, left)

Courtesy of Lauren Kelley: pp. 91 (all), 92 (bottom right)

Courtesy of the Kilgore Rangerettes: p. 21 (bottom)

Courtesy of Kuumba House: p. 28 (chrono, center)

Amy Kweskin, Courtesy Aurora Picture Show: p. 102 (chrono, right)

Tom LaFaver: pp. 39, 41 (top and bottom), 43, 45 (top and bottom)

Courtesy of Lawndale Art Center: p. 94 (chrono, left)

Eric Leshinsky: pp. 24 (top right), 99–100 (all), 101 (top left and right)

Lee Littlefield: pp. 78 (chrono, left), 103

© Estate of Mark Lombardi, courtesy of pierogi 2000: p. 23 (chrono)

Courtesy Bert L. Long, Jr.: p. 82 (chrono, left)

Courtesy of Rick Lowe: p. 107 (top)

Laurie MacDonald: p. 34 (chrono, right: top and bottom)

Michael Mallow: p. 23

Frank Martin: p. 24 (chrono, left)

Courtesy Benjy Mason and Zach Moser: p. 111 (bottom)

© Estate of Gordon Matta-Clark, courtesy of Canadian Centre for Architecture, Montréal: p. 21 (top left)

Connie McAllister: p. 68 (top)

Michael McCall: p. 36 (chrono, left)

Courtesy of Midtown Art Center: p. 28 (chrono, right)

Courtesy Zach Moser: p. 111 (top left)

Courtesy of Not Ant Farm: p. 17 (chrono, right)

The Orange Show: pp. 15 (chrono, left), 39 (chrono, center and left)

Courtesy of Michael Peranteau: p. 29 (chrono, left)

Courtesy of Performance Art Lab: p. 106 (chrono, right)

John Powers: p. 116 (all)

Don Quaintance: pp. 4–5 (frontispiece), 16 (chrono, left), 19 (chrono,), 24 (chrono, right), 25 (chrono, right), 32 (chrono, left), 34 (center), 35 (left and right), 36 (left, center, and right), 37 (left and right), 38 (chrono, right), 40 (bottom), 44 (chrono, right), 56–57 (top), 74 (chrono, right)

Michelle Rosenberg: p. 112 (all)

Courtesy of Magda Sayeg: pp. 22 (top), 95 (all), 102 (chrono, left)

Ed Schipul: pp. 31 (chrono, left), 71 (top)

Wilbur Seiders: p. 14 (chrono, right)

Mark Seliger: p. 51 (bottom)

Courtesy of Sketch Klubb: p. 94 (chrono, right)

Courtesy of Skydive: p. 118 (chrono, right)

Debora Smail, courtesy Aurora Picture Show: p. 70 (chrono, right)

Courtesy of Dolan Smith: p. 58 (chrono, left)

Everett Taasevigen: pp. 18, 52 (right), 53 (top and bottom left)

Courtesy of The Station Museum: p. 86 (chrono, left)

Courtesy of Nestor Topchy and Si Dang: p. 121

Randy Twaddle: p. 90 (chrono, right)

Sarah Wagner and John Brummit: p. 118 (chrono, left)

Watershed Collective: p. 78 (chrono, right)

Patrick Waugh: p. 32 (chrono, right)

Roger Wells, courtesy Menil Archives, Houston: p. 20 (chrono, left)

Amanda Wiles: p. 75 (bottom)

Courtesy Workshop Houston: pp. 24 (top), 111 (top right)

Catalogue

Editors: Polly Koch and Heather Brand
Publication Coordinators: Toby Kamps, Meredith Goldsmith, and Justine Waitkus
Design: Don Quaintance, Public Address Design, Houston
Design/Production Assistant: Elizabeth Frizzell, Public Address Design
Typography: Composed in Solex
Printing and Binding: CS Graphics, Singapore

Authors' Biographies

Cameron Armstrong is a Houston-based architect with a practice focused on new building types and construction technologies. Prior to forming Cameron Armstrong Architects (CAA), he worked in various jobs, ranging from commercial real estate to minerals prospecting. In recent years, CAA's projects have attracted tours, publications, and sometimes controversy, and have been widely featured in United States news media. Born in Edmonton, Alberta, Cameron grew up primarily in Canada and England. Following studies at Oberlin College and the Institute for Architecture and Urban Studies (IAUS), he graduated from Yale University, M.Arch, 1981.

The Art Guys (**Michael Galbreth** and **Jack Massing**) began working together in 1983 after meeting while students at the University of Houston. Since that time their work has been included in more than 150 exhibitions in museums, galleries, and public spaces throughout the United States and in Europe and China. The Art Guys have experimented with a wide range of materials and activities in their attempt to expand the dialogue about, and boundaries of, art. Described in the *New York Times* as "a cross between Dada and David Letterman, John Cage and the Smothers Brothers," The Art Guys often use humor and everyday materials as a way to demystify contemporary art.

Meredith Goldsmith was a curatorial associate at the Contemporary Arts Museum Houston (2008–2009), where she organized the exhibition *Stephanie Syjuco: Total Fabrication*. She was a critical studies resident in the Core Fellows Program at the Museum of Fine Arts, Houston, from 2006 to 2008, where she organized the exhibition *You Are Here* featuring Beth Campbell, Leslie Hewitt, Shana Lutker, and Peter Lynde. She earned her M.A. in Visual and Critical Studies from the California College of the Arts, San Francisco, and her B.A. in Art History from California State University, Chico.

Tony Hoagland came to Houston in 2002 to teach in the University of Houston graduate writing program. His work has received many awards, including the Mark Twain Award, a Guggenheim Fellowship, and the Jackson Poetry Prize. His most recent book of poems is *What Narcissism Means To Me*. Over his time here, his poetry has grown increasingly urban, political, and economic in its palette. He is also interested in theater; *Enron, the Opera* is a gleam in his eye.

Caroline Huber was visual arts director (1985–86) and co-director (1987–93) at DiverseWorks, one of Houston's seminal alternative spaces. She was artistic manager for the development of the Market Square Park Project (1988–92). She serves on the board of directors of the Orange Show Center for Visionary Art and on the advisory boards of the the Cornudas Mountain Foundation, which supports the completion and preservation of James Magee's *The Hill*, a monumental art environment near El Paso, and the William A. Graham Artist Emergency Fund.

Toby Kamps, senior curator at the Contemporary Arts Museum Houston, has organized solo exhibitions by artists such as Claes Oldenburg, Ellsworth Kelly, Vanessa Beecroft, Martin Kersels, Adi Nes, Michael Queenland, and Torolab, a design collaborative in Tijuana, Mexico. He has curated thematic survey and catalogue projects, including *The Old, Weird America*; *Small World: Dioramas in Contemporary Art*; and, with a curatorial team, *Baja to Vancouver: The West Coast and Contemporary Art*. A graduate of the Williams College Graduate Program in the History of Art and the Getty Museum Leadership Institute, Kamps has written on contemporary art and artists for numerous exhibition catalogues and periodicals.

Susanne Demchak Theis served as the first executive director of the Orange Show Center for Visionary Art from 1983 until 2007, a site that she was instrumental in listing on the National Register of Historic Places. She helped to create Orange Show programs such as Eyeopener tours and the Art Car Parade. During her tenure, this small local organization developed a national following and acquired a second visionary art environment, the Beer Can House. In 1996, she curated *Wind in My Hair* for the American Museum of Visionary Art in Baltimore. She has lectured at museums around America and in Europe. In 2007 she became the first programming director of Discovery Green, Houston's new downtown park, which opened in 2008.